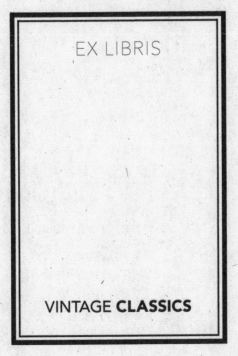

EX LIBRIS

VINTAGE **CLASSICS**

HOMER

Homer is generally believed to have composed
the two great Ancient Greek epics, the *Iliad* and the
Odyssey, in the eighth century BC. No information
about Homer has survived and today there are
many varied theories about the authorship of
these two poems.

Caroline Alexander is the author of seven books of
non-fiction including the international bestsellers
*The Endurance: Shackleton's Legendary Antarctic
Expedition* and *The Bounty: The True Story of
the Mutiny on the Bounty*. A contributing writer
for *National Geographic* for many years,
Alexander has also written for the *New
Yorker*, *Smithsonian* and *Granta* among other
publications. Alexander's latest books are *Lost
Gold of the Dark Ages: War, Treasure and
the Mystery of the Saxons* and *The War That
Killed Achilles: The True Story of the Iliad
and the Trojan War*. Between 1982 and 1985,
Alexander established a department of Classics
at the University of Malawi, in central-east Africa.

ALSO BY CAROLINE ALEXANDER

Lost Gold of the Dark Ages: War, Treasure, and the Mystery of the Saxons
The War That Killed Achilles: The True Story of Homer's Iliad and the Trojan War
The Bounty: The True Story of the Mutiny on the Bounty
The Endurance: Shackleton's Legendary Antarctic Expedition
Mrs Chippy's Last Expedition: The Remarkable Journal of Shackleton's Polar- Bound Cat
Battle's End: A Seminole Football Team Revisited
The Way to Xanadu: Journeys to a Legendary Realm
One Dry Season: In the Footsteps of Mary Kingsley

HOMER

The Iliad

TRANSLATED FROM THE ANCIENT GREEK BY
Caroline Alexander

VINTAGE

11

Vintage
20 Vauxhall Bridge Road
London SW1V 2SA

Vintage Classics is part of the Penguin Random House group of companies
whose addresses can be found at global.penguinrandomhouse.com

First published in Great Britain by Vintage Classics in 2015
This paperback edition published by Vintage Classics in 2017
Published by arrangement with HarperCollins Publishers,
New York, USA

penguin.co.uk/vintage

A CIP catalogue record for this book is
available from the British Library

ISBN 9781784870577

Printed and bound in Great Britain by Clays Ltd, Elcograf S.p.A.

Penguin Random House is committed to a sustainable future
for our business, our readers and our planet. This book is made
from Forest Stewardship Council® certified paper.

TO ELIZABETH ANN KIRBY

My mother,

Who always knew that I would do this

CONTENTS

INTRODUCTION

The *Iliad* begins its story in the tenth and final year of the Trojan War, which has ground to a stalemate between the two opposing armies—the invading Achaeans, as Homer calls the Greeks, and the besieged Trojans, who are fighting for their city, which lies only a few days' sail from the Greek mainland, and which they call both "Troy" and "Ilion". The cause of the war was the seduction and abduction of Helen, the beautiful wife of king Menelaos of Sparta, by handsome Paris, (also called Alexandros) one of the many sons of Troy's king, Priam. Mustered from all over the Greek mainland and islands under the command of Menelaos' wealthy and powerful brother, Agamemnon, king of Mycenae, the Achaeans have grown weary of the war. Their ships, beached at the edge of the Trojan plain, are decaying with disuse. Their greatest warrior, Achilles, has just publicly denounced, in the most bluntly brutal terms, both the war and his commander, and it appears that much of the Achaean host shares Achilles' view that the war is no longer worth fighting.

For their part, the besieged Trojans are increasingly desperate. Hemmed inside their city walls, they and their regional allies have long been preyed upon by marauding Achaeans, and their resources are dwindling. Suddenly, unexpectedly, feckless Paris turns to his brother, Hector, the heroic warrior upon whom the Trojans most depend, and makes a welcome suggestion: he will personally challenge Menelaos to a duel. The two chief protagonists of the conflict, then, will fight it out man to man and the rest of their armies, Achaean and Trojan, can leave in friendship and peace. Swiftly Hector announces this offer to the Achaeans and after an anxious hush—the *Iliad* gives a number of tactful hints that the Achaeans do not regard Menelaos as the mightiest of their warriors—Menelaos accepts, and a treaty is cut to sanctify the outcome of the duel.

> *So he spoke, and both Achaeans and Trojans rejoiced,*
> *hoping to make an end of the sorrowful war.*
> *And they reined the chariots into line, and themselves descended*
> *and took off their armour, and placed it on the ground*
> *close together, and there was little earth left between. . . .*
> *And thus would a man speak, both Trojan and Achaean;*
> *"Zeus most glorious and greatest, and all you immortal gods,*
> *those who first do harm in violation of the sacred treaty—on*
>   *whichever side they be—*
> *may their brains flow—thus—upon the ground, like this wine,*
> *and the brains of their children, and may their wives be forced by other*
>   *men."*
> *So they spoke; but the son of Cronus did not accomplish this for them.*[1]

It is a remarkable scene in a great war epic—the warriors of both armies making violent prayer to go home in peace. The scene is wholly consistent with the epic's depiction of war as something loathed and dreaded by all who must participate. *Lugrós, polúdakrus, dusēlegēs, ainós*—wretched, accompanied by many tears, bringing much woe, dread —these are the adjectives the *Iliad* uses for war. Every mortal being at Troy, man and woman, warrior and civilian, wants the bloody and exhausting Trojan War to end.

The *Iliad*, above all else, is a powerful, first-rate story, whose dramatic action is wrapped around such time-tested themes as insulted honour, love, loss, and revenge. Its cast of characters, mortal and divine, is among the most enduring and compelling in all of literature, and it is through their words and fates that the epic asserts its tragic vision. But central to this tragic vision is the Trojan War. The war is not merely a dramatic backdrop for heroic action, nor, as I was taught at times, a poetic metaphor for the human struggle and experience. The *Iliad* is riveted on what may be called the enduring realities of war: the fact that an individual warrior must risk his life for a cause in which he does not believe, or must subject himself to the command of a lesser man; or that a successful warrior needs not only skill, but the good luck of being loved by the gods—and that these same gods are fickle, and the outcome of any combat mission is therefore fraught with mortal uncertainty; above all that war blights every life it touches. Warriors, Greek and Trojan, the women they capture and the women they love, those too young to fight and those too old, the victorious and the vanquished, the wounded, the dying, the dead—the fates of all are evoked by the *Iliad*. And all the while looming ever closer through the dust of battle is the imminent destruction of the city of Troy and all her people as casualties of the hated war. Compassionate but clear-eyed, the *Iliad* evokes the bedrock fact of the human experience, namely that every mortal being, even the greatest—even an Achilles—cannot escape death. And this terrifying truth is seen in high relief because this is a war story, and tragic loss and mortality are never more nakedly revealed than in time of war.

The *Iliad* opens upon a scene of plague raging through the Achaean camp. The Achaean hero Achilles, the greatest warrior fighting at Troy, calls an emergency assembly. Here Calchas, prophet and seer to the army, reveals that the god Apollo sent the plague as retribution for the mistreatment of one of his priests at the hands of Agamemnon, the king of wealthy Mycenae and commander-in-chief of the diverse Achaean host. The priest's daughter had been seized along with other plunder on a recent raid, and when the aged priest came to the Achaean camp to offer ransom for her, Agamemnon harshly rebuffed him. Now, Calchas declares, the only remedy is for Agamemnon to surrender the girl to her father. This straightforward solution is angrily rejected by Agamemnon, who sees himself diminished by the loss of his prize. When Achilles steps in both to rebuke and to encourage compliance, a bitter quarrel erupts between the two men. Agamemnon threatens to take Achilles' own prize, a young woman named Briseïs, who was also captured in a raiding party, but whom Achilles has come to love. Achilles in his turn angrily withdraws himself and his men, the Myrmidons, from the war, and also threatens to return to his home in

Thessaly. Stubbornly, Agamemnon refuses to relent. He duly returns the priest's daughter, but then dispatches heralds to conduct Briseïs from Achilles' quarters to his own.

The subsequent action is concerned with the repercussions of Achilles' wrath. At Achilles' request his mother, the sea goddess Thetis, goes to Zeus, the almighty ruler of Olympus, to beg a favour for her son. Achilles is destined to be short-lived, she reminds him, and therefore he should at least win honour. Her request of Zeus is that he safeguard this honour by ensuring that Agamemnon be made to feel the loss of his greatest warrior, and so come to regret his taking of Achilles' prize. Zeus bows his head in assent, and the tide of battle turns disastrously against the Achaeans. At length, with all his other best warriors wounded, Agamemnon sends a delegation to Achilles, who has been sitting idle by his ships, to beg that he return to battle in exchange for a dazzling array of gifts. But Achilles, during this unaccustomed absence from fighting, has come to see the value of his life. He has two possible fates, he tells the delegation:

> For my mother tells me, the goddess Thetis of the silver feet,
> that two fates carry me to death's end;
> if I remain here to fight around the city of the Trojans,
> my return home is lost, but my glory will be undying;
> but if I go home to the beloved land of my father,
> outstanding glory will be lost to me, but my life will be long.[2]

His choice, he announces, is to live long and obscurely rather than die with glory, and he repeats his threat to sail back home. Achilles' shocking renouncement of the warrior's creed comes in Book 9 of the *Iliad's* twenty-four books (as by long convention the chapters are called) and his speech here is one of the finest in the epic. The speech makes poignant all that follows; from this point on, the *Iliad* cannot be mistaken for glorifying war's destructive violence. Rather, it makes explicit the tragic cost of such glory, even to the greatest warrior.

The embassy to Achilles returns defeated, and the men must continue fighting. But Patroclus, Achilles' closest companion, stricken by the suffering of their comrades, begs Achilles to lend him his armour—seeing him armed like Achilles, the Trojans will retreat in fear, believing Achilles has returned. Reluctantly Achilles agrees, but his deepest fear is realized when Patroclus is slain by Hector with significant help from the god Apollo. At the death of his beloved companion, Achilles, filled with shame and anger as well as loss, returns to the war with the single-minded intent of avenging his friend. This he does, in a momentous showdown that ends with the death of Hector. After Achilles buries Patroclus with full honours, Hector's father, Priam, the king of Troy, comes at night to the Achaean camp to beg for the body of his dead son. Achilles relents and returns the body, and Hector is buried by the Trojans. The epic ends with the funeral of Hector.

From ancient times, this epic has been called the *Iliad* (the first mention of its title is made by Herodotus in the fifth century B.C.[3]), meaning "the poem about Ilios", Ilios being another name for Troy. With the death of Hector the imminent fall of Troy is made explicit.

Homer's epic, then, relates the events of a narrow period within the legendary ten-year-long Trojan War. The complete story of the war, supported by a sprawling web of subplots and a broad cast of both momentous and minor characters, was told by a series of six other epics, known collectively as the Trojan war poems of the Epic Cycle. Of various dates beginning from approximately 625 B.C., these other epics were composed considerably later than the *Iliad*, but, like the *Iliad*, are thought to have drawn upon much older common traditions. Long lost to time, the epics are known today only by rough summaries and a few surviving lines. From these we learn that the epic *Cypria* told of the origins of the war, for example, while the *Aethiopis* told of the death and funeral of Achilles. Other epics told of the capture of Troy by the Greeks, the destruction of Troy, and the return of the Greek veterans to their homes[4] (although not part of the Epic Cycle, Homer's *Odyssey*, which tells the story of the long voyage home of the veteran hero Odysseus, is such an epic of return).

Because the *Iliad*'s action occurs over the course of a few weeks toward the end of the war, many well-known events are not included. The epic does not tell of the fatal beauty competition between the goddesses Hera, Athena, and Aphrodite, of which Paris was judge, for example, although a few lines in the last Book of the *Iliad* appear to refer to this event.[5] Likewise, the seduction of Helen by Paris is not described, but is referred to on several occasions, most poignantly by Helen herself, as in her words to Priam, in Book 3:

> *And Helen shining among women answered him with these words:*
> *"Honoured are you to me, dear father-in-law, and revered,*
> *and would that evil death had pleased me at that time when*
> *I followed your son here, abandoning my marriage chamber and*
> > *kinsmen,*
> *my late-born child, and the lovely companions of my own age.*
> *But that did not happen; and so I waste away weeping."*[6]

Given the wide array of dramatic events encompassed by the sprawling legend, the *Iliad*'s chosen subject is striking— the quarrel between a warrior and his commander-in-chief during a protracted stalemate. Behind this choice there undoubtedly lay a much older story built on the familiar themes of wrath, revenge, and return of a slighted warrior. As it is, the *Iliad*'s choice necessarily rivets attention on Achilles. This epic thus does not focus directly on the launching of fleets, or the fall and plundering of cities, but on the tragedy of the best warrior of the Trojan War, who, as the *Iliad* makes relentlessly clear, will die in a war in which he finds no meaning.

The *Iliad* evokes a mythological world, one in which Olympian deities descend to the field of battle to fight alongside mortals, or whisk a favourite warrior to safety. Yet this poetic, mythological world is grounded in recognisable human experience. When the god Hephaestus forges a new shield for Achilles, he decorates it with scenes drawn from the lives of men:

> *And on it he made two cities of mortal men,*
> *both beautiful; and in one there were weddings and wedding feasts,*

and they were leading the brides from their chambers beneath the
   gleam of torches
through the city, and loud rose the bridal song;
and the young men whirled in dance, and in their midst
the flutes and lyres raised their hubbub; and the women
standing in their doorways each watched in admiration.[7]

Majestic similes evoking the natural world flash through the epic, similes that are effective because the scenes they describe are enduringly familiar:

As when on a mountain height the South Wind spills dark mist—
no friend to the shepherd, but to the thief better than night—
and a man sees before him only so far as he throws a stone;
so the thick dust rose beneath the feet
of the advancing men; and in all swiftness they traversed the plain.[8]

Or the description of Achilles' divinely forged helmet:

   As when to sailors at sea there appears the light
of a watchfire burning, which blazes high on the mountains
in a lonely folding, as storm winds carry them unwilling
across the fish-filled sea far from their friends,
so the flare from Achilles' shield, beautiful and intricately wrought,
reached the high clear air. And lifting his heavy four-ridged helmet
he placed it about his head; and it shone far like a star.[9]

The mythological world of the *Iliad* is also grounded in a specific period of history. The epic's references to geographical place-names, types of armament and clothing, to fortified cities and other artefacts, can be correlated with archaeological finds dating to the Greek Bronze Age. In broad and somewhat fuzzy outline, then, the world evoked by

the *Iliad* falls within the period dating from the seventeenth to the end of the thirteenth century B.C., which historians call "Mycenaean," after Mycenae, the principal Greek citadel-state of the time.[10]

The Mycenaeans came to power on the Greek mainland in the seventeenth century B.C. and by the fifteenth century had achieved ascendancy throughout the Aegean. Sailors, and traders, they were also warriors and raiders. Cuneiform documents in the royal archives of the contemporary Hittites (the ruling power of Anatolia, now Turkey) refer to marauding Mycenaean troublemakers, suggesting that bands of individuals, if not organised armies, roamed the Anatolian coast, looking for plunder.[11] The *Iliad* also mentions such raiding. *"Twelve cities of men I have sacked from my ships,"* boasts Achilles,

> *"and eleven, I say, on foot throughout Troy's rich-soiled land;*
> *and from all these I carried off as spoil many treasures, valuable*
> *treasures."*[12]

The height of Mycenaean power was reached in the late fourteenth and thirteenth centuries B.C., the so-called palatial period, named for the great palace complexes built at this time. Mycenae, Tiryns, Pylos, Argos, Thebes, Iolkos—the *Iliad* names many of the sites that archaeology has uncovered. This is the period to which most historians would ascribe any historical Trojan War.[13] Like other great civilisations of the Bronze Age, the Mycenaeans kept written records, in this case tablets of baked clay inscribed with a syllabic ideogram script called Linear B. These records have yielded no diplomatic documents, treaties, or letters, as have the Hittite, Egyptian, or Assyrian royal archives; no historical accounts of skirmishes or battles; no poems, or prayers, or fragmentary epics—nothing but the careful inventories of possessions:

> *Kokalos repaid the following quantity of olive oil to Eumedes: 648*
> *litres of oil.*

One footstool inlaid with a man and a horse and an octopus and a
    griffin in ivory.
One pair of wheels, bound with bronze, unfit for service.
Twenty-one women from Cnidus with their twelve girls and ten boys,
    captives.
Women of Miletus.
And:
To-ro-ja — Woman of Troy. [14]

How a woman of Troy ended up in the inventory of a Mycenaean palace
cannot be known from one slender entry. Like the women of Cnidus, she
may have been a captive, taken as booty in a raid. But she may also have been
acquired through trade, for the Mycenaeans had trading settlements along
the Anatolian coast, and as the archaeological record indicates, Mycenaean
traders had substantial contact with Troy. A small Bronze Age cemetery,
apparently a burial ground for foreign mariners, unearthed west of Troy's
ancient harbour, contained a mass of Mycenaean pottery and objects. [15]

Situated at the entrance to the Dardanelles, which Homer calls the
Hellespont, Troy in the late Bronze Age was a prosperous settlement sur-
mounted by a palace citadel. As the mariners' cemetery suggests, the site
was visited by diverse ships of trade, and it is possible that the city's wealth
came from its control of the Dardanelle strait and thus access to the Black
Sea beyond. The city's influence extended throughout the Troad, as the sur-
rounding region is still known, and to islands such as Lesbos to the south.

The earliest, very small Trojan settlement had been built around
2900 B.C., on a low hill above a marshy and possibly malarial plain cut by
two rivers that the *Iliad* calls Simoeis and Scamander.[16] Archaeologists
have identified seven major levels of settlements built on this site that span
nearly two thousand years, the last being abandoned around 950 B.C.[17] Of
these seven levels of settlement, that at the very end of Troy VI (dated from
1700 to 1250 B.C.) is the usual candidate for the Troy of any Trojan War.

Built on the ashes of its predecessors, Troy VI was constructed with novel skill and style, suggesting that a new people had claimed the ancient site; the Luwians, an Indo-European people related to the powerful Hittites, are known to have settled at this time in northwest Anatolia, and are the most likely candidates. A palatial citadel was rebuilt on the hill, with handsome, gently sloping defensive walls constructed of blocks of carefully dressed limestone. Standing some seventeen feet in height, the stone walls were in turn surmounted by a mud-brick superstructure, so that from stone base to brick summit the walls rose to nearly thirty feet. Strategic towers strengthened the defences, and stone ramps led to gateways in and out of the city.[18] These details are known to the *Iliad*, which describes Troy's wide ways and gateways, its towers and its "well-built walls." Below the citadel, a lower city housed a population of an estimated six thousand souls.[19] The last of Troy VI's stages—Troy VIh—ended in 1250 B.C., falling to what appears to have been a combination of earthquake and enemy action.[20]

There is no material evidence to connect the Mycenaeans to the fall of Troy. The Hittite royal archives, however, have yielded tantalising clues about the historical relationship between the two peoples of the *Iliad*. A reference to the Ahhiyawa, ruled by a great king across the sea, for example, is now generally taken to refer to the Achaeans—the name the *Iliad* most commonly uses for the Bronze Age Greeks, whom we call Mycenaeans.[21] Similarly, Hittite Wilusa is now confirmed to be the place Homer calls Ilios or Troy; or more properly, with the restoration of its original ancient *w*-sounding letter, the "digamma," "Wilios."[22] Particularly intriguing is a reference made by the Hittite king Hattusili III in a letter to an unnamed king of Ahhiyawa, around 1250 B.C.: "Now as we have reached agreement on the matter of Wilusa over which we fought . . ."[23]: This, then, is evidence that on one occasion, at least, a Mycenaean king had come to blows with an Anatolian power over the town called Ilios.

If Troy VIh did indeed fall to Mycenaean invaders, the Mycenaeans did not have long to savour their victory. Despite the strength and watchfulness of their great citadels, the Mycenaeans could not forestall the cataclysmic disaster that ended their own civilisation, dramatically and suddenly, around 1200 B.C., a generation or so after the fall of Troy—a time that saw the collapse of many Eastern Mediterranean and Near Eastern powers. Numerous explanations are offered for this collapse—natural disaster, plague, internal unrest, disruption of trade, foreign marauders. Most recently, a study of fossilised pollen from the Late Bronze Age points to severe and widespread drought between 1250 and 1100 B.C., findings that are corroborated by a thirteenth-century B.C. letter from a Hittite queen to Ramses II: "I have no grain in my lands," she wrote at what would have been the start of this devastating drought.[24]

Remarkably, it was the view of later ancient writers that the Trojan War itself was the cause of Greece's undoing. The *Odyssey* gives evidence of social unrest in the wake of the war, with its depiction of the return of the veteran hero Odysseus to his own land, where he finds his estate has been plundered in his absence by usurpers who did not fight at Troy. "It was long before the army returned from Troy, and this fact in itself led to many changes," wrote Thucydides in the fifth century B.C., "There was party strife in nearly all the cities and those who were driven into exile founded new cities."[25]

The collapse of the Mycenaean kingdoms led to the abandonment of the major palace sites, with waves of refugees striking out for other parts of Greece or the Aegean. Throughout Greece, the archaeological record shows diminished populations living in reduced conditions. In most parts of Greece, trade is lost. Literacy is lost. This Dark Age of Greece was to last some four hundred years.[26]

The fact that the *Iliad* has preserved memories of the great palaces, certain types of armour, and other elements of Mycenaean life must mean that the epic tradition was carried across this protracted period of illiteracy by oral storytelling. Like a snowball rolling down the hill of time, the tradition accumulated material from each age through which it passed. A mix of words and syntax from different ages and different dialects, studded with conscious archaisms, the language of the *Iliad* is "artificial," which is to say never spoken by any particular people, but rather the legacy of generation after generation of oral poets.

Close study of the *Iliad* indicates that this epic-making process is in fact even older than the Bronze Age, and indeed draws on sources from outside the Greek world. For example, the name of Helen of Troy can be traced to the Indo-European **Swelénā*, associated with burning and sun glare. Helen's prototype was a Daughter of the Sun, the abduction of the Sun-maiden being a recurrent motif in old Indo-European myth.[27] The comradeship of Achilles and Patroclus has long invited comparison with that of Gilgamesh and Enkidu in the Near Eastern epic of *Gilgamesh*, variants of which can be dated as far back as the third millennium B.C. Nearly half of the *Iliad's* 15,693 lines are in direct speech, meaning that to some degree the epic is as much a drama as it is a narrative. The prototypes for this kind of dramatic presentation are also found in the Near East, in tales, myths, and poems in Sumerian, Akkadian, Egyptian, Ugaritic, and Hittite.[28]

The antiquity of the *Iliad's* tradition is also apparent in the poem's distinctive metre—its rhythm—which is called dactylic hexameter; *dactyl* is the Greek word for "finger," and like a finger the poetic dactyl has one long and two short units. *Hex* is Greek for "six," and accordingly the dactylic hexameter line consists of six such metrical units—more or less; the metre allows the substitution of two longs (a spondee) for a dactyl, and the last unit always has a two-beat ending (usually a spondee, sometimes a trochee, which is long-short). This flexibility affords great variety in the metrical shape of every line of verse, avoiding monotony. It is a striking fact that certain Homeric phrases are closely related to phrases found in Vedic Sanskrit literature. For example, the Greek phrase *kléos áphthiton*—meaning "everlasting glory," a concept central to the heroic ethos—has a close cognate in the Sanskrit *śrávas ákṣitam*. Both the Greek and Sanskrit phrase, moreover, are in hexameter—suggesting they descend from a common Indo-European, or even Proto-Indo-European, heroic poetic tradition.[29]

The *Iliad's* oldest linguistic stratum is Aeolic, a dialect that was spoken in Boeotia in central Greece and in Thessaly, on the northern edge of the Mycenaean world. Significantly, Achilles is a Thessalian hero, and the *Iliad* refers to legends relating to Thessaly, Boeotia, and other regions with Thessalian connections. Following the collapse of the Mycenaean kingdoms, these Aeolic speakers drifted east as far as the western coast of Anatolia and the island of Lesbos, just off the Anatolian mainland.[30] There is compelling evidence from the Hittite archives that Mycenaeans had been present on Lesbos from as early as the fifteenth century B.C., and it may be that these later Aeolic-speaking immigrants were now joining kin or countrymen. Archaeological excavations show that the inhabitants of the island shared the culture of the Troad. Thus, by chance or destiny, Greek poets carrying the epic tradition had settled among a people who were, in terms of culture, Trojans.[31]

While these Aeolic-speaking immigrants had lost their land, their cities, the graves of their ancestors, they still brought with them much of value, such as the gods they worshipped, the language they spoke, and the stories they told. Here in the region of Lesbos, memories of the lost Mycenaean world were handed down to subsequent generations in stories and poems: Tales of great cities rich in gold, remembrances, often muddled, of battles waged and types of armour, exploits of warriors who fought like lions and communed with the gods.[32]

And at some point, a new and electrifying character strode into the evolving narrative, a semi-divine hero indelibly associated with the Aeolian homeland in faraway Thessaly, called Achilles. There is much evidence to suggest that Achilles was originally a folk hero possessed of supernatural gifts that made him invulnerable—a horse, a spear, magic armour—and that he was swept into the epic tradition at a relatively late date. In the *Iliad*, he bears indelible traces of his folk origins but has been stripped of all magically protective powers, and indeed his divine gifts only underscore his mortality. Thus in the *Iliad*, the immortal horse of Achilles does not carry him to safety, but prophesies his death; his wondrous armour is forged by the divine smith Hephaestus, who clearly states to Achilles' grieving mother that the armour cannot protect her son from dying:

> "Would that I were so surely able to hide him away from death and its
>   hard sorrow,
> when dread fate comes upon him,

as he will have his splendid armour, such as many a man
of the many men to come shall hold in wonder, whoever sees it." [33]

Although born of a goddess, the hero of the *Iliad* is wholly mortal, and indeed his mortality is one of the unmoving poles about which the epic turns.[34]

The archaeological record on Lesbos indicates that despite the waves of migrations that continued over several generations, the Aeolic-speaking newcomers made very little impact upon the local Anatolian culture. This would suggest that there was no hostile conquest of one people by another.[35] A few scattered Anatolian words and phrases embedded in the *Iliad* give further evidence of contact between colonisers and native people, and the *Iliad*'s descriptions of the geography of the Troad shows close acquaintance with the region.[36] This period during which Aeolic poets shaped the epic tradition while in the shadow of Troy possibly accounts for one of the most striking features of the *Iliad*: namely, that this Greek epic derives much of its emotional power from the tragedy of the Trojans. It is not unreasonable to speculate that the epic's deeply sympathetic depiction of the enemy was the result of close acquaintance during this period; possibly the Aeolic poets heard stories of the legendary war from the Trojan side.[37]

Just as Aeolic speakers travelled from their homelands eastward, so others were migrating from other parts of Greece. From their homelands in the Peloponnese and Athens, speakers of Ionic Greek migrated to the central western coast of Anatolia and its adjacent islands. And sometime around 800 B.C., the epic tradition—the *Iliad*-in-the-making—passed from Aeolic-speaking poets into the hands and dialect of Ionian poets. Thus despite its anciently embedded Aeolic words and phrases, its Aeolian hero Achilles, and its emphasis on Aeolian-speaking regions of Greece, the *Iliad* we have today is composed in Ionic Greek, and ancient tradition held Homer to be a poet of Ionia.

How the transference from one people and dialect to another happened is unknown, but not wholly mysterious. Ionic Euboea, the long slender island close to the central Greek mainland, which had significant contact with Lesbos, is thought to be a likely place for this transference.[38] The distances between the Aeolic and Ionic settlements were in any case not great, and the eighth century B.C. was a time of energetic trade and movement. The centuries of Dark Age had ended. Enterprising individuals and communities were leaving Greece to establish colonies, from the Black Sea to southern Italy and Sicily. Evidence of significant social upheaval is seen in the fact that the new age opened upon an entirely different political landscape. The old palace complexes and their feudal societies were gone, and the city-state with its vocal citizenry was ascendant—a fact perhaps reflected in the *Iliad*'s depiction of Achilles' fearless challenge of his inept superior, Agamemnon, king of Mycenae.

And this is the age in which literacy is rediscovered. Of the two earliest known examples of the new Greek alphabetic writing, one is an inscription incised on a wine jug from a cemetery near the Dipylon Gate in Athens, and dated to 740 B.C., preserving enigmatic lines of hexameter verse: ". . . / *the dancer who dances most delicately. . . .*" The other, scratched on a clay cup found in the grave of a ten-year-old boy in the Greek colony of Ischia, in Italy, is also in hexameter (with the first line in prose). Dated to 735–720 B.C., the inscription reads: *"I am the cup of Nestor, a joy to drink from. / Whoever drinks from this cup, straightway that man / the desire of beautiful-crowned Aphrodite will seize."*[39] Astonishingly, these early lines of written verse apparently make playful reference to a scene in Book 11 of the *Iliad*, in which the magnificent cup of the Achaeans' aged counsellor Nestor is described. We have come, then, to the age of Homer.

To the ancient Greeks, "Divine Homer" was a professional poet from Ionia, with the island of Chios and the city of Smyrna on the Anatolian mainland being the usual contenders for his place of birth. This plausible tradition apart, his identity is lost in the mythic past; according to one testament, for example, his father was the river Meles and his mother a nymph. The *Odyssey* gives a portrait of a professional singer working at the court of a noble family who is blind, a fact that inspired the tradition that Homer himself was a blind bard—the truth of which is impossible to know.[40]

As indistinct as was the ancient view of Homer, it is straightforwardly clear compared with modern views about him. Who Homer was, or was not, how he composed, whether he wrote or dictated, and whether he composed both the *Iliad* and *Odyssey* are the subjects of the so-called Homeric Question, and the most contentiously debated aspects of Homeric scholarship. Modern views range from the belief that Homer was the last and defining poet writing at the end of the long epic tradition; to the belief that there never was a Homer at all, but only a shared tradition passed down by generations of bards; and on to the extreme view that there is no single definitive *Iliad*, only versions of its various performances.[41]

Modern scholarship on the subject is dated to the work of Milman Parry in the late 1920s and early 1930s, which securely established the oral heritage of the Homeric poems. A hallmark of Homeric language are the formulaic expressions. People, places, things, events are regularly evoked by standard, recurrent phrases. Thus swift-footed Achilles; godlike Paris; resourceful Odysseus; white-armed Hera; black ships; the nourishing earth. Parry demonstrated that the epic system of formulaic phrases was not merely poetic or aesthetic, but functional: in other words, the formulaic language serves a formally useful purpose. Therefore the choice of a particular noun-epithet phrase, according to Parry, was determined by its metrical position in a line of verse, and not by the poet's interest in the attribute. So ships in Homer are black, well-balanced, seagoing, many-benched, many-oared, and swift. In Greek, as in English, each of these attributes, with its different number of differently emphasized syllables, has a different metrical "shape", appropriate to different parts of the verse-line. The poet's use of "swift ships" as opposed to "well-benched ships", then, has nothing to do with a desire to emphasise speed over construction; the choice is determined only by the metrical phrasing that is needed.

Oral poets in living traditions generally do not recite works strictly word for word from memory (although some do), but improvise to some extent with each performance. A ready stock of noun-epithet units serving any metrical need is very handy for a poet singing his song "live" and without opportunity for the kind of reflection and revision that writing allows.

As Parry observed, the Homeric formulaic system ensured both that key nouns possessed a formulaic phrase for any given metrical position in a line of hexameter verse, but *no more than* one such phrase. Such a combination of both scope and economy, Parry claimed, could have been achieved only by the refinement of use over many centuries.[42] Once taken as conclusive proof of the strict orality of the Homeric poems *themselves*, Parry's work has come to receive more critical scrutiny. While few today would dispute the epic's evident debt to traditional oral poetry, there is wide debate concerning the ultimate authorship, or compilation of the poems.

In addition to these short formulaic phrases, a variety of repeated themes, scenes, and patterns inform the *Iliad*. The causative event of the Trojan War, the abduction of Helen, for example, is mirrored by the causative event of Achilles' anger, the abduction of his prize Briseïs. Passing references are made to the anger of Paris and of Aeneas, which hint at larger stories, now unknown to us, that mirrored the *Iliad*'s grand subject, the anger of Achilles. Scenes of battle are built on repeated patterns: A suggests to comrade B that they attack the enemy together; B agrees and they charge; party C stands firm but calls for aid, and so on.[43]

Similarly, lengthy set pieces describing a variety of activities such as making sacrifice, arriving or setting out on a journey, bathing, making an oath, and arming are repeated throughout the epic. So in the *Iliad*, a ritual of sacrifice is described in solemn detail:

> *Then when they had prayed and thrown the scattering barley*
> > *before them*
> *they first drew back the heads of the sacrificial animals and cut*
> > *their throats, and flayed them,*
> *and cut out the thighbones and covered them over with fat*
> *they had made into double folds, and placed raw flesh upon them;*
> *the old man burned these on a cleft-stick and over them poured in*
> > *libation*
> *dark-gleaming wine; and the youths beside him held sacrificial forks*
> > *in hand.*

> Then when the thighbones had been consumed by fire and they had
>   tasted the entrails,
> they cut up the other parts and pierced them through on spits
> and roasted them with care, and then drew off all the pieces.
> And when they had ceased their work and prepared their meal,
> they feasted, nor did any man's appetite lack his due portion.[44]

The scene is from Book 1 but is repeated with minor variations on two other occasions in the epic. Such repetition is not only stylistically impressive, creating an elevated, solemn tone, but also highly practical: ready-made scenes, like ready formulaic phrases, are of obvious value to the performing poet.

While such repetitions—of formulaic phrases, scenes, and themes—are characteristic of oral poetry (although not characteristic of only oral poetry), it is evident that these traditional features still afforded a gifted poet great latitude. Presumably the themes sketched above, of abduction and wrath, could have been exploited more fully had the poet so chosen. The type scenes of arming, as the reader will see, display staggering variety, with each scene adapted to characterise a particular warrior: in the case of the arming of Agamemnon, Homer has dramatically adapted the arming template so as to mirror the power, prestige and materialism of Agamemnon, and in so doing stretched the template almost beyond its recognisable limits (11.5–46). And while many formulaic phrases are indeed only functional, a number have been exploited to great dramatic purpose. When, in Book 6, for example, Hector removes his helmet because its fierce crest terrifies his infant son, we can be sure that the poet was playing off Hector's most famous epithet—"Hector of the shimmering helm," which elsewhere is a symbol of his fierceness. When, in Book 22, Hector flees for his life as Achilles chases him around the walls of Ilion, the fact that his pursuer is "swift-footed Achilles" adds an element of horror to the scene.

We have no way of knowing whether such exploitation of traditional elements, or a bravura adaptation such as the scene of Agamemnon's arming, are authentically traditional, meaning part of a living oral process, or innovations occurring at the end of a long tradition. The *Iliad*, one must bear in mind, is not only informed by a long tradition, it is the last iteration of that long tradition. There is no other *Iliad* after the *Iliad*. Did centuries of tradition simply end because the performance of the last poet, Homer, was so exceptional as to deter all other competing bards and versions? Or had the tradition, as an oral process, already ended, allowing an individual poet—Homer—to address the inherited material with untraditional liberty?

Central to the question as to how the Homeric epics achieved their final form is the role that may have been played by the rediscovered art of writing. It is a very striking coincidence that a long epic poem comprising 15,693 lines of verse should happen to have been unveiled to the world precisely around the time that writing was rediscovered. Furthermore, the new system of writing was unlike any other of time past. Hitherto, writing systems had been encoded in hieroglyphs, cuneiform, the ideograms of Mycenaean Linear B—systems devised for an inner circle of professional scribes, but wholly unpronounceable to the uninitiated. The new Greek system, however, based upon the so-called Phoenician, or West Semitic, script, was a true alphabet; it was designed to capture the sounds of words as they were spoken. *Menin aeide thea*—anyone knowing the sound of each letter of the Greek alphabet can roughly make out the first three words of the *Iliad*, even with no knowledge of what the words mean. In theory, then, an epic poem that had for centuries flowed forth only by means of the spoken word could now be written as it was spoken.[45]

The Homeric poems themselves contain a single, enigmatic reference to writing: In the *Iliad* Book 6, the story is told of a wicked king who sent the hero Bellerophon to Lycia *"and gave him baneful signs, / scratching on a folded tablet many destructive things."*[46] Does this reference reflect an oral poet's genuine and total ignorance of any form of writing? Is it a knowing reference to an artefact—in this case, some stray shard of Linear B scratching—belonging, like types of armour and palatial ruins, to the distant, dimly remembered past? Or could it be a witty reference to the re-emergence of writing in the poet's own time, after the Dark Age had ended?

That the earliest known examples of phonetic Greek should date from the time of Homer, be written in hexameter verse, and in one case make reference to Homer has struck many scholars as more than coincidence. Might it not be the case, they argue, that the Greek alphabet was devised precisely in order to capture the sounds of the spoken words of hexameter poetry? If so, two possible theories emerge in response to the Homeric Question: that an individual poet, Homer, wrote his poems; or that as he sang or recited them, they were written down in dictation by someone adept in the new alphabetic art. History offers several examples of the latter possibility: a long poem dedicated to the god Baal was written in West Semitic script as dictated to a scribe around 1400 B.C., accompanied by a note naming both the poet-priest and the scribe; and a Hittite birth incantation appears to have been hastily written by a scribe taking dictation.[47]

My own views are shaped by my experience in the 1980s establishing a small department of classics at the University of Malawi, in south-east Africa. In discussing Homer, my Malawian students and colleagues, who had grown up with genuine, living oral traditions and knew the genre intimately, were emphatic that the *Iliad* did not "feel" like an oral poem. To their sensibilities, despite the obvious evidence of an oral legacy, Homer was a literary poet. He did not honour oral conventions. In particular, his characters are "round", which is to say fully formed. The *Iliad*'s dramatic speeches serve as much to reveal a speaker's character as to further epic action, for example, while traditional oral poetry, being intensely communal, is not similarly invested in individual characterisation. Homer is celebrated by literary people in literary cultures, my associates maintained, because his compositions meet literary expectations.

The attention lavished on the question of whether the Homeric poems owe their final form to oral or to literary composition has focused excessively on mechanics, on the physical act of recitation versus that of writing. The more interesting question is not whether a traditional poem was ultimately recorded by the spoken or the written word, but rather in what relationship the final poet stood to his tradition. Did Homer see himself as simply one poet in a long line of traditional poets, improvising and transmitting the tradition he had inherited, more or less as it had always been done? Or did he see himself as standing in a different relationship to the traditional material than the poets before him? Regardless of whether he sang, dictated, or wrote—did he see himself as doing something with the traditional material that had never been done before? This, it seems to me, is the fundamental Homeric Question.

The duel between Menelaos and Paris, the description of which began this introductory overview, ends inconclusively. Its stated purpose was to allow the chief protagonists to decide the issue of the Trojan War. Achaeans and Trojans alike are united, *"hoping to make an end of the sorrowful war"*. But the immortal gods, who direct all human action, decree otherwise. Despite the fears of his Achaean comrades, Menelaos gets the upper hand, only to have Paris whisked to safety by Aphrodite, the goddess of love and his adoring protector. High on Olympus, Zeus turns to the assembled deities who have been intently watching the human activity below: *"Yet let us consider how this matter will be,"* he declares;

> *"whether, then, we again rouse evil war and dread battle,*
> *or cast friendship between the two sides.*
> *And if somehow this plan should be desirable and pleasing to all,*
> *then the city of lord Priam may still remain a place of habitation."*

Although Zeus himself tends toward a peaceful conclusion, his strong-willed wife, Hera, passionately objects. Zeus surrenders the argument, and so peace is averted and the war rolls on:

> *for many Trojans and Achaeans on that day*
> *lay sprawled face down in the dust beside one another.*[48]

Even when no one desires it, war still happens, whether by the will of the gods or the nature of man. If we were to take any random hundred-year period within the last five thousand years, it has been calculated, we would find on average ninety-four of that hundred to have been occupied with large-scale conflicts in one or more regions of the globe.[51] The result of at least three thousand years of storytelling, the *Iliad* is still with us because it has resonated powerfully with every passing age. Majestic similes that conjure the world of nature; magnetic characters defined by stirring and momentous speeches; and a broad and generous humanity that reveals a panorama of human life locked in heroic struggle beneath a mischievous or indifferent heaven—these are the hallmarks of Homeric poetry. Through such high artistry did this mysterious master poet transform an ancient tale of one obscure campaign into a sublime and sweeping evocation of the devastation of every war, of any time.

NOTES

1. Book 3.111–15; 3.297–302.
2. 9.410–15.
3. Herodotus, *The Histories*, 2.116.
4. For a survey of the dates and possible authorship of the poems of the Trojan Epic Cycle, see M. L. West, *Greek Epic Fragments* (Cambridge, Mass., 2003). For an examination of the Trojan poems (and other lost epics of the cycle covering different mythic themes) and their relation to the poems of Homer, see Jonathan S. Burgess, *The Tradition of the Trojan War in Homer and the Epic Cycle* (Baltimore, 2001).
5. 24:25ff.; for the authenticity of these lines, see Nicholas Richardson, *The Iliad: A Commentary, Vol. VI: books 21–24* (Cambridge, 1996), sub vv. 23–30, 276ff.
6. 3.171–76.
7. 18.490–96.
8. 3.10–14.
9. 19.375–81.
10. While there are numerous specialized studies of the Mycenaean world, the most accessible overview is K. A. Wardle and Diana Wardle, *Cities of Legend:*

The Mycenaean World (London, 1997). Nic Fields, *Mycenaean Citadels c. 1330–1200 B.C.* (Botley, Oxon., 2004) is a well-illustrated, up-to-date guide to the great Mycenaean sites.

11. For Mycenaean interference in Anatolia, see Trevor Bryce, *Life and Society in the Hittite World* (Oxford, 2004), 259.

12. 9.328–30.

13. A very few objects mentioned appear to date back to the sixteenth century B.C.—well before the conjectured thirteenth-century B.C. date of the Trojan War. Arguing from this, and other evidence, some scholars have suggested that a fourteenth-century B.C. date for the war is more defensible; a counter-view is that the story of Troy was drawn into an already established tradition about seaborne raids: See Carol G. Thomas and Craig Conant, *The Trojan War* (Westport, Conn., 2005) 41ff. and 63ff.

14. The story of the Linear B tablets is excitingly told by John Chadwick, *The Decipherment of Linear B* (Cambridge, 1990). After Michael Ventris cracked the code, he and Chadwick were largely responsible for making the contents of the Linear B tablets accessible to the world; for the documents themselves, see M. Ventris and J. Chadwick, *Documents in Mycenaean Greek*, 2nd ed. (Cambridge, 1973). The different categories of women's work are described in John Chadwick, "The Women of Pylos", in *Texts, Tablets and Scribes: Studies in Mycenaean Epigraphy and Economy*, ed. J.–P. Olivier and T. G. Palaima (Salamanca, 1988), 43–96.

15. Manfred Korfmann, "Beşik Tepe: New Evidence for the Period of the Trojan Sixth and Seventh Settlements," in *Troy and the Trojan War*, ed. Machteld J. Mellink (Bryn Mawr, Pa., 1986), 17–28.

16. The topography of Troy is described in Manfred Korfmann, "Troy: Topography and Navigation", in ibid., 1–16. For the likelihood of malaria, and Trojan health in general, see J. Lawrence Angel, "The Physical Identity of the Trojans", in ibid., 63–76. Skeletal remains for the Trojans of any of its eras are slight—forty-five samples from Troy VI to VIIb, mostly from cremations. An infant-to-child-to-adult death ratio is calculated at 6:2:10, "possibly better than in contemporary Greece" (p. 68).

17. After a lapse of some centuries, later levels were built from the eighth century B.C. on into Roman times.

18. For a guide to Troy, see Nic Fields, *Troy c. 1700–1250 B.C.* (Botley, Oxon., 2004). The detailed and excellent field reports from the excavation at Troy, under the auspices of the University of Tübingen, and under the direction of Manfred Korfmann until his untimely death, in 2005, have been published since

1991 in the periodical *Studia Troica*. Michael Wood, *In Search of the Trojan War*, rev. ed. (London, 2005), 46ff., gives a a very good—and very readable—account of the history of excavation on the site from Heinrich Schliemann onwards. H. Craig Melchert, ed., *The Luwians* (Leiden, 2003) contains a collection of essays about Luwian culture and history.

19. The size and significance of Troy VI has been the subject of unexpectedly heated debate. For an assessment and succinct overview of the site and its probable population, see D. F. Easton, J. D. Hawkins, A. G. Sherratt, and E. S. Sherratt, "Troy in Recent Perspective", *Anatolian Studies* 52 (2002):75–109.

20. For the evidence and date of Troy's fall, see Manfred Korfmann, "Altes und Neues aus Troia", *Das Altertum* 36 (1990):230–40, and especially p. 232.

21. See Trevor R. Bryce, "Ahhiyawans and Mycenaeans—An Anatolian Viewpoint", *Oxford Journal of Archaeology* vol. 8, no. 3, (1989):297–310.

22. Confirmation of the Hittite geographical and political landscape was made only relatively recently with the translation of a key monumental and much weathered cliff-face inscription; see J. D. Hawkins, "Karabel, 'Tarkondemos' and the Land of Mira: New Evidence on the Hittite Empire Period in Western Anatolia", *Würzburger Jahrbücher für die Altertumswissenschaft* 23 (1998):7–14; and J. D. Hawkins, "Tarkasnawa King of Mira: 'Tarkondemos', Boğazköy sealings and Karabel", *Anatolian Studies* 48 (1998):1–31.

23. For the full, fragmented text of this letter, see John Garstang and O.R. Gurney, *The Geography of the Hittite Empire* (London, 1959): 111–14; the referece to Wilusa is at p. 113.

24. Dafna Langgut, Israel Finkelstein, and Thomas Litt, "Climate and the Late Bronze Collapse: New Evidence from the South Levant", *Tel Aviv* 40 (2013):149–75.

25. Thucydides, *History of the Peloponnesian War*, rev ed. trans. Rex Warner (New York, 1972), i.11–12, p. 42.

26. For the end of the Mycenaean world and the Dark Age that followed, see Carol G. Thomas and Craig Conant, *Citadel to City-State: The Transformation of Greece, 1200–700 B.C.E.* (Bloomington, Ind., 1999); and Robin Osborne, *Greece in the Making: 1200–479 B.C.* (London, 1996).

27. Helen's origins are paraphrased from M. L. West, *Indo-European Poetry and Myth* (Oxford, 2007), 229ff.

28. The percentage of direct speech is given in Jasper Griffin, "Homeric Words and Speakers", *Journal of Hellenic Studies* 106 (1986):36–57. Dramatic versus narrative and the dramatic character of Near Eastern literature closely follows G. S. Kirk, *The Iliad: A Commentary*, Vol. II, books 5–8 (Cambridge, 1990), 28ff.

29. On the Vedic cognates see Gregory Nagy, *Comparative Studies in Greek and Indic Meter* (Cambridge, Mass., 1974), 229–61; for a succinct overview of the different theories about the origin of the hexameter, see Richard Janko, *The Iliad: A Commentary, Vol. IV, books 13–16,* (Cambridge, 1992), 9ff.

30. Later Greeks, recounting fragmentary knowledge of their post-Mycenaean history, called these colonists Aeolians, from Aeolis, a son of Hellen, the eponymous clan hero of the Hellenes, or Greeks, and the term is used by historians today. For Mycenaean Thessaly, see Brian Feuer, *The Northern Mycenaean Border in Thessaly* (Oxford, 1983). V. R. d'A Desborough, *The Greek Dark Ages* (New York, 1972), 87ff., discusses the Thessalian migration.

31. For a survey of the evidence for early Mycenaean control of Lesbos, see Annette Teffeteller, "Singers of Lazpa: Reconstructing Identities on Bronze Age Lesbos", in *Luwian Identities: Culture, Language and Religion Between Anatolia and the Aegean*, ed. Alice Mouton, Ian Rutherford, and Ilya Yakubovich (Leiden, 2013), 567–89. For the numerous associations of Lesbos with the Trojan War tradition, see Emily L. Shields, "Lesbos in the Trojan War", *Classical Journal* 13 (1917–1918):670–81.

32. For the evolution of the epic and the Aeolic phase, see M. L. West, "The Rise of the Greek Epic", *Journal of Hellenic Studies* 108 (1988):151–72.

33. 18.464–67.

34. For Achilles' complex origins, see Caroline Alexander, *The War That Killed Achilles* (New York, 2009), 87ff.

35. For the the arrival of the Mycenaeans on Lesbos and their apparent coexistence with the Lesbian population, see Nigel Spencer, "Early Lesbos between East and West: A 'Grey Area' of Aegean Archaeology", *Annual of the British School at Athens* 90 (1995): 273ff.

36. For Anatolian phraseology in the *Iliad,* see, for example, Emile Benveniste, *Indo-European Language and Society*, trans. Elizabeth Palmer (Coral Gables, Fla., 1973), 371ff., on the Aeolo-Phrygian word for "the people" of the king in Homer; and Jaan Puhvel, "An Anatolian Turn of Phrase in the *Iliad*", *American Journal of Philology* 109 (1988):591–93. For the Troad landscape, see John Victor Luce, *Celebrating Homer's Landscapes: Troy and Ithaca Revisited* (New Haven, 1998).

37. A fragment of verse in Luwian, the presumed language of the Trojans, embedded in a thirteenth-century Hittite ritual text, gives a tantalising hint of just such a story: *"ahha-ta-ta alati awienta wilusati . . ."* This has been translated as *"When they came from steep Wilusa . . .";* "steep" is a common epithet of Ilios in the *Iliad*, thus suggesting that this may have been a fragment of a

Trojan account of the Trojan War. See Calvert Watkins, "The Language of the Trojans", in Mellink, ed., *Troy and the Trojan War*, 58ff. This translation has, however, been disputed. Alternative versions range from *"When they came from the sea, from Wilusa"* to *"when they came from the meadow-lands"*, the latter suggesting not an epic but a shepherd's song. For these alternative readings see, respectively, F. Starke, "Troja im Kontext des historisch-politischen und sprachlichen Umfeldes Kleinasiens im 2 Jahrtausend," *Studia Troica* 7 (1997):473, n. 78; and G. Neumann, "Wie haben die Troer im 13. Jahrhundert gesprochen," *Würzburger Jahrbücher für die Altertumswissenschaft*, n.f. 23 (1999):20ff., n. 20.

38. The likelihood of Euboea as the place of transference, and similar examples of transferences across languages of other cultures, are described in West, "The Rise of the Greek Epic", 166ff. Compelling evidence of Euboean diffusion is also given in Thomas and Conant, *The Trojan War*, 65ff.

39. B. B. Powell, *Homer and the Origins of the Greek Alphabet* (Cambridge, 1991), 49. The Homeric lines referenced are 11.632–37.

40. The "Homeric" *Hymn to Delian Apollo* also perpetuates this tradition: *"Think of me in future, if ever some long-suffering stranger comes here and asks, 'O Maidens, which is your favourite singer who visits here, and who do you enjoy most?' Then you must all answer with one voice. . . ' It is a blind man, and he lives in rocky Chios: all of his songs remain supreme afterwards."* M.L. West, *Homeric Hymns. Homeric Apocrypha. Lives of Homer.* (Cambridge, Mass., 2003) vv.166ff. p. 85.

41. On the Homeric Question, see Robert Fowler, "The Homeric question", in *The Cambridge Companion to Homer*, ed. Robert Fowler (Cambridge, 2004), 220–32.

42. Parry's legacy is most accessible in a single volume collection of his papers: Adam Parry, ed., *The Making of Homeric Verse: The Collected Papers of Milman Parry* (Oxford, 1997); owing to the necessarily technical nature of his work, nonspecialist readers may find these landmark papers more complex and obscure than rewarding. More suitable for the general reader is Albert B. Lord, *The Singer of Tales* (Cambridge, Mass., 1981). A more extensive bibliography can be found in the Further Reading section at the end of this translation.

43. For an overview of typical scenes and how they are adapted in the epics, see Mark W. Edwards, *The Iliad: A Commentary; Vol. 5: Books 17–20* (Cambridge, 1991), 11ff.

44. 1:458–68; repeated at 2:421ff. and adapted at 7:316ff.

45. This overview of the evolution of the Greek alphabet and its relationship to

hexameter verse closely follows Barry B. Powell, *Homer* (Oxford, 2007), 17 and 35ff.

46. 6.168–69.

47. For scribal dictation, see Powell, *Homer*, 37ff.; and Mary R. Bachvarova, "CTH 767.7—The Birth Ritual of Pittei: Its Occasion and the use of Luwianisms," in Mouton et al., ed., *Luwian Identities*, 145ff.

48. Quotations from 4.14–18 and 4.543–44.

49. Paraphrased from Trevor Bryce, *Life and Society in the Hittite World* (Oxford, 2004), 98.

A NOTE ON THE TRANSLATION

This translation is based upon the Greek text prepared by Martin L. West and published in two volumes by Teubner between 1998 and 2000. An editor compiles the text of any ancient work of literature by collating all surviving ancient examples and citations. In the case of the *Iliad*, over 1,500 manuscripts and papyrus fragments dating from the third century B.C. to the fourteenth century A.D., together with considerable ancient scholarly commentary and quotations, have all to be consulted. The preparation of a new text of the *Iliad*, then, represents an extraordinary act of sustained and dedicated scholarship.

Despite the antiquity of the *Iliad*'s textual (as opposed to oral) transmission, the Greek text we use today is virtually the same as the "official" text compiled and approved by the great scholars of the Alexandrian library, in Egypt, by around 150 B.C.—a remarkable fact, given the many opportunities for editorial interference over the centuries. Despite this stability, there are numerous places in the poem where the textual tradition offers different choices for a particular word, phrase, or even line. An editor's task is to determine which of the competing choices is attested by the most reliable sources—a decision often informed by surviving comments and decisions of ancient editors addressing the same puzzle.

The edited, published Greek text indicates those places where such a decision was made. The editor denotes, for example, whole verse lines that appear to be later interpolations, often lines "borrowed" from other parts of the poem and repeated for effect. Verses that appear "suspect" but cannot satisfactorily be disproven, are bracketed but retained. An editor omits entirely verses for which the evidence of interpolation is strong. In this translation, following West, verse numbers indicate those places where such lines have been omitted, as in Book 1, where verse 264 is directly followed by verse 266. Since new evidence, chiefly in the form of papyrological fragments, continually comes to light, Greek texts published decades apart will subtly differ.

My approach has been to render a line-by-line translation as far as English grammar allows; my translation, therefore, has the same number of lines as the Greek text and generally accords with the Greek lineation. I have tried to carve the English as close to the bone of the Greek as possible. The translation is in unrhymed verse, with a cadence that attempts to capture the rhythmic flow and pacing, as well as the epic energy, of the Greek, and which like the Greek varies from verse to verse. It is meant to follow unforced rhythms of natural speech.

I have given all major proper names in their Latin-based anglicised form: thus Athena, not Athene; Achilles, not Akhilleus; Mycenae, not Mykenai. This decision is based upon my object in making the text as accessible as possible to the English-language reader, for whom familiarity with the centuries-old (technically incorrect) transliterations is a great asset. Minor characters and place-names of less familiarity, however, are rendered as in the Greek—in this practice I share the inconsistency of many a translator!

A few notes on general pronunciation. I have used a diaeresis (¨) to indicate where adjacent vowels are to be pronounced as distinct syllables rather than a diphthong; so Briseïs is pronounced *Bri-see-is*. Similarly "–aa" is pronounced as two syllables; thus, "Danaans" is *Dan-a-anz*. Final "e" is sounded as a long syllable, "Ariadne" is pronounced *A-ri-ad-nee*.

A few other points of terminology: Homers's Greeks are called Achaeans, Argives and Danaans. Similarly the Trojans are also called Dardanians. The two warriors with the name Ajax (Aias in the Greek) are frequently referred to in the Greek dual form, a feature preserved with the phrase "the Aiantes".

Notes on obscure mythological references can be found at the end of the poem.

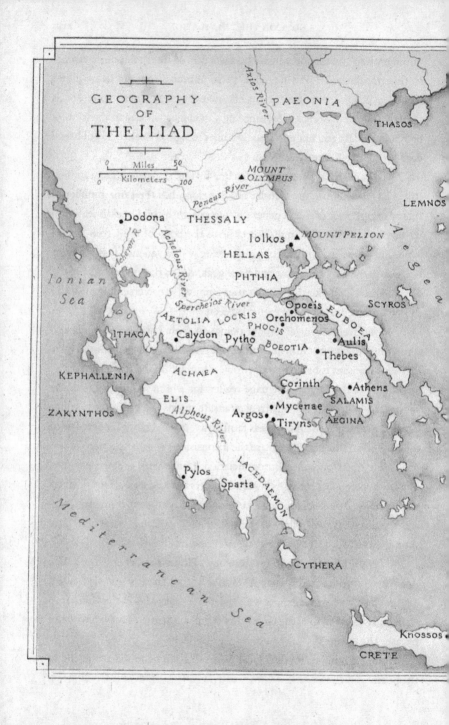

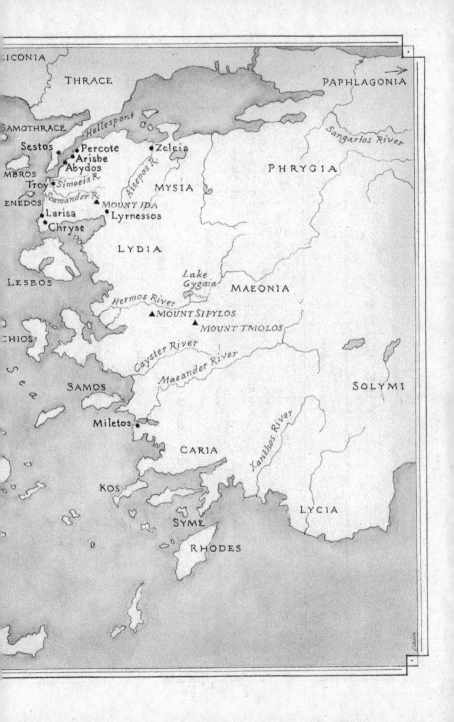

THE GODS

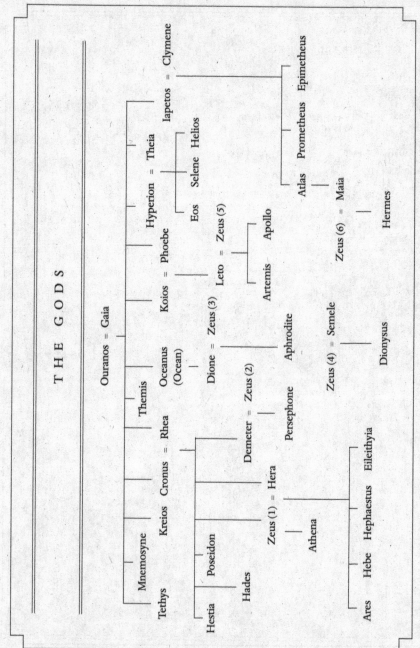

THE HOUSE OF ATREUS

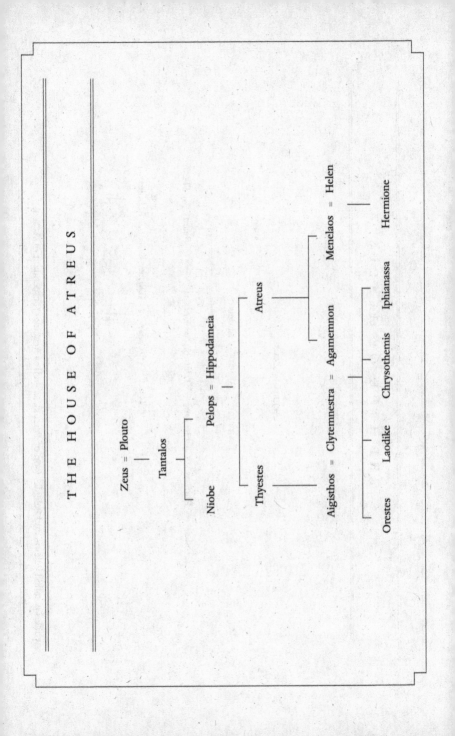

THE LINE OF AEACUS

Asopos

Aegina = Zeus

Asterodeia = Phokos   Psamathe = Aeacus = Endeis   Hesione = Telamon = Eriboia   Peleus = Thetis

Teucer   Ajax = Tekmessa   Achilles

Eurysakes   Neoptolemos

Achilles is called Peleion and Peleides (son of Peleus), as well as Aeacides (descendant of Aeacus).

THE HOUSE OF PRIAM

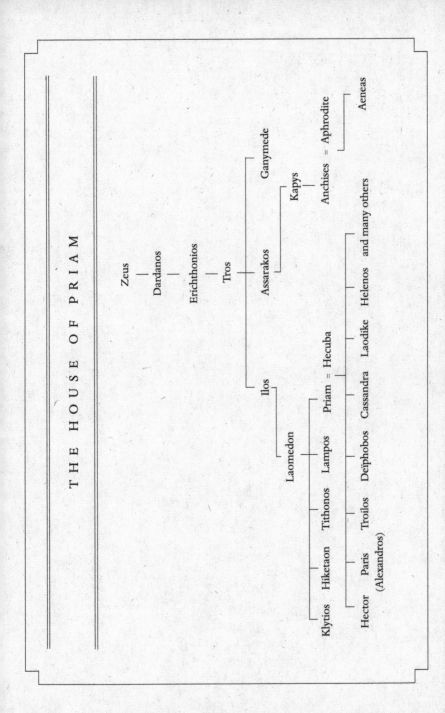

THE
ILIAD

ILIÁDOS A

Wrath—sing, goddess, of the ruinous wrath of Peleus' son Achilles,
that inflicted woes without number upon the Achaeans,
hurled forth to Hades many strong souls of warriors
and rendered their bodies prey for the dogs,
for all birds, and the will of Zeus was accomplished;
sing from when they two first stood in conflict—
Atreus' son, lord of men, and godlike Achilles.

      Which of the gods, then, set these two together in conflict, to fight?
Apollo, son of Leto and Zeus; who in his rage at the king
raised a virulent plague through the army; the men were dying   10
because the son of Atreus dishonoured the priest Chryses.
For he came to the Achaeans' swift ships
bearing countless gifts to ransom his daughter,
holding in his hands on a golden staff the wreaths of Apollo
who strikes from afar, and beseeched all the Achaeans—
but mostly the two sons of Atreus, marshallers of men:
"Sons of Atreus and you other strong-greaved Achaeans,
may the gods who have homes on Olympus grant you
to plunder the city of Priam, and reach your home safely;
release to me my beloved daughter, take instead the ransom,   20
revering Zeus' son who strikes from afar—Apollo."

    Then the rest of the Achaeans all shouted assent,
to respect the priest and accept the splendid ransom;
but this did not please the heart of Atreus' son Agamemnon,

and violently he sent him away and laid a powerful warning upon him:
"Let me not find you, old man, near our hollow ships,
either loitering now or coming again later,
lest the god's staff and wreath not protect you.
The girl I will not release; sooner will old age come upon her
in our house, in Argos, far from her homeland,   30
pacing back and forth by the loom and sharing my bed.
So go, do not make me angry, and you will return the safer."

        Thus he spoke; and the old man was afraid and obeyed his word,
and he went in silence along the shore of the tumultuous sea.
And going aside, the old man fervently prayed
to lord Apollo, whom lovely-haired Leto bore:
"Hear me, God of the silver bow, you who stand over Chryse
and Killa most holy, you whose might rules Tenedos,
God of Plague; if ever I roofed over a temple that pleased you,
or if ever I burned as sacrifice to you the fatty thighbones   40
of bulls and of goats—grant me this wish:
May the Danaans pay for my tears with your arrows."

        Thus he prayed, and Phoebus Apollo heard him,
and set out from the heights of Olympus, rage in his heart,
with his bow on his shoulders and his hooded quiver;
the arrows clattered on his shoulders as he raged,
as the god himself moved; and he came like the night.
Then far from the ships he crouched, and let loose an arrow—
and terrible was the ring of his silver bow.
First he went after the mules and sleek dogs,   50
but then, letting fly a sharp arrow, he struck at the men themselves,
and the crowded pyres of the dead burned without ceasing.

        Nine days the shafts of the god flew through the army,
and on the tenth Achilles summoned the people to assembly;
the goddess of the white arms, Hera, put this in his mind,
for she was distressed for the Danaans, since she saw them dying.
And when they were gathered together and assembled,

Achilles of the swift feet stood and addressed them:
"Son of Atreus, I now think that, staggering back,
we shall go home again—if we escape death that is—   60
if after all war and plague alike are to rout the Achaeans;
but come—let us ask some seer, or priest,
or even an interpreter of dreams, for a dream, too, is from Zeus,
who may tell us why Phoebus Apollo is so greatly angered,
if perhaps he faults our vows and sacrifice,
and whether receiving the burnt fat of sheep, of goats without blemish,
he may somehow be willing to avert our destruction."

       Thus Achilles spoke and sat down. Then stood among them
Calchas the son of Thestor, far the most eminent of bird-seers,
who knew things that are, and things to come, and what had gone
   before,   70
and had guided the ships of the Achaeans to Troy,
through his divination, which Phoebus Apollo gave him.
He in his wisdom spoke and addressed them:
"O Achilles, dear to Zeus, you bid me state the reason
for the wrath of Apollo, the lord who strikes from afar.
Then I will speak, but you listen closely and swear an oath to me
that in good earnest you will stand by me in word and strength of hand;
for I well know that I will anger a man who
has great power over the Argives, and whom the Achaeans obey.
For a king has the upper hand when he is angered with a
   base-born man;   80
if he does swallow his anger for that day,
yet he also holds resentment for later, until he brings it to fulfilment,
within his breast. You now declare whether you will protect me."

       Then answering him Achilles of the swift feet spoke:
"Take courage, and speak freely of any omen you know;
for by Apollo beloved of Zeus, to whom you, Calchas,
pray when you reveal the gods' omens to the Danaans,
no man while I live and see light upon this earth

will lay heavy hands upon you by the hollow ships—
none of all the Danaans, not even if you speak of Agamemnon,   90
who now makes claim to be far the best man in the army."

   And then the blameless priest took courage and spoke:
"It is not with prayer nor with sacrifice that he finds fault,
but for the sake of his priest, whom Agamemnon dishonoured,
and did not release his daughter, and did not accept the ransom—
for that reason the god who shoots from afar has sent these sufferings,
 and will send yet more;
nor will he drive this foul plague away from the Danaans
until we give back the dark-eyed girl to her dear father
without price, without ransom, and lead a holy sacrifice
to Chryse; propitiating him in this way we might persuade him."   100

   Thus speaking he sat down; and then rose among them
the warrior son of Atreus, wide-ruling Agamemnon,
greatly distressed, his darkening heart consumed with rage,
his eyes like gleaming fires.
Glaring, he first addressed Calchas:

   "Prophet of evil, never yet have you spoken anything good for me,
always to prophesy evil is dear to your heart.
You have never spoken nor yet accomplished any good word;
and now you speak in assembly of the Danaans, declaiming god's will—
that for this reason, you say, the Archer who shoots from afar causes their
 affliction—   110
because I was not willing to accept his splendid ransom
for the girl Chryseïs, since I greatly desire to have her
at home; for I prefer her to Clytemnestra,
my wedded wife, as she is not inferior to her,
not in figure or bearing, nor even in disposition or handiwork.
Yet, even so, I am willing to give her back—if this is for the best.
I wish my men to be safe rather than perish.
But make ready another prize at once, so that I alone
of the Achaeans am not unrecompensed, since that is not fitting.

For all of you are witness that my own prize goes elsewhere."   120

      Then answered him swift-footed, godlike Achilles:
"Most honoured son of Atreus, of all men most covetous of possessions,
how then can the great-hearted Achaeans give you a prize?
We do not know of any great common store laid up anywhere,
but those things we carried from the cities, these have been distributed—
and it is not fitting to go about gathering these things again from the men.
But no, relinquish the girl to the god now; we Achaeans
will pay you back three times, four times over, if ever Zeus
gives us the well-walled city of Troy to plunder."

      Then answering him spoke powerful Agamemnon: 130
"Do not in this way, skilled though you be, godlike Achilles,
try to trick me, for you will not outwit nor persuade me.
Or do you intend—while you yourself have a prize—that I just sit here
without one—are you ordering me to give the girl back?
No, either the great-hearted Achaeans will give me a prize
suited to my wishes, of equal value—
or if they do not give one, then I myself will go and take
either your own prize, or that of Ajax, or I will
take and carry away the prize of Odysseus; and whomever I visit will be
    made angry;
but we shall consider these things later.   140
For now, come, let us drag one of our dark ships to the bright salt sea,
and assemble in it suitable rowers, and place the sacrifice in it,
and take on the girl herself, Chryseïs of the lovely cheeks;
and let there be one man in command, some man of counsel,
either Ajax or Idomeneus, or noble Odysseus,
or you, son of Peleus, most terrifying of all men,
you might reconcile to us Apollo who works from afar, and perform
    the sacrifice."

      Then looking at him from under his brows swift-footed Achilles
    spoke:
"O wrapped in shamelessness, cunning in spirit—

how can any man of the Achaeans obey your words with good heart,   150
to journey with you or join men in violent battle?
For it was not on account of Trojan warriors I came
to wage battle here, since to me they are blameless—
never yet have they driven off my cattle, or my horses,
nor ever in Phthia, where the rich earth breeds warriors,
have they destroyed my harvest, since there is much between us,
both shadowy mountains and clashing sea.
But we followed you, O great shameless one, for your pleasure,
to win recompense for Menelaos and for you, dog-face,
from the Trojans; none of this do you pause to consider or care for.   160
And now you boast you will personally take my prize from me,
for which I suffered much hardship, which the sons of the Achaeans
     gave me!
Never do I receive a prize equal to yours when the Achaeans
sack some well-settled city of the Trojans;
it is my hands that conduct the greater part of furious war,
yet when it comes to division of the spoils
yours is the far greater prize, and I bearing some small thing, yet also prized,
make my way to my ships, wearied with fighting.
Now I am going to Phthia, since it is far better
to go home with my curved ships, and I do not intend   170
to stay here dishonoured, hauling up riches and wealth for you."
          Then Agamemnon lord of men answered him:
"Run, then, if your spirit so moves you. Nor will I
beg you to stay here for my sake. Other men stand by me,
who will pay me honour, and especially all-devising Zeus.
You are most hateful to me of the kings cherished by Zeus;
always contention is dear to you, and fighting and battles.
If you are so very powerful, a god doubtless gave this to you.
Go home with your ships and your companions—
be lord of the Myrmidons; of you I take no account,   180
nor do I care that you are angered. But I promise you this:

As Phoebus Apollo robs me of Chryseïs,
whom I will send away, on my ship, with my companions—
so I will take Briseïs of the pretty cheeks,
yes, your prize, going myself to your hut, so that you will discern
how much I am your better and so another man will be loath
to speak as my equal, openly matching himself with me."

So he spoke. And anguish descended upon the son of Peleus
and the heart in his rugged breast debated two ways,
whether he should draw the sharp sword by his side   190
and scatter the men and slay and despoil the son of Atreus,
or check his anger and restrain his spirit.
While he churned these things through his heart and mind,
as he was drawing from its sheath his great sword, Athena came to him
down from heaven; for Hera the goddess with white arms dispatched her,
who in her heart loved and cared for both men alike.
She came up behind and grabbed the son of Peleus' tawny hair,
appearing to him alone, and none of the others saw her.
Thunderstruck, Achilles turned behind him and at once recognised
Pallas Athena; for her eyes gleamed terribly.   200
And addressing her, he spoke winged words:
"Why do you come again, daughter of Zeus who wields the aegis?
Is it to witness the outrage of Agamemnon, the son of Atreus?
But I state openly to you, and I think that it will be accomplished,
that by these insolent acts he will shortly lose his life."

Then the gleaming-eyed goddess addressed him:
"From heaven I have come to stop your anger, if you will heed me;
Hera the white-armed goddess sent me forth,
who in her heart loves and cares for you both alike.
Come, leave off this contention, stay your hand on your sword,   210
but rather cut him with words, telling him how things will be.
For I will tell you this, and it will be accomplished;
someday you will have three times as many shining gifts
because of this outrage; restrain yourself and obey me."

Then in reply Achilles of the swift feet addressed her:
"I must obey the word of you both, goddess,
enraged in spirit though I am; for so is it better.
If a man heeds the gods, then they also listen to him."
He spoke and checked his powerful hand on the silver sword hilt
and back into the sheath thrust the great sword, nor did he disobey   220
the word of Athena. Then she was gone to Olympus,
to the house of Zeus who wields the aegis and the company of the other
    gods.

And the son of Peleus once more with menacing words
addressed Agamemnon, and he did not hold back his anger:
"Wine-besotted, you who have the eyes of a dog and the heart of a deer,
never do you have courage to gear up for battle with your people,
nor go on ambush with the best of the Achaeans;
to you that is as death.
Far better it is, all through, the broad army of the Achaeans,
to seize the gifts of the man who speaks against you.   230
King who feeds upon your people, since you rule worthless men;
otherwise, son of Atreus, this now would be your last outrage.
But I say openly to you, and I swear a great oath to it—
yes, by this sceptre, that never again will put forth leaves and shoots
when once it has left behind its stump in the mountains,
nor will it flourish again, since the bronze axe has stripped it round,
leaf and bark; and now in turn the sons of the Achaeans
busy with justice carry it around in their hands, they who
safeguard the ordinances of Zeus—this will be my great oath:
some day a yearning for Achilles will come upon the sons of the
    Achaeans,   240
every man; then nothing will save you, for all your grief,
when at the hands of man-slaying Hector
dying men fall in their multitude; and you will rip the heart within you,
raging that you paid no honour to the best of the Achaeans."
Thus spoke the son of Peleus, and hurled the gold-studded

sceptre to the ground, and sat down,

while the son of Atreus raged on the other side. Then between them rose
   Nestor,

the sweet-sounding, the clear speaker from Pylos,

whose voice flowed from his tongue more sweetly than honey.

In his time two generations of mortal men had already   250

perished, those who were born and raised with him in days of old,

in sacred Pylos, and he was ruler among the third generation.

With kindly thoughts to both he advised and addressed them:

        "Oh look now, surely great trouble comes to the land of the
Achaeans!

Surely Priam and the sons of Priam would be gladdened

and the rest of the Trojans greatly rejoiced in heart

if they were to learn you two were fighting over all this—

you who surpass the Danaans in counsel, who surpass them in fighting!

But hearken; you are both younger than me.

For once upon a time I banded with better   260

men even than you, and never did they slight me.

Never yet have I seen, nor shall see such men—

Peirithoös and Dryas, shepherd of his people,

and Kaineus and Exadios and Polyphemos like a god.   264

These were raised to be strongest of earthly men;   266

they were the strongest and they fought with the strongest—

the Centaurs who lie in the mountains—and terribly they slaughtered
   them.

And yet with these men I kept company, coming from Pylos,

far away, from a distant land; for they summoned me.   270

And I fought by myself, I alone; against these men no

mortal now upon earth could fight.

And yet they marked my counsels and heeded my word.

Now you two heed me, since it is better to do so.

You should not, great though you are, deprive him of the girl,

but let her be, as it was to him the sons of the Achaeans gave her as prize;

nor you, son of Peleus, venture to contend face to face
with your king, since the king bearing the sceptre partakes of
a very different honour, and is he to whom Zeus has given distinction.
And if you are the stronger man, and the mother who bore you a
    goddess,   280
yet is this one more powerful, since he rules over more men.
Son of Atreus, restrain your spirit; for I—yes, I—
entreat you to relinquish your anger with Achilles, who is for all
Achaeans the great wall of defence against this evil war."

      Then in turn lord Agamemnon spoke:
"Indeed all these things, old sir, you rightly say;
but this man wants to be above all other men;
he wants to be lord over all, to rule all,
to give orders to all—which I think that one man at least will not obey.
And if the eternal gods have made him a spearman   290
they do not on that account appoint him to speak insults."

      Interrupting, godlike Achilles answered him:
"May I be called a coward and of no account
if I submit to you in everything you should say.
Give such orders to other men, but do not act as master to me.
For I do not think it likely I will obey you.
And I will tell you something else and put it away in your mind—
I will not fight for the girl with strength of hand,
not with you, nor with any other man, since you who take her from me
    also gave her.
But of other possessions beside my ships, swift and dark,   300
of these you can take nothing lifted against my will.
And I invite you to try, so that these men too will know—
very quickly will your dark blood gush round my spear."

      Having fought like this with words, blow for blow,
they both stood, and broke up the assembly by the ships of the
    Achaeans.
Peleus' son went to his shelter and balanced ships

with the son of Menoetius and his companions.

But the son of Atreus then drew a swift ship down to the sea,

and chose twenty rowers to go in her, and put on board the sacrificial
    hecatomb

for the god, and fetching Chryseïs of the lovely cheeks   310

put her on board; and resourceful Odysseus came on as leader.

          Then, embarked, they sailed upon the watery way,

and the son of Atreus charged the men to purify themselves.

They cleansed themselves and cast the impurities into the sea,

and to Apollo they made perfect sacrificial hecatombs

of bulls and goats along the shore of the murmuring sea;

and the savour rose to heaven amid a swirl of smoke.

          So they attended to these tasks throughout the army; but
    Agamemnon did not

leave off the quarrel, in which he first threatened Achilles,

but spoke to Talthybios and Eurybates,   320

who were heralds and ready henchmen:

"Go to the shelter of Peleus' son Achilles;

take by the hand Briseïs of the lovely cheeks and lead her away.

And if he does not give her up, I myself will take her,

coming in force, and it will be the worse for him."

          So saying, he sent them forth, and enjoined on them a harsh
    command.

And they two went unwilling along the shore of the murmuring sea,

and came to the camp and ships of the Myrmidons.

They found Achilles by his shelter and dark ship,

sitting; and he did not rejoice to see them.   330

The two stood in fear and awe of the king,

and neither addressed him, nor questioned.

But Achilles understood in his heart, and spoke to them:

          "Hail heralds, messengers of Zeus, as also of men—

come close; you are not to blame in my eyes, but Agamemnon,

who sends you two forth on account of the girl Briseïs.

But come, Patroclus, descended from Zeus, bring out the girl
and give her to these two to take away. And let them both be witnesses
before the blessed gods and mortal men alike,
and before him, this stubborn king, if ever hereafter   340
other men need me to ward off shameful destruction.
For he surely raves in his ruinous heart,
and knows not to look ahead as well as behind
as to how the Achaeans shall fight in safety beside the ships."

      Thus he spoke and Patroclus obeyed his beloved companion,
and from the shelter led Briseïs of the lovely cheeks,
and gave her to be taken away. And straightway the heralds left for the
    ships of the Achaeans.
She the young woman, unwilling, went with them. But Achilles,
weeping, quickly slipping away from his companions, sat
on the shore of the grey salt sea, and looked out to depths as dark
    as wine;   350
again and again, stretching forth his hands, he prayed to his beloved
    mother:
"Mother, since you bore me to be short-lived as I am,
Olympian Zeus who thunders on high ought to
grant me at least honour; but now he honours me not even a little.
For the son of Atreus, wide-ruling Agamemnon
has dishonoured me; he keeps my prize, having seized it, he personally
    taking it."

      So he spoke, shedding tears, and his lady mother heard him
as she sat in the depths of the salt sea beside her aged father.
At once she rose from the clear salt sea, like mist,
and sat before him as he wept,   360
and caressed him with her hand, and spoke to him and said his name:
"Child, why do you cry? What pain has come to your heart?
Speak out, don't hide it, so that we both know."

      Groaning deeply, Achilles of the swift feet spoke to her:
"You know; why should I recount these things to you who know them all?

We came to Thebes, the holy city of Eëtion;

we sacked it and brought everything here.

The sons of the Achaeans fairly divided the things among them,

and to the son of Atreus they gave out Chryseïs of the lovely cheeks.

Then Chryses, a priest of Apollo who strikes from afar,   370

came to the swift ships of the bronze-clad Achaeans

bearing untold ransom to set free his daughter,

holding in his hands the wreaths of Apollo who strikes from afar

on a golden staff, and beseeched all the Achaeans,

but mostly the two sons of Atreus, marshallers of men.

Then all the rest of the Achaeans shouted assent,

to respect the priest and take the splendid ransom;

but this did not please the heart of Atreus' son Agamemnon,

but violently he drove him away and laid a strong injunction upon him.

And in anger the old man went back; and Apollo   380

heard him when he prayed, since he was very dear to him,

and he let fly an evil arrow against the Argives; and now the men

died in quick succession as the arrows of the god ranged

everywhere through the broad army of the Achaeans. But then a seer

possessed of good knowledge publicly declared to us the wishes of the

    god who works his will.

Straightway I led in urging that the god be appeased;

but then anger seized the son of Atreus, and suddenly rising to speak

he declared aloud a threat, which is now fulfilled.

For the dark-eyed Achaeans are sending the girl on a swift ship

to the town of Chryse, taking gifts for lord Apollo;   390

just now the heralds set out from my shelter leading,

the daughter of Briseus, whom the sons of the Achaeans gave to me.

But you, if you have the power, defend your son;

go to Olympus and petition Zeus, if ever in any way

in word or in deed you delighted the heart of Zeus.

For many times in the halls of my father I have heard you

boast when you said that from the dark-clouded son of Cronus,

alone among immortals, you warded off shameful destruction,
at that time when the other Olympians sought to bind him—
Hera and Poseidon and Pallas Athena;   400
but you coming to him, goddess, released his bonds,
swiftly summoning to high Olympus the Hundred-Handed One,
whom the gods call Briareos the Strong—but all men call
Aigaion—he in turn is stronger than his father;
and this one seated himself beside the son of Cronus, rejoicing in his glory.
And the blessed gods trembled before him, and did no more binding.
Now remind Zeus of these things, seat yourself beside him and clasp his
    knees
and see if he might be willing to aid the Trojans,
and to pen the Achaeans around the sterns of their ships and the sea,
dying, so that all may have profit of their king,   410
and he will know, Atreus' son, wide-ruling Agamemnon,
his delusion, when he paid no honour to the best of the Achaeans."

        Then Thetis answered him, with tears flowing down:
"Ah me, my child, why did I, bitter in childbearing, raise you?
Would that you sat by your ships without tears, without pain,
for indeed your measure of life is so very small, not long at all.
And now you are at once short-lived and unlucky beyond all men;
so I bore you to an unworthy fate in my halls.
To speak your request to Zeus who hurls the thunderbolt
I myself shall go to Olympus of the deep snow; perhaps he will heed me. 420
But you stay now by your fast-running ships,
nurse your wrath at the Achaeans, and leave off the war entirely.
Zeus went yesterday to the river of Ocean among the blameless Aethiopians,
to attend a feast, and all the gods accompanied him.
On the twelfth day he will come back to Olympus
and then at that time I will go for you to the bronze-floored house
of Zeus, and I will clasp his knees in supplication, and I think I will
    persuade him."

        Then speaking thus she went away and left him there,

angered in his heart on account of the fair-belted woman,
whom they were taking by force against his will. And Odysseus   430
was drawing near the town of Chryse, bearing the sacred hecatomb.
When they had come inside the deep harbour,
they furled the sails, and placed them in the dark ship,
and deftly lowering the mast by the forestays, laid it in the mast-gallows,
and rowed her to her mooring under oars;
then they threw the anchor stones, and made fast the stern lines,
and themselves disembarked into the broken surf,
and disembarked the hecatomb for Apollo, who strikes from afar;
and Chryseïs disembarked from the seagoing ship.
Then leading her to the altar resourceful Odysseus   440
placed her in her father's hands and addressed him:
"O Chryses, Agamemnon, lord of men, dispatched me
to lead your child to you and to perform sacred hecatombs to Phoebus
on behalf of the Danaans, so that we might propitiate lord Apollo,
who has now sent sufferings, much lamented, upon the Argives."
          So speaking, he placed her in the priest's arms, and he, rejoicing,
     received
his beloved daughter; and the men swiftly set up the splendid hecatomb
     for the god
in good order around the well-built altar,
then they washed their hands and took up the barley for scattering.
And Chryses prayed aloud for them, lifting his hands: 450
"Hear me, thou of the silver bow, you who stand over Chryse
and Killa most holy, you whose might rules Tenedos,
surely once before this you heard me when I prayed;
honouring me you smote hard the host of the Achaeans.
Now, as once before, fulfil this wish for me;
now this time ward off shameful destruction from the Danaans."
Thus he spoke praying, and Phoebus Apollo heard him.
          Then when they had prayed and thrown the scattering barley
     before them

they first drew back the heads of the sacrificial animals and cut their
    throats, and flayed them,
and cut out the thighbones and covered them over with fat   460
they had made into double folds, and placed raw flesh upon them;
the old man burned these on a cleft-stick and over them poured in libation
dark-gleaming wine; and the youths beside him held sacrificial forks in
    hand.
Then when the thighbones had been consumed by fire and they had
    tasted the entrails,
they cut up the other parts and pierced them through on spits
and roasted them with care, and then drew off all the pieces.
And when they had ceased their work and prepared their meal,
they feasted, nor did any man's appetite lack his due portion.
And when they had put away desire for eating and drinking,
the young men filled mixing bowls brimful with wine,   470
and after pouring libations in each cup, distributed it to all;
then all day long they sought the favour of the god in dance and song,
the young Achaean men beautifully singing a hymn of praise,
celebrating the god who works from afar; and the god rejoiced in his
    heart as he listened.
        When the sun sank and dusk came on,
then they lay down to sleep by the stern lines of their ship;
and when dawn, born of the morning, shone forth her fingers of rosy light,
then they sailed out for the broad army of the Achaeans.
And to them Apollo who works from afar sent a following wind.
They stepped the mast and spread the glistening sails,   480
and the wind blew gusts in the middle of the sail, and around
the cutwater the bow-wave, shimmering dark, sang loud as the ship
    proceeded.
She swept over the swell, making her course.
And when they arrived at the broad army of the Achaeans,
they dragged the dark ship ashore
high on the sand, and splayed long struts beneath,

and themselves scattered to their ships and shelters.

      But, he, sitting idle by his fast-running ships, remained full of
  wrath—
the Zeus-descended son of Peleus, Achilles of the swift feet;
never did he go to the assembly where men win glory,
never to war, but consumed his own heart   490
biding his time there; yet he yearned for the war shout and battle.

      But when at length the twelfth dawn arose,
then all the gods who live forever went to Olympus,
together, with Zeus as their leader; and Thetis did not neglect her son's
directives, and she rose from the heaving surface of the sea
and at dawn ascended to towering Olympus.
She found the far-thundering son of Cronus sitting apart from the others
on the topmost peak of ridged Olympus;
and she sat before him and clasped his knees   500
with her left hand, and with her right took hold of him beneath his chin,
and in supplication addressed lord Zeus, the son of Cronus:
"Father Zeus, if ever among the immortals I helped you
by word or by deed, accomplish this wish for me:
honour my son, who was born short-lived beyond all men,
and yet now the lord of men Agamemnon has
dishonoured him; he holds his prize, having seized it, he personally taking it.
Do you now revenge him, Olympian Zeus, all-devising;
give strength to the Trojans until that time the Achaeans
recompense my son and exalt him with honour."   510

      So she spoke; but Zeus who gathers the clouds did not answer her,
but sat silent a long while. And as she had clasped his knees, so Thetis
now held on, clinging closely, and beseeched him again:
"Promise me faithfully, and nod your assent,
or refuse me—you have nothing to fear—so that I may learn
how much I am of all gods the most dishonoured."

      Greatly troubled, Zeus who gathers the clouds addressed her:
"This is a deadly business, when you set me up to quarrel

with Hera, when she will harass me with words of abuse.
As it is, she is always quarrelling with me in the presence of the
    immortal gods,   520
and maintains, as you know, that I help the Trojans in battle.
Now go back, lest Hera notice anything;
I will make these matters my concern, to bring them to accomplishment.
Come, I will my bow my head for you, so that you may be convinced;
for among immortals this is the greatest
testament of my determination; for not revocable, nor false,
nor unfulfilled is anything to which I have bowed my head."
The son of Cronus spoke, and nodded with his blue-black brows,
the ambrosial mane of the lord god swept forward
from his immortal head; and he shook great Olympus.

　　　　　Thus the two parted after conspiring; and she
sprang into the deep salt sea from shining Olympus,   530
and Zeus went to his home; and all the gods rose as a body
from their seats before their father; nor did any dare
remain seated as he approached, but all stood to meet him.
So he took his seat there upon his throne; nor did Hera
fail to perceive at a glance that silver-footed
Thetis, the daughter of the old man of the sea, had conspired with him.
Straightway she addressed Zeus, the son of Cronus, with taunting words:
"Which of the gods now, O cunning schemer, has conspired with you?   540
Always you love being away from me, mulling over your secrets
to make your decisions. Never yet to me
have you willingly dared state what you are thinking."

　　　　　Then the father of gods and men answered her:
"Hera, do not hope to know all my thoughts;
they will be hard for you, although you are my wife.
However, that which is fitting for you to hear, no other,
of gods or men, will know before you;
but that which I may wish to consider apart from the gods—
do not press me about each and every thing, nor make inquiry."   550

Then answered him the ox-eyed lady Hera:
"Most dread son of Cronus, what sort of word have you spoken?
Certainly before now I have neither pressed you, nor made inquiry,
and entirely without interference you devise whatever you want.
But now my heart is terribly afraid lest
silver-footed Thetis, daughter of the old man of the sea, won you over;
for at dawn she came to your side and clasped your knees.
And I suspect you pledged faithfully to her that you would honour
Achilles, and destroy many by the ships of the Achaeans."

Then in answer Zeus who gathers the clouds addressed her: 560
"What possesses you? You always suspect something, I never get past you.
Nonetheless, you can accomplish nothing at all, but will only be
further from my heart—and it will be the worse for you.
If this is the way things are—then you may be sure this is the way that
    pleases me.
Sit down and be silent, and obey my word,
lest the gods in Olympus, as many as there are, be of no avail to you
    against me
as I close in, when I lay my unassailable hands upon you."

Thus he spoke and the ox-eyed lady Hera was afraid,
and she sat down in silence, bending her own heart into submission;
and throughout the house of Zeus the heavenly gods were troubled.   570
To them Hephaestus, famed for his art, began to speak,
comforting his dear mother, white-armed Hera:
"To be sure this will be a deadly business, not to be borne,
if you two quarrel this way for the sake of mortals,
carrying on this jabbering among the gods; nor
will there be any pleasure from our noble feast if unseemliness prevails.
I advise my mother, sensible as she is,
to be agreeable to our dear father Zeus, so that our father
will not reproach us again, and throw our feast into disorder.
For what if the Olympian wielder of lightning wished to   580
blast us from our seats—for he is much the strongest.

Rather address him with gentle words;
then straightway will the Olympian be favourable to us."

      Thus he spoke, and springing to his feet placed a double-handled
  cup
in his dear mother's hands, and addressed her:
"Endure, my mother, and restrain yourself, distressed though you be,
lest, dear as you are, I with my own eyes see you
struck down; then for all my grief I will have no power
to help you; for it is painful to oppose the Olympian.
For at another time before this, when I was trying to ward him
  off from you,   590
he grabbed me by the foot and cast me from the threshold of heaven;
the whole day I drifted down, and as the sun set
I dropped on Lemnos, and there was but little life still in me.
It was there the Sintian men quickly ministered to me after my fall."
So he spoke and Hera, goddess of the white arms, smiled
and smiling accepted the cup from her son's hand.
Then to all the other gods, serving to the right,
he poured sweet nectar like wine, drawing from a mixing bowl;
and unquenchable laughter broke out among the blessed gods
as they watched Hephaestus bustling through the halls.   600

      Then all day long until the sun went down,
they feasted, nor was the appetite of any stinted of fair portion—
nor stinted of the beautifully wrought lyre, which Apollo held,
or of the Muses, who sang, one following the other, with lovely voice.
Then when the sun's bright light went down,
they left to go to bed, each in his own house,
where the famous crook-legged god,
Hephaestus, had made a house for each with skilful understanding.
Olympian Zeus, wielder of lightning, went to his bed
where he was wont to retire when sweet sleep came to him;   610
here mounting his bed, he went to sleep, with Hera of the golden
  throne beside him.

So the other gods as well as chariot-fighting men
slept through the night; but no sweet sleep held Zeus,
and in his mind he pondered how he might bring honour to
Achilles, and destroy a multitude beside the ships of the Achaeans.
And this plan seemed to his mind best—
to send to Atreus' son Agamemnon ruinous Dream.
And calling out, he addressed him with winged words:
"Come, ruinous Dream, go to the swift ships of the Achaeans;
enter the shelter of Agamemnon, Atreus' son,
utter every word exactly as I charge.   10
Bid him arm the long-haired Achaeans
in full force; for now he might take the wide-wayed city
of the Trojans; no longer are the immortal dwellers of Olympus
divided—she has bent all to her will,
has Hera, with her entreaties—and we grant him to win this triumph."

          So he spoke; and Dream set out when he heard the command,
and swiftly reached the swift ships of the Achaeans,
then made his way to the son of Atreus, Agamemnon; and found him
sleeping in his shelter, immortal slumber poured around him.
And Dream stood above his head in the likeness of Nestor,   20
son of Neleus, whom of all the elders Agamemnon most esteemed;
and in this likeness divine Dream addressed him:
"You sleep, son of Atreus, skilled breaker of horses:
a man of counsel should not sleep night long,

a man to whom his people turn, and who has so many cares.
Now, in all haste, mark me; I am a messenger of Zeus,
who, though far away, takes great thought for and pities you.
He bids you arm the long-haired Achaeans
in full force; for now you might take the wide-wayed city
of the Trojans; no longer are the immortal dwellers of Olympus   30
divided—she has bent all to her will,
has Hera, with her entreaties—and woes are latched upon the Trojans,
sent from Zeus. Hold this firm in your mind and do not let
   forgetfulness
take you, once sleep with its honeyed thoughts releases you."

      So speaking he went away, and left Agamemnon there
thinking over in his heart these things that were not to be;
for he supposed he would take Priam's city on that day—
fool, he knew not those deeds that Zeus devised;
for Zeus intended to inflict woe and groaning sorrow
on both Trojans and Danaans, through the mighty combat.   40

      He woke from sleep and the divine voice flowed around him.
He sat upright and donned his soft tunic,
fresh and fine, and cast his great cloak round him,
and beneath his smooth feet he bound his splendid sandals;
and then he cast about his shoulders his silver-studded sword,
took up the sceptre of his fathers, imperishable, eternal,
and with this set out along the ships of the bronze-clad Achaeans.

      Dawn the goddess set her foot on high Olympus,
heralding light of day to Zeus and the immortals;
and to the clear-voiced heralds Agamemnon gave commands   50
to summon to assembly the long-haired Achaeans.
They made the summons and with all speed the men assembled.

      But first Agamemnon held a council of great-hearted elders
beside the ship of Nestor, king of the Pylians.
And having called these men together, he laid out his clever plan:
"Listen, friends; divine Dream came to me in my sleep

through the immortal night; to godlike Nestor
in appearance and size and physique was he most wonderfully like!
He stood above my head and spoke this speech to me:
'You sleep, son of Atreus, skilled breaker of horses;   60
a man of counsel should not sleep night long,
a man to whom his people turn, and who has so many cares.
Now, in all haste, mark me; I am a messenger of Zeus
who, though far away, takes great thought for and pities you.
He bids you arm the long-haired Achaeans
in full force; for now you might take the wide-wayed city
of the Trojans; no longer are the immortal dwellers of Olympus
divided—she has bent all to her will,
has Hera, with her entreaties—and woes are latched upon the Trojans,
sent from Zeus; hold this firm in your mind.' Speaking thus,   70
he left, flying away, and sweet sleep released me.
Come, let us arm the sons of the Achaeans—
but first I will test them with a speech, which is my right,
and I will order them to flee with their many-benched ships;
you, on all sides, check them with your words."

   Having said all this, he then sat down; and among them rose
Nestor, lord of Pylos by the sandy shore.
He with wise regard for them spoke and addressed them:
"O friends, leaders and counsellors of the Argives—
if any other of the Achaeans had told of this dream then   80
we would deem it a delusion and stay clear of it;
as it is, he who saw it claims to be the best by far of the Achaeans.
Come—let us see if we can arm the sons of the Achaeans."

   Thus speaking, he led the departure from the council,
and they rose at his bidding and obeyed the shepherd of the people,
they the sceptre-bearing kings. And the army host surged after them;
as when there goes a swarm of densely buzzing bees
streaming ever anew from a hollowed rock,
in clusters like grapes, zipping towards spring flowers

in a throng on the wing, hither and thither—
so the many troops of men from the ships and shelters
marched before the broad seashore
in throngs to the assembly; and blazing in their midst Rumour
urged them on, Zeus' envoy; and so they gathered.
The assembly was thrown into disorder, the earth groaned beneath
the men as they were seated, there was a roar of voices from the throng.
Nine heralds bellowing were trying to restrain them, to make them
cease their shouting and listen to the Zeus-cherished kings.

     With difficulty the men were seated, settled in their seats,
and ceased their clamour. Then rose lord Agamemnon,   100
holding his sceptre; this Hephaestus had toiled to make;
Hephaestus gave it to Zeus, the lord, the son of Cronus,
then Zeus gave it to Hermes, the messenger and slayer of Argos,
and lord Hermes gave it to Pelops, driver of horses,
then Pelops in turn gave it to Atreus, shepherd of the people;
and Atreus on dying left it to Thyestes, rich with many sheep,
and Thyestes in turn left it to Agamemnon to carry about,
and to be lord of many islands and of all Argos.
Propped on this, Agamemnon addressed the Argives with his words:

     "O friends, Danaan warriors, companions of Ares,   110
greatly has Zeus the son of Cronus entangled me in grave delusion;
hard he is, who before promised me and pledged
that I would return home after sacking well-walled Troy.
But as it is, he devised base deception, and he bids me
go back to Argos in dishonour, since I have destroyed a multitude of my men.
This, it seems, must please Zeus, supreme in might,
who has brought to ruin the citadels of many cities,
and will destroy yet more; for his is the greatest power.
And this is a disgrace even for future men to hear of—
that in this way, to no purpose, so great and so numerous a host of
   Achaeans   120
waged an ineffectual war and fought against

fewer men, and no accomplishment was ever shown.
Indeed, if Achaeans and Trojans alike were willing
to cut a sacred truce and be counted on both sides,
and those Trojans who have homes in the city were numbered,
and we Achaeans were to be divided into companies of ten,
and each of our divisions chose a man of Troy to pour their wine,
there would be many tens of men lacking a wine pourer.
So much more numerous, I say, are we sons of the Achaeans
than the Trojans, those who reside throughout the city; yet there are
    allies   130
from many cities, spear-wielding men,
who have knocked me wide off course and do not allow me, as I desire,
to sack the well-settled town of Ilion;
nine years have passed under mighty Zeus,
and the ship planks have rotted, the lines frayed;
no doubt our wives and our young children
sit in our homes watching for us; the task
for which we came here is utterly unaccomplished.
But come—let us all be persuaded to do as I say;
let us flee with our ships to our beloved fatherland,   140
for we will not ever take Troy of the wide ways."

          Thus he spoke and stirred the heart in every breast
among the multitude, all who had not heard his plan.
The assembly was shaken like the towering waves of the sea,
the open sea of Icaria; waves which the South and East Winds
raise, rushing down from the clouds of Zeus the father.
As when the West Wind's coming shakes a deep stand of corn
rushing onward in its fury, and the corn bends its ears before the blast—
so all the assembly was shaken; with a shout
the men rushed to the ships, and dust raised beneath their feet   150
hung in the air. They urged one another
to seize the ships and drag them to the bright sea,
and to clear out the launching tracks. The cry reached heaven

of men longing for home; and they. They lifted the props from beneath
　　the ships.

　　　　　Then against fate, would there have been homecoming for the
　　Argives
had not Hera spoken a word to Athena:
"Shame, shame! Child of Zeus who bears the stormy aegis, Unwearied
　　One—
is it in this way now the Argives will flee homeward to their beloved
fatherland, across the broad back of the sea?
They would leave as trophy for Priam and the Trojans　　　　　　　160
Helen of Argos, on whose account many Achaeans
have died at Troy, far from the soil of their fatherland.
But now go throughout the host of the bronze-clad Achaeans;
check each man with your calming words,
do not allow them to drag their double-ended ships to the sea."

　　　　　Thus she spoke, and the gleaming-eyed goddess Athena did not
　　disobey,
and she left, shooting down from the heights of Olympus.　　　　　167
Then she found Odysseus, like Zeus in wiles,　　　　　　　　　　169
just standing; he had not touched his dark, well-benched ship　　170
since anguish gripped him in his heart and soul.
Standing close, gleaming-eyed Athena addressed him:
"Son of Zeus-descended Laertes, Odysseus of many stratagems,
is it in this way you Argives will flee homeward now to your beloved
fatherland, falling into your ships with their many oars?
You would leave as a trophy for Priam and the Trojans
Helen of Argos, on whose account many Achaeans
have died at Troy, far from the dear soil of their fatherland.
Come, go now throughout the host of the Achaeans, hold back no longer;
check each man with your calming words,　　　　　　　　　　　180
do not allow them to drag their double-ended ships to the sea."

　　　　　Thus she spoke, and he recognised the voice of the goddess
　　speaking,

and departed at a run, casting off his cloak; this
Eurybates gathered up, the herald from Ithaca who attended him.
And Odysseus, coming straight up to the son of Atreus Agamemnon,
took from him the sceptre of his fathers, imperishable, eternal,
and with this he strode to the ships of the bronze-clad Achaeans.
Encountering a king, or some man of prominence,
he would check him with soothing words, standing beside him:
"What possesses you? It is not seemly that I should frighten you as if you
   were a base-born man,   190
but come, sit yourself down and get your people seated.
For you do not yet fully know the plan of the son of Atreus;
he is testing now, but shortly will bear hard upon the sons of the Achaeans.
We did not all hear what he said in council;
may he not in anger commit some violence against the sons of the
   Achaeans—
the anger of the king Zeus cherishes is mighty,
his rank is from Zeus, and Zeus all-devising loves him."
But if he saw and came upon some man of the ranks crying out,
he beat him with the sceptre and shouted a threat:
"Mad man, be still and heed the word of others   200
who are your betters; you are craven and cowardly,
and count for nothing in war or council.
It seems not all we Achaeans can be kings here;
the rule of many is not a good thing; let there be one ruler,
one king, to whom the son of devious Cronus gave sovereignty."   205
So giving commands he brought the army to order; the men
   rushed back   207
to the assembly from the ships and shelters
with a shout, as when a wave of the tumultuous sea
roars mightily on the shore, and the whole sea crashes.   210
      The other men were seated, settled in their seats;
Thersites alone still jabbered his unbridled speech,
who knew in his mind many incoherent things to say—

vain, indecent—to antagonise kings,

but which seemed to him to be amusing to the Argive men.

The most repellent man to come beneath the walls of Ilion;

he was a dragger of feet, lame in one leg, his humped-over shoulders

came together at his chest; above them

his head was misshapen to a point and meagre stubble sprouted on it.

Above all he was detested by Achilles and Odysseus   220

for he was always reviling the two. But now it was against godlike
   Agamemnon

he noisily gave his litany of shrill abuse; for at him the Achaeans

were greatly angered and resentful in spirit.

Shouting loudly, he abused Agamemnon with his speech:

"Son of Atreus, what thing now do you fault and covet?

Your huts are full of bronze, many choice women

are within your shelter, whom we Achaeans gave you

as first spoils when we sacked a city.

Or do you lack yet more gold, which some man

of the horse-breaking Trojans will carry from Ilion as ransom for his
   son,   230

whom I, or another Achaean, have bound and led away—

or a new woman so you can join in fornication,

a woman you can possess apart? It is indecent

that you, the leader, march the sons of the Achaeans into evil.

Wretches, cowardly disgraces, Achaean women, no longer men of Achaea!

Let us return to our homes with our ships, let us leave this man

here in Troy to brood upon his prizes, so that he may know

whether we too, in some way, are of use to him, or whether not.

And now he has dishonoured Achilles, a far better man than him;

for he keeps his prize, having seized it, he personally taking it.   240

Why, there is no gall in the heart of Achilles, rather he is slow to action!

Otherwise, son of Atreus, now would be your last outrage."

         Thus Thersites spoke reviling Agamemnon, the shepherd of the
   people;

but straightway godlike Odysseus confronted him,

and looking at him from under his brows upbraided him with hard words:

"Thersites, incoherent in speech, clear speaker though you may be,

restrain yourself, and do not seek to contend on your own with kings.

For I say there is no other mortal man baser than you,

however many came with the sons of Atreus beneath the walls of Ilion;

therefore do not have kings on your tongue when you hold forth in the

    assembly   250

and cast abuse at them and be vigilant for departure.

We have no clear idea how this business will turn out,

whether we sons of Achaeans will return home well or badly.

So; now at the son of Atreus—Agamemnon, shepherd of the people—

you sit hurling abuse, because the Danaan warriors

gave him much; your declaiming in assembly is mockery.

I say this outright to you, and it will be accomplished—

if ever again I find you ranting as you do now,

then let Odysseus' head stand no longer on his shoulders,

nor may I still be called the father of Telemachos,   260

if I don't take hold of you and strip off your very clothes,

your cloak and tunic that conceal your private parts,

and send you wailing to the swift ships,

after being flogged round the assembly with shameful blows."

       Thus he spoke and with the sceptre beat the other's back

and shoulders; Thersites doubled over and shed welling tears;

a bloody welt started up between his shoulders

under the gold-studded sceptre; and he sat down, terrified,

in pain and looking helplessly around wiped away his tears.

And distressed as they were, the men laughed heartily at him,   270

and a man looking at his neighbour would speak in this way:

"Oh me! Odysseus has accomplished thousands of good deeds,

both leading good councils and marshalling battle—

but this now is the best thing he has accomplished among the Argives,

he has shut out this flinger of scurrilous words from speaking in

assemblies.
Likely his bold heart will not drive him again
to contend against kings with abusive words!"

       Thus the multitude spoke. Odysseus the sacker of cities
stood up holding the sceptre, and beside him gleaming-eyed Athena
in the likeness of a herald commanded the host to silence,   280
so that the sons of Achaeans, both in front and behind,
might hear his word and learn his plan.
He, with wise regard for them, spoke and addressed them:
"Son of Atreus, now, my lord, the Achaeans have a mind
to make you most contemptible in the eyes of all mortal men,
nor do they fulfil the promise that they undertook
at that time that they were leaving for here from the horse-grazed
    pastures of Argos—
that they would return home after sacking well-walled Ilion.
For like young children and widowed women
they wail among themselves about returning to their homes.   290
But surely it is also hardship to return home sick at heart!
For even a man away from his wife for a single month
chafes as he waits with his many-benched ship, he whom the whirling
    storm winds
of winter hold, and the tempestuous sea;
for us this is the ninth revolving year's turning
we tarry here. Therefore, I do not blame the Achaeans
for chafing beside their curved ships; but for all that
it is shameful to tarry a long time and also return empty-handed.
Endure, my friends! And stand firm until that time when we learn
whether Calchas prophesised truthfully, or not.   300
For this we know well in our minds—you are all
witnesses, you whom the fates of death have not carried off,
only yesterday, as it seems—when the Achaean ships in Aulis
were gathered, bearing evil for Priam and Troy,
and we around a spring and about the sacred altars
performed perfect sacrificial hecatombs for the immortals,

beneath a lovely plane tree, from where bright water flowed;
and there appeared a momentous portent; a snake, its back mottled
   blood-red,
a thing of dread that the Olympian himself dispatched into the light,
darting from beneath the altar sped toward the plane tree—   310
where a sparrow's nestlings were, innocent young,
on the tip-top branch, cowering beneath the leaves,
eight of them, and the mother made nine, who gave them life.
There it devoured them as they cheeped piteously,
the mother fluttering around, crying for her beloved children.
Then, having coiled itself up, it seized her by the wing as she cried about.
And when it had devoured utterly both the young and the mother sparrow,
the god removed him from sight, the god who had brought it to light;
for the son of devious Cronus turned it to stone;
and we standing by marvelled at what happened—   320
in this way, then, the terrible portent of the gods broke into our hecatombs.
Thereupon Calchas spoke at once, prophesying:
'Why are you become silent, O long-haired Achaeans?
Zeus, all-devising, brought to light this great omen for us,
late arriving, late to be fulfilled, and the fame of which will never die.
As this thing devoured the sparrow's young and the sparrow herself—
eight they were, but the mother made nine, who gave the young life—
so we for as many years shall wage battle here,
and in the tenth we shall take the city of the wide ways.'
Thus he was telling us; and now all these things are being fulfilled.   330
Come—stay, all you strong-greaved Achaeans,
stay here until we take the great city of Priam."

       So he spoke, and the Argives shouted loud assent—the ships
   around them
echoed terribly with the force of the Achaeans' shouting—
approving the speech of godlike Odysseus.
Then among them also spoke the Gerenian driver of horses, Nestor:
"For shame! You debate like children,

infants with no concern for warlike deeds.

Where go our covenants and oaths?

Let the counsels and plans of men be burned in fire,   340

and solemn libations of treaty and the pledges in which we trusted!

To no end do we contest with words, nothing expedient

are we able to find, for all the long time we have been here.

Son of Atreus, hold firm yet, as before, to your unshaken plan,

lead the Argives through the mighty combat,

and let those perish, the one or two who

make their plans apart from the Achaeans—they will accomplish nothing—

to return early to Argos, before knowing

whether the promise of Zeus who wields the aegis was false, or not.

For I say that the almighty son of Cronus nodded his assent   350

on that day, when in fast-running ships the Argives departed

bringing death and slaughter to the Trojans,

flashing lightning to our right, showing forth a true sign.

Therefore, let no one press to return home,

before he has bedded the wife of a Trojan man

to exact requital for the struggle and groaning over Helen.

And if any man strongly wishes to go home,

let him only touch his black well-benched ship,

so that before the others he may meet his death and destiny.

But, my lord, both plan carefully yourself and also listen to another;   360

not to be disregarded is the word I say.

Separate the men by tribes, then by clans, Agamemnon,

so that clan stands by clan, and tribe by tribe.

If you do this, and the Achaeans obey you,

then you will know which of the leaders is worthless, as well as which of
     the ranks,

and which is outstanding; for they will fight in separate divisions on their
     own,

and you will learn too whether it is by the will of god you do not sack the
     city,

or by the cowardice of man and ignorance of war."

       Then answering him lord Agamemnon spoke:

"Once again, old man, you have outdone the sons of the Achaeans in
   speech.

Father Zeus, Athena and Apollo! Would that

there were ten such advisers among the Achaeans!

The city of lord Priam would swiftly totter

beneath our hands, captured and sacked.

But Zeus who wields the aegis, the son of Cronus, gave me woes,

who cast me into useless quarrels and contentions.

So I and Achilles have fought over a girl,

confronting each other with words, and I was first to be angry.

If ever we should be at one in counsel, then there would be no further

respite from evil for the Trojans, not even a little.

Now go to your dinner, so that we may assemble our battle.

Let each man sharpen his spear, let him get his shield at the ready,

let him feed well his swift-footed horses.

And when he has inspected his chariot, let each man turn his attention
   to war.

Daylong we shall be measured in hateful warfare.

There will be no interlude in it, not even a little,

until night descending separates the raging men;

around a man's chest the strap of his body shield

will be wet with sweat, his hand will grow weary around his spear,

and the horse will be wet with sweat that draws his burnished
   chariot.

That man I find away from battle, seeking

to linger around the curved ships—for him

there will be no surety of escaping the dogs and birds."

       So he spoke and the Argives roared assent, like a wave

when the coming South Wind rouses it, upon a high headland,

a jutting prominence; one which the surge, wind-driven from all quarters,

never leaves in peace, coming on this side and that.

Rising to their feet, the men set to work, scattering toward the ships,
and made their smoking fires besides the shelters, and took their meal.
And each man offered sacrifice to one or another of the ever-living
    gods,   400
praying to escape death and battle's tumult.

        Then the lord of men Agamemnon sacrificed an ox,
rich with fat, five years of age, to the almighty son of Cronus,
and summoned the senior nobles from the whole Achaean force.
Nestor first of all, and lord Idomeneus,
then the two Aiantes and the son of Tydeus, Diomedes,
and then sixth, Odysseus, like Zeus in wiles;
Menelaos of the war cry came of his own accord;
for his heart perceived how his brother laboured.
They stood around the ox and scattered sacrificial barley,   410
and praying for them lord Agamemnon spoke:
"Zeus most glorious, mightiest, you of the dark clouds, dwelling in heaven—
let not the sun go down or darkness descend upon us
until I have hurled headlong Priam's smoke-blackened palace,
enflamed its gates with deadly fire,
and rent from Hector's breast his tunic
slashed with bronze; while in droves around him his companions,
headlong in the dust, bite the earth between their teeth."
So he spoke. But the son of Cronus did not grant him this,
but accepted his sacrifice, and multiplied the unwished hardship.   420

        Then when they had prayed and thrown the scattering barley
    before them,
they first drew back the head of the sacrificial animal and cut its throat,
    and flayed it,
and cut out the thigh bones and covered them over with fat
they had made into double folds, and placed raw flesh upon them;
and these they then roasted on spits of stripped wood,
and spitting the entrails they held them over the fire of Hephaestus.
Then when the thighbones had been consumed by fire and they had

tasted the entrails,
they cut up the other parts and pierced them through on spits
and roasted them with care, and then drew off all the pieces.
And when they had ceased their work and prepared their meal,   430
they feasted, nor did any man's appetite lack his due portion.

    And when they had put away desire for drinking and eating,
then Nestor the Gerenian horseman began a speech:
"Most glorious son of Atreus, lord of men Agamemnon,
let us no longer talk about these things, nor yet longer
delay our task, which god has handed us.
Come, let the heralds of the bronze-clad Achaeans
make proclamation and assemble the people by the ships,
and let us go together as we are throughout the broad army of the
    Achaeans,
so that we may more swiftly bring about the piercing war."   440

    So he spoke and lord of men Agamemnon did not disobey,
but at once commanded the clear-voiced heralds
to summon the long-haired Achaeans to war.
They made their summons and the men were swiftly assembled;
and around the son of Atreus the kings cherished by Zeus
hastened about marshalling them, and with them went gleaming-eyed
    Athena,
holding the stormy aegis—revered, ageless and deathless,
a hundred tassels of solid gold floated from it,
each intricately woven, each worth a hundred oxen;
with this she darted and flashed through the host of Achaeans,   450
and she stoked the strength in each man's heart, urging him to go,
to fight on without respite and do battle;
and suddenly war became sweeter to them than going home
in hollow ships to their beloved fatherland.

    As when obliterating fire rages through an immense forest
on the mountain height, and from afar the flare shows forth,
so the gleam from the sublime bronze of marching men

glinting through the clear sky reached heaven.
These, as great flocks of winged birds,
of geese or cranes or long-necked swans,   460
in the Asian meadow amid the waters of the river Cayster,
flying hither and thither exulting in their wings,
ever settling, one before the other, with ringing cries, and the meadow
    resounds—
so the many tribes of men from the ships and shelters
poured forth onto the plain of Scamander; and the earth
thundered terribly beneath their feet and beneath the horses.
They took position in the flowering meadow of Scamander,
thousands of them, as many as there are leaves and flowers in springtime,
as the many swarms of incessant flies
that flit about a shepherd's stall   470
in spring, when milk splashes the pail,
so the long-haired Achaeans took their stand against the Trojans
on the plain, urgent to shatter them.

        As goat-herding men easily separate
wide-ranging herds of goats, when they are mingled in pasture,
so the leaders marshalled the men here and there
to go into combat, and with them was lord Agamemnon—
his eyes and head like Zeus who hurls the thunderbolt,
his girth like Ares, his chest like Poseidon's.
As when an ox stands out from all others in the herd,   480
a bull who is pre-eminent among the gathered cattle,
so did Zeus on that day render the son of Atreus
conspicuous amid the multitude, outstanding among warriors.

        Tell me now, Muses, who have your homes on Olympus—
for you are goddesses, and ever-present, and know all things,
and we hear only rumour, nor do we know anything—
who were the leaders and captains of the Danaans.
As for the multitude, I could not describe nor tell their names,
not if I had ten tongues, and ten mouths,

or a voice that never tired, and the spirit in me were as bronze;   490
not unless the Muses of Olympus, daughters of Zeus who wields the aegis,
should remember all who came beneath the walls of Ilion.
Yet the leaders of ships I will recite, and the ships themselves, from
    start to finish.

      Of the Boeotians, Peneleos and Leïtos were leaders,
and Arkesilaos, Prothoënor and Klonios;
those who dwelt in Hyria and in rocky Aulis,
in Schoinos and Skolos and the spurred mountains of Eteonos,
in Thespeia and Graia and Mykalessos with its wide places for dancing,
those who dwelt around Harma and Eilesion and Erythrai,
those who held Eleon and Hyle and Peteon,   500
Okalea and Medeon, a well-established city,
Kopai and Eutresis and Thisbe of the many doves,
those who held Koroneia and grassy Haliartos,
those who held Plataia and those who dwelt in Glisas,
those who held Lower Thebes, a well-established city,
and holy Onchestos, the splendid grove of Poseidon;
those who held Arne rich in grapes, and those who held Mideia,
and Nisa the holy and furthest Anthedon—
of these there went fifty ships, and in each there embarked
one hundred and twenty young men of Boeotia.   510

      Those who dwelt in Aspledon and Minyan Orchomenos,
of these were Askalaphos and Ialmenos were leaders, sons both of Ares,
whom Astyoche bore in the house of Aktor, the son of Azeus—
a shy maiden, who entered the upstairs chamber
with mighty Ares; and in secret he lay with her;
of these there sailed thirty hollow ships.

      Then Schedios and Epistrophos led the Phocians,
sons of Iphitos, the son of great-hearted Naubolos;
these held Kyparissos and rocky Pytho,
and sacred Krisa and Daulis and Panopeus,   520
and those dwelling around Hyampolis and Anemoreia,

those who lived by the shining river Kephisos,
and those who held Lilaia by the fountains of Kephisos;
forty black ships followed with these leaders.
They marshalled the ranks of Phocians,
stationed them under arms on the left, hard by the Boeotians.

Of Locrians, swift Ajax, son of Oïleus, was leader—
the lesser Ajax, not so great as Telamon's son Ajax,
but lesser by far; for he was a small man, and his breastplate of linen,
yet in work of spear he excelled all Achaeans and Hellenes—   530
they who dwelt in Kynos and Opoeis and Kalliaros
and in Bessa and Skarphe and also lovely Augeiai
and in Tarphe and Thronion and round the streams of Boagrios—
with him there followed forty black ships
of Locrians, those who dwell beyond holy Euboea.

Those who held Euboea, the Abantes who breathe fury,
Chalcis and Eretria and Histiaia rich in grapes,
and Kerinthos by the sea and the steep city of Dion,
those who held Karystos and those who dwelt in Styra—
of these Elephenor was leader, companion of Ares,   540
the son of Chalkodon, lord of the great-hearted Abantes;
the swift Abantes followed with him, their hair grown long behind,
spearmen straining with out-held spears
to shatter the breastplates round their enemies breasts;
and with him there followed forty black ships.

And then those who held Athens, a well-built city,
realm of great-hearted Erechtheus, whom once Athena,
Zeus' daughter, reared—Erechtheus born of the grain-giving fields—
and established him in Athens, in her own rich temple;
where Athenian youths with bulls and rams   550
supplicate him through the turning years;
of these Menestheus was leader, son of Peteos.
There was not any man born his equal on earth
at marshalling horses and shield-bearing men;

Nestor only rivalled him; for in age he was older.
And with him there followed fifty black ships.

From Salamis, Ajax led twelve ships,
and arrayed them where the ranks of Athenians were stationed.

Those who held Argos and walled Tiryns,
and Hermione and Asine enfolding its deep bay,   560
Troizen and Eïonai and Epidauros rich in vines,
those who held Aegina and Mases, sons of the Achaeans—
of these Diomedes of the war cry was leader,
and Sthenelos, the beloved son of glorious Kapaneus.
With them Euryalos went as a third, a man like the gods,
the son of lord Mekisteus, from the line of Talaos,
all these Diomedes of the war cry led;
and with them there followed eighty black ships.

Those who held Mycenae, the well-built city,
and prosperous Corinth and well-built Kleonai   570
and they who dwelt in Orneai and lovely Araithyrea
and Sikyon, where Adrestos first ruled as king,
and those who held Hyperesia and sheer Gonoëssa
and Pellene and those who dwelt around Aigion
throughout all Aigialos and around broad Helike—
of their hundred ships was lord Agamemnon leader,
Atreus' son. And with him followed by far the most men
and the best; he himself was clad in blinding bronze,
triumphant, conspicuous among all warriors,
because he was best—since he led by far the most men.   580

Those who held Lacedaemon, set low in ravines,
and Pharis and Sparta and Messe haunted by doves,
and those who dwelt in Bryseiai and lovely Augeiai,
and those who held Amyklai and Helos, the seaside city,
those who held Laas and those who dwelt round Oitylos,
of these his brother Menelaos of the war cry
led sixty ships; they were stationed apart,

and he came emboldened by ardour,
driving them to battle; above all his heart desired
to exact requital for the struggle and groaning over Helen.   590

      Those who dwelt in Pylos and lovely Arene,
and Thryon, where Alpheus is crossed, and well-built Aipu,
and those who lived in Kyparisseïs and Amphigeneia,
and Pteleos and Helos and Dorion, where the Muses
accosted Thamyris, the Thracian, and put an end to his singing
as he came from Oichalia and Oichalian Eurytos—
for boasting he declared he would prove winner should the Muses
    themselves
sing against him, the daughters of Zeus who wields the aegis;
stung with anger, they paralysed him, took away
his divine gift of song, and caused him to forget his lyre-playing—   600
of these Nestor the Gerenian horseman was leader;
of these there sailed ninety hollow ships.

      Those who held Arcadia under sheer Mount Kyllene,
by the tomb of Aipytos, where men fight at close quarters,
those who dwelt in Pheneos and Orchomenos, with its many flocks,
and in Rhipe and Stratia and windswept Enispe,
and held Tegea and lovely Mantineia,
who held Stymphalos and dwelt in Parrhasia—
lord Agapenor, son of Ankaios, was leader
of their sixty ships; and in each ship went many   610
men of Arcadia, well skilled in warfare,
Agamemnon, lord of men, gave them
well-benched ships to cross a sea as dark as wine,
the son of Atreus himself, since the work of the sea was of no
    concern to them.

      Then those who lived in Bouprasion and shining Elis,
all that is bounded by Hyrmine and the borders of Myrsinos,
and the rock of Olen and Alesion—
of these were there four leaders, and with each

there followed ten swift ships, with many Epeans on board.
Of these Amphimachos and Thalpios were two leaders,   620
sons of Aktor's line, one by Kteatos and one by Eurytos;
powerful Diores was also their leader, son of Amarynkeus;
and godlike Polyxeinos was their fourth leader
son of lord Agasthenes, who was son of Augeias.

      Those from Doulichion and from Echinai, sacred
islands that lie across the sea facing Elis—
of these Meges was leader, equal to Ares,
son of Phyleus—Phyleus begot him, driver of horses, beloved of Zeus,
who angered at his father in time past departed to settle Doulichion;
and with him there followed forty black ships.   630

      Then Odysseus led the high-hearted Kephallenians,
those who held Ithaca and Neritos of fluttering leaves
and those who dwelt in Krokyleia and rugged Aigilips,
those who held Zakynthos and those who dwelt around Samos,
those who held the mainland and those who dwelt about the facing shore;
of these Odysseus was leader, Zeus' match in wisdom;
and with him there followed twelve scarlet-prowed ships.

      Thoas, son of Andraimon, led the Aetolians,
those who dwelt in Pleuron and Olenos and Pylene,
and Chalkis near the sea and rocky Calydon;   640
for the sons of great-hearted Oineus were no longer alive,
nor did Oineus himself still live, and tawny Meleager had died,
so to Thoas was charged the rule of all Aetolians;
and with him there followed forty black ships.

      Of the Cretans was spear-famed Idomeneus the leader,
those who held Knossos and high-walled Gortyn,
Lyktos and Miletos and gleaming Lykastos
and Phaistos and Rhytion, a well-settled city,
and those others who dwelt around Crete of the hundred cities.
Of these Idomeneus the famed spearman was leader   650
and Meriones, equal to Enyalios, the murderous war.

And with them there followed eighty black ships.

      Tlepolemos, son of Heracles, a good man and great,
led nine ships from Rhodes with noble Rhodians,
those who dwelt about Rhodes marshalled into three states,
from Lindos and Ialysos and gleaming Kameiros;
of these Tlepolemos, famed spearman, was leader,
whom Astyocheia bore to strong Heracles,
she whom he led out of Ephyra, from the river Selleeïs,
after sacking many cities of Zeus-cherished young warriors.   660
Then when Tlepolemos came of age in the well-built palace,
he soon killed his father's dearly loved uncle,
a man already grown old, Likymnios, companion of Ares.
Quickly he fitted out ships, gathering a great band of followers,
and left, fleeing over the deep sea; for other
sons and grandsons of strong Heracles threatened him.
He came to Rhodes after wandering, after suffering misfortunes;
and they settled in three companies according to tribe, and were favoured
by Zeus, who is lord of gods and of men,
and on them the son of Cronus bestowed marvellous wealth.   670

      Nireus from Syme led three balanced ships,
Nireus, son of his mother Aglaïa and lord Charopos,
Nireus, the most beautiful man to come beneath Ilion
of all the Danaans, after blameless Achilles,
but he was weak and few men followed with him.

      Then those who held Nisyros and Karpathos and Kasos
and Cos, the city of Eurypylos, and the Kalydnian islands,
these both Pheidippos and Antiphos ruled,
the two sons of lord Thessalos, son of Heracles;
of these there sailed thirty hollow ships.   680

      Now too all those who dwelt in Pelasgian Argos,
those who dwelt in Alos and Alope and those dwelling in Trachis,
those who held Phthia and Hellas of beautiful women—
those called Myrmidons and Hellenes and Achaeans;

their fifty ships were led by Achilles.
But these paid no heed to grievous war;
for there was no man to lead them to the ranks of battle;
since swift-footed godlike Achilles lay low by his ships,
angered for the girl, lovely haired Briseïs,
whom he had taken from Lyrnessos after much labour,   690
after sacking Lyrnessos and the walls of Thebes,
and struck down Mynes and Epistrophos, spear-fighters,
sons of lord Euenos, who was son of Selepos—
for her sake he lay grieving; but soon he would rise.

    Those who held Phylake and flowering Pyrasos,
the sanctuary of Demeter, and Iton, mother of flocks,
and Antron by the sea, and grass-banked Pteleos;
of these Protesilaos the warlike was leader—
while he lived; for already the dark earth held him,
and his wife, her cheeks torn in mourning, was left in Phylake,   700
his house half built; a Dardanian man killed him
as he leapt from his ship, first by far of the Achaeans;
but they were not leaderless, though they mourned their leader.
Podarkes arrayed them, companion of Ares,
the son of Iphiklos, son of flock-rich Phylakos,
a full brother of great-hearted Protesilaos,
younger by birth; but the older and better
was the warrrior Protesilaos; yet his men were not leaderless,
although they mourned him, noble as he was.
And with Podarkes there followed forty dark ships.   710

    Those who dwelt in Pherai beside Lake Boibeïs,
and in Boibe and Glaphyrai and well-built Iolkos,
of these the beloved son of Admetos led eleven ships,
Eumelos, he whom Alcestis, resplendent of women, bore to Admetos,
the most beautiful of all daughters of Pelias.

    Those who dwelt in Methone and Thaumakia
and held Meliboia and rugged Olizon—

Philoctetes well skilled in the bow was the leader
of their seven ships; and in each were embarked fifty rowers,
well skilled in the bow to fight strongly in battle.   720
But on an island he lay, suffering powerful afflictions,
on Lemnos the sacred, where the Achaeans had left him
tormented by the baneful wound of a deadly water serpent;
there he lay suffering; but soon the Argives,
camped by their ships, were to turn their minds to lord Philoctetes.
Nor were they leaderless, for all they mourned their leader;
but Medon, bastard son of Oïleus, marshalled them,
Medon whom Rhene bore to Oïleus sacker of cities.

      Those who held Trikka and rugged Ithome,
those who held Oichalia, city of Oichalian Eurytos,   730
of these the two sons of Asclepius were leaders,
both good healers, Podaleirios and Machaon;
of these there sailed thirty hollow ships.

      Those who held Ormenion and the spring Hypereia,
who held Asterion and the shining white summits of Titanos,
of these Eurypylos was leader, splendid son of Euaimon;
and with him there followed forty dark ships.

      Those who held Argissa and dwelt in Gyrtone,
and Orthe and Elone and the white city Oloösson—
of these steadfast Polypoites was leader,   740
the son of Peirithoös, whom immortal Zeus fathered,
he whom Hippodameia the glorious bore to Peirithoös
on that day when he wreaked vengeance on the shaggy Centaurs,
and drove them from Mount Pelion into the land of the Aithikes;
not alone, for with him was Leonteus, companion of Ares,
son of high-hearted Koronos, of the line of Kaineus;
and with these there followed forty dark ships.

      Gouneus from Kyphos led twenty-two ships;
the Enienes followed him and the steadfast Peraiboi,
they who made their homes around wintry Dodona,   750

they who settled the tilled fields around the lovely Titaressos,
who pours forth his waters, lovely flowing, into the Peneus—
Titaressos does not mingle with the silver eddies of Peneus,
but rather floats above, like oil, on the surface;
for this is a branch of the Styx, dread river of oath.

      Prothoös, son of Tenthredon, led the Magnesians,
those who dwelt around the Peneus and fluttering-leaved Mount Pelion;
of these swift Prothoös was leader,
and with him there followed forty dark ships.

      Such, then, were the commanders and leaders of the Danaans.   760
Tell me, Muse, who of these was very best,
of the men and the horses, who followed Atreus' sons?
The best horses by far were belonging to the line of Pheres,
mares that Eumelos drove, swift-moving as birds,
matched in colour, in age, their backs across as level as a plumb line—
horses that Apollo of the silver bow had reared in Pereia,
both females, bearers of terror in battle.
And of men far the best was Telamonian Ajax—
while Achilles was wrathful; for Achilles was far strongest,
as were his horses, who always carried the blameless son of Peleus.   770
But he lay idle among his curved seagoing ships,
raging against Agamemnon, shepherd of the people,
the son of Atreus; and along the breaking surf of the sea his men
amused themselves casting discus and hunting spears,
and aiming with their bows; and each horse stood beside its chariot
munching clover and marsh parsley.
The well-covered chariots were laid away
in the shelter of their lords. They, bereft of their warlike leader,
roaming here and there throughout the army, did not fight.

      But the others advanced as if fire were grazing all the land,   780
and the earth rumbled as when Zeus, who hurls the thunderbolt rages,
when he lashes the earth around Typhoeus
in the land of the Arimoi, where men say monstrous Typhoeus has his lair.

So the earth loudly thundered beneath the feet
of the approaching men; and with lightning speed they traversed the plain.
     Then to the Trojans, swift Iris with feet like the wind came as
    messenger,
sent from Zeus who wields the aegis with a painful message.
They were gathered in assembly by Priam's gates
all together, both young and old.
Standing close, swift-footed Iris addressed them;   790
she likened her voice to that of Priam's son Polites,
who confident in the swiftness of his feet, sat as sentinel of Troy
on the highest point of the tomb of old Aisyetes,
on the lookout for when the Achaeans might sally forth from the ships.
In his likeness, swift-footed Iris addressed them:
"Old sir, endless talk is always dear to you
as before, in the days of peace; but war unceasing has arisen.
And to be sure I have entered into many a battle with men,
but never have I beheld such a force and in such numbers;
more numerous than leaves or grains of sand   800
the men advance across the plain towards the city to do battle.
Hector, on you above all I lay this injunction, to do as I say;
many allies are around the great city of Priam,
and every language of these widely scattered men is different from the
    others;
let each man give orders to those troops he leads,
and once he has marshalled his fellow citizens, have him lead them forth."
    So Iris spoke, and Hector did not fail to recognise the word of a
    goddess,
and at once he broke the assembly; and the men rushed to their arms.
All the gates were opened, and the host surged forth,
on foot and on horse; and a great roar rose.   810
There is a steep hill in front of the city
on its own in the plain, with running room on every side.
This men call by the name "Batieia", or the place of brambles,

but the gods know it as the tomb of the far-dancing Amazon Myrine;
there the Trojans and their allies were arrayed.

      Great Hector of the shimmering helm was leader of the Trojans,
Priam's son; with him by far the most numerous and best
troops were mustered, at the ready with their spears.

      Next the noble son of Anchises led the Dardanians,
Aeneas, whom divine Aphrodite bore to Anchises,   820
a goddess lying with a mortal man in the foothills of Mount Ida;
he was not alone, for with Aeneas were two sons of Antenor,
Archelochos and Akamas, both skilled in all manner of fighting.

      Those who dwelt in Zeleia below the furthest foot of Ida,
wealthy men who drank the dark water of Aisepos,
Trojans; of these Lykaon's splendid son,
Pandaros, was leader, to whom Apollo himself had given a bow.

      Those who held Adresteia and the country of Apaisos,
and held Pityeia and the steep mountain Tereia—
of these was Adrestos leader and Amphios too, in his breastplate of
    linen,   830
both sons of Merops of Percote, who beyond all men
was skilled in divination, and forbade his sons
to go to man-destroying war. But these two did not
obey him; for the forces of dark death drove them.

      Those who dwelt around Percote and Praktion,
and held Sestos and Abydos and shining Arisbe,
of these Asios the son of Hyrtakos was leader, a chief among men,
Asios son of Hyrtakos, whose great blazing
horses carried him from Arisbe, away from the river Selleeïs.

      Hippothoös led the tribe of Pelasgian spear-fighters,   840
they who inhabited Larisa with its rich soil.
Of these Hippothoös and Pylaios, companion of Ares, were leaders,
two sons of Pelasgian Lethos, who was son of Teutamos.

      Akamas and the warrior Peiroös led the Thracians,
all those whom the strong-flowing Hellespont bounds within.

Euphemos led the Ciconian spearmen,
a son of Troizenos, cherished by Zeus, and the son of Keas.

Pyraichmes led the Paeonians with their curved bows,
from faraway Amydon and the wide-flowing Axios—
Axios, whose water flows loveliest on earth.   850

Rough-hearted Pylaimenes led the Paphlagonians
from the land of the Enetoi, the place of wide-ranging mules
they who held Kytoros and who dwelt around Sesamos,
and who lived in their splendid homes around the river Parthenios,
at Kromna and Aigialos and Erythinoi on high.

Then Odios and Epistrophos led the Halizones
from far-off Alybe, where silver is born.

Of the Mysians, Chromis was leader, with Ennomos augur of
    birds;
but not by birds did he ward off dark death,
but was broken under the hands of swift-footed Achilles
in the river, where he cut down other Trojans.

Phorkys and godlike Askanios led the Phrygians   860
from faraway Askania; for they hungered to go to battle in the combat.

Mesthles and Antiphos commanded the Maeonians,
sons of Talaimenes, whom Lake Gygaia bore;
these led the Maeonians, those reared beneath Mount Tmolos.

Nastes led the wild-speaking Carians,
those who held Miletos and Phthires, the mountain of dense leaves,
and the stream of Maeander and the steep peak of Mykale.
Of these Amphimachos and Nastes were leaders,   870
Nastes and Amphimachos, splendid sons of Nomion;
Nastes who came to the war wearing gold like a girl—
fool, nor did this ward off from him miserable death,
but he was killed at the hands of swift-footed Aeacides
in the river, and blazing Achilles attended to his gold.

And Sarpedon and blameless Glaukos led the Lycians,
from faraway Lycia, and the whirling eddies of Xanthos.

Then when all the contingents were marshalled with their leaders
the Trojans set out with ringing cries and clamour, like birds—
as when the ringing cry of cranes goes up before heaven
when they flee the winter storms and monstrous rains,
and with a ringing cry fly to the rivers of Ocean,
bearing bloodshed and death to Pygmy men,
and high in the air display their evil battle strife—
but the Achaeans advanced in silence, breathing fury,
intent in their hearts to stand by one another.
As when on a mountain height the South Wind spills dark mist—   10
no friend to the shepherd, but to the thief better than night—
and a man sees before him only so far as he throws a stone;
so the thick dust rose beneath the feet
of the advancing men; and in all swiftness they traversed the plain.
Then when they had advanced almost upon each other,
godlike Alexandros stepped out before the Trojans as their champion,
a leopard skin and curved bow upon his shoulders,
and a sword; shaking two bronze-tipped spears
he called forth all the best of the Argives
to fight him man to man in dread combat.   20
As he did, Menelaos beloved by Ares caught sight of him
as he came striding before the throng of battle;
and as a lion rejoices when he comes upon a great carcass,
finding a horned deer or a wild goat

in his hunger, and devours it greedily, for all
the swift dogs and sturdy young men rush him;
so Menelaos rejoiced seeing godlike Alexandros
before his own eyes; for he thought to take vengeance on his offender;
and straightway he leapt from his chariot in his armour to the ground.

　　　As he did, godlike Alexandros saw him　　　　　　　　　　30
emerging among the front fighters, and was shaken in his heart,
and he drew back into the band of his companions, shunning death.
As when a man sees a snake in a mountain glen
and leaping back stands at a distance, and trembling seizes his limbs
and he draws back again, and pallor claims his cheeks,
so godlike Alexandros slipped back into the company
of noble Trojans, fearing the son of Atreus.

　　　And seeing him Hector reviled him with contemptuous words:
"Accursed Paris, outstanding only in beauty, woman crazed, seducer—
would that you were never born and died unwed;　　　　　　　40
so I would wish, and it would have been far better
than to be as now an outrage and something sneered at by others.
The long-haired Achaeans howl in laughter
thinking you our first champion, because your appearance
is beautiful—but there is no strength in your heart, nor any courage.
Were you such a man when in seagoing ships
you sailed the deep sea, assembling your trusty comrades,
and coming among foreign people led away a beautiful woman
from a distant land, a woman related to spearmen—
mighty ruin to your father and city and all your people,　　　　50
but great joy to our enemies and disgrace to yourself?
You will not stand to face Menelaos, beloved by Ares?
You would learn what kind of man was he whose luscious wife you
　　hold.
Your lyre and the gifts of Aphrodite would be of no use to you,
nor your hair and looks when you coupled with the dust.
The Trojans are great cowards; else before now

you would have worn a shirt of flying stones for your evils,
such things you have done."
    Then in turn godlike Alexandros addressed him:
"Hector, since you rebuke me fairly, and not beyond what is fair—
your heart is ever unyielding, like an axe   60
that goes through wood wielded by a man who skilfully
carves timber for a ship, and the axe increases the man's swing;
just so is the spirit in your breast relentless—
do not cast in my teeth the desirable gifts of golden Aphrodite.
Not to be thrown away are the glorious gifts of the gods,
whatever it is they might give; not at will can a man obtain them.
If you wish for me now to go to war again and do battle,
have all the other Trojans seated and all the Achaeans,
and match me and Menelaos beloved by Ares in the space between
to fight for Helen and all her possessions;   70
whichever of us proves winner and is mightier,
let him take all the possessions and duly lead the woman home—
and the others, swearing faithful oaths of friendship, let them
dwell in Troy where the soil is rich, or return
to the horse-grazed pastures of Argos and Achaea with its beautiful
    women."
    So he spoke; and Hector rejoiced greatly hearing his word,
and going into the midst of the Trojans he restrained the battle lines,
taking hold of his spear by the middle; and they all sat down.
But the long-haired Achaeans turned their bows on him,
and taking aim with arrows and stones, tried to hit him.   80
Then the lord of men Agamemnon shouted loudly:
"Hold back, Argives, do not strike, Achaean men;
for Hector of the shimmering helm has come forward to say something."
    So he spoke, and the men held off and were silent
in expectation. And Hector spoke between both sides:
"Hear from me, Trojans and strong-greaved Achaeans,
the word of Alexandros, for whose sake this strife arose.

He bids the other Trojans and all the Achaeans
lay their fine armour aside on the nourishing earth,
and in the space between, he and Menelaos beloved by Ares   90
alone will fight for Helen and all her possessions;
whichever of them proves winner and is mightier,
let him take all the possessions and duly lead the woman home—
and let the others swear faithful oaths of friendship."

      So he spoke, and all the men were hushed in silence.
Then spoke to them Menelaos of the war cry:
"Listen now to me also; for pain seizes my heart
above all others, and I think that now Argives and Trojans
can be parted, as they have suffered much evil
on account of my quarrel, and on account of Alexandros who
   began it.   100
To whichever of us death and fate are prepared,
let him die; but let the others be parted with all speed.
Bring sheep—a white ram and a black female
for the Sun and the Earth; and we Argives shall bring another besides
   for Zeus.
And fetch strong Priam, so that he may cut the sacred oath
himself, seeing that his sons are reckless and faithless,
lest any man violate Zeus' sacred treaty with a transgression.
The wits of younger men are ever fluttering in the air;
but an older man looks both before and behind for those he
is with, so that the very best comes about for both sides."   110

      So he spoke, and both Achaeans and Trojans rejoiced,
hoping to make an end of the sorrowful war.
And they reined the chariots into line, and themselves descended
and took off their armour, and placed it on the ground
close together, and there was little earth left between.
At once Hector sent two heralds to the city
to bring the lambs and to summon Priam.
And lord Agamemnon dispatched Talthybios

to the hollow ships, and ordered a lamb
brought forth; and he did not disobey illustrious Agamemnon.   120

      Then Iris went as messenger to white-armed Helen,
in the likeness of her husband's sister, the wife of Antenor's son,
she whom Antenor's son, lord Helikaon, held—
Laodike, most outstanding in beauty of all of Priam's daughters.
She found Helen in her chamber; she was weaving a great cloth,
a crimson cloak of double thickness, and was working in the many
    trials
of the Trojan horse-breakers and bronze-clad Achaeans,
trials which for her sake they had suffered under the hand of Ares.
Standing close, Iris of the swift feet addressed her:
"Come this way, dear bride, and see the marvellous deeds   130
of the Trojan horse-breakers and bronze-clad Achaeans,
who earlier carried war and all its tears against each other
into the plain, in their longing for deadly battle;
these men now sit in silence, the war stopped,
leaning on their shields, their great spears fixed upright beside them;
and Alexandros and Menelaos beloved by Ares
are to fight with their great spears on your account;
and you will be called wife of that man who is victor."

      So speaking the goddess aroused in Helen's heart sweet longing
for her husband of old, her city and her children.   140
At once, veiling herself with gleaming white shawls,
she started up from her chamber, weeping soft tears,
and not on her own; for with her followed her two handmaids.
Aithra daughter of Pittheus and ox-eyed Klymene.

      Swiftly they arrived where stood the Scaean gates;
and those men by Priam—Panthoös and Thymoites
and Lampos, Klytios and Hiketaon, companion of Ares,
as well as Oukalegon and Antenor, both sound men—
elders of the city, sat above the Scaean gates,
having ceded war to their old age, but were fine speakers all,   150

like chirping cicadas, which settling themselves throughout the forest
on trees, issue forth their lily-soft voice.
Such then were the leaders of Troy sitting upon the tower.
And they, as they saw Helen approaching the tower,
in undertones spoke winged words to one another:
"No blame that the Trojans and strong-greaved Achaeans
have suffered so long on account of such a woman;
terribly does she seem like the immortal goddesses to look on.
But even so—such as she is, let her go back home in the ships,
let her not stay as a bane to us and our children after."   160

      So they spoke; but Priam called aloud to Helen:
"Come here, dear child, and sit in front of me
so that you may see your husband of old, your friends and his
    kinsmen—
to me you are not in any way to blame, but in my eyes it is the gods who
    are blameworthy,
who stirred up against me this sorrowful war of the Achaeans—
so tell me the name of this gigantic man,
who is this Achaean man, good and great?
To be sure there are other men even greater in height,
but I have never beheld with my eyes a man so handsome,
nor so majestic; for he seems a kingly man."   170

      And Helen shining among women answered him with these
    words:
"Honoured are you to me, dear father-in-law, and revered,
and would that evil death had pleased me at that time when
I followed your son here, abandoning my marriage chamber and kinsmen,
my late-born child, and the lovely companions of my own age.
But that did not happen; and so I waste away weeping.
but this I will tell you, which you asked me and questioned;
that man is the son of Atreus, wide-ruling Agamemnon,
both a good king and a powerful spear-warrior.
He was my brother-in-law, dog-faced as I am—if that ever happened."   180

So she spoke; and the old man marvelled at him and exclaimed:
"O most fortunate son of Atreus, child of fortune, heaven-blessed;
many indeed are the young men of the Achaeans subject to you.
In time before I went to Phrygia, rich in vines,
where I saw a multitude of Phrygian men and their flashing horses,
the armies of Otreus and godlike Mygdon,
who were camped along the banks of the Sangarios;
and I too, being young, was numbered with them
on that day when came the Amazons, a match for men—
but they were not so numerous as the dark-eyed Achaeans."   190

Then seeing Odysseus, the old man inquired a second time:
"Come, tell me this too, dear child, who this man is;
he is lesser in height than Agamemnon son of Atreus,
but he seems broader in the shoulders and chest.
His armour lies upon the nourishing earth,
and he himself like a ram ranges the ranks of men.
I would liken him to a deep-fleeced ram,
who moves through a great flock of gleaming white sheep."

Then answered him Helen, born of Zeus:
"Now this is the son of Laertes, resourceful Odysseus,   200
who was raised in the country of Ithaca, rough though it is,
knowing every kind of stratagem and shrewd plan."

Then wise Antenor in turn addressed her:
"O lady, unerring indeed is this word you spoke!
For shining Odysseus once before came here too
as an embassy with Menelaos, beloved by Ares, concerning you;
I received them as guests and treated them kindly in my hall,
and I got to know the character and shrewd plans of both.
And when they took their places among the assembled Trojans,
Menelaos standing towered with his broad shoulders,   210
but when both were seated, Odysseus was the more majestic;
and when they began to weave for everyone their web of words and
    counsels,

Menelaos, to be sure, was a fluent speaker,

but brief, although very clear, as he was not a man of many words,

nor a rambler—and yet indeed he was younger;

but when resourceful Odysseus rose to speak,

he would stand and fixing his eyes on the ground would raise his gaze

   from time to time,

and he did not gesture with his staff back and forth,

but held it without moving, like an ignorant man;

you would think him to be surly and some mere simpleton.   220

But when he let go the great voice from his chest

and words like snowflakes in winter—

then no other mortal man could rival Odysseus.

Then we marvelled no longer at Odysseus' appearance."

     Again, seeing Ajax, the old man then inquired a third time:

"Who is this other Achaean man, good and great,

outstanding among the Argives in height and broad shoulders?"

And Helen, shining among women with her trailing gown, answered:

"That man is huge Ajax, bulwark of the Achaeans.

And on the other side Idomeneus stands like a god among the Cretans,   230

and the leaders of Crete are gathered around him.

Many times Menelaos beloved by Ares received him as a guest

in our home, whenever he came from Crete.

I see them all now, the rest of the dark-eyed Achaeans,

those I know well and could name—

but I cannot see the two marshals of the people,

Castor, breaker of horses, and the skilful boxer Polydeukes,

my two brothers, born with me of the same mother.

Perhaps they did not follow the others from lovely Lacedaemon;

or they did follow here in the seagoing ships,   240

but now are not willing to enter the combat of men,

fearing the many insults and reproaches against me."

She spoke, but already the life-giving earth covered them

back there, in Lacedaemon, in their beloved fatherland.

Then through the city the heralds bore the trusted oath offerings
   for the gods,
two sheep and cheering wine, fruit of the field,
in a goatskin wine sack; and the herald Idaios
carried a shining wine bowl and cups of gold.
And standing beside him he roused the old man with his words:
"Rise up, son of Laomedon, you are summoned by the best   250
of the horse-breaking Trojans and bronze-clad Achaeans alike,
to come down to the plain, to cut faithful oaths of treaty.
For Alexandros and Menelaos beloved by Ares
are to fight with their great spears for the woman;
and to that man who is victor will go the woman and her possessions,
but the rest of us will cut faithful oaths of friendship,
and we will live in Troy where the soil is rich, and they will return
to the horse-grazed pastures of Argos and Achaea with its beautiful
   women."

So he spoke, and the old man shuddered, but bade his companions
yoke the chariot horses; and quickly they obeyed.   260
Then Priam mounted and drew the reins back tight
and beside him Antenor mounted the beautifully wrought chariot;
and so through the Scaean gates they drove the swift horses to the
   plain.
And when they arrived among the Trojans and Achaeans,
descending from the chariot to the nourishing earth
they strode into the midst of the Trojans and Achaeans.
Then at once lord of men Agamemnon stood to his feet,
and resourceful Odysseus; the noble heralds
led forth the sacrificial offerings of oath for the gods, and mixed wine
in the bowl, and poured water over the hands of the kings.   270
Then with his hands the son of Atreus drew his knife,
which always hung beside the great scabbard of his sword,
and cut fleece from the heads of the sheep; then
the heralds distributed this to the Trojans and Achaean leaders.

And raising his hands, the son of Atreus prayed aloud for all:
"Father Zeus, ruling from Mount Ida, most glorious and greatest,
and thou the Sun, who oversees and overhears all things,
and Rivers and Earth, and those of you beneath the earth
who take vengeance on men who have died, on whomever has sworn
    false oath—
you be witnesses, you guard these trusted oaths.   280
If Alexandros kills Menelaos,
let him then have Helen and all her possessions,
and we return home in our seagoing ships;
but if fair-haired Menelaos kills Alexandros,
then the Trojans must give back Helen and all her possessions,
and pay recompense to the Argives, whatever is proper,
and which will stand even for men who come hereafter.
And if Priam and the sons of Priam are unwilling
to pay me recompense, should Alexandros fall,
then I will surely fight for compensation,   290
remaining here, until I reach the conclusion of this war."

      He spoke, and cut the throats of the sheep with the pitiless
  bronze.
And he deposited them gasping on the earth,
their life force failing, as the bronze took their strength,
and drawing wine from the bowl in cups
they poured libations and prayed to the immortal gods.
And thus would a man speak, both Trojan and Achaean:
"Zeus most glorious and greatest, and all you immortal gods,
those who first do harm in violation of the sacred treaty—on whichever
    side they be—
may their brains flow—thus—upon the ground, like this wine,   300
and the brains of their children, and may their wives be forced by other
    men."
So they spoke; but the son of Cronus did not accomplish this for them.
      Then Dardanian Priam spoke a word among them:

"Listen to me, Trojans and strong-greaved Achaeans.
Now I go back again to windswept Troy,
since I cannot bear to see with my own eyes
my dear son locked in combat with Menelaos beloved by Ares.
Zeus no doubt knows, and the other deathless gods,
to which is decreed the finality of death."
He spoke, a man like a god, and placed the lambs in the chariot,   310
and then himself mounted, and drew the reins back taut,
and Antenor mounted the splendid chariot beside him.

      Then the two turning back returned to Ilion;
and Priam's son Hector and godlike Odysseus
first measured out a space, and then
choosing lots, they shook them in a brazen helmet,
to see which of the two men should first hurl his bronze spear.
And the armies prayed, raising their hands to the gods,
and thus would a man speak, both Trojan and Achaean:
"Father Zeus, ruling from Mount Ida, most glorious and greatest,   320
whichever man inflicted these troubles between us both,
grant that he die and make his way into the house of Hades,
but to us grant friendship and that the sacred treaty stand."
So they spoke. And great Hector of the shimmering helm shook the lots,
his eyes averted; and Paris' lot was swiftly shaken out.

      And thereupon the men seated themselves in their ranks, at the
   place where
each man's embellished armour lay by his high-stepping horses.
But shining Alexandros put his fine armour upon his broad shoulders,
he, the husband of Helen of the lovely hair.
First he strapped the splendid greaves around his shins,   330
fitted with silver bindings around his ankles;
next he girt about his chest a breastplate,
his brother Lykaon's, but it fitted him;
across his shoulders he slung his bronze sword
studded with silver; and then his great strong shield.

Over his powerful head he placed his well-forged helmet
with flowing horsehair; and terribly the crest nodded over it.
He took his strong spear, fitted to his hand.
And in this way too did warlike Menelaos also arm.
        When they had armed themselves on their opposite sides of the
    throng,   340
they strode into the middle of the Trojans and Achaeans,
looking terror at each other; and awe held those watching,
both horse-breaking Trojans and strong-greaved Achaeans;
and taking their stands close to each other in the marked-out space,
they shook their spears, and raged at each other.
        Alexandros was first to hurl his long-shadowed spear,
and he struck the circle of the son of Atreus' shield;
but the spear-point was bent back
in the mighty shield. And Menelaos son of Atreus attacked next
with his bronze spear, having made prayer to Zeus the father: 350
"Lord Zeus, grant me vengeance on the man who first wronged me with
    his evil deeds,
Alexandros the godlike, and break him beneath my hands,
so that even generations to come will shudder
to wreak evil on a host, a man who has given friendship."
He spoke, and balancing the long-shadowed spear he hurled it,
and struck the circle of the son of Priam's shield.
The heavy spear ran through the gleaming shield,
and was forced through his elaborate breastplate;
straight through his tunic beside his ribs
the spear cut; but Paris turned aside and evaded dark death.   360
And the son of Atreus drew his silver-studded sword
and raising his arm, struck the helmet ridge; and on both sides of the
    ridge
his sword—shattered into three, into four pieces—fell from his hand.
        Then the son of Atreus cried out, looking up to broad heaven:
"Father Zeus, no other one of the gods is more malicious than you!

I thought I surely had my revenge on Alexandros for his wickedness;
but now my sword has shattered in my hand, my spear
flown from my hand in vain, and I have not beaten him."
He spoke, and springing forward seized Alexandros' horsehair-crested
    helmet,
and wheeling about, dragged him toward the strong-greaved
    Achaeans;   370
and the elaborately embellished strap choked Alexandros beneath his
    soft throat,
stretched tight under his chin to secure his helmet.
And indeed Menelaos would have dragged him away and won for himself
    glory everlasting,
had not Aphrodite Zeus's daughter taken sharp notice;
she snapped the strap, the leather of a slaughtered ox;
and the helmet came empty in his massive hand.
Then the warrior hurled it among the well-greaved Achaeans,
whirling around, and his loyal companions caught it up;
and he himself rushed forward again, raging to kill
with his bronze spear—but Aphrodite snatched Alexandros away,   380
easily, goddess that she was, enfolded in dense mist,
and set him down in his incense-perfumed bedroom.

        At once she set out to summon Helen; and found her
by the lofty tower, thronged around by the women of Troy.
Grasping with her hand, she twitched Helen's fragrant robe;
and addressed her in the likeness of an old woman, a woolworker of
    advanced years
who, when she lived in Lacedaemon,
used to fashion for her beautiful wools, and Helen loved her above all
    others;
in likeness of this woman divine Aphrodite addressed her:
"Come here; Alexandros summons you home;   390
he is there, in his bedroom, on his bed that is inlaid with rings,
shining in beauty and raiment—you would not think

that he came from fighting a man, but rather that he was going
to a dance, or had just left the dance and was reclining."
        So she spoke; and stirred the anger in Helen's breast.
And when she recognised the goddess' beautiful cheeks
and ravishing breasts and gleaming eyes,
she stood amazed, and spoke out and addressed her by name:
"Mad one; why do you so desire to seduce me in this way?
Will you drive me to some further place among well-settled cities,   400
to Phrygia or lovely Maeonia?
Perhaps there too is some mortal man beloved by you—
since now Menelaos has vanquished godlike Alexandros
and desires that I, loathsome as I am, be taken home.
Is it for this reason you stand here now conniving?
Go, sit yourself beside him, renounce the haunts of the gods,
never turn your feet to Olympus,
but suffer for him and tend him forever,
until he makes you either his wife, or his girl slave.
As for me, I will not go there—it would be shameful—   410
to share the bed of that man. The Trojan women
will all blame me afterward; the sufferings I have in my heart are
    without end."
        Then in anger divine Aphrodite addressed her:
"Do not provoke me, wicked girl, lest I drop you in anger,
and hate you as much as I now terribly love you,
and devise painful hostilities, and you are caught in the middle of both,
Trojans and Danaans, and are destroyed by an evil fate."
So she spoke; and Helen born of Zeus was frightened;
and she left, covering herself with her shining white robe,
in silence, and escaped notice of the women of Troy; and the divine
    one led her.   420
        When the women arrived at the splendid house of Alexandros,
the handmaids swiftly turned to their work,
and she, shining among women, entered into the high-roofed chamber;

then laughter-loving Aphrodite, taking a stool for her,
placed it opposite Alexandros, the goddess herself carrying it.
There Helen took her seat, daughter of Zeus who wields the aegis,
and averting her eyes, reviled her husband with her words:
"You're back from war; would that you had died there
broken by the stronger man, he who in time past was my husband.
Yet before this you used to boast that you were stronger   430
than Menelaos beloved by Ares in your courage and strength of hand and
    skill with spear;
go now and challenge Menelaos beloved by Ares,
to fight again, face to face—but no, I
recommend you give it up, and not fight fair-haired Menelaos
man to man, or recklessly do battle,
lest you be swiftly broken beneath his spear."

        But in answer Paris addressed her with his words:
"Do not, woman, rebuke my spirit with hard reproaches.
Now Menelaos is victorious, with Athena's help,
but another time I'll defeat him; for the gods are with us too.   440
But come, let us go to bed and pleasure ourselves with love;
for never at any time has desire so overwhelmed my senses—
not when I first carried you off from lovely Lacedaemon
and sailed in my seagoing ships,
and on that rocky island first joined in love and sex—
as now I desire you and sweet passion holds me."
He spoke and led the way toward the bed; and his wife followed with him.

        Then the two lay together in the decorated bed;
but Atreus' son ranged along the host like a wild beast,
trying to catch sight of godlike Alexandros.   450
But none of the Trojans, or their famous allies, was able
then to hand over Alexandros to Menelaos beloved by Ares;
nor for love would they have concealed him, if any had seen him;
since he was detested by them all as dark death.
Then to them the lord of men Agamemnon spoke:

"Hear me, Trojans and Dardanians and allies.
The victory plainly belongs to Menelaos, beloved by Ares;
surrender Argive Helen and the possessions with her
and pay recompense, whatever is proper,
and which will stand even for men who come hereafter."   460
So spoke the son of Atreus, and the rest of the Achaeans gave their
    applause.

Now the gods were seated in assembly by Zeus' side
on a floor of gold; and among them lady Hebe
poured nectar, and with goblets of gold
they pledged one another, looking down upon the city of the Trojans.
And straight off the son of Cronus set himself to provoke Hera
with taunting words, speaking wilfully:

      "Two of you goddesses are allies of Menelaos—
Argive Hera and Athena who stands guardian in Boeotia;
and even now they sit apart enjoying themselves
as they look on; yet laughter-loving Aphrodite in her turn   10
has always stood by Paris and defends him from death.
And now she has saved him when he expected to die.
To be sure, victory belongs to Menelaos beloved by Ares,
yet let us consider how this matter will be;
whether, then, we again rouse evil war and dread battle,
or cast friendship between the two sides.
And if somehow this plan should be desirable and pleasing to all,
then the city of lord Priam may still remain a place of habitation,
and Menelaos would take back Argive Helen."

      He spoke; and Athena and Hera muttered against him;   20
for they sat close to each other, devising evil for the Trojans.
And Athena was silent and said not a thing,
seething at Zeus the father as savage anger seized her;

but Hera's spirit could not contain her anger and she spoke out:
"Most dread son of Cronus, what kind of word have you spoken?
How can you seek to render useless and futile my labour,
the labour for which I sweated my sweat and my horses grew weary
rallying the people, for the evil of Priam and his sons?
Do it; but not all the rest of us gods will approve."

     Greatly troubled, Zeus who gathers the clouds addressed her: 30
"Strange one; how ever did Priam and the sons of Priam
do you such great wrong that you rage so furiously
to destroy the well-built city of Ilion?
If entering its gates and high walls
you could eat Priam and the sons of Priam raw,
and all the other Trojans, would you then be cured of your anger?
Do as you want; hereafter let this small quarrel not
become for you and me a cause of strife between us both.
But I will tell you something else, and put it away in your mind;
whenever I too should be bent on laying waste a city   40
of my choice, where men dear to you live—
do not in any way put off my anger, but let me proceed;
for I grant this to you of my own will, although unwilling in heart.
For of all the cities beneath the sun and star-strewn heaven
lived in by earthly men,
of these is holy Ilion especially honoured in my heart,
and Priam and the people of Priam of the fine ash-spear.
For never has my altar lacked fair portion
of libations and smoke of burnt offerings; since we receive this as our
    honoured privilege."

     Then answered him ox-eyed lady Hera: 50
"In truth, three cities are dearest to me by far,
Argos and Sparta and Mycenae with its wide ways;
destroy these, whenever they become hateful to your heart.
I will not stand in defence of them against you nor grudge you.
For even if I did begrudge you and would have you not destroy them,

I could accomplish nothing, for all my objecting, since you are far the
    stronger.
And yet my labour must not be rendered worthless;
for I too am a god, and my parentage is from the same place as yours,
and devious Cronus bore me to be his eldest daughter.
For both these reasons, my birth and also because I am called   60
your wife, and you are lord among all the immortals.
Yet come, let us yield to each other on these matters;
I to you, and you to me; the other immortal
gods will follow on. Quickly tell Athena
to enter into the dread fray of Trojans and Achaeans
and try to work it so that the Trojans first commence hostilities
against the triumphant Achaeans, in violation of their sacred oaths."

       Thus she spoke, nor did the father of men and gods refuse;
immediately he addressed Athena with winged words:
"With all speed go to the armies of the Trojans and Achaeans,   70
and try to work it so that the Trojans first commence hostilities
against the triumphant Achaeans, in violation of their sacred oaths."

      So speaking he urged Athena, who had been eager even before,
and she left, shooting down from the peaks of Olympus.
As when the son of devious Cronus hurls forth a star,
a glittering portent to sailors or a vast army of men,
from which shards of fire stream in multitude—
so Pallas Athena flashed toward earth,
and dashed down in their midst; amazement seized the onlookers,
both Trojans, breakers of horses, and strong-greaved Achaeans.   80
Thus each man spoke as he looked to his neighbour:
"Now either war and evil and dread battle will again
take place, or Zeus will settle friendship between both sides,
Zeus who dispenses war for men."

     So each man would speak, Trojan and Achaean.
But Athena descended into the battle throng in the likeness of a Trojan
    man,

Laodokos, Antenor's son, a powerful spearman,
searching for godlike Pandaros, in the hope that she could come
    upon him.
She found him, the strong blameless son of Lykaon,
standing by; around him were powerful ranks of shield-bearing   90
men, who had followed him from the flowing waters of Aisepos.
Standing close, she addressed him with winged words:
"Surely now, you would listen to me, son of wise Lykaon?
Would you dare let fly a sharp arrow against Menelaos?
You would win gratitude and honour in the eyes of all Trojans,
above all from king Alexandros.
You, before all others, would carry away shining gifts from him,
were he to behold warlike Menelaos son of Atreus,
broken by your arrow and placed upon a sorrow-making funeral pyre.
Come, shoot an arrow at glorious Menelaos;   100
pray to Lycian Apollo, famed for the bow, vowing
to perform a glorious sacrificial hecatomb of firstborn sheep
when you return home to the city of holy Zeleia."

        So spoke Athena, and persuaded the fool's wits;
immediately he drew forth his bow, well made from a running wild
goat, which in time past he himself—taking aim below its heart
as it descended from a rocky place, while he watched in ambush—
had struck in the chest, and it fell on its back onto the rock.
The horns from its head had grown sixteen palms across;
and these a craftsman who worked in horn, labouring, joined
    together,   110
and having smoothed it all skilfully, had fitted on a string-notch of
    gold.
And bending the bow for the string, Pandaros positioned it carefully,
bracing it against the ground; and his brave companions held their
    shields before him
lest the warrior sons of the Achaeans should rush him first
before he struck warlike Menelaos, Atreus' son.

Then he removed the cover of his quiver, took out an arrow,
feathered and never shot before, a bearer of dark pain,
swiftly fitted the sharp-pointed arrow to the bowstring,
and prayed to wolf-born Apollo, famed for the bow, vowing
to perform a glorious sacrificial hecatomb of firstborn sheep   120
when he returned home to the city of holy Zeleia.
He drew, holding together the arrow-notch and the oxhide bowstring;
then brought the bowstring to his chest, and the iron-point to the bow.
And when he had stretched the great bow to an arc,
the bow rang, the bowstring sang loud, and the sharp-pointed
arrow sprang forth, straining to fly to the battle-throng.

      Nor, Menelaos, did the blessed immortal gods forget
you, and Zeus' daughter was first to remember, she who carries off the
    spoils of war,
and who taking her stand in front of you warded off the sharp arrow.
She brushed it from his skin, just so, as when a mother   130
brushes a fly from her child, when he lies down in sweet slumber;
with her own hand she directed it straight to where the golden buckles of
    his belt
came together and the two halves of the breastplates met.
The sharp arrow landed on the fitted belt;
through the decorated belt it drove,
and was pressed through his elaborate breastplate
and belt-guard, that he wore to protect his skin, a barrier against
    shafts,
which best protected him; but it went straight through even this,
and the utmost point of the arrow grazed his skin.
Instantly a dark cloud of blood flowed from the wound;   140
as when a woman of Maeonia or Caria stains ivory with
crimson dye, to be a cheek piece for horses—
it lies unused in a storeroom, and many horsemen pray that they
may bear it, but it lies away to delight the king,
both an ornament for the horse and an honour for the rider—

in such fashion, Menelaos, were your thighs stained with blood,
and your muscular calves and down to your fine ankles.

       Then Agamemnon lord of men shuddered,
when he saw dark blood flowing down from the wound,
and Menelaos beloved by Ares shuddered too,   150
but when he saw the binding thread and arrow barb were outside,
his spirit was rallied again back in his breast.
But groaning deeply lord Agamemnon spoke among their comrades,
holding Menelaos by the hand, and they groaned in response:
"Beloved brother, the oath I cut was your death,
when I put you forward before the Achaeans to fight alone with the
    Trojans,
seeing now that the Trojans have struck you, and trampled underfoot the
    sacred treaty.
Yet in no way is our oath in vain, and the blood of lambs,
and the unmixed libations and pledges of hand which we trusted.
For even if the Olympian does not accomplish this at once,   160
he will accomplish it in full, though late, and they will pay greatly
with their heads and their women and their children.
For I know this well in my mind and in my heart;
there will some time be a day when holy Ilion is destroyed,
and Priam and the people of Priam of the fine ash-spear—
Zeus, son of Cronus, who sits on high, dwelling near heaven,
himself will brandish at them all his lowering stormy aegis,
in rage for this deception. These things will not pass unaccomplished;
but my grief will be bitter for your sake, O Menelaos,
if you should die and fulfil your life's destiny,   170
and I return disgraced to the parched land of Argos.
Immediately the Achaeans would turn their thoughts to their
    fatherland,
and we would leave as trophy for Priam and the Trojans
Helen of Argos; a field would rot your bones
as you lay in Troy on an unaccomplished mission.

And thus will some Trojan speak in his overweening manhood,
as he leaps onto the tomb of glorious Menelaos:
'Would that Agamemnon brought his anger to completion in this way
    against all his enemies,
as he once led an army of Achaeans here to no purpose,
and then went home to his beloved fatherland   180
with his empty ships, leaving behind brave Menelaos.'
Thus in time to come a man will speak; then let the broad earth gape
    beneath me."
        Then cheering him, fair-haired Menelaos addressed him:
"Courage, do not in any way alarm the Achaean people.
The sharp arrow did not fix in a mortal place, but before it did
my war-belt, all-gleaming, protected me, and beneath it
the underbelt and belt-guard, which bronze-working men toiled to
    make."
        Then answering him lord Agamemnon spoke:
"I pray that it is so, O dear Menelaos.
A healer will lay hands and place medicines on the wound,   190
which will put a stop to the dark pains."
He spoke, and addressed Talthybios, the divinely protected herald:
"Talthybios, quickly as you can summon here Machaon,
the man who is the son of Asclepius, the blameless healer,
so that he may see Menelaos, warlike leader of Achaeans,
whom some archer well skilled in bows, a Trojan or Lycian,
has struck—a thing of glory to him, but grief to us."
        So he spoke, and hearing him the herald did not disobey,
and he left to go to the army of the bronze-clad Achaeans,
to search out the warrior Machaon; he recognised him   200
as he stood by; around him were powerful ranks of shield-bearing
men, who had followed him from the horse-grazed pastures of Trikka.
Standing close, he addressed him with winged words:
"Up, son of Asclepius, lord Agamemnon summons,
so that you may see Menelaos, warlike leader of Achaeans,

whom some archer well skilled in bows, a Trojan or Lycian,
has struck—a thing of glory to him, but grief to us."

      So he spoke and stirred the spirit in the other's breast;
They set out to go through the throng and along the broad army of the
    Achaeans.
And when he arrived where fair-haired Menelaos   210
was wounded, and all the best men were gathered around him
in a circle, Machaon, a man like a god, went to his side in their midst,
and at once he drew out the arrow from the fitted war-belt;
the sharp barbs were broken back as it was drawn out.
He loosened the war-belt, all-gleaming, and beneath it
the underbelt and belt-guard, which bronze-working men toiled to make.
Then when he saw the wound, where the pointed arrow had entered,
sucking out the blood, he then expertly sprinkled on soothing
herbs, which once upon a time Chiron with kind intent gave to his father.

      While they attended to Menelaos of the war cry,   220
all the while the ranks of shield-bearing Trojans drew near;
and the Achaeans again put on their armour, and recollected their
    fighting spirit.
Then you would not have seen godlike Agamemnon dozing,
or cowering, or reluctant to fight,
but rather rushing to battle where men win glory.
For he left aside his chariot, intricate with bronze, and his horses—
these, breathing hard, his attendant Eurymedon held apart,
Eurymedon, son of Ptolemaios, the son of Peiraios;
and on him Agamemnon laid a strong injunction to hold them in
    readiness, until the time when
exhaustion might take hold of his limbs, through being lord to
    so many—   230
then going on foot he ranged around the ranks of men.
And those of the Danaans of swift horses whom he saw were eager;
these men, standing close, he encouraged further with his words:
"Argives, never yet, in any way, relax your fierce courage;

for Zeus the father will be no abettor to those who deceive,
and these men who have done harm contrary to their sacred oaths,
surely, vultures will devour their tender flesh,
and their dear wives and tender children
we shall lead off in our ships, when we take their city."

       Yet those men he saw hanging back from the hated war,   240
these he reviled with angry words:
"Argive blusterers, disgraces, are you not ashamed?
Why do you stand in this way like bewildered fawns,
who exhausted after racing around a great plain
come to a stand, and there is no spirit of resistance in their hearts?
Just so you stand bewildered, and do not fight.
Or are you waiting for the Trojans to come close, to where the ships
are drawn up, strong-sterned, onto the beach of the grey sea,
to see whether the son of Cronus will hold over you his protective hand?"

       Thus giving his commands he ranged around the ranks
  of men.   250
And he came upon the Cretans as he went through the throng of men;
they were arming around brilliant Idomeneus.
Idomeneus was in the front ranks, like a wild boar in courage,
while Meriones urged on the rear lines.
Seeing them, Agamemnon lord of men rejoiced,
and straightway addressed Idomeneus with winning words:
"Idomeneus, I honour you above all the Danaans of swift horses
in battle and for every type of deed,
and in the feast, when the Argive elite mix in a bowl
the dark-gleaming wine of kings.   260
For although the rest of the long-haired Achaeans
drink down their portion, your cup stands always full
as does mine, to drink whenever our spirit desires.
But rouse yourself to war, as such a man you boast you were before."
Then Idomeneus leader of the Cretans addressed him in reply:
"Son of Atreus, a trusty comrade I will surely be to you,

as at the first I undertook and promised.
But rally the other long-haired Achaeans,
so that we can fight without delay, since the Trojans
have destroyed their sacred oaths; there will be death and sorrows for
    them 270
in time to come, since they were first to do harm against the sacred
    treaty."

          Thus he spoke, and the son of Atreus departed, rejoicing in his
    heart;
he came upon the two Aiantes as he went through the throng of men.
Both were in armour, and a cloud of foot soldiers followed with them;
as when a goat-herding man watches a cloud from a mountain peak
when it bears down over the sea by the power of the West Wind's blast,
and, being far away, to him it seems blacker than pitch
as it moves over the sea, and carries a great tempest with it,
and he shudders seeing it, and drives his flocks into a cave,
just so did the dark ranks of young men cherished by Zeus move with
    the two Aiantes   280
close-pressed to war's destruction,
and bristling with spears and shields.
And seeing them lord Agamemnon rejoiced,
and lifting his voice he addressed them with winged words:
"Aiantes, you two leaders of the bronze-clad Argives,
it is not fitting to urge you two, nor to give orders;
for you yourselves strongly command your people to fight.
Father Zeus, Athena and Apollo, would that
such a spirit were in the breast of every man!
The city of lord Priam would swiftly totter   290
beneath our hands, captured and sacked."

          So speaking he left them there, and went among the other men.
There he came on Nestor, the clear speaker from Pylos,
arraying his companions and urging them to fight,
great Pelagon and Alastor and Chromios about him

and powerful Haimon and Bias, shepherd of the people;
in front he positioned the horsemen with their horses and chariots,
and the foot soldiers behind them, numerous and warlike,
to be a defensive wall against the war; and the spiritless men he drove
    into the middle,
so that even an unwilling man would by constraint do battle.   300
And in the front ranks he commanded the horsemen; and he urged them
to restrain their horses so they would not be fouled in the throng of
    battle:
"Let no man trusting in his horsemanship and manhood
on his own, in front of the other men, strive to do battle with the
    Trojans,
nor let him retreat; for you will be too weak.
And a man who from his own chariot can reach chariots of the enemy,
let him thrust with his spear, since this is more effective.
In this way the men of time before sacked walls and cities,
holding this purpose and this spirit in their breasts."
      So the old man urged them on, skilled in warfare of long ago;   310
and seeing him lord Agamemnon rejoiced,
and speaking out addressed Nestor with winged words:
"O old man, would that, like the spirit in your very breast,
your knees' strength might keep pace with you, and your power be
    unwavering;
but old age wears you, which levels all alike. Would that some
other man had your age, and you were among the younger men."
      Then answered him the Gerenian horseman Nestor:
"Son of Atreus, indeed I myself could also wish
to be so, as when I slew godlike Ereuthalion.
But the gods never grant all things to men at the same time.   320
If then I was a youth, now in turn old age comes upon me.
Yet even so I will take my station and command the horsemen
with advice and counsel; for this is the privilege of age;
younger men will throw the spear, men

later born than me and who put their trust in strength."

So he spoke; and the son of Atreus went on his way rejoicing in
   his heart.
He found the son of Peteos, Menestheus, driver of horses,
standing idle; about him were the Athenians, raisers of the battle cry;
and close by resourceful Odysseus had taken position,
and beside and around him unwearying ranks of the Kephallenians   330
stood by; for the people had not yet heard the cry for battle,
and the lines of horse-breaking Trojans and Achaeans had only just
begun to move; those waiting
stood by for the time when some other line of advancing Achaeans
might make onslaught on the Trojans and begin the war.
Seeing them, the lord of men Agamemnon spoke words of revilement;
and lifting his voice he addressed them with winged words:
"O son of Peteos, Zeus-cherished king,
and you surpassing all in craven schemes, cunning in spirit,
why do you hang back, cowering in fear, waiting out the other men?   340
It is only decent that you two take your stand
among the front ranks and have your share of searing battle,
for you two are the first to hear me when it comes to feasting,
whenever we Achaeans make ready a feast for the ruling counsellors.
There it is your pleasure to eat roasted meats and to drink
cups of honey-sweet wine for so long as you wish;
but now you would gladly look on, even should ten battalions of Achaeans
fight before your eyes with pitiless bronze."

Then looking at him from under his brows resourceful Odysseus
   addressed him:
"Son of Atreus, what kind of word has escaped the barrier of your
   teeth?   350
How do you say that we hang back from battle? Whenever we Achaeans
rouse shrill battle against the Trojans, breakers of horses,
you will see, if you have a wish to and if these things concern you,
the beloved father of Telemachos grappling with the foremost fighters

of the horse-breaking Trojans; these words you talk are so much
   wind."
Then smiling on him lord Agamemnon addressed him,
as he knew he was angry, and he took back his word:
"Son of Laertes descended from Zeus, Odysseus of many stratagems,
I neither rebuke you needlessly, nor give you orders.
For I know that the spirit in your own breast   360
has well-disposed intentions; for you think the same things I do.
But come, we will redress these matters later, if anything unworthy
has been said now; may the gods make all these things come to
   nothing."
       So speaking he left them there, and went among the other men.
And he found the son of Tydeus, high-spirited Diomedes,
standing among his horses and bolted chariot;
and beside him stood Sthenelos, the son of Kapaneus.
And seeing him lord Agamemnon rebuked him;
and lifting his voice he addressed him with winged words:
"O me! Son of Tydeus, the skilled breaker of horses,   370
why do you skulk, why gape between the lines of battle?
It did not please Tydeus to crouch this way in fear,
but rather to fight the enemy far in front of his beloved comrades—
so they say who saw him at work; I myself never
saw nor encountered him; but they say he surpassed all men.
Indeed he once came to Mycenae, although not for war,
but as a guest friend with godlike Polyneikes, recruiting men;
they were at that time on campaign against the sacred walls of Thebes,
and greatly did they beseech us to offer our renowned men as allies.
Our men were willing to give them, and were assenting to what the
   others desired,   380
but Zeus changed their purpose, showing forth ill-omened signs.
After that, then, the two departed and were forward on the road,
and arrived at the Asopos, with its grassy banks and deep rushes,
where the Achaeans appointed Tydeus as their ambassador;

and he went on his way, and came upon a large number of Thebans from
   the city of Cadmus,
taking their meal at the home of strong Eteocles.
There, stranger though he was, Tydeus striker of horses was not
frightened, although alone among so many Cadmeians,
but he challenged them to contests of strength, and won all events
easily. Such an ally to him was Athena.   390
Then angered, the Thebans, skilled drivers of horses,
set a cunning ambush for him as he returned home—
fifty young warriors, and there were two leaders,
Maion the son of Haimon, a man resembling the gods,
and the son of Autophonos, Lykophontes, steadfast in war.
Tydeus sent these men a shameful death;
he slew them all—one man alone he permitted to return home;
for he let Maion go, obedient to signs from the gods.
Such a man was Aetolian Tydeus; but he begat a son
inferior to him in battle, but more skilled in public speaking."   400

      So he spoke; and powerful Diomedes did not answer him at all,
respecting the rebuke of the honoured king.
But the son of glorious Kapaneus gave him answer:
"Son of Atreus, do not lie when you know how to speak clearly.
We claim to be far better than our fathers;
we sacked the very seat of seven-gated Thebes,
leading fewer men beneath a stronger wall,
trusting in the signs of the gods and the help of Zeus;
the others died by their own reckless folly.
Therefore never in my presence accord our fathers the same honour."   410

      Then looking at him from beneath his brows powerful Diomedes
   addressed him:
"My friend, keep silent, and heed my word.
I myself do not blame Agamemnon the shepherd of the people
for rallying the strong-greaved Achaeans to fight.
For honour will follow him, if the Achaeans should

cut down the Trojans and capture sacred Ilion,
and in turn great will be his pain should the Achaeans be cut down.
But come, and let us two also remember our fierce courage."
He spoke and leapt from his chariot in his armour to the ground,
and terribly did the bronze clash on the chest of the king   420
as he moved; thereon would fear have seized even a steadfast man.

      As when waves of the sea dash on the thundering shore,
one after another under power of the West Wind moving—
the wave rises first in the open sea, then
shattering on land it roars mightily, and curling as it goes
breaks around the headland, and spatters foam of the salt sea—
so in this way did the ranks of Danaans move one after another
ceaselessly to war. Each leader commanded his
own men; the rest of the men were silent, nor would you have thought
that so large an army could restrain its voice and follow,   430
keeping silent, for fear of their commanders; and on them all
shone the elaborate armour that they wore as they marched.
But the Trojans, as the numberless ewes of a wealthy man
stand in their pen to be milked of their white milk,
bleating incessantly as they hear the cries of their lambs,
so the war cries of the Trojans rose through the broad army;
for the speech of all the men was not the same, nor was there one voice,
but the tongues were mixed in confusion; the men were summoned from
    many places.

      These men Ares drove on, and gleaming-eyed Athena drove the
    Achaeans
and Terror and Panic and Strife, raging, insatiable,   440
the sister and companion of man-slaughtering Ares,
she is small when she first rises up, but in the end
she leans her head against the heavens even as she strides upon the
    earth.
She too hurled into their midst war strife that levels all alike
as she advanced through the throng, multiplying the groans of men.

Then when the armies arrived in one place, pitted against each
    other,
they hurled their oxhide shields together, their spears, even the strength
    of their
bronze-armoured men; and their bossed shields
met each the other, and a great roar rose.
Then came at once cries of distress and vaunts of men   450
killing and being killed, and the earth flowed with blood.
As when rivers in winter torrent, flooding down from a mountain
to where valleys meet, hurl together their heavy weight of water,
fed from mighty springs within a cleft ravine,
and to a long distance a shepherd hears their roaring in the mountains—
such was the shouting and panic of men as they came together.

Antilochos was first to kill a Trojan commander, an outstanding
    man
in the front ranks, Echepolos son of Thalysios;
he struck him first on the crest of his helmet, bristling horsehair,
and the bronze spear-point plunged in his brow, then penetrated
    bone;   460
darkness covered his eyes,
and he fell like a tower in the mighty combat.
Taking hold of the fallen man by the feet, lord Elephenor
son of Chalkodon, leader of the great-hearted Abantes,
dragged him away from the range of thrown spears in eager haste,
with all speed to strip his armour. But his haste was short-lived.
For great-hearted Agenor, seeing him dragging the dead man,
thrust at his ribs, which showed forth beneath his shield as he bent over,
with his bronze-headed spear, and unstrung his limbs.
So Elephenor's spirit left him, and over his body there was wrought
    hard   470
work of war by Trojans and Achaeans; like wolves they
rushed at one another, man flung at man.

Then Telamonian Ajax struck the son of Anthemion,

virginal Simoeisios in the flower of youth, whom time ago his mother,
descending from Mount Ida bore by the banks of the river Simoeis,
when she followed with her parents to watch the flocks.
And for this reason they named him Simoeisios; his parents
he did not repay for his nurture, and short was the life allotted to him,
who was broken under the spear of great-hearted Ajax.
For Ajax struck him as he came among the front fighters, on the chest,
    beside his right   480
nipple, and straight on through the shoulder the bronze spear
came; and he fell to the ground in the dust like a poplar,
which in the lowland of a great marsh-meadow has grown
smooth-trunked, and yet branches are brought forth on its topmost part;
and these a man, a chariot maker, with gleaming iron axe
cuts away, so that he may bend from them a wheel rim for a splendid
    chariot;
and the poplar lies drying by the banks of the river;
such then was Simoeisios, son of Anthemion, whom
Zeus-descended Ajax killed. And Antiphos of glinting armour,
Priam's son, cast at him through the crowd with his sharp spear;   490
he missed Ajax, but struck Leukos, noble companion of Odysseus,
hard in the groin as he was dragging a body to one side;
and the body dropped from his hand, and he fell upon it.
And at the killing of this man Odysseus was greatly angered in his heart,
and he strode through the front rank of fighters, helmeted with gleaming
    bronze,
and drawing near the body, took his stand and menaced with his shining
    spear,
looking close about him; and the Trojans gave way before
the man as he cast his spear. And not in vain did he hurl the shaft,
but he struck Demokoön, a son of Priam, a bastard,
who had come from Abydos, from the place of swift mares;   500
this man Odysseus in anger for his comrade, struck with his spear
in the temple; through the other temple the sharp bronze

passed; darkness covered his eyes,
he fell with a thud, and his armour clashed shining upon him.

      The front ranks fell back, even shining Hector,
and the Argives gave a great cry and dragged away the dead,
and kept charging forward. But Apollo was watching from the height of
Pergamos, outraged, and crying out he called to the Trojans:
"Rise up, Trojan breakers of horses, do not yield the battle
to the Argives; for their skin is not rock or iron   510
that withstands flesh-cutting bronze when they are struck.
Nor now does Achilles, the son of Thetis of the lovely hair,
fight in the battle, but by his ships he broods upon his heart-grieving
    anger."
So from the citadel spoke the terrifying god; but the daughter of Zeus,
most glorious Athena Tritogeneia, urged the Achaeans on
as she advanced through the host to where she saw men malingering.

      And there fate bound Diores son of Amarynkeus;
for he was struck beside the ankle by a jagged stone
on his right shin; the leader of the Thracian men hurled it,
Peiros son of Imbrasos, who had come from Ainos.   520
Bone and both tendons the ruthless stone
utterly crushed; and he fell on his back in the dust,
stretching his hands to his beloved companions,
breathing out his soul; and he—Peiros, the man who wounded him—
    ran up,
and with his spear struck Diores beside his navel; all his
bowels were poured out upon the ground, and darkness covered his
    eyes.

      But Thoas the Aetolian, rushing up, struck Peiros with his
    spear
in the chest below the nipple, and the bronze point fixed in his lung.
Thoas moved close to him, pulled the heavy spear
from his chest, and drew his sharp sword;   530
and smote him in the middle of his stomach, and snatched his life away.

But he did not strip the armour; for the dead man's companions stood
  around him,
top-knotted Thracians, holding their long spears in their hands,
and big though he was and strong and illustrious,
they drove Thoas from them; and he retreated, staggering.
So the two men were stretched beside each other in the dust,
both leaders, he of the Thracians, the other of the bronze-clad Epeans;
and many others were slain around them.

      There, a man coming upon the scene would not make light of the
  work of war,
someone still unharmed and unwounded by sharp bronze,   540
who whirled through their midst with Pallas Athena to lead him
by the hand and to ward off the onslaught of spears thrown;
for many Trojans and Achaeans on that day
lay sprawled face down in the dust beside one another.

And then to Tydeus' son Diomedes, Pallas Athena
gave strength and daring, that he be pre-eminent among all
Argives and win glory outstanding;
from his helmet and shield she blazed forth unwearying fire,
like the star of late summer, which gleams brightest of all,
washed clean by Ocean.
Such was the fire she made blaze from his head and shoulders,
as she drove him through the midst, to where the tumult was the greatest.

        Among the Trojans was a certain Dares, a rich and blameless man,
a priest of Hephaestus; he had two sons, 10
Phegeus and Idaios, well skilled in all kinds of battle;
these two, peeling off from the throng, charged against the son of
   Tydeus,
they from their chariot, and he on foot charged from the ground.
Then when they had advanced almost upon each other,
Phegeus was first to hurl his long-shadowed spear;
over the son of Tydeus' left shoulder the spear-point
passed, nor struck him. But the son of Tydeus attacked next with his
bronze-headed spear; and not in vain did his cast escape his hand,
but he struck Phegeus in the chest between the breasts, and knocked him
   from his chariot.
And Idaios abandoning the splendid chariot leapt away, 20
nor had he courage to stand over his slain brother;
nor indeed would even he have escaped dark death,

had not Hephaestus brought him from danger and saved him, concealed
   in darkness,
so that the old man, his priest, not be wholly broken with sorrow.
And driving their horses off, the son of great-spirited Tydeus
gave them to his comrades to lead down to his hollow ships.

      But when the great-hearted Trojans saw the two sons of Dares,
the one fleeing, the other dead by his chariot,
the hearts in all were stirred to panic; then gleaming-eyed Athena,
taking furious Ares by the hand, addressed him with words: 30
"Ares, Ares, ruinous to mortals, murderous sacker of walled cities,
shall we not leave the Trojans and Achaeans
to fight, for whichever of them father Zeus should grant victory?
Let us two withdraw and avoid Zeus' wrath."
So speaking she led furious Ares from the field of war.
Then she sat him down on the banks of Scamander;
and the Danaans turned the Trojans to flight, and each of the leaders
killed a man. First Agamemnon lord of men
struck great Odios leader of the Halizones from his chariot;
he was killed first, for as he was turning Agamemnon fixed his spear in
   his back   40
between the shoulders, and drove it through his chest;
he fell with a thud, and his armour clashed upon him.

      Then Idomeneus killed Phaistos, son of Maeonian
Boros, who came from Tarne where the soil is rich.
With his long spear Idomeneus, famed spearman,
stabbed him down through his right shoulder as he was about to mount
   behind his horses;
he fell from his chariot, and the hateful darkness took him.
And Idomeneus' henchmen stripped his armour;
then Menelaos son of Atreus killed with his sharp spear
the son of Strophios, Scamandrios, cunning in the chase,   50
an outstanding hunter; for Artemis herself had taught him
to strike down all kinds of wild beasts, those the mountain forest rears;

but now Artemis who showers arrows did not protect him,
nor did the far-shooting in which he had before excelled;
but Atreus' son famed spearman Menelaos, struck
him with his spear in the back as he was fleeing before him
between the shoulders, and drove the spear through his chest,
and he fell headlong and his armour clattered about him.

      Meriones stripped the life of Phereklos, the son of Tekton
son in turn of Harmon, who knew how to make with his hands all   60
elaborate things, for greatly had Pallas Athena loved him;
he it was who had built for Alexandros the balanced ships
that began the troubles, which came to be evil for all Trojans
and for himself, since he knew nothing of what the gods had
   determined.
And when Meriones, pursuing, caught him,
he struck him down through the right buttock; straight through
into the bladder under the bone the spear-point passed;
he dropped to his knees screaming, and death embraced him.

      Then Meges slew Pedaios, the son of Antenor,
whom, bastard though he was, noble Theano, Antenor's wife, nurtured
   closely,   70
like her own children, to gratify her husband.
Drawing near, Meges the spear-famed son of Phyleus
struck him through the tendons at the back of the head with his sharp
   spear;
straight through his teeth and tongue the bronze cut,
and he fell in the dust, and bit the cold bronze with his teeth.

      Eurypylos the son of Euaimon slew godlike Hypsenor,
the son of high-spirited Dolopion, who served as priest
of the river Scamander, and was honoured like a god by the people,
this man it was Eurypylos, Euaimon's splendid son,
struck on the shoulder, running in pursuit as Hypsenor fled before
   him,   80
and slashing with his sword, he sheered away Hypsenor's massive arm;

covered with gore, the arm fell to the ground, and over his eyes
crimson death and powerful destiny seized him.

      So they toiled through the mighty combat;
and you would not have known with which side the son of Tydeus stood,
whether he fought in company with Trojans or Achaeans.
For he surged across the plain like a river swollen
with winter flood that, racing swiftly, dashes its embankments,
and the dams fenced close around cannot restrain it,
nor the protective walls hold it from the fertile gardens   90
in its sudden coming, when the rain of Zeus pounds down,
and crushes beneath it many fine plots tilled by vigorous young men;
so the close-pressed ranks of Trojans were roiled
by the son of Tydeus, nor did they withstand him although they were
    many.

      Then Pandaros, the splendid son of Lykaon, saw him
as he surged across the plain, roiling the battle lines before him,
and he swiftly pulled his curved bow upon the son of Tydeus,
and struck him as he rushed forward, hitting him by the right shoulder,
in the hollow of his breastplate, and the bitter arrow flew on,
and held straight through, and the breastplate was spattered with
    blood.   100
And at this the splendid son of Lykaon shouted loud:
"Rise up, great-hearted Trojans, spurrers of horses;
for the best of the Achaeans is hit, and I do not think he
will long endure the strong arrow, if truly lord Apollo
the son of Zeus stirred me to set forth from Lycia."

      So he spoke, vaunting; but the swift arrow had not defeated
    Diomedes,
and drawing back, he stood before his horses and chariot,
and spoke to Sthenelos, the son of Kapaneus:
"Rise up, son of Kapaneus, my ready friend, get down from the chariot,
so that you can withdraw this bitter arrow from my shoulder."   110
So he spoke, and Sthenelos leapt from behind his horses to the ground,

and standing close pulled the swift arrow right through his shoulder;
and blood spurted up through his supple tunic.
 And then Diomedes of the war cry prayed:
"Hear me, child of Zeus who wields the aegis, Weariless One, Athena;
if ever you stood by my father in kindness of heart
in deadly battle, now also be my friend, Athena;
and grant that I kill this man and come within spear-cast of him,
who struck me before I saw him and boasts about it, and declares that
I will not look long upon the shining light of the sun."   120
So he spoke, praying; and Pallas Athena heard him,
and made his limbs light and his feet and his arms above,
and standing close she addressed him with winged words:
"With good heart now, Diomedes, go to battle with the Trojans;
for in your breast I have caused to flow the mighty spirit of your father,
unshakeable, such as the shield-wielding horseman Tydeus possessed.
I have taken from your eyes the mist that was before upon you,
so that you may well distinguish god and also mortal man.
Therefore now, should a god come here to test you,
do you in no way wage head-on battle with the immortal gods,   130
with any of the others—only if Aphrodite daughter of Zeus
comes to war, her you can wound with sharp bronze."
 Speaking thus, gleaming-eyed Athena left,
and at once the son of Tydeus setting forth took his place among the front
     fighters,
hungry in spirit as he was even before to do battle with the Trojans;
but now three times greater was the fighting spirit that seized him, like a
     lion
that a shepherd in wild pasture among his wool-fleeced flock
has grazed as it leapt over the enclosure, but did not kill;
he rouses the lion's strength, and thereafter does not come out to aid his
     flock,
but ducks into his shelter, and they, forsaken, scatter in fear;   140
they are huddled together in a heap,

but the lion in fierce haste bounds forth from the high enclosure;
so powerful Diomedes in eager haste took his stand among the Trojans.

       There he killed Astynoös and Hypeiron shepherd of the people,
smiting the one above the breast with his bronze-headed spear,
and the other he struck on the collarbone beside the shoulder
with his great sword, and from neck and back severed the shoulder.
He left them, and went after Abas and Polyidos,
sons of Eurydamas the aged interpreter of dreams;
but the old man interpreted no dreams for them as they went forth,   150
and powerful Diomedes killed them.
And he went after Xanthos and Thoön, both late-born
sons of Phainops; he was worn out with pitiful old age,
and did not bear another son to be left behind for his possessions.
There Diomedes killed them, took away the dear life of
both, and left for the father lamentation and pitiful cares,
since he did not receive them alive, returned home from battle,
and kinsmen divided up his possessions.
Then Diomedes slew the two sons of Dardanian Priam
who were in the same chariot, Echemmon and Chromios.   160
As a lion leaping among cattle shatters the neck
of a calf or cow of a herd feeding in a woodland copse,
so the son of Tydeus brought both down from their chariot
with evil intent, against their will, then stripped their armour,
and gave the horses to his companions to drive to the ships.

       And Aeneas saw him wreaking havoc on the ranks of men,
and he left to go through the fighting and through the spears' confusion
seeking out godlike Pandaros, in the hope that he would come upon him.
He found the blameless and mighty son of Lykaon,
and stood close to him, and spoke a word straight to him: 170
"Pandaros, where is your bow and your feathered arrows
and your glory, with which no man here can compete,
nor any man in Lycia boast to be your better?
Come, lift your hands to Zeus, let fly an arrow at this man,

whoever this is who holds sway over us and has worked so much evil
on the Trojans, since he has unstrung the knees' strength of many and
   outstanding men—
unless he is some god angered at the Trojans,
wrathful over failed sacrifices; and the wrath of the god be heavy upon us."
      Then the splendid son of Lykaon addressed him:
"Aeneas, leader in counsel of the bronze-clad Trojans,   180
to the skilled son of Tydeus do I liken him in all respects,
judging by his shield and ridged helmet with the hollow eyes, and
looking at his horses; but I do not know for sure that he is not a god.
And if indeed he is the man I think, the skilled son of Tydeus,
he does not rage this way without a god, but some one of the immortals
stands close by him, wrapping his shoulders round with cloud,
who turned my swift arrow elsewhere, away from him, as it reached its
   mark.
For I have already shot a shaft at him, and it struck him on his right
shoulder straight on through the hollow of his breastplate;
and I thought I had sent him to the house of death,   190
yet all the same I did not kill him; surely, then, this is an angry god.
I do not have horses or a chariot that I could mount,
yet, I tell you, eleven chariots stand in the house of my father Lykaon,
beautiful, fitted together for the first time, newly made, covers
spread around them; and by each paired horses
stand, munching wheat and white barley.
And the old man, spearman Lykaon, instructed me again and again
in our sturdy home, as I was setting out;
he bade me mount behind my horses and chariot
to lead the Trojans throughout the mighty combat;   200
But I was not persuaded—which would have been far better—
and spared my horses, in fear that with men besieged
I might lack pasture, they being accustomed to eating their fill.
So I left them, and came on foot to Ilion,
trusting to my bow; but it was to be of no help to me.

For I have already let fly at two of their best men,
Tydeus and the son of Atreus, and from them both
as I struck I made real blood flow, but only aroused them the more.
Therefore it was in an evil hour I took my curved bow from its peg
on that day, when to lovely Ilion   210
I came as leader among the Trojans, bearing aid to godlike Hector.
But if I return home and look with my own eyes
upon my homeland and wife and great high-roofed house,
then let some outlander cut off my head at once
if I do not put this bow in the gleaming fire
broken in two by my hands; for its service to me is useless as the wind."

          Then in reply Aeneas commander of the Trojans answered him:
"Don't talk this way; there will be no change
until we two set out against this man with horse and chariot
to test him strength for strength with arms.   220
Come, mount my chariot so you may see
what kind of horses are these of Tros, expert
in making swift pursuit or flight here and there, across the plain—
These two will bring us safely to the city, even if once more
Zeus gives honour to Diomedes son of Tydeus.
But come now, take the whip and glossy reins,
and I will dismount the chariot to fight;
or you take on this man, and the horses will be my care."

          Then in turn the splendid son of Lykaon answered him:
"Aeneas, you hold the reins yourself and drive your horses;   230
they will carry their curved chariot better under their accustomed
     driver
should we flee back from the son of Tydeus.
May these two not baulk in fear, unwilling
to carry us out of battle when they miss your voice,
and the son of great-hearted Tydeus rush at us and
kill us both and drive off the single-hoofed horses.
No, you drive your own chariot and paired horses,

and I will wait with my sharp spear for this man as he advances."

So speaking they mounted the elaborate chariot,
and held the swift horses as they sped toward the son of Tydeus.   240
Sthenelos saw them, the splendid son of Kapaneus,
and at once he addressed the son of Tydeus with winged words:
"Son of Tydeus, Diomedes, delighting my heart,
I see two powerful men eager to fight against you,
both of immeasurable strength; one is well skilled in the bow,
Pandaros, who boasts he is the son of Lykaon;
and Aeneas, who boasts he is the son born of blameless
Anchises, and whose mother is Aphrodite.
Come, let us withdraw with our horses, do not, I beg you, rush so
through the frontlines, lest you destroy your own life."   250

Then looking at him from under his brows powerful Diomedes
  addressed him:
"Do not speak of flight, since I do not think you will persuade me.
For it is not in my blood to do battle by fleeing,
nor to cower; my nerve is still steady,
and I am unwilling to mount my chariot, but even as I am
I will go to meet them; Pallas Athena will not allow me to retreat.
The swift horses will not bring both these two men back again
from us, even should one or the other escape.
And I will tell you something else and put it away in your mind;
if Athena in her great wisdom should grant me the glory   260
of killing both men, you hold these swift horses of ours
here, drawing the reins tight to the chariot rail
and dash for the horses of Aeneas—remember all this—
and drive them from the Trojans to the strong-greaved Achaeans;
for they are of that stock that far-thundering Zeus gave to Tros
as recompense for his son Ganymede, since they were the best
of horses, of all beneath the sun and dawn.
Anchises lord of men stole from this stock,
for in secret from Laomedon he bred mares to the horses;

and from these six were born in his halls as offspring;   270
four of these, keeping for himself, he raised at the manger,
but two he gave to Aeneas, master of the rout.
If we should take these two, we would win outstanding glory."

          So they talked these things among each other,
and the two driving the swift horses drew swiftly closer.
And the splendid son of Lykaon first called in challenge to Diomedes:
"Strong-hearted, skilled son of glorious Tydeus,
I see the swift shaft did not kill you, my bitter arrow;
now I will try you again with my spear, if I make good my aim."
He spoke, and balancing his long-shadowed spear he hurled,   280
and hit the son of Tydeus on the shield; and flying straight through it
the bronze point brushed his breastplate.
And the splendid son of Lykaon cried aloud to him:
"You are struck in the side, right through, and I do not think you
will suffer long; but you have given me great cause for glory."

          Then not afraid powerful Diomedes addressed him:
"You missed, nor did you hit your mark; and I do not think you two
will desist, until one of you at least in falling
gluts with his blood the shield-bearing warrior Ares."
So speaking he let fly, and Athena directed his cast   290
to Pandaros' nose, beside the eye, and it passed through his white teeth;
the unyielding bronze cut away his tongue at the root,
and the spear-point came out beneath his chin.
He fell from the chariot, and his armour clashed about him
glinting, gleaming, and the swift-footed horses shied to one side;
and there his soul and strength were undone.

          Aeneas sprang away from the chariot with his shield and great
     spear,
fearing lest the Achaeans somehow drag the dead man away.
And he took his stand over him like a lion who trusts in his prowess,
holding before him his spear and the circle of his shield,   300
straining to kill any man who might come against him,

crying a fearsome cry. But the son of Tydeus took in his hand
a boulder, a great feat, which two men could not lift,
such as mortal men are now; but he even alone brandished it with ease;
with this he struck Aeneas on the hip joint, where the thigh-bone
turns in the hip joint, and which they call the socket cup.
And the jagged stone crushed his hip socket, snapped the tendons on both
    sides,
and forced the skin away. And the warrior
fell on his knees and remained there and leaned with his massive hand
upon the earth; and around his eyes the black night closed.   310
And there and then would Aeneas lord of men have perished
had Aphrodite, Zeus' daughter, not taken sharp note,
his mother, she who conceived him with Anchises when he was out with
    his cattle;
and around her beloved son she poured her white arms,
and folded the loose parts of her shining robe in front
to be a defence against missiles, lest one of the Danaans of swift horses,
hurling a bronze shaft in his breast, take his life away.

        She carried her beloved son away from the war;
nor did the son of Kapaneus forget the agreements
which Diomedes of the war cry had enjoined on him,   320
but he checked their own single-hoofed horses
away from the tumult, drawing the reins tight to the chariot rail,
and dashing for the horses of Aeneas with their beautiful manes,
he drove them off from the Trojans toward the strong-greaved
    Achaeans;
he gave them to Deïpylos, a beloved companion, whom beyond all
of his peers he honoured, because in their hearts they thought alike,
to drive to the hollow ships. Then the warrior himself
mounting behind his own horses took up the glossy reins,
and at once drove the strong-footed horses after the son of Tydeus
in fierce haste; but the son of Tydeus was ranging after Cyprian
    Aphrodite   330

with his pitiless bronze spear, knowing that she was not a fighting god,
nor of those goddesses who hold sway throughout the war of men,
not Athena, nor city-sacking Enyo.
And when, pressing hard through the great throng, he caught her,
there the son of great-hearted Tydeus reaching out,
charging with his sharp spear, wounded the tip of her
soft hand; the spear pierced her skin straight
through her immortal robe, which the Graces themselves toiled to make
    for her,
above the base of her palm; the immortal blood flowed from the
    divinity—
ichor, which alone flows in the blessed gods.   340
For they do not eat grain, nor drink shining wine;
and for this reason they are bloodless and are called immortals.
Shrieking loudly, she flung her son from her;
but Phoebus Apollo kept him safe in his arms
within a blue-black cloud, lest some one of the Danaans of swift horses
hurling bronze into his breast should rob him of his life.
And at her, Diomedes of the war cry shouted loud:
"Give over, daughter of Zeus, from war and battle!
Is it not enough that you beguile defenceless women?
If you make a habit of coming to war, then I think you   350
will shudder at war all right, even if you should only hear of it from
    somewhere else."

       So he spoke; and she, beside herself with pain, departed in
    dreadful distress.
And Iris with feet like the wind, taking her up, led her out of the throng
weighed down with pain, her beautiful skin blood-dark.
Then Aphrodite found furious Ares towards the left of the fighting,
sitting, his spear propped against the mist, with his two swift horses;
and falling to her knees before her dear brother,
beseeching again and again, she asked for his gold-bridled horses:
"Dear brother, rescue me and give me your horses,

that I may go to Olympus, where stands the seat of the immortals.   360
I am crushed with pain in this wound, which a mortal man struck me,
the son of Tydeus, who now would fight with even Father Zeus."

So she spoke. And Ares gave her the gold-bridled horses.
She got in the chariot grieving in her dear heart,
and beside her Iris mounted and took hold of the reins in her hands,
and lashed the whip to start the horses; and they two not unwilling
    flew on.
Swiftly they arrived at the seat of the gods, steep Olympus;
here swift Iris with feet like the wind drew up the horses,
released them from the chariot, and cast before them ambrosial fodder.

Divine Aphrodite fell upon the knees of Dione,   370
her mother; and she held her daughter tight in her arms,
and caressed her with her hand, and spoke to her and said her name:
"Who now, dear child, of the Olympians has done such a thing to you
without purpose, as if you had committed some crime in the sight of all?"
Then laughter-loving Aphrodite answered her:
"The son of Tydeus struck me, high-hearted Diomedes,
because I carried my beloved son away from the war,
Aeneas, who to me is far dearest of all men.
For this is no longer a dread battle between Trojans and Achaeans,
but now the Danaans fight with the very immortal gods."   380
Then Dione shining among goddesses answered her:
"Endure, my child, and bear up for all your pain.
For many of us who have homes on Olympus have suffered
from men, inflicting hard woes upon one another.
Ares suffered, when Otos and strong Ephialtes,
sons of Aloeus, bound him in bonds too strong for him;
they trussed him in a bronze jar for thirteen months.
Then surely Ares, the insatiable in war, would have perished,
had not their stepmother, surpassingly lovely Eëriboia,
carried word to Hermes; he took Ares away by stealth   390
by now worn to extremity, for the bronze bonds defeated him.

And Hera too endured, when the powerful son of Amphitryon
struck her, down into her right breast, with a three-barbed arrow;
then pain that could not be soothed gripped even her.
Among these too mighty Hades endured a swift arrow
when the very same man, the son of Zeus who wields the aegis,
struck him amid the dead in Pylos, and delivered him to pain;
but he went to the house of Zeus and high Olympus
hurt in heart, pierced with pain, the arrow
lodged in his powerful shoulder, stricken in spirit;   400
Paiëon sprinkling medicines that kill pain
healed him; for Hades was not born for death.
Wicked man! Evil-doer, who cared nothing as he performed his evil
    deeds,
who with his bow brought pain to the gods who hold Olympus!
Yet this deed against you the gleaming-eyed goddess Athena incited;
the fool, the son of Tydeus does not know this in his wits—
that not at all long for life is the man who battles with the gods,
his children do not call him papa at his knee
when he comes home from war and dread battle.
Now therefore, let the son of Tydeus, for all his surpassing
    strength,   410
think carefully, for fear that someone stronger than you do battle with
    him—
for fear that for a long time to come his wife Aigialeia, wise daughter of
    Adrestos,
will wake her dear servants from sleep with her wailing,
yearning for her wedded husband, the best of Achaeans,
the goodly wife of Diomedes breaker of horses."
She spoke, and with both her hands wiped the ichor away from her
    daughter's wrist;
the hand grew whole, and the heavy pangs of pain subsided.
        But Athena and Hera looking on
teased Zeus the son of Cronus with mocking words,

and the gleaming-eyed goddess Athena began to speak among
   them: 420
"Father Zeus, will you in any way be angry with me, if I should say
   something?
It seems Cypris, goading some Achaean woman
to follow after the Trojans, whom she so terribly loves,
as she caressed one of the fine-robed Achaean women
scratched her slender hand on a golden brooch."
So she spoke; and the father of gods and men smiled,
and calling her over, addressed golden Aphrodite:
"Not to you, my child, are given the deeds of war;
rather, you attend to the pleasurable deeds of marriage,
all these things will be the concern of furious Ares and Athena."   430

       Thus they spoke of such things to one another;
but Diomedes of the war cry rushed after Aeneas,
knowing though he did that Apollo himself held his hands above him,
but he was not awed by the great god, but ever pressed
to kill Aeneas and strip away his splendid armour.
Three times he rushed forward raging to kill,
and three times Apollo smote back his bright shield;
but when for the fourth time he charged like something more than
   human,
he who works from afar, Apollo, shouted out in a voice of terror:
"Take care, son of Tydeus, and give way; do not seek to think   440
yourself like the gods, since never the same is the race
of immortal gods and of men who walk upon the ground."
So he spoke, and the son of Tydeus withdrew a little back,
shrinking from the wrath of Apollo who strikes from afar.
And Apollo set Aeneas apart from the throng of battle
in holy Pergamos, where his temple stood.
Here Leto and Artemis who showers arrows
healed and glorified him within the great inner shrine.
But Apollo of the silver bow created an image

in the likeness of Aeneas himself and like his armour,   450
and around the image Trojans and glorious Achaeans
kept tearing at the oxhide shields about each other's chests,
well-rounded shields and bristling hides fluttering with tassels.

Then Phoebus Apollo spoke to furious Ares:
"Ares, Ares, ruinous to mortals, murderous sacker of walled cities,
will you not go and haul this man from battle,
the son of Tydeus, who now would fight with even Father Zeus?
First at close quarters he stabbed Cyprian Aphrodite's hand at the wrist,
and then he charged at even me like something more than human."
So speaking the god seated himself on the heights of Pergamos,   460
and murderous Ares set out to rally the Trojan ranks,
in the likeness of Akamas the swift leader of the Thracians;
and to the sons of Priam cherished by Zeus he gave orders:
"O sons of king Priam, cherished by Zeus,
for how long will you permit your people to be killed by the Achaeans?
Even until they fight about your well-made city gates?
A man lies fallen whom we honour equal to glorious Hector,
Aeneas, the son of great-hearted Anchises.
Come, let us save our noble companion from the tumult of battle."

So speaking he stirred the strength and spirit of each man.   470
But then in turn Sarpedon strongly rebuked glorious Hector:
"Hector, where has your courage gone, which you before possessed?
You used to say that you would hold the city without an army, without
    allies,
you alone with your brothers-in-law and your blood brothers;
now I am not able to see nor discern a one of them,
but they cower like dogs about a lion.
We are the ones fighting, we who are your allies.
Indeed I too, an ally, have come from very far away;
Lycia is a long way off, on the swirling river Xanthos,
where I left a dear wife and little son,   480
and many possessions, which some man in his need might covet.

But even so I urged on the Lycians and myself was eager
to go to battle with this man; yet there is nothing of mine here
that the Achaeans would carry off or lead away as spoil.
You stand here, but you do not bid the rest of
your men stand firm and defend their wives.
May you not, as if caught in the mesh of a trawling net,
become the spoil and prey of enemy men,
who soon will sack your well-settled city.
All these things must be your care through both the nights and in the
    day—   490
to entreat the leaders of your far-famed allies
to hold the line relentlessly, and from yourself to put away any cause for
    strong reproach."

        So spoke Sarpedon; and his speech bit into the heart of Hector.
At once he leapt from his chariot in his armour to the ground,
and brandishing his sharp spears he made his way to every place
    throughout the army
rallying the men to fight, and he stirred up the dread battle.
The men wheeled themselves about and stood facing the Achaeans;
but the Argives stood firm together, nor did they flee.
And as the wind carries chaff hither and thither across the sacred
    threshing floor
of men as they winnow, when golden Demeter   500
sifts grain and chaff beneath the gusting winds,
and the heaped chaff grows white, so the Achaeans
grew white beneath the cloud of dust that through their ranks
their horses' feet pounded to the brazen sky
as they fought close again; and the charioteers wheeled with them.
They carried the might of their hands straight on; and bolstering the
    Trojans
furious Ares wrapped night around the battle,
ranging everywhere; he brought to pass the wishes
of Apollo of the sword of gold, who ordered him

to stir the spirit of the Trojans when he saw Pallas Athena   510
had departed; for she it was who gave aid to the Danaans.
And out of his rich sanctuary Apollo sent forth Aeneas,
and cast strength in the breast of the shepherd of his people.
Aeneas took his stand among his comrades; and they rejoiced
when they saw him alive and unharmed as he came toward them
and possessed of his outstanding strength; but they asked no questions;
for their other work did not permit them, the work of war that the god of
    the silver bow had raised,
and Ares, ruinous to mortals, and Strife, who is zealous always.

        But the two Aiantes and Odysseus and Diomedes
urged the Danaans to wage war; they themselves   520
did not shrink before the Trojan might, nor their attacks,
but stood firm, like clouds that the son of Cronus
sets on a windless day upon the topmost part of mountains,
motionless, when the North Wind's power is hushed, and the other
violent winds'—winds that with piercing blasts
scatter the shadowy clouds when they blow hard—
so the Danaans withstood the Trojans steadfastly nor did they flee.

        But the son of Atreus roamed throughout the host giving many
    orders:
"O friends, be men and take hold of your courageous spirit
and fear shame before each other throughout the mighty combat;   530
when men fear shame, more are safe than slain,
but when men flee, neither glory nor any victory is seen."
He spoke, and swiftly casting with his spear, he struck the foremost man,
a companion of great-hearted Aeneas, Deïkoön
the son of Pergasos, whom the Trojans esteemed as equal to the sons of
Priam, since he was always quick to fight among the first ranks.
Lord Agamemnon struck him across the shield with his spear;
and it did not protect him from the spear, but the bronze passed straight
    through,
and piercing his war-belt, into the pit of his stomach it drove.

He fell with a thud, and his armour clashed upon him.   540

      But then Aeneas slew the best of Danaan men,

the sons of Diokles, Krethon and Ortilochos,

whose father dwelt in well-built Phere,

a man who lived richly, a descendant of the river

Alpheus, who flows wide through the land of Pylos;

he begat Ortilochos lord of many men,

and Ortilochos then begat great-hearted Diokles,

and from Diokles were born twin sons,

Krethon and his namesake Ortilochos, both well skilled in all kinds of
    battle.

These two, then, in the flower of their youth, on dark ships   550

followed with the Argives to Ilion with its fine horses,

to win honour for the sons of Atreus, for Agamemnon

and Menelaos; and there the finality of death enfolded both.

They were as two lions reared on the heights of

a mountain by their mother in the thickets of deep forest;

who seizing cattle and fat flocks

lay waste people's farmsteads, until even they

are killed at the hands of men with sharp bronze;

as such did the two youths broken under the hands of Aeneas

fall, like towering firs.   560

      And as they fell Menelaos beloved of Ares pitied them,

and he made his way through the front-rank fighters armed in gleaming
    bronze,

shaking his spear; Ares encouraged his passion,

with this in mind—that Menelaos would be killed at the hands of Aeneas.

But Antilochos, son of great-hearted Nestor, saw him,

and he made his way through the front-rank fighters, for he was afraid for
    the shepherd of the people,

lest he should suffer death and wholly defeat the purpose of their war toil.

And when Menelaos and Aeneas held up their hands and sharp spears

against each other, ready to fight,

Antilochos took his stand close by the shepherd of the people;   570
and Aeneas did not stay, swift fighter though he was,
when he saw the two men standing firm beside each other.
They then dragged the dead bodies toward the Achaean host,
and so placed the unlucky pair in the hands of comrades,
and themselves, turning back, went to battle among the front fighters.

      Thereupon they killed Pylaimenes the equal of Ares,
leader of the Paphlagonians, the great-hearted shield-bearers.
For Atreus' son spear-famed Menelaos
smote him as he stood, striking at his collarbone;
and Antilochos let fly at Mydon his charioteer and henchman,   580
the noble son of Atymnios—he was wheeling around his single-hoofed
    horses—
with a great stone, striking the middle of the elbow; and from his hands
the reins gleaming white with ivory fell to the ground in the dust.
Springing forward Antilochos drove with his sword at Mydon's temple;
and he, gasping, dropped from the well-wrought chariot,
helmet first, on his head and shoulders in the dust.
A long time he stayed there, for he chanced to hit deep sand,
while his two horses pounding the ground with their hooves beat him
    into the dust—
horses that Antilochos then lashed on, and drove toward the Achaean
    army.

      And through the lines of battle Hector marked them, and sprang
    for them   590
crying aloud; and with him followed the ranks of Trojans
in their power; and Ares led them and lady Enyo, spirit of war,
bringing Panic with her, the ruthless turmoil of war,
and Ares wielded in his hand his great spear,
as he ranged now before Hector, now behind him.
And seeing him Diomedes shuddered, he of the war cry;
as when a man making his way over a great plain stands helpless
by a river, swift flowing as it rushes to the sea,

watching it roaring with foam, and runs forward and back,
so then the son of Tydeus drew back and spoke to his men: 600
"O friends, how we marvelled at glorious Hector
for being a spearman and bold warrior!
Always one of the gods is by his side, who wards off destruction.
And now Ares is that one beside him, in the likeness of a mortal man.
Come, face the Trojans and keep withdrawing
back, and do not seek to fight with force against the gods."

     Thus he spoke; and the Trojans approached almost upon them.
There Hector killed two men wise in the art of war
who were in one chariot, Menesthes and Anchialos.
As they both fell great Telamonian Ajax pitied them,   610
and coming up he stood hard by, and cast with his shining spear,
and struck Amphios, the son of Selagos, who in Paisos
lived rich in possessions, rich in corn-land; but destiny led him
to serve as ally with Priam and with his sons.
Telamonian Ajax struck him down across his war-belt,
the long-shadowed spear fixed in the pit of his stomach,
and he fell with a thud; glorious Ajax ran toward him
to strip the armour; the Trojans poured their spears upon him,
glinting sharp, but his shield caught many.
With his foot against the dead body, he dragged out   620
his bronze spear; but still was not able to strip
the splendid armour from the dead man's shoulders , for he was assailed
    by hurled spears.
And he feared the strong encirclement of noble Trojan spearmen,
the many and the excellent men who drew up to take their stand holding
    spears;
and big though he was and strong and illustrious,
they drove him from them; and he retreated, staggering.

     Thus they toiled throughout the mighty combat;
and Tlepolemos descended from Heracles, a good man and great,
was driven toward godlike Sarpedon by powerful destiny.

And when they had advanced almost upon each other—   630
the son and the grandson of Zeus who gathers the clouds—
Tlepolemos spoke the first word to Sarpedon:
"Sarpedon, leader of Lycians in counsel alone, what compels you
to cower here, a man ignorant of battle?
They lie who say you are born of Zeus who wields the aegis,
since you fall far short of those men
who were born of Zeus in the days of men of old.
Heracles they say was a different sort of man—
my father, bold-spirited, lionhearted,
who, in time past, coming here for Laomedon's horses   640
did with his six ships and with fewer men
utterly sack the city of Ilion, and widow its streets.
But in you is a coward's heart, and your people waste away,
nor do I think you will be any defence for the Trojans
in your coming from Lycia, not even if you are very strong,
but broken under my hand you will pass through the gates of Hades."
        But Sarpedon leader of the Lycians answered him in turn:
"Tlepolemos, Heracles did indeed destroy sacred Ilion
through the witlessness of one man—illustrious Laomedon—
who abused with an evil word one who had done him well,   650
and did not give up the mares, for which Heracles had come so far.
But I say to you here that bloodshed and dark death
are what will be wrought by me, and broken by my spear
you will give glory to me, and your soul to Hades of famed horses."
So spoke Sarpedon; and Telepolemos lifted his ash-spear;
and the long spears flew from their hands together.
Sarpedon struck the middle of his neck,
and the grievous point passed all the way through,
and from his eyes down murky night enveloped Tlepolemos;
but he had wounded Sarpedon with his long spear   660
in the left thigh, and the eager spear-point sped through,
shaving the bone; but for this time Zeus his father averted destruction.

His glorious companions carried godlike Sarpedon
from the fighting; the long spear weighed him down
as it dragged—no one noticed it or took thought
to pull the ash-spear from his thigh, so that he might stand,
in their haste; for such was their trouble handling him—
and on the other side the strong-greaved Achaeans carried Tlepolemos
from the fighting. Godlike Odysseus saw,
he whose spirit was unflinching, and his heart shook for action;   670
and he weighed in his mind and in his heart,
whether he should further pursue the son of far-thundering Zeus,
or he should strip the life from yet more Lycians.
But it was not fated for great-hearted Odysseus
to kill the powerful son of Zeus with his sharp bronze;
and therefore Athena turned his anger toward the multitude of Lycians.
And there he killed Koiranos and Alastor and Chromios
and Alkandros and Halios and Prytanis and Noemon;
and now godlike Odysseus would have killed even more of the Lycians,
if great Hector of the shimmering helm had not taken sharp note.   680
He came through the front fighters armoured in gleaming bronze,
bearing terror to the Danaans; and Sarpedon rejoiced at his coming,
the son of Zeus, and spoke an imploring word:
"Son of Priam, do not let me lie as spoil for the Danaans,
but fight for me. Then life may forsake me
in your city, as it seems I was not destined
to return to my home, to the beloved land of my fathers
and to make happy my dear wife and young son."
      So he spoke; but Hector of the shimmering helm said nothing to
   him,
and sped past in eager haste, so that he might quickly   690
force back the Achaeans, and strip the life away from many.
So his glorious companions laid godlike Sarpedon
beneath a beautiful oak, sacred to Zeus who wields the aegis;
and from his thigh the ash-spear was forced out

by noble Pelagon, who was his beloved companion;
and his soul left Sarpedon and mist seeped down from his eyes.
But about him the breath of the North Wind's
blowing revived the life-spirit he had cruelly panted out, and he breathed
     again.
          The Argives under force of Ares and bronze-armoured Hector
never turned to their dark ships   700
nor ever engaged in fighting, but ever backward
kept withdrawing, for they saw Ares was with the Trojans.
Who there was the first man, who the last that
Priam's son Hector and bronze Ares killed?
Godlike Teuthras, and then Orestes driver of horses,
and Trechos the Aetolian spearman and Oinomaos
and Helenos son of Oinops and Oresbios of the shimmering belt-guard,
who had lived in Hyle greatly concerned for his riches,
aslope the shore of the Kephisian lake; and beside him lived other men
of Boeotia, who held the luxuriant country.   710
          Then when the white-armed goddess Hera saw the
Argives perishing in the mighty combat,
she at once addressed winged words to Athena:
"O for shame, daughter of Zeus who wields the aegis, Athena Atrytone,
now the word we pledged to Menelaos is come to nothing,
that he would return home having sacked well-walled Ilion,
if we allow murderous Ares to rage in this way.
But come, and let us two also take thought of our fierce courage."
So she spoke, nor did the gleaming-eyed goddess Athena disobey.
Departing, Hera got ready the gold-bridled horses,   720
she, elder of goddesses, daughter of great Cronus;
And on both sides of the chariot Hebe swiftly fitted its curved wheels—
bronze, eight-spoked around an iron axle;
their inner rim is imperishable gold,
bronze tyres are close fitted round, a wonder to look upon,
and hubs of silver spin on either side;

the chariot car is braced tight with gold and silver bindings,
and front and back, curved rails run round.
A silver yoke-pole protrudes from it; and on its end
Hebe secured the golden, splendid yoke, and fitted on the splendid
   harness   730
also of gold; and under the yoke Hera led
the swift-footed horses, eager as she was for strife and battle.

       And Athena, daughter of Zeus who wields the aegis,
let fall her rippling robe upon her father's floor,
elaborate with embroidery, which she herself had made and laboured on
   with her own hands,
and putting on the cloak of Zeus who gathers clouds,
she armed herself for tearful war.
Around her shoulders she flung the tasselled aegis
a thing of dread, crowned on every side with Panic all around,
and Strife was on it, and Battle Spirit and chilling Flight,   740
and on it too the terrible monstrous Gorgon head,
a thing of awe and terror, portent of Zeus who wields the aegis;
and on her head Athena placed her helmet, ridged on both sides,
with four golden bosses, adorned with fighters of a hundred cities;
she made her way on foot toward the flame-bright chariot, and seized her
   spear,
heavy, massive, powerful, with which she beats down the ranks of warrior
men, with whom she, born of the mighty Father, might be angered.

       Hera with her whip swiftly touched the horses;
of their own accord the gates of heaven groaned, which the Seasons guard,
they to whom broad heaven and Olympus are entrusted   750
to push back the thick-pressed clouds and also close them over.
Through these they held the goad-sped horses;
they found the son of Cronus sitting apart from other gods
on the topmost peak of ridged Olympus.
There the white-armed goddess Hera, bringing the horses to a stop,
spoke out to Zeus the high son of Cronus and addressed him:

"Father Zeus, do you not find fault with Ares for these violent deeds,
seeing he has destroyed so many and such good Achaean warriors,
heedlessly, without seemliness, to my sorrow? And, untroubled,
Cypris and silver-bowed Apollo, are exultant,   760
having let this madman loose, who knows nothing decent.
Father Zeus, would you then be angry with me if I
were to drive Ares, thrashed sorely, from the battle?"
Then in answer Zeus who gathers the clouds addressed her:
"Go to then, set Athena the spoiler at him,
who above all others is practised in bringing him close to evil pains."

      So he spoke, nor did the goddess of the white arms Hera disobey.
She put whip to the horses, and they two not unwilling flew on
between the earth and star-strewn heaven.
As far as a man can see with his eyes into the haze of distance   770
as he sits on a peak, looking on sea as dark as wine,
so far the horses of the gods leapt in one stride, thundering on high.
But when they came to Troy and its two flowing rivers,
where Simoeis and Scamander meet their streams,
there Hera the goddess of the white arms drew up the horses,
released them from the chariot, and around them poured abundant mist;
and Simoeis brought forth for them ambrosia to be grazed.

      Like wild doves the two goddesses strutted forth,
in eagerness to defend the Argive men.
And when then they arrived where the most and the best men   780
stood massed around strong Diomedes breaker of horses,
like lions who eat flesh,
or wild boars, whose strength is unflagging,
there taking her stand, the goddess of the white arms Hera cried out,
like Stentor, great-hearted and bronze-voiced,
whose shouting cry is as great as that of fifty other men:
"For shame, Argives, cowardly disgraces, admirable only in appearance!
During the time Achilles the godlike came to battle,
never did the Trojans go beyond the Dardanian gates;

for they feared his heavy spear;   790
now far from the city, they fight beside the hollow ships."
So speaking she stirred the strength and spirit of every man.

      And the gleaming-eyed goddess Athena rushed to the son of
  Tydeus.
She found the king beside his horses and chariot
cooling off his wound that Pandaros had struck with his arrow.
For the sweat wore him beneath the broad strap
of his man-surrounding shield; he was worn with it, and his arms were
  weary;
lifting his shield strap he wiped away the dark-clouded blood.
But the goddess grasped his horse's yoke and spoke to him:
"Surely Tydeus begot a son only a little like him.   800
Tydeus to be sure was small in build, but he was warlike;
even at the time when I forbade him to go to war,
or to rush to the fray, when he went alone without the Achaeans
as messenger to Thebes among many Cadmeians,
and I bade him dine with them peacefully in their halls,
yet keeping his spirit strong, as ever before,
he challenged the young men of Cadmus, and vanquished them
  entirely—
easily; such an ally to him was I.
And surely I stand by and watch over you,
and gladly bid you do battle with the Trojans;   810
but either the weariness of many assaults has entered in your limbs,
or, perhaps, it is spiritless fear that holds you. Not then are you
the child of Tydeus, the brilliant son of Oineus."

      Then answering her, powerful Diomedes spoke:
"I know you, goddess, daughter of Zeus who wields the aegis;
therefore gladly do I speak to you nor will I hold my thoughts.
Neither any spiritless fear holds me, nor any shirking,
but I am yet mindful of your commands, which you charged;
you did not permit me to engage in head-on battle with the other

blessed gods; but if Aphrodite daughter of Zeus   820
came to war, her I could wound with sharp bronze.
For this reason now I have withdrawn and ordered
the other Argives all to mass together here.
For I know it is Ares who lords it across the battlefield."

      Then the gleaming-eyed goddess Athena answered him:
"Son of Tydeus, Diomedes, delighting my heart,
do not fear Ares on this account nor any other
of the immortals; such an ally to you am I.
But come, hold your single-hoofed horses straight for Ares,
strike at close quarters, do not stand in awe of furious Ares   830
this madman, created for evil, double-faced,
who only yesterday to myself and Hera declaiming aloud pledged
to fight the Trojans, and defend the Argives,
and now he bands with the Trojans, and has no thought of this."

      So speaking she pulled Sthenelos from the chariot to the ground,
drawing him backwards with her hand, and he quickly sprang away;
and she the goddess mounted into the chariot beside brilliant Diomedes
in eager haste; and the oaken axle groaned mightily
with weight; for it bore a dread goddess and a noble man.
And Pallas Athena seized the whip and reins;   840
straightway she held the single-hoofed horses straight for Ares.
He was just stripping huge Periphas,
the best by far of the Aetolians, the splendid son of Ochesios;
this man murderous Ares was stripping; but Athena
put on the cap of Hades, so that massive Ares would not see her.
And when Ares, ruinous to mortals, saw brilliant Diomedes,
he let huge Periphas lie flat on the spot
where he first had stripped his life and killed him,
and then made straight for Diomedes breaker of horses.

      And when they had advanced almost upon each other,   850
Ares lunged first over the yoke and the reins of the horses
with his bronze spear, bent on stripping away his life;

but the gleaming-eyed goddess Athena taking the spear with her hand
thrust it up and away from the chariot to fly in vain.
Then Diomedes of the war cry charged
with his bronze spear; and Pallas Athena pressed it
in low beneath the ribs, where Ares was girt by his war-belt.
Striking there she wounded him and ripped through his splendid skin,
and drew the spear out again. And brazen Ares roared,
as loud as nine thousand men shout, or ten thousand   860
men in battle joined in strife of war;
and at this trembling took hold of both Achaeans and Trojans
in their fear; so loud did he roar, Ares insatiate of war.
As darkling mist appears from the clouds
after the heat of weather, and a violent wind is stirred,
so did Ares the bronze god appear to Diomedes son of Tydeus
among the clouds, as he rose up to broad heaven.
          Swiftly he came to the seat of the gods, steep Olympus,
and seated himself at the side of Zeus the son of Cronus grieving in his
     heart,
and he showed the ambrosial blood flowing from his wounds,   870
and making lament spoke winged words:
"Father Zeus, do you not find fault seeing these violent deeds?
We gods always are undergoing the most dreadful evils
by each other's will, as we bear our service to mankind.
And we are all at war with you; for you bore this witless, accursed
girl, whose concern is always unseemly deeds.
All the others, as many as are gods on Olympus,
are obedient to you and each of us is your subject,
but this one you rebuke neither with word nor any deed,
but you incite her, since you yourself begot this ruinous child.   880
Now she has incited the son of Tydeus, prideful Diomedes,
to rage like a madman against the immortal gods;
first he wounded Cypris at close quarters on the wrist of her hand,
and then he rushed at even me like something more than human.

But my swift feet bore me away; else I assure you for some long time
I would have suffered pain there among the terrible piles of dead.
Or I would have been alive but powerless, through the blows of his
    bronze spear."

        Then looking at him from under his brows Zeus who gathers the
    clouds addressed him:
"Do not, you double-faced, sit beside me whimpering complaint.
You are to me most hateful of the gods who hold Olympus;   890
always contention is dear to you, and fighting and battles.
The rage of your mother Hera is uncontainable, unyielding;
and I with difficulty control her with my words.
Therefore I think that you will suffer for her promptings.
Yet I will not allow you to bear your pain for long;
for you are born of me, and your mother bore you to me.
But had you been born so ruinous of any other god,
you would long ago have been made even lower than the fallen
    Titans."
So he spoke, and bade Paiëon heal him;
and Paiëon sprinkled medicines that kill pain on the wound.   900
As when fig juice hastens the curdling of white milk,   902
which is liquid, but instantly thickens as one stirs,
so then he instantly healed furious Ares.
And Hebe bathed him, and put fine clothes on him;
and he seated himself beside Zeus the son of Cronus, exulting in his
    glory.

        And they returned back to the house of great Zeus,
Hera of Argos and Athena who stands guardian in Boeotia,
having stopped Ares, ruinous to mortals, of his man-slaughtering.

So left to itself was the grim battle of Trojans and Achaeans.
Back and forth, the fighting pressed on across the plain,
as they sent their bronze-fitted spears straight at one another
between the flowing waters of Xanthos and Simoeis.

      Ajax son of Telamon, a wall of defence for the Achaeans, first
broke the Trojan lines, and brought light to his companions,
striking a man who was best among the Thracians,
the son of Eüssoros, Akamas, a good man and mighty.
Ajax struck him first, on the ridge of his horsehair-crested helmet,
and fixed him between the eyes; into the bone the brazen point   10
passed, and darkness enclosed his eyes.

      Then Diomedes of the war cry killed Axylos,
the son of Teuthras, who lived in strong-built Arisbe,
a rich man, he was a friend to mankind;
for he welcomed all men, dwelling as he did in a house by the wayside;
but no man now warded off his sorrowful destruction
coming out to defend him, and Diomedes stripped both of life,
Axylos himself and his attendant Kalesios, who was driver
of his horses; and both went down to the realm beneath the earth.

      And Euryalos, son of Mekisteus, killed Dresos and Opheltios;   20
and then went after Aisepos and Pedasos, whom in time past the water
   nymph
Abarbarea bore to blameless Boukolion.
Boukolion was the son of noble Laomedon,

the eldest in birth, whom his mother bore in secret darkness.
While tending his sheep, Boukolion lay with the nymph in love and sex;
and she conceived and bore twin sons.
But the son of Mekisteus undid the strength of their shining limbs
and stripped the armour from their shoulders.

       Then Polypoites, steadfast in battle, slew Astyalos;
and Odysseus killed Pidytes from Perkote   30
with his bronze spear, and Teucer killed noble Aretaon;
and Antilochos son of Nestor dispatched Ableros
with his shining spear-shaft, and lord of men Agamemnon dispatched
    Elatos;
he had lived by the banks of lovely flowing Satnioeis
in steep Pedasos; and the warrior Leïtos slew Phylakos
as he fled; and Eurypylos killed Melanthios.

       And then Menelaos of the war cry took Adrestos
alive; for his two horses bolting in panic across the plain
were caught on a branch of tamarisk, and shattering
the curved chariot at the yoke-pole's end they made for   40
the city, where others bolting in panic had fled,
and Adrestos was spun out of his chariot headfirst in the dust upon
    his face
beside the wheel; and standing there beside him was
the son of Atreus, Menelaos, holding his long-shadowed spear.
Then Adrestos, grasping his knees, beseeched him:
"Take me alive, son of Atreus, take the worthy ransom.
Many valuables lie in the house of my rich father,
bronze and gold and iron wrought with labour;
from these my father would satisfy you with priceless ransom,
were he to know that I am alive by the ships of the Achaeans."   50

       So he spoke, and was persuading the spirit in Menelaos' breast;
and he was about to give Adrestos forthwith to his attendant
to lead down to the Achaeans' swift ships; but Agamemnon
came running toward him, and shouting out he spoke his word:

"O soft one, O Menelaos, why are you so caring
of these men? I suppose only the noblest things were done in your house
by the Trojans? Let not a man of them escape sheer destruction
at our hands, not even he whom the mother carries in her womb,
the male child, may even he not escape, but together, all of them,
may they be expunged from Ilion, without burial and without a trace."   60
So speaking the noble warrior turned his brother's heart,
urging what was justified; and Menelaos with his hand shoved
the warrior Adrestos from him. Lord Agamemnon struck him
beneath the ribs; he fell back face upward, and the son of Atreus
stepping with his foot upon the dead man's chest drew out his ash-spear.

Then Nestor, shouting aloud, called to the Argives:
"O friends, Danaan warriors, companions of Ares,
let no man now tarry behind to throw himself upon the
spoils, in order to reach the ships with the biggest haul,
but rather let us kill men; then at your leisure these things too   70
you can plunder from the bodies of those who died all along the plain."
So speaking he rallied the strength and spirit of each man.

Then once more would the Trojans have gone up into Ilion,
defeated by their lack of spirit before the warlike Achaeans
had not Priam's son Helenos, far the best augur of birds,
spoken to Aeneas and Hector as he stood beside them:
"Aeneas and you too Hector, since on you both above all rests
the Trojans' and Lycians' toil of war, because you are the best
in every course, both fighting and strategy—
take your stand here, check your people before the gates,   80
patrol in every direction, before they fall, fleeing back
into the arms of their women, and become a source of joy to our enemies.
Then when you both have roused all lines of battle,
we will fight with the Danaans, standing firm here,
hard pressed though we surely be; for necessity propels us;
but Hector, you make your way to the city, and speak to
your mother and mine; let her summon the elder women

to the temple of gleaming-eyed Athena on the city height,

and open with her key the doors of the sacred shrine,

and place a robe, one which seems to her to be the loveliest and most
    ample   90

in her house, and which is most precious to her,

let her place this upon the knees of the statue of Athena of the lovely
    hair;

and pledge to sacrifice to her in the temple twelve young cows,

yearlings, unbroken, if she would have mercy

on the city and on the wives of the Trojans and their infant children,

if she would ward off the son of Tydeus from holy Ilion—

savage spearman, violent master of the rout,

who I say has become the mightiest of Achaeans.

We did not so fear Achilles, leader of men,

who they say is sprung from a goddess; but this one rages beyond all
    bounds,   100

nor has any man power to contend with his strength."

      So he spoke; and Hector did not disobey his brother.

At once he sprang from his chariot in his armour to the ground,

and brandishing his sharp spears he made his way to every place
    throughout the army

rallying the men to fight, and stirred the dread battle.

The Trojans wheeled about and stood facing the Achaeans.

And the Argives withdrew, and ceased their slaughter—

they thought some one of the immortals from the star-strewn heaven

had descended to defend the Trojans; just so had they wheeled.

      And Hector called to the Trojans, shouting loud: 110

"High-spirited Trojans and allies far-renowned,

be ready men and defend the city from outrage,

so that I may go to Ilion and speak with

the elder counsellors and our wives

to pray to the divine ones, and promise hecatombs."

So speaking, Hector of the shimmering helm departed;

the black oxskin of his shield struck him at both neck and ankles,
the rim which ran on the edge of his bossed shield.

      Then Glaukos the son of Hippolochos and the son of Tydeus
came together in the space between both armies, straining to fight.   120
And when they had advanced almost upon each other,
Diomedes of the war cry first addressed the other:
"Who are you, brave friend, of men consigned to death?
For I have never seen you in battle where men win glory
before this time, but now striding far in front of all men
in your bold courage, you stand to wait my long-shadowed spear—
and they are sons of brokenhearted men, who face my might.
But if you are one of the immortals come down from heaven,
I would not go to battle with the gods of heaven.
For not long, not long at all, did the son of Dryas live, powerful
   Lykourgos,   130
who competed with the gods of heaven;
who in time past drove the nurses of raving Dionysus
down the mountain slopes of holy Nysa, and all of them as one
scattered their sacred staffs to the ground, when struck by the cattle goad
that man-slaughtering Lykourgos wielded. And Dionysus, fleeing,
plunged beneath a wave of the salt sea, and Thetis took him, terrified,
in her embrace; for powerful trembling held him at the man's bellowing.
Then the gods who live at ease were enraged with Lykourgos,
and the son of Cronus struck him blind; nor was he still long
for life, once he incurred the hatred of all immortal gods.   140
So I would not wish to do battle with the blessed gods.
But if you are a man, of mortals who eat the fruit of worked land,
draw near, so that you may more swiftly arrive at death's border."

      And in turn the glorious son of Hippolochos addressed him:
"Great-hearted son of Tydeus, why do you ask my lineage?
As a generation of leaves, so is the generation of men.
The wind scatters some leaves to the ground, but the forest grows
   others

that flourish and in the time of spring come to succeed them;
so a generation of men either grows, or it dies.
But if you indeed wish to learn these things, so as to know well   150
my family's lineage, many men know of it.
There is a city, Ephyre, in a corner of horse-pasturing Argos,
where Sisyphus ruled, who was born most cunning of men,
Sisyphus the son of Aeolus; he fathered a son, Glaukos;
then Glaukos fathered blameless Bellerophon.
And to Bellerophon the gods gave beauty, and also attractive
manliness; but Proitos intended evil things against him in his heart,
and since he was more powerful by far, he drove Bellerophon from
    the land
of Argives; since Zeus had subjugated them beneath Proitos' sceptre.
For the wife of Proitos, regal Anteia, was mad   160
to lie with him in secret love; but she did not
persuade wise-thinking Bellerophon, for he was noble-hearted.
So speaking a lie, she addressed king Proitos:
'May you die, O Proitos, or kill Bellerophon,
who desired to lie in love with me, I who was not willing.'
So she spoke; and anger seized the king at what he heard.
Yet he refrained from killing Bellerophon, for in his heart he felt shame
    to do so,
but sent him to Lycia, and gave him baneful signs,
scratching on a folded tablet many destructive things,
and instructed him to show them to his father-in-law, so that he might
    die. 170
And Bellerophon went to Lycia under blameless escort of the gods.
And when he came to Lycia and the flowing river Xanthos,
the lord of wide Lycia honoured him graciously;
for nine days he gave him hospitality and sacrificed nine cattle.
But when the tenth dawn shone forth her rosy fingers of light,
then it was he questioned him and asked to see the symbols,
whatever it was he had brought with him from his son-in-law Proitos.

And when he was given his son-in-law's evil message,
first he ordered Bellerephon to slay the invincible Chimaira;
a thing of divine origin, not of men,   180
a lion in front, its hind part a serpent, and its middle a goat,
breathing forth a fearsome raging blaze of fire.
But Bellerophon killed it, following signs from the gods.
Second, he now fought the legendary Solymi;
it was, he used to say, the most violent battle of men he entered.
The third time, he killed the man-battling Amazons.
And then the king contrived another cunning trick for him as he returned;
choosing the best men from wide Lycia
he set an ambush. But it was these men who did not return back home,
for blameless Bellerophon slew them all.   190
And when the king perceived that he was from the noble lineage of a god,
he detained Bellerophon there, and indeed offered him his daughter,
and gave him half of all his royal honour;
and the Lycians cut out a plot of land surpassing all others,
a beautiful plot, with orchards and tilled fields, for him to enjoy.
And the king's daughter bore three children to wise Bellerophon,
Isandros and Hippolochos and Laodameia.
And with Laodameia Zeus all-devising lay,
and she bore godlike Sarpedon of the bronze armour.
But when Bellerophon too became hateful to all gods,   200
he wandered alone across the Aleian plain,
consuming his own heart, avoiding the paths of men,
and his son Isandros was killed by Ares, insatiate of war,
as he fought the glorious Solymi,
and Artemis of the golden reins killed his daughter in anger.
And Hippolochos begot me, and I say I am born of him;
he sent me to Troy, and gave many directives to me,
always to be best and to be better than all others,
not to disgrace the line of my fathers, who were far the best
in Ephyre and in broad Lycia.   210

Of such descent and blood do I claim to be."
      So he spoke; and Diomedes of the war cry rejoiced.
He fixed his spear in the nourishing earth,
then with friendly words addressed the shepherd of the people:
"Now then, surely you are my guest friend from my father's side of long
    ago;
for noble Oineus once received blameless Bellerophon
as guest friend in his halls, detaining him for twenty days.
They even gave to each other splendid gifts of friendship;
Oineus gave a war-belt bright with crimson,
and Bellerophon a two-handled cup of gold;   220
and I left it in my home when setting forth;
I do not remember Tydeus, since I was still small
when he left me, that time the Achaean people perished at Thebes.
Now therefore I am guest friend to you in the heart of Argos,
as you to me in Lycia, whenever I should come to their country.
Let us avoid each other's spears, even in the thick of battle;
for there are many Trojans and their famed allies for me
to kill, whom god might put in my hands, or let me catch with my feet,
and in turn many Achaeans are there for you to kill, whomever of them
    you can.
Let us exchange armour with each other, so that these others here   230
will know that we claim to be guest friends from our fathers."
      Having so spoken, they both leapt from their chariots
and took each other's hands and pledged their trust.
But Zeus the son of Cronus took away the wits from Glaukos,
who exchanged with Diomedes son of Tydeus armour
of gold for that bronze, a hundred oxen's value for nine.
      But as Hector came to the Scaean gates and rampart,
the wives and daughters of the Trojans ran to surround him,
asking about their sons and brothers and kinsmen and
their husbands; but he urged them to pray to the gods,   240
each woman in turn; for woes had been bound upon many.

When he came to the sumptuous house of Priam
built with its smooth-wrought colonnades—within it
were fifty chambers of polished stone,
close built to one another, where the sons
of Priam slept beside their wedded wives;
on the other side, facing them inside the courtyard, were his daughters'
twelve roofed chambers of polished stone,
close built to one another; where the sons-in-law
of Priam slept beside their modest wives—   250
there Hector's mother, giver of kindness, came to meet him,
leading Laodike, the most outstanding in beauty of her daughters,
and clung to him with her hand and spoke to him and said his name:
"Child, why have you come, leaving the reckless fighting?
Truly, the sons of the Achaeans, of cursed name, have worn you out
with their battling round the city, and your spirit has impelled you to
    come here,
to lift your hands to Zeus in supplication from the high place of the city.
But wait, while I bring you wine, honey-sweet,
for you to make libation to Zeus the father and the immortals
first, and then yourself have enjoyment, should you drink it.   260
Wine greatly strengthens the spirit in a weary man,
as you have been wearied protecting your people."

        And then great Hector of the shimmering helm answered her:
"Do not to me offer up wine, sweet to the spirit, my lady mother,
lest you sap my limbs of strength, and I forget my courage.
And I shrink from pouring a libation of dark-gleaming wine to Zeus
with unwashed hands; a man cannot pray to the son of Cronus
of the dark clouds spattered with blood and gore.
But you to the temple of Athena of the Spoils
go with burnt offerings, summoning the elder women,   270
and place a robe, one which seems to you to be the loveliest and most
    ample
in your house, and which is most precious to you,

and place this on the knees of the statue of Athena of the lovely hair;
and pledge to sacrifice to her in the temple twelve young cows,
yearlings, unbroken, if she would have mercy
on the city and on the wives of the Trojans and their infant children,
if she would ward off the son of Tydeus from holy Ilion—
savage spearman, violent master of the rout.
But you go to the temple of Athena of the Spoils,
and I will seek after Paris, to summon him,   280
if he should choose to hear me speak. Would that the earth
would gape to swallow him on the spot! For the Olympian has raised him
     to be a great affliction
to the Trojans and to great-hearted Priam and to his children.
If I could see him on his way down into the house of Hades,
I would declare my heart had forgotten sorrow."
So he spoke; and his mother going to the house called for
her handmaids, and they gathered the elder women throughout the city.
And she herself went down into the scented chamber,
where were robes of intricate design, the work of women of Sidon
whom Alexandros, godlike in beauty, himself   290
led from Sidon, sailing upon the wide deep sea
on that journey, on which he brought away high-born Helen.
Taking up one of these, Hecuba carried it as a gift to Athena,
the robe that was most beautiful in decorations and the largest,
which gleamed like a star; it had been lying beneath the others.
Then she set out on her way, and many women elders went with her.
          And when they came to the temple of Athena on the citadel
     height,
Theano of the lovely cheeks opened the doors for them,
the daughter of Kisseus, wife of Antenor breaker of horses;
for the Trojans had appointed her priestess of Athena.   300
With a wailing cry, all the women raised their hands to Athena;
and taking the robe, Theano of the lovely cheeks
laid it on the knees of the statue of lovely haired Athena;

and praying, she entreated the daughter of mighty Zeus:
"Lady, Athena protector of the city, shining of goddesses,
break the spear of Diomedes, and grant that he
drop headlong before the Scaean gates,
so we will now, without delay, sacrifice to you in your temple twelve
    young cows,
yearlings, unbroken, if you would have mercy
on the city and on the wives of the Trojans and their infant children."   310
Thus she spoke beseeching; but Pallas Athena turned away her head.

       So the women were praying to the daughter of almighty Zeus;
but Hector went to the house of Alexandros,
a thing of beauty, which he himself had built by men who were the very
    best
craftsmen in Troy's rich-soiled land,
and who built for him a sleeping chamber, hall and courtyard
close by that of Priam and Hector, on the citadel height.
Therein entered Hector, beloved by Zeus, and in his hand
he held his spear of eleven cubits length; before him gleamed
the bronze point of the spear shaft, round which ran a golden binding
    ring.   320
He found Alexandros in his splendid chamber handling his armour,
his shield and breastplate, and turning over his curved bow;
Argive Helen was sitting with her serving women,
and directing her maids' fine handwork.
And seeing him, Hector reviled him with contemptuous words:
"Unnatural man, it is not good to store this anger in your heart.
Men are perishing about the city and steep walls
as they do battle, and it is on your account the battle shout and war
blaze all around this city; you would confront another man
were you to see him anywhere hanging back from hated war.   330
Up now; lest the town be soon made hot by enemy fire."

       In turn godlike Alexandros addressed him:
"Hector, since you fairly rebuke me, nor beyond what is fair,

on this account I will speak to you, and you mark and hear me.

It was not so much in anger and resentment of the Trojans

I was sitting in my room; no, I wished to yield myself to grief.

Just now, my wife was coaxing me with gentle words,

urging me into battle. And it seems to me too that this

will be better; victory shifts from man to man.

But come, wait a bit, let me put on the armour of Ares;   340

or go, and I will come after; I expect I'll catch you up."

      So he spoke, and Hector of the shimmering helm said nothing
   to him.

But Helen addressed him softly:

"Brother-in-law of me, an evil-thinking dog who strikes cold fear,

would that on the day when first my mother gave me birth,

some foul-weather storm of wind carrying me had borne me

to a mountain or a swelling wave of the tumultuous sea,

where the wave would have swept me away before these deeds had
   happened.

But since the gods have so decreed these evils,

then would I were the wife of a better man,   350

a man who knew what righteous blame was and the many reproaches
   that men make.

But the wits of this man here are not steady now, nor will they be

hereafter; and I think that he will reap the fruit of this.

But come now, come in and take your seat upon this stool,

brother-in-law, since the toil of fighting has mostly stood astride your heart

because of me, a dog, and Alexandros' infatuation,

we on whom Zeus has laid this evil fate, so that even after this

there will be songs of us for men to come."

      Then answered her great Hector of the shimmering helm:

"Do not have me sit, Helen, for all your love; you will not persuade me.   360

For my spirit has already set me to defend

the Trojans, who have great longing for me when I am away.

But you rouse this one, and let him hurry,

so that he might catch me up while inside the city.
For my part I am going home, so that I may see
my household and my beloved wife and little son.
For I do not know whether, returning once more to them, I will come
    back again,
or if, already now, the gods will defeat me beneath the hands of the
    Achaeans."
            So speaking, Hector of the shimmering helm departed;
and quickly he reached his well-established home.   370
But he did not find white-armed Andromache in his halls,
for she with her child and fair-robed attendant
had taken her stand upon the tower, weeping and shedding tears.
And when Hector did not find his blameless wife,
he paused upon the threshold as he was going, and spoke among the
    servants:
"Come, maids, and tell me clearly;
where has white-armed Andromache gone from the hall?
To some house of my sisters, or of my brothers' fair-robed wives,
or has she set out for the temple of Athena, where the other
Trojan women with lovely hair propitiate the dread goddess?"   380
And in turn his ready housekeeper addressed him:
"Hector, since you strongly bid me speak the truth,
it is not to some house of your sisters, or of your brothers' fair-robed wives,
nor has she set out for the temple of Athena, where the other
Trojan women with lovely hair propitiate the dread goddess,
but she has gone to the great tower of Ilion, because she heard
the Trojans are worn down, and that Achaean strength is great,
by now she has arrived at the tower in urgent haste
like a madwoman; the nurse with her carries the baby."
            The housekeeper spoke, and Hector ran from the house   390
back the same way through the well-built streets.
When he arrived at the Scaean gates, having crossed the great city,
there where he intended to pass through to the plain,

there his worthy wife came to meet him, running,
Andromache, daughter of great-hearted Eëtion—
Eëtion, who once lived below wooded Plakos,
in Thebes below Mount Plakos, ruling the Cilician men;
his daughter was held as wife by bronze-armoured Hector.
She met him then, and her attendant came with her,
the child held against her breast, tender-hearted, just a baby,   400
the cherished only child of Hector, beautiful like a star,
whom Hector used to call Scamandrios, but all others
Astyanax, lord of the city; for his father alone protected Ilion.

         And looking at his child in silence, Hector smiled,
but Andromache came and stood close to him shedding tears
and clung to him with her hand and spoke to him and said his name:
"Inhuman one, your strength will destroy you, and you take no pity
on the child and young one, or on me who have no future, who will
    soon be
bereft of you; the Achaeans will soon kill you,
the whole of them rushing in attack. And for me it would be better   410
with you lost to go down beneath the earth; for no other
comfort will there be hereafter, when you meet your fate,
but grief. I have no father or lady mother;
it was godlike Achilles who slew my father,
when he sacked the well-established town of the Cilicians,
high-gated Thebes, and killed Eëtion;
yet he did not strip his body, for in his heart he thought it shameful,
but he cremated him with his decorated war-gear,
and heaped a burial mound over. And around it elms were grown
by nymphs of the mountains, daughters of Zeus who wields the
    aegis.   420
And they who were my seven brothers in our halls,
they all on a single day entered the house of Hades;
all of them swift-footed godlike Achilles slew
as they watched over their shambling cattle and white sheep.

And my mother, who was queen under wooded Plakos,

when he led her here with the rest of his plunder,

he set her free again, accepting untold ransom;

and, in the hall of her father, Artemis who showers arrows struck her down.

Hector, so you are father to me, and honoured mother,

and my brother, and you are my strong husband.   430

So have pity now and stay here by the ramparts,

do not make your child fatherless, your wife a widow.

Station your men by the wild fig tree, where the city is

easiest to scale and the walls can be overrun.

Three times they came there and tested it, the best men

with the two Aiantes and illustrious Idomeneus,

and with the sons of Atreus and Tydeus' daring son;

perhaps some seer, well skilled, told them of it,

or it was their own spirit that urged and compelled them."

   And great Hector of the shimmering helm answered her: 440

"Surely, all these things concern me too, my wife; but greatly

I would dread what they would think, the Trojans and the Trojan women

  with their trailing robes,

if like a coward I should shirk away from fighting.

My spirit does not allow me, for I have learned to be brave

always and to fight among the front rank of Trojans,

winning great glory for my father, and for me.

But I know this well in my mind and in my heart;

there will some time be a day when holy Ilion is destroyed,

and Priam and the people of Priam of the fine ash-spear;

but it is not the coming suffering of the Trojans that so much

  distresses me,   450

nor of Hecuba herself, nor of lord Priam,

nor of my many and brave brothers who

will fall in dust at the hands of enemy men,

so much as distress for you, when some bronze-armoured Achaean

leads you off in tears, taking away your day of freedom.

And in Argos you will work the loom for another woman,
and carry water from the spring of Messeïs or Hypereia
time and again under compulsion, and necessity will lie harsh
    upon you.
And one day someone seeing you shedding tears may say:
'This is the wife of Hector, who used to be best of the horse-breaking
    Trojans   460
in waging battle, at that time when men fought round Ilion.'
So one day someone may speak; and for you the pain will be new again,
bereft of such a husband to ward off the day of slavery.
But may the heaped earth cover me over dead
before I ever hear your cry as you are dragged away."

            So speaking, shining Hector reached out for his son;
but the child turned away, back to the breast of his fair-belted nurse,
crying, frightened at the sight of his own father,
struck with terror seeing the bronze helmet and crest of horsehair,
nodding dreadfully, as he thought, from the topmost of the helmet.   470
They burst out laughing, his dear father and lady mother.
At once shining Hector lifted the helmet from his head,
and placed it, gleaming, on the earth;
then he rocked his beloved son in his arms and kissed him,
and prayed aloud to Zeus and to the other gods:
"Zeus, and you other gods, grant now that this child too,
my son, will become, even as I am, conspicuous among Trojans,
likewise skilled in courage, and rule Ilion in strength.
And one day may someone say of him, 'This man is far better than his
    father'
as he returns from war, and may he bear back bloodstained spoils of
    armour,   480
having killed an enemy man, and his mother's heart rejoice."

            So speaking he placed in the hands of his beloved wife
his son; and she took him to her perfumed breast,
laughing as she cried. And her husband took pity, watching,

and with his hand he caressed her and spoke to her and said her
     name:
"Foolish one, do not, I beg you, distress your heart too much.
No man against fate will hurl me to Hades;
 for no man, I think, escapes destiny,
not the cowardly, nor the brave, once he is born.
But go to the house and tend to your work,   490
to your loom and distaff, and direct your handmaids
to ply their work; war is the concern of men,
all men, and me most of all, who live in Ilion."

     So speaking, shining Hector took up his helmet
crested with horsehair; and his beloved wife went home,
turning to look back all the while, letting the full tears fall.
Soon she reached the well-established home
of man-slaying Hector, and inside found her many
handmaids; and she stirred all of them to lamentation.
They lamented Hector in his own house while he was yet alive;   500
for they did not think that he would come home again,
returned from war, escaping the might and hands of the Achaeans.

     Nor did Paris linger in his high-roofed house,
but when he had put on his glorious armour, elaborate in bronze,
then he sped through the city, confident in the swiftness of his feet.
As when a horse confined to a stall, fed on barley at the manger,
breaking his tether runs with pounding feet across the plain
to immerse himself in the fair-flowing waters of his accustomed river,
triumphant, and he holds his head high, his mane
streaming about his shoulders; emboldened by his beauty,   510
his knees bear him lightly to the pasture and places horses love;
so Paris, son of Priam, from the heights of Pergamos
set out radiant in his armour like the sun,
laughing out loud, his swift feet carrying him. Quickly
he found shining Hector, his brother, as he was about
to turn from the place where he had spoken fondly with his wife.

Godlike Alexandros addressed him first:
"Elder brother of mine, to be sure I have delayed you as you hurried
by my tarrying, I did not come in proper time, as you were urging."
Answering him spoke Hector of the shimmering helm: 520
"Strange one, no man who is fair
could slight your work in battle, since you are brave;
but you hang back by choice and are not willing. And for that I
grieve deep in my heart, when I hear insults about you
from the Trojans, who suffer much hardship on your account.
But let us go. We will redress these matters later, if ever Zeus
grants us to dedicate in our halls a feast bowl of freedom
to the heavenly gods who live forever,
after driving out of Troy the strong-greaved Achaeans."

So speaking, shining Hector exploded through the city gates,
and with him went his brother Alexandros; and in their hearts
both hungered to do battle and wage war.
As a god grants to yearning sailors
a fair wind, when they labour at their well-worn oars
flogging the sea, and their limbs with fatigue are weak beneath them,
so now the two appeared to the yearning Trojans.
          There they each slew a man, Alexandros the son of lord
    Areïthoös,
Menesthios, who dwelt in Arne, he whom Areïthoös
of the battle mace and ox-eyed Phylomedousa bore;   10
and Hector struck Eïoneus with his sharp spear
on the neck below his bronze-wrought helmet rim, and unstrung his limbs.
And Glaukos the son of Hippolochos, leader of Lycian men,
struck Iphinoös son of Dexios with his spear in the midst of mighty combat,
on the shoulder, as he was springing for
his swift mares; he fell from his chariot to the ground, the strength of his
    limbs undone.
          But when the gleaming eyed-goddess Athena perceived them
destroying the Argives in mighty combat,
she went, shooting down from the heights of Olympus
into holy Ilion. Watching from the height of Pergamos,   20
Apollo started up to face her, and he plotted victory for the Trojans;
and the two met up beside the oak tree.

Lord Apollo the son of Zeus addressed her first:
"Why do you come this time in eagerness, daughter of great Zeus,
down from Olympus, why does that great spirit of yours impel you?
Is it perhaps to give the Danaans victory, reversing the tide of battle?
Since you do not pity at all the Trojans who are being destroyed.
But if you would be persuaded by me, it would be far better;
Let us now halt the war and the fighting
this day; later, let them fight again, until they learn first hand the fated
    end   30
of Ilion, since thus has it been dear to the heart
of you immortal ladies, to destroy utterly this town."
          In turn the gleaming-eyed goddess Athena addressed him:
"Let it be so, you who shoot from afar; for it was with the same things
    in mind I too
came from Olympus among the Trojans and Achaeans.
But come, how do you intend to halt this war of mortal men?"
And lord Apollo son of Zeus spoke to her again:
"Let us rouse the strong spirit of Hector, breaker of horses,
to see if he will challenge any of the Danaans
to fight man to man, face to face, in dread combat,   40
then they, the bronze-greaved Achaeans, grudging him honour
will send out one man alone to do battle with shining Hector."
So he spoke, nor was the gleaming-eyed goddess Athena unpersuaded.
          Then Helenos, beloved son of Priam, inferred in his heart
their plan, the plan that was pleasing to the scheming gods.
Making his way to Hector, he stood beside him and spoke a word:
"Hector son of Priam, you who are equal to Zeus in counsel,
will you now be persuaded by me? For I am your brother.
Have all the other Trojans seated and all the Achaeans,
and yourself, you challenge whoever is best of the Achaeans   50
to fight man to man, face to face, in dread combat.
For it is not yet your destiny to die and meet fate;
for so I heard the very word of the ever-living gods."

So he spoke; and Hector rejoiced greatly hearing his word,
and going into the midst of the Trojans he restrained the battle lines,
taking hold of his spear by the middle; and they all sat down.
And Agamemnon seated the strong-greaved Achaeans,
and Athena and Apollo of the silver bow
crouched down, like birds, like vultures,
on the towering oak tree of their father Zeus, who wields the
    aegis,   60
delighting in the spectacle of men. Ranks of them, pressed close, were
    seated,
bristling with shields and helmets and spears.
As the ruffling of the West Wind spreads across the open sea
when the wind is first roused, and the sea grows dark beneath it,
so rank on rank of Achaeans and Trojans were settled
on the plain. And Hector spoke between both sides:
"Hear me, Trojans and strong-greaved Achaeans,
while I speak those things the spirit in my breast urges.
The son of Cronus seated on high has not fulfilled our oaths,
but is minded to decree evil for both sides,   70
until that time either you take Troy with its fine walls,
or yourselves are broken beside your seagoing ships.
Since among you are the best of all Achaeans,
he of you whose spirit stirs to fight me,
let him come forth from all of you as champion against great Hector.
This I declare, and may Zeus be our witness;
if he should slay me with tapered point of bronze,
stripping my armour, let him bear this to the hollow ships,
but give my body to be borne home again, so that
the Trojans and the wives of Trojans may give to me when I have died my
    portion of the fire;   80
but if I should slay him, and Apollo gives the right to vaunt to me,
stripping his armour, I will carry it to sacred Ilion
and hang it on the temple of Apollo who shoots from afar,

but the dead body I will give back to the well-benched ships,
so that the long-haired Achaeans may give him due burial,
and heap a commemorative mound for him beside the broad Hellespont.
And one day someone even of generations to come will say,
as he sails in a ship with its many oars upon a sea as dark as wine:
'This is the memorial of a man who died long ago,
a man whom, fighting his best, shining Hector slew in days of old.'   90
So someone will speak one day, and my glory will never die."
So he spoke, and all the men were hushed in silence;
they were ashamed to refuse, but afraid to accept.

      At length Menelaos rose up and addressed them;
reproaching them with abuse, he groaned mightily in spirit:
"Oh me! braggarts, Achaean women no longer men of Achaea;
to be sure this will be a most dreadful disgrace,
if no one of the Danaans goes now to face Hector.
May you all turn to earth and water
who sit here, each of you, spiritless, of no account—   100
I myself will arm against this man; the strings of victory
are held above among the immortal gods."

      Then so speaking he donned his splendid armour.
And there, Menelaos, would have appeared the end of your life
at the hands of Hector, since he was far the stronger,
had not the Achaean kings, starting up, grabbed at you;
And the son of Atreus himself, wide-ruling Agamemnon,
took hold of his right hand, and spoke to him and said his name:
"You play the fool, Menelaos, god-cherished, there is no need
of such madness from you. Restrain yourself, distressed though
    you be,   110
nor from rivalry seek to fight with a better man,
with Hector the son of Priam, whom even other men dread.
Even Achilles shuddered to encounter this man
in battle where men win glory, who is by far a greater warrior than you.
But you now sit down, go to your band of companions,

the Achaeans will put forward another man as champion against him.
Even if he is fearless and even if he is insatiable for battle tumult,
I say that he will willingly kneel in rest, should he escape
from deadly war and grim battle."

So speaking the warrior won over his brother's heart,   120
urging what was justified, and Menelaos obeyed. But when his
rejoicing henchmen took the armour from his shoulders,
Nestor stood and addressed the Argives:
"O look now, surely great trouble comes to the land of the Achaeans!
Surely the aged horseman Peleus would greatly lament,
the excellent counsellor of the Myrmidons and their speaker,
who in days before, having questioned me in his house, greatly rejoiced,
asking the birth and parentage of all the Argives.
If all these men, he now should hear, cowered before Hector,
he would raise his hands again and again to the immortals,   130
to pray that his life-spirit leave his limbs to go down to the house of Hades.
Father Zeus, Athena and Apollo, if only
I were young, as when beside the swift-flowing river Keladon there fought
the gathered Pylians and the spear-fighting Arcadians
near the walls of Pheia, around the streams of Iardanos;
Ereuthalion stood as their champion, a man like to a god,
bearing on his shoulders the armour of lord Areïthoös,
godlike Areïthoös, he whom men and fair-belted women
called by the name Mace-Fighter,
because it was not with bows he used to fight, nor with the long spear,   140
but with an iron mace he shattered battle lines.
Lykourgos slew him, by craft, not at all by strength,
in a narrow pass, where his mace did not ward off his destruction,
for all that it was iron; for Lykourgos got his blow in first,
and speared him through the middle, and he lay stretched face up upon
    the ground;
he stripped the armour that the brazen war god gave him,
which he himself then bore through the trial of war.

But when Lykourgos grew old within his halls,
he gave it to Ereuthalion his beloved henchman to wear;
and it was wearing his armour that Ereuthalion challenged all the best
    men.   150
And they trembled greatly before him and were afraid, and no man dared,
but my much enduring spirit compelled me to fight
in reckless boldness; and in age I was the youngest of all;
and I—I did battle with him, and Athena granted my prayer.
And I killed him, the tallest and mightiest man;
a vast man who lay sprawled out from here to there.
Would that I were young as then, and my strength unfailing!
In short order would Hector of the shimmering helm find his fight!
But you men who are best of all Achaeans,
not even you with good heart seek to go against Hector."   160

      Thus the old man reproached them, and nine men all stood up;
First by far to rise was the lord of men Agamemnon,
and after him the son of Tydeus rose, powerful Diomedes,
and after them the two Aiantes, wrapped in fierce courage,
and after them Idomeneus and the henchman of Idomeneus
Meriones, equal to the man-slaughtering war god Enyalios,
and after them Eurypylos, the splendid son of Euaimon,
and Thoas stood up, the son of Andraimon, and shining Odysseus;
since all these wished to fight with shining Hector.

      These were the men the Gerenian horseman Nestor addressed:170
"Now shake the lots thoroughly to see who is chosen;
for that man will profit the strong-greaved Achaeans,
and he will profit his own spirit, if he escapes
from war's destruction and dread battle."
So he spoke, and each man marked his lot
and cast it into the helmet of Agamemnon son of Atreus.
And the army prayed, lifting their hands to the gods,
and thus would a man speak looking up to broad heaven:
"Father Zeus, grant that Ajax is chosen, or the son of Tydeus,

or he who is king of gold-rich Mycenae."   180

       So they spoke, and Nestor, the Gerenian horseman, shook the lots;
and one leapt from the helmet, the one which the men themselves
   desired,
the lot of Ajax. A herald carrying it everywhere through the crowd,
displayed it, left to right, to all the best of the Achaeans;
but they not recognising it, disavowed it, each man in turn.
But when at length, carrying it all about the crowd, he came to that man,
the man who had marked the lot and cast it in the helmet—glorious
   Ajax—
Ajax held out his hand, and the herald, standing close, dropped it in,
and Ajax recognised the lot, seeing the mark upon it, and rejoiced in his heart.
He flung it to the ground by his feet and spoke: 190
"O friends, surely this lot is mine; myself, I am glad
in my heart, since I think that I will vanquish shining Hector.
But come, while I put on my war armour
do you pray to Zeus the son of lord Cronus,
in silence among yourselves, so that the Trojans may not know.
Or even openly, since in truth we fear no man.
For no one, for all his will, shall drive me away against my will by force,
nor by any skill—since that I lack knowledge in this respect
I do not think likely, born and raised as I was in Salamis."
So he spoke; and the men prayed to Zeus the son of lord Cronus,   200
and thus a man would speak looking up to broad heaven:
"Father Zeus, ruling from Mount Ida, most glorious, most mighty,
grant victory to Ajax and grant that he win a splendid triumph.
But if you love also Hector and have care for him,
give equal strength and equal glory to both."

       Thus they spoke. And Ajax armed himself with gleaming bronze.
But when he had sheathed his body in all his armour,
then he moved swiftly, and set forth like gigantic Ares,
who goes to war among men whom the son of Cronus
has pitted together to do battle in heart-devouring strife.   210

So did Ajax then start up, gigantic, bulwark of the Achaeans,
his face savage with its smile, he went with his feet beneath him
taking long strides, shaking his long-shadowed spear.
And looking on him the Argives rejoiced greatly,
while dreadful trembling seized the limbs of the Trojans, every man;
And the heart in Hector's own breast beat hard;
but still he did not have means to flee, nor to duck
back into the throng of men, since it was by will to fight he made the
    challenge.
        Ajax drew near, bearing his shield like a tower,
bronze, of seven layers of oxhide, which had been made for him with toil
    by Tychios,   220
best by far of leather workers, dwelling in his house in Hyle,
and who made for him the glistening shield of seven layers of hide
from well-fed bulls, and onto these he hammered an eighth of bronze.
Bearing this before his chest Telamonian Ajax
took his stand hard by Hector, and in a threatening voice addressed him:
"Hector, now will you know well, alone in single combat,
what kind of men are pre-eminent among the Danaans,
even besides Achilles the lionhearted, who shatters men.
He in his curved seagoing ships
sits idle, consumed with wrath for Agamemnon shepherd of the
    people,   230
but we are such men as will fight against you,
and we are many. Come, make a start of battle and of fighting."
        Then answered him in turn great Hector of the shimmering
    helm:
"Ajax, son of Telamon born of Zeus, leader of the people,
do not make trial of me as if of some feeble boy
or woman, or one ignorant of deeds of war.
For I well know of battles and the killing of men;
I know how to wield to the right, to wield to the left my shield
of tanned hide, which is my strong shield in fighting.

I know how to charge at the tumult of swift horses,   240
I know how in close fighting to dance for the deadly god of war.
But being the man you are I do not wish to strike you
in stealth, eyeing my chance, but rather openly, and take my chance."

      He spoke, and balancing the long-shadowed spear he hurled it,
and struck the dread shield of Ajax, of seven layers of hide,
on the outermost bronze, which was the eighth layer upon it.
Tearing through six layers the weariless bronze passed,
and stopped in the seventh hide. And next in turn
Zeus-descended Ajax hurled his long-shadowed spear,
and struck the circle of the son of Priam's shield.   250
The heavy spear ran through the gleaming shield,
and was forced through his elaborate breastplate;
straight through his tunic beside his ribs
the spear cut; but he bent aside and evaded dark death.

      Then wrenching out the long-shadowed spears with their hands,
  they both together
fell on each other like lions who eat flesh,
or wild boars, whose strength does not flag.
And the son of Priam stabbed with his spear the middle of Ajax's shield,
but the bronze did not penetrate, and its point bent back;
and Ajax springing forward thrust at Hector's shield, and right
  through   260
went the spear, and beat back Hector as he raged,
and cut his neck as it went, and dark blood gushed forth.

      Even so Hector of the shimmering helm did not relinquish battle,
and drawing back he seized a stone in his massive hand
that lay on the plain, dark and jagged and huge.
With this he struck the dread, seven-layered hide shield of Ajax
on the boss in the middle, and the bronze rang out all around.
Then in turn lifting a far greater stone Ajax
hurled it, whirling about, so as to heave it hard;
he smashed Hector's shield inward, striking it with a rock like a

millstone, 270
and broke the strength of Hector's very knees; and he was laid out on his
    back
pressed by the shield; but straightway Apollo righted him,
and surely now with swords they would have been stabbing at close
    quarters,
had not the heralds, messengers of Zeus and men,
come up, one from the Trojans, the other from the bronze-clad Achaeans,
Talthybios and Idaios, both men of sound sense.
They held their staffs between both men, and
the herald Idaios, skilled in sound counsels, spoke:
"Fight no longer, my sons, nor do battle.
For Zeus who gathers the clouds loves you both, 280
and you are both good spearmen; this we all surely know;
but night comes on already; and it is good to yield to night."
            Then answering him spoke Telamonian Ajax:
"Idaios, bid Hector declare these things;
for he it was who by his will to fight challenged all the best men.
Let him take the lead; and I heartily will yield, to what this one decides."
In reply, great Hector of the shimmering helm spoke to him:
"Ajax, since god gave you stature and strength
and good understanding, and with the spear you are most outstanding of
    Achaean men,
let us now stop the battle and fighting 290
for today; later we shall fight again, until the power above
parts us, and grants victory to one side or the other.
Night comes on already; and it is good to yield to night,
and so you will make happy all the Achaeans by their ships
and most of all your own people and companions, who are with you,
and I through the great city of lord Priam
will make happy the Trojans and Trojan women with their trailing robes,
who giving thanks on my account will enter the sacred place of assembly.
Come, let us give to each other illustrious gifts, both of us,

so that someone might speak in this way, Achaean and Trojan: 300
'The two fought in heart-devouring strife,
but then parted united in friendship.'"
So speaking, he gave over his silver-studded sword,
bringing with it the sheath and well-cut baldric;
and Ajax gave his war-belt bright with crimson.

      Both separating, Ajax went among the Achaean people,
and Hector made his way to the company of Trojans; and they rejoiced,
when they saw him alive and unharmed as he came toward them,
escaping Ajax's might and his invincible hands,
and they led him to the city, having despaired of his safety;   310
in turn, for their part the strong-greaved Achaeans led Ajax,
he rejoicing in victory, to godlike Agamemnon.
And when they were all in the shelters of the son of Atreus,
the lord of men Agamemnon sacrificed an ox for them,
a male, five years of age, to the almighty son of Cronus;
they flayed it and dressed it properly
and skilfully sliced the flesh and pierced it on spits
and roasted it with care, and then drew off all the pieces.
And when they had ceased their work and prepared their meal,
they feasted, nor did any man's appetite lack his due portion;   320
and Ajax was honoured with a gift of the whole unbroken chine
by the warrior son of Atreus, wide-ruling Agamemnon.

      And when they had put away desire for eating and drinking,
the old man taking the lead began to weave his plan to them,
Nestor, whose counsel in time past had proved best,
and he in his wisdom spoke and addressed them:
"Son of Atreus and you others who are chiefs of all Achaeans,
so many long-haired Achaeans have died,
whose dark blood around the fair-flowing waters of Scamander
the sharp point of war has now scattered, and whose souls have gone
    down to the house of death;   330
therefore, at dawn you must halt the war of the Achaeans,

and assembling them, let us cart the dead here
with oxen and mules; then let us burn them
at safe distance from the ships, so that each man carries bones
home for someone's sons, whenever we return to our fatherland.
And let us make one common mound around the pyre, bringing
the material from the plain; and let us swiftly build against it
high ramparts, defence for the ships and for ourselves.
And in them let us build gates, close-fitting,
so there can be a road through them for driving horses.   340
And outside, let us dig a deep ditch nearby,
which encircling round us could hold back horse and people,
so that the host of noble Trojans never crush us."
So he spoke; and all the kings approved him.

        And there was in turn an assembly of the Trojans on the heights
   of Ilion,
a fearful one, stirred to panic, at Priam's doors,
and to the Trojans Antenor, wise in understanding, began to speak:
"Hear me, Trojans and Dardanians and allies,
while I speak those things the spirit in my breast urges.
Come now, let us give Argive Helen and the possessions with her   350
to the sons of Atreus to lead away. We fight now
having rendered false our sacred oaths; therefore nothing good for us
I think will be accomplished, unless we do this."

        So speaking in this way, he then sat down; and there stood
   among them
godlike Alexandros, husband of Helen of the lovely hair,
who answering him spoke swift flying words:
"Antenor, these things you declare are no longer pleasing to me.
You know how to think up some other speech better than this.
But if you now make this declaration truly, in earnest,
then the gods themselves have utterly deprived you of your wits.   360
But I will speak out among the Trojans, breakers of horses.
And outright I say no; I will not give back the woman,

but her possessions, as many as I took out of Argos to our house,

all these I am willing to give, and to add yet others from my own house
   store."

      So speaking in this way, he then sat down; and there stood
  among them

Dardanian Priam, equal to the gods as counsellor,

he in his wisdom spoke and addressed them:

"Hear me, Trojans and Dardanians and allies,

while I speak those things the spirit in my breast urges.

Now all of you take your evening meal throughout the city, as before,   370

but be mindful of your watch and stand alert, each of you,

and at dawn let Idaios go to the hollow ships

to declare to the sons of Atreus, to Agamemnon and Menelaos,

the word of Alexandros, on whose account the strife arose.

And also to make this sound proposal; if they would be willing

to halt this hard and painful war, until the time we can cremate

our dead; later we shall fight again, until the time when the power above

parts us, and grants victory to one side or the other."

      So he spoke; and they listened closely to him and obeyed.

Then through the host they took their evening meal at their posts.   380

And at dawn Idaios went to the hollow ships;

he found the Danaans, Ares' henchmen, in assembly

by the stern of Agamemnon's ship. And standing in their

midst, the herald with raised voice spoke out:

"Son of Atreus and you others who are chiefs of all Achaeans,

Priam and the other noble Trojans bid me

speak, if this be welcome and sweet to you,

the word of Alexandros, on whose account the strife arose.

Those possessions, as many as in his hollow ships Alexandros

carried off to Troy—would that he had perished—   390

all these he is willing to give, and to add yet others from his own house
   store;

but the lawful wife of glorious Menelaos

he says he will not give back; although the Trojans urged it.
And he also bade me say this; if you would be willing
to halt this hard and painful war, until the time we can cremate
our dead; later we shall fight again, until the power above
parts us, and grants victory to one side or the other."
So he spoke, and all the men were hushed in silence.

At length Diomedes of the war cry addressed them:
"Let no one now accept possessions from Alexandros,   400
nor accept Helen. It is known to everyone, even he who is a fool,
that the snares of death are already fastened on the Trojans."
So he spoke; and all the sons of the Achaeans shouted assent,
in admiration of the word of Diomedes breaker of horses.

And then lord Agamemnon addressed Idaios:
"Idaios, you yourself have heard the word of the Achaeans,
as they have made plain to you; and this is what is pleasing to me.
Concerning the dead, I do not begrudge cremating them;
for there should be no grudging of the corpses of those who have died,
to give them swift consolation of fire, once dead.   410
Let Zeus be witness to this oath, the far-thundering husband of Hera."
So speaking he raised his sceptre to all the gods;
and Idaios went back again to sacred Ilion.
And the Trojans and sons of Dardanos were in assembly,
all of them gathered together, on the lookout for when Idaios
might come; and he came and delivered his message
as he stood in their midst. And straightway they made ready
on two fronts, to bring in the dead, and others to go after wood;
and across the way the Argives from their well-benched ships
were preparing some to bring in the dead, and others to go after
    wood.   420

The sun then was just striking ploughed fields,
climbing out of the silent deep-flowing Ocean
into heaven, as the two sides met each other.
It was difficult there to identify each man,

but washing away with water the bloody gore,
shedding warm tears, they lifted the dead onto the wagons.
Nor did great Priam allow lament; but the Trojans in silence
kept heaping the dead upon the place of fire, grieving at heart,
and having burned them on the pyre, they went to sacred Ilion.
And likewise across the way the strong-greaved Achaeans   430
kept heaping the dead upon the place of fire, grieving at heart,
and having burned them on the pyre, they went to their hollow ships.

    And when it was not quite dawn, but still night's twilight,
then around the pyre there gathered an appointed band of Achaeans,
and made one common mound around it, bringing
the material from the plain; and against it they built a wall,
with high ramparts, defence for the ships and for themselves.
And in them they built gates, close-fitting,
so there could be a road through them for driving horses.
And outside against it they dug a deep ditch,   440
wide and massive, and on it they fixed stakes.

    So the long-haired Achaeans toiled;
and the gods sitting beside Zeus wielder of lightning
gazed with wonder on the great work of the bronze-clad Achaeans.
And Poseidon the earth-shaker was first to speak to them:
"Father Zeus, who is there now of mortal men upon the boundless earth
who will to the immortal gods make known his mind and purpose?
Do you not see, that now again the long-haired Achaeans
have built a wall to defend their ships, and around it driven
a ditch, but did not give to the gods illustrious hecatombs?   450
Surely, its fame will spread as far as the morning light,
and they will forget that wall that I and Phoebus Apollo
built for the warrior Laomedon with much toil."

    Then greatly troubled Zeus who gathers the clouds addressed him:
"Oh me, Earth-Shaker whose might is wide, what kind of thing have you
    said?
Some other god might fear this scheme,

one who is much weaker than you in strength of hand and might;
surely, your own fame will spread as far as the morning light.
Go to then; whenever the long-haired Achaeans again
depart with their ships for their own fatherland,   460
tear the wall apart and heap the whole of it into the salt sea,
and bury again the entire great shore with sand,
so that the Achaeans' great wall is obliterated."
Thus the gods debated these things with one another.
The sun went down, and the Achaeans' task was completed.

They slaughtered oxen all along the line of shelters and took their
    evening meal.
And ships from Lemnos came to them bringing wine,
many ships, which Euneos son of Jason sent,
whom Hypsipyle bore to Jason, shepherd of the people;
and to the sons of Atreus separately, to Agamemnon and to Menelaos,   470
the son of Jason gave wine for them to bear away, a thousand measures.
Then from the ships, the long-haired Achaean men bartered for wine,
some with bronze, some with gleaming iron,
some with hides, some with oxen themselves,
some with captives of war; and they made a luxurious feast.

Then the whole night long the long-haired Achaeans
feasted, as did the Trojans through their city, and their allies;
and the whole night long all-devising Zeus plotted evil for the men,
thundering dreadfully. And pale fear gripped them,
and they poured the wine from their cups to the ground, and no man
    dared   480
to drink again before he made libation to the all-powerful son of Cronus.
Then they lay down and took the gift of sleep.

Dawn robed in saffron spread over all the earth;
and Zeus who hurls the thunderbolt made assembly of the gods
on the topmost peak of ridged Olympus.
And he himself addressed them, and all the gods paid heed:
"Hear me, all you gods, and all you goddesses too,
while I speak such things as spirit in my breast commands.
Let no god, female or male,
attempt to cut across my stated purpose, but without exception all
    of you
assent, so that I can accomplish these matters forthwith.
That one whom I see intending without the knowledge of the
    other gods   10
to assist either Trojans or Danaans,
thunderstruck against all dignity will he return to Olympus;
or I will seize and hurl him into murky Tartaros,
a very long way, where the deepest chasm is beneath the earth,
where the gates are iron and the threshold bronze,
as far below Hades as heaven is from earth;
he will know then by how much I am most powerful of all gods.
Come then, make this trial, you gods, so that you all may know—
hang a rope of gold from heaven,
all you gods, and all goddesses too, and grasp it;   20
but you will not pull Zeus from heaven to the ground,
he the highest lord of counsel, no, not if you should labour greatly—

but whenever I should wish, in earnest, to pull you,
I would pull you all, along with the earth itself, along with the very ocean.
The rope I would then bind around the summit of Olympus,
and everything would then be dangling in mid-air.
By so much do I surpass the gods, and do I surpass mortals."

      So he spoke, and all were hushed in silence,
amazed at his words; for he had spoken very powerfully.
At length the gleaming-eyed goddess Athena addressed him: 30
"O father of ours, son of Cronus, most exalted of rulers,
indeed, well do we know that your strength is not to be resisted;
but nonetheless we pity the Danaan spearmen,
who filling their measure of evil destiny will perish.
To be sure, we shall keep away from the war, if you bid us,
but we will put counsel in the minds of the Argives, which may profit
    them,
so that not all will perish by your anger."
And smiling on her, Zeus who gathers the clouds spoke:
"Take heart, Tritogeneia, dear child; for not in all seriousness
do I speak, and I wish to be kind to you."   40

      So speaking he yoked to his chariot a pair of horses shod with
    bronze,
swift-flying, with luxuriant manes of gold,
and he clad himself in gold, and grasped his golden
well-wrought whip, and stepped into his chariot,
and lashed his whip to start the horses; and they two not unwilling flew on,
between the earth and star-strewn heaven.
He arrived at Mount Ida of the many springs, mother of wild beasts,
and at the peak of Gargaros; there was his sanctuary and his altar
    smoking with sacrifice;
and here the father of gods and men drew up his horses,
released them from the chariot, and around them poured abundant
    mist,   50
and he himself sat down upon the mountain height, exulting in his glory,

looking down upon the city of the Trojans and the ships of the Achaeans.

The long-haired Achaeans took their meal
swiftly beside their shelters, then rising forthwith armed for battle;
the Trojans in turn across the way prepared their arms,
fewer in number, but even so intent on fighting in the combat
through urgent necessity, for their women and for their children.
All the gates were opened, and the host surged forth,
on foot and on horse; and a great roar rose.

Then when the armies arrived in one place, pitted against each
    other,   60
they hurled their oxhide shields together, their spears, even the strength
    of their
bronze-armoured men; and their bossed shields
met each the other, and a great roar rose.
Then came together the cries of distress and the vaunting of men
killing and being killed, and the earth flowed with blood.

As long as it was dawn and the heaven-sent day was rising,
so long the missiles of both sides reached their marks, and the people fell;
but when the sun stood astride the middle part of heaven,
then Zeus the father levelled his gold scales,
and placed in them two portions of death that brings enduring grief,   70
that of the horse-breaking Trojans and that of the bronze-clad
    Achaeans,
and lifted them, holding by the middle; and the measured day of the
    Achaeans sank.
The fates of the Achaeans settled towards the nourishing
earth, those of the Trojans were lifted towards broad heaven.
And Zeus himself from Ida thundered loudly, and let fly
a blazing flash into the host of the Achaeans; and they seeing it
were stunned, and pale fear gripped them all within.

Then Idomeneus did not dare to remain, nor Agamemnon,
nor did the two Aiantes keep their stand, Ares' henchmen.
Only Gerenion Nestor remained, guardian of the Achaeans,   80

not at all of his own will, but his horse was stricken, his horse that
    godlike Alexandros,
husband of Helen of the lovely hair, struck with an arrow
across the top of its head, where a horse's forelock
grows on the skull, and where is most fatal.
The horse reared in agony, and the arrow entered into his brain,
and he flung the horses with him into panic as he writhed around the
    arrow-point.
            While the old man cut away the traces,
lunging with his sword, Hector's swift horses came
through the scrum bearing their fierce chariot lord—
Hector! And there, surely, the old man would have lost his life   90
had not Diomedes of the war cry paid sharp notice,
and shouted in a voice of dread, rallying Odysseus:
"Son of Laertes descended from Zeus, Odysseus of many stratagems,
how can you flee, guarding your back, into the throng like some low-
    born coward?
Take care lest someone plants his spear in your back as you flee.
Come, stand firm, so that we may ward off this savage from the old man."
So he spoke, but godlike, enduring Odysseus did not heed him,
but darted past toward the hollow ships of the Achaeans.
And the son of Tydeus alone as he was moved amid the front fighters,
and took his stand before the horses of the old son of Neleus,   100
and lifting his voice, addressed him with winged words:
"Father, surely now the young warriors wear you out,
and your strength is broken, and age and its difficulties dog you,
your charioteer is shaky, and your horses slow.
Come, mount my chariot so you may see
what kind of horses are these of Tros, expert
in making swift pursuit or flight here and there across the plain,
which once I took from Aeneas, master of the rout:
let the two attendants take care of yours, and these we two
will drive straight for the horse-breaking Trojans, so that even Hector 110

will know whether my spear rages in my hands too."

So he spoke, nor did the Gerenian horseman Nestor disobey.
The two attendants then looked after Nestor's horses,
powerful Sthenelos and courteous Eurymedon,
while the other two mounted the chariot of Diomedes.
And Nestor took in his hands the crimson reins,
and lashed the horses; swiftly they closed on Hector.
And as he came straight for them, the son of Tydeus cast his spear,
but missed him, and it was Hector's henchman and charioteer,
Eniopeus, the son of high-hearted Thebaios,   120
he struck in the chest beside his breast as he held the horses' reins;
he fell from the chariot, the swift-footed horses started,
and there his soul and strength were undone.
Dreadful grief closed over Hector's heart for his charioteer;
but he let him lie, grieving though he was for his companion,
and drove in search of a bold charioteer; nor was it long
his horses lacked a master; for Hector swiftly found
the bold son of Iphitos, Archeptolemos, whom he then
made mount behind the swift-footed horses, and gave the reins into his
    hands.

Then there would have been destruction and works of war
    without remedy,   130
and the Trojans would have been penned in Ilion like sheep,
had the father of gods and of men not taken sharp notice;
and thundering dreadfully he let fly a glaring thunderbolt,
and down before Diomedes' horses he hurled it to the ground;
a dreadful flare of fire shot from the burning sulphur,
the two horses, terrified, cowered against their cart.
And from Nestor's hands the crimson reins escaped,
and in his heart Nestor was afraid, and he spoke to Diomedes:
"Son of Tydeus, come, drive the single-hoofed horses back to flight.
Do you not see that Zeus-sent victory does not follow with you?   140
Now Zeus the son of Cronus grants glory to this man

for today; tomorrow, in turn, he will give it to you, if he chooses.
No man wards off the design of Zeus,
not even if he is very strong, since Zeus is by far more powerful."
Then answered him Diomedes of the war cry:
"Yes, all these things, old sir, you rightly say,
but this is a bitter pain that comes upon my heart and spirit;
for Hector, someday, speaking among the Trojans, will say:
'The son of Tydeus fled to his ships before me.'
So he will claim one day; then let the broad earth gape beneath me."   150
Then answered him the Gerenian horseman Nestor:
"Oh, come! Son of wise Tydeus, what do you say!
If ever Hector will declare you cowardly or craven,
still the Trojans and Dardanians would not believe it,
nor the wives of great-hearted shield-bearing Trojans,
whose vigorous husbands you struck down in the dust."

         So speaking he turned the single-hoofed horses to flight
back through the scrum; and Hector and the Trojans
with unearthly din poured their doleful spears and arrows after them;
and to Diomedes, in a voice that carried far, called great Hector of the
     shimmering helm: 160
"Son of Tydeus, the Danaans of swift horses honoured you excessively
with a seat of honour, with cuts of meat and goblets filled;
but now they will dishonour you; you are after all no better than a woman.
Be off! Poor puppet, since you will not set foot upon our ramparts
on account of my retreating, nor will you lead our women
in your ships; before that I will hand you your fate."

         So he spoke; and the son of Tydeus weighed whether
to turn the horses and fight face to face.
Three times he pondered in his mind and his heart,
and three times from the peaks of Ida thundered all-devising Zeus,   170
giving signal to the Trojans that battle victory was changing sides.
And Hector urged the Trojans, calling in a voice that carried far:
"Trojans and Lycians and Dardanian spearmen,

be men, friends, and remember your fierce carnage.
I know now the son of Cronus of his will grants me
victory and glory, and grants to the Danaans their destruction.
Fools, who contrived these walls,
feeble things, not worth the thought; they will not ward off my strength;
and the horses easily will leap the ditch they dug.
And when I should come beside their hollow ships,   180
let someone remember to bring blazing fire,
so that I may torch the ships with fire, and kill them,
the Argives by their ships, stupefied by the smoke."

        So speaking he urged and called to his horses:
"Xanthos and you Podargos, and Aithon and shining Lampos,
now repay me for your care, the great abundance that
Andromache daughter of great-hearted Eëtion
has placed before you of honey-hearted wheat,
and wine she mixed for you to drink, whenever you wished—
to you before even me, though I boast to be her strong husband!   190
Follow on, make haste, so we can seize
Nestor's shield, the fame of which goes up to heaven,
all gold, grips and body,
and seize from the shoulders of horse-breaking Diomedes
his elaborate breastplate, which Hephaestus toiled to make.
If we should take these two things, I think the Achaeans
this very night might embark in their swift ships."

        So he spoke, vaunting; and lady Hera was angered,
and started on her throne, shaking great Olympus,
and she addressed the great god Poseidon: 200
"oh me, Earth-Shaker, wide-ranging in might, does not your
heart in your very breast feel for the Danaans who are dying?
They bring gifts for you up into Helike, and Aigai too,
many of them and pleasing; you used to wish them victory.
If only we were willing, we who aid the Danaans,
to thrust the Trojans back and check far-thundering Zeus,

then he would be sorry sitting there alone on Ida."
Then greatly troubled the lord Earth-Shaker addressed her:
"Hera, reckless in speech, what kind of word have you spoken?
I would not wish for the rest of us to fight   210
with Zeus the son of Cronus, since he is far the stronger."
So they argued such things with one another;
as for the Achaeans, all the space beyond the ships bounded by wall and ditch
was full of both shield-bearing men and horses,
packed in together; and equal to swift Ares was he who packed them—
Hector, son of Priam, at that time when Zeus gave glory to him.

   And now he would have torched the well-balanced ships with
  burning fire,
if lady Hera had not put in Agamemnon's mind,
as he was hastening about, that with all speed he must rally the Achaeans.
He went beside the shelters and the ships of the Achaeans   220
holding his great shimmering cape in his massive hand,
and took his stand upon Odysseus' dark, great-bellied ship,
which was in the middle, so he could be heard in both directions,   223
and with a piercing voice he shouted so as to be heard by the
  Danaans: 227
"For shame, Argives, cowardly disgraces, admirable only in
  appearance!
Where went our boasts, that time we said we were pre-eminent,
those boasts you once declaimed in Lemnos, vaunting idly,   230
as you consumed quantities of straight-horned cattle meat,
drinking bowls up to the brim with wine,
that each of you would stand up against one hundred, two hundred
  Trojans   230
in war? And now we are not the equal of one,
of Hector, who will very soon torch our ships with burning fire.
Father Zeus, did you before strike blind any other powerful king
with such delusions, and strip him of his great glory?
Not ever, at any time, I say, did I pass by your splendid altars

in my many-benched ships, coming here on this ruinous journey,
but on every one I burned the fat of oxen and their thighbones,   240
eager as I was to sack well-walled Troy.
But, Zeus—this prayer at least accomplish for me;
at least let us ourselves escape and get away,
do not let the Achaeans be broken like this by Trojans."
So he spoke, and as he shed tears Zeus the father pitied him.
And he bowed his head in promise that the men would be saved and
      would not perish.
And straightway he sent an eagle, the surest omen of winged birds,
grasping in its talons a fawn, the young of a swift deer;
and down by Zeus' splendid altar it cast the fawn,
where the Achaeans were wont to perform sacrifice to Zeus who
      speaks all omens.   250
And when the men then saw the bird had come from Zeus,
they sprang the more against the Trojans, and recollected their fighting
      spirit.
            Then not one of the Danaans, many though there were,
could boast he held his swift horses ahead of the son of Tydeus,
to drive beyond the ditch and take up the fight, man to man,
for Diomedes was first by far to kill a Trojan leader,
Agelaos son of Phradmon. He had turned his horses to flight,
and Diomedes fixed his spear in his back as he turned about,
between the shoulders, and drove it through his chest.
He fell from his chariot, and his armour clashed upon him.   260
After Diomedes came the sons of Atreus, Agamemnon and Menelaos,
and after them the two Aiantes, wrapped in fierce courage,
and after them Idomeneus and the henchman of Idomeneus
Meriones, equal to the man-slaughtering war god Enyalios,
and after them Eurypylos, the splendid son of Euaimon;
and Teucer came ninth, bending his back-curved bow,
and took his stand beneath the shield of Telamonian Ajax.
There Ajax would move his shield away, and the warrior

would look sharply out, then, shooting his arrow, when
he struck someone in the throng, who dropping there died,   270
he went back, like a child to his mother's embrace, ducking
to the protection of Ajax, who would shelter him with his shining shield.

      Then who was the first of the Trojans blameless Teucer killed?
Orsilochos was first and Ormenos and Ophelestes,
Daitor and Chromios and godlike Lykophontes,
and the son of Polyaimon, Amopaon, and Melanippos.   276
And seeing him Agamemnon lord of men rejoiced   278
as Teucer with his powerful bow destroyed ranks of the Trojans,
and Agamemnon went and stood beside him and spoke a word
   to him: 280
"Teucer, dear man, son of Telamon, leader of men,
strike just so, if you would be a shining light to the Danaans
and to your father Telamon, who raised you when you were little
and, illegitimate though you were, cared for you in his own house.
You will transport him to glory, although he is far away.
And I will say outright to you, and thus it will be accomplished:
if Zeus who wields the aegis and Athena grant me
to sack the well-built city of Ilion,
to you first, after myself, I will place a prize of honour in your hands,
either a tripod, or two horses with their own chariot,   290
or a woman, who will enter into your shared bed."
And answering, blameless Teucer addressed him:
"Most lordly son of Atreus, why do you urge me when I myself
am already eager? Never, as far as my strength holds, do I let up
but from the time we pushed the Trojans back to Ilion,
from that time, lying in wait with my bow, I have been killing men.
Eight long-barbed arrows have I shot,
and all have fixed in the flesh of vigorous men, swift in fight;
but this mad dog I cannot hit."
He spoke, and let loose another arrow from his bowstring   300
straight at Hector, and his heart strained to hit him;

but he missed him, and struck instead blameless Gorgythion
in the chest with his arrow, Priam's worthy son,
whom his mother bore, she who was taken as wife from the town of
   Aisyme,
beautiful Kastianeira like to a goddess in figure;
his head hung to one side like a garden poppy
made heavy with seed and the showers of spring;
so his head drooped, weighed down by his helmet.

      Teucer let loose another arrow from his bowstring
straight at Hector, and his heart strained to hit him;   310
but he missed even this time, for Apollo thwarted him,
and it was Archeptolemos, Hector's bold charioteer,
he struck in the chest beside his breast as he rushed to the fighting;
he fell from the chariot, the swift-footed horses started,
and there his soul and strength were undone.
Dreadful grief closed over Hector's heart for his charioteer;
but he let him lie, grieving though he was for his companion,
and summoned Kebriones, his brother, who was nearby,
to take the horses' reins; and when he heard he did not disobey.
Hector leapt from his gleaming chariot to the ground   320
crying a dreadful cry; and took a stone in his hand
and made straight for Teucer, his heart urgent to strike.
And Teucer had taken from his quiver a piercing arrow,
and placed it on the bowstring; but as he was drawing back the bowstring
   to his shoulder;
Hector of the shimmering helm struck him, there where the collarbone
   separates
the neck and the chest, and where is most fatal,
there, Hector struck with a jagged stone as Teucer aimed at him,
and broke the string; Teucer's hand went numb at the wrist,
and falling on his knees, he remained there, and dropped the bow from
   his hand.
And Ajax was not careless of his brother's falling,   330

but running stood astride and put his shield to cover him.
Then getting their shoulders under him, two faithful comrades,
Mekisteus the son of Echios and godlike Alastor,
bore him, groaning heavily, to the hollow ships.

    And once again the Olympian aroused courage in the Trojans;
and straight across the deep ditch they thrust the Achaeans.
And Hector went among the front ranks exulting in his strength;
as when a dog seizes a wild boar or lion
from behind as he pursues with his swift feet,
snatching at the flanks and hindquarters and watching closely for it to
    turn,   340
so Hector pressed hard upon the long-haired Achaeans,
killing always the hindmost man; and they fled.
But when they passed through the palisade and ditch
in flight, many were broken at the hands of the Trojans,
and the rest were checked beside the chariots, and there stood their ground,
calling out to one another and lifting their hands
to all the gods, each man crying aloud in prayer.
And Hector wheeled right and left his horses with their splendid manes,
his eyes like the Gorgon's or the eyes of Ares ruinous to mortals.

    And seeing them Hera the goddess of the white arms felt pity,
and she at once addressed Athena with winged words:
"Alas, daughter of Zeus who wields the the aegis, are we no longer
to care for the dying Danaans, at this their last hour,
they who filling their measure of evil destiny will perish
by the storm of one man's force? For he rages beyond endurance,
this Hector son of Priam, and he commits much evil."

    Then in turn the gleaming-eyed goddess Athena answered her:
"How I wish this man would lose his strength and spirit,
dying at the hands of the Argives in his own fatherland;
but my father rages in his unbalanced mind,   360
hard-hearted, always wicked, thwarting my plans,
he remembers nothing of those times, when again and again

I kept on saving his son Heracles who was worn down by the trials set by
   Eurystheus.
The man kept calling out to heaven, but it was me Zeus
dispatched from heaven to his aid.
If I had known the things now in his bitter mind,
that time when Eurystheus sent Heracles off to the guarded gates of Hades,
to bring the hound of hateful Hades out of Erebus,
then he would not have escaped the steep plunging waters of the Styx.
And now he hates me, and he has brought to pass the plans of Thetis,   370
who kissed his knees and took his chin in her hand,
imploring him to honour Achilles sacker of cities.
The time will yet come when he calls me again his dear gleaming-eyed girl.
But now ready for us the single-hoofed horses,
while I, entering into the house of Zeus who wields the aegis,
arm myself for war, so that I might see
whether Priam's son Hector of the shimmering helm
rejoices when we two appear between the lines of battle,
or whether any of the Trojans will also sate the dogs and birds
with their fat and flesh, falling by the ships of the Achaeans."   380

      So she spoke, nor did Hera goddess of the white arms disobey.
Departing, she got ready the gold-bridled horses
she, elder of goddesses, daughter of great Cronus;
And Athena, daughter of Zeus who wields the aegis
let fall her rippling robe upon her father's floor,
elaborate with embroidery, which she herself had made and laboured on
   with her own hands,
and putting on the cloak of Zeus who gathers clouds,
she armed herself for tearful war.
She made her way on foot toward the flame-bright chariot, and seized her
   spear
heavy, massive, powerful, with which she beats down the ranks of
   warrior   390
men, with whom she, born of the mighty Father, might be angered.

And Hera with her whip swiftly touched the horses;
of their own accord the gates of heaven groaned, which are guarded by
    the Seasons,
to whom broad heaven and Olympus are entrusted,
to push back the thick-pressed clouds and also close them over.
There, through these, they held the goad-sped horses.

   But when Zeus the father saw from Ida, his rage was extreme,
and he summoned Iris with her wings of gold to go as messenger:
"Come, swift Iris, set out and turn them back, do let them advance
    against me;
for it is not good that we should clash in war.   400
For I say this outright and it will be accomplished;
I will lame their swift horses beneath their chariot,
and I will hurl them from their seat, and shatter the chariot;
and not in the turning of ten years
will the wounds be healed that my thunderbolt will fasten on them;
so will my gleaming-eyed girl know what it is to battle with her father!
Hera I do not blame so much, nor am I angered with her,
for it is always her way to thwart me, whatever I propose."

   So he spoke, and storm-footed Iris sprang up to take his message,
and set out from the peaks of Ida to high Olympus.   410
And at the outer gates of Olympus with its many folds,
she caught the two goddesses and checked them, and spoke to them the
    word of Zeus:
"Where do you two hasten? What mad plan is in your minds?
The son of Cronus does not permit you to defend the Argives!
For thus the son of Cronus threatens, and thus it will be accomplished:
he will lame the swift horses beneath your chariot,
and he will hurl you from your seat and shatter your chariot;
and not in the turning of ten years
will your wounds be healed that his thunderbolt will fasten on you;
so, gleaming-eyed one, you will know, what it is to battle with your
    father.   420

Hera he does not blame so much, nor is he angered with her,
for it is always her way to thwart him, whatever he proposes.
But you are an intolerable, brazen dog if you truly
dare to raise your monstrous spear against the face of Zeus."

She spoke, and so speaking swift-footed Iris departed;
and Hera addressed Athena with a word:
"O dear daughter of Zeus who wields the aegis, I can no longer
allow us two to battle Zeus for the sake of mortals.
Let one of them perish, let another live,
as his luck may be. And let Zeus pondering those plans of his   430
decide for Trojans and Danaans, as is his right."
So speaking, she turned back the single-hoof horses;
and the Hours released the horses with their splendid manes for them,
and tethered them at their ambrosial mangers,
and the chariots they leaned against the gleaming inner walls.
And the goddesses seated themselves on divans of gold
among the other gods, stricken at their very hearts.

And from Ida, Zeus the father swiftly drove his well-wheeled
    chariot and horses
to Olympus, and arrived at the assembly of the gods.
And the illustrious Earth-Shaker released his horses for him,   440
and placed the chariot on a stand, spreading a cover over.
And he himself, far-thundering Zeus, on a throne of gold took
his seat, and great Olympus shook beneath his feet.
And alone of all the gods, Athena and Hera stayed apart from
Zeus, nor did they speak a word to him, nor question him.
But in his mind he understood and he called to them:
"Why are you two so stricken, Hera and Athena?
You did not, I think, exhaust yourselves in battle where men win
    glory,
destroying Trojans, on whom you have settled your terrible rancour.
Such is my might and my unassailable hands   450
that not the whole band of gods upon Olympus could turn me back.

But trembling seized your shining limbs even
before seeing war or the baneful deeds of war.
For I say this outright, and it will be accomplished;
blasted from your chariot by my lightning bolt,
you two would not have returned to Olympus, where is the seat of the
    gods."

              So he spoke; and they, Athena and Hera, muttered.
They sat close together, devising evil for the Trojans.
And Athena was silent and said nothing,
seething at Zeus her father, savage anger gripping her.   460
But Hera's breast could not contain her anger, and she spoke out:
"Most dread son of Cronus, what sort of word have you spoken?
Indeed we too well know that your strength is not to be resisted;
but nonetheless we pity the Danaan spearmen,
who filling their measure of evil destiny will perish."   465

              And answering her spoke Zeus who gathers the clouds: 469
"In the morning, you will see an even more powerful son of Cronus,   470
if you should wish, lady Hera of the brown eyes,
destroying a great army of Argive spearmen.
For mighty Hector will not cease from fighting
before Peleus' swift-footed son is stirred beside the ships,
on that day when the men fight beside their sterns
in a most terrible narrow space about dead Patroclus;
for thus it is decreed by heaven. And I take no care of your
anger, not if you were to go to the lowest limits
of the earth and sea, where Iapetos and Cronus
sit, cheered neither by the light of Helios Hyperion,   480
nor by winds, but Tartaros is deep about them;
not if you arrived there in your wandering, I have no care for
your being angry, since nothing is more dog-like than you."
So he spoke; and to him, Hera of the white arms said not a thing.

              The sun's radiant light dropped into Ocean,
and dragged black night upon the grain-giving fields.

For the Trojans the light sank against their will, but for the Achaeans
welcome, thrice prayed for, came the murky night.

       And shining Hector made assembly of the Trojans,
leading them away from the ships to the eddying water,   490
in a clear space, where the ground could be seen through the bodies.
Descending from their chariots to the ground, they listened to his word,
the word Hector beloved by Zeus spoke in the assembly; in one hand
he held his spear of eleven cubits length; before him gleamed
the bronze point of the spear shaft, round which ran a golden binding ring.
Leaning on this, he addressed the Trojans:
"Hear me, Trojans and Dardanians and allies.
I thought now that having destroyed the ships and all Achaeans
we would return back home to windy Ilion.
But the darkness came before, which most of all has now saved   500
the Argives and their ships beside the breaking surf.
Let us yield now to night's darkness
and let us prepare our meals; release the horses with their splendid manes
from under their chariot yokes, and drop fodder by them;
and fetch from the city oxen and fat sheep
with all speed, and get honey-hearted wine
and grain from the houses, and collect a mass of firewood besides,
so that the whole night long until dawn, born of morning,
we can burn our many fires, and the blaze go up to heaven,
lest by chance, even in the night, the long-haired Achaeans   510
move themselves to flight across the broad back of ocean.
And let them not embark their ships without a struggle, without
    hindrance,
but in such a way that many a one of them will nurse a wound even back
    home,
struck by an arrow or sharp spear
as he leapt upon his ship—so that another man will shudder
to carry war and all its tears to the horse-breaking Trojans.
And let the heralds, beloved by Zeus, announce throughout the city

that the boys in the bloom of youth and the white-headed elders
will camp out all around the city, on our ramparts that were built by gods;
and let the females, the women each in her own home,   520
kindle a great fire; and let each man stand firm guard
lest an ambush enter the city while the army is away.
Let this be, great-hearted Trojans, as I declare;
let the speech I have spoken serve for the present—
that for tomorrow I will announce later to the horse-breaking Trojans.
I hope, after praying to Zeus and the other gods,
to drive from here these dogs carried by the fates of death,
those whom the fates bore on their black ships.
We shall guard ourselves for night,
and in early morning, having armed in our weapons with the dawn,   530
let us by the hollow ships awaken piercing war;
and I shall see whether the powerful son of Tydeus, Diomedes,
will drive me from their ships to the wall, or whether
slashing him with bronze, I shall carry away the bloody spoils of his armour.
Tomorrow he will learn the value of his courage, and whether
he can withstand the approach of my spear; but I think among the front
    fighters
he will lie wounded with his many comrades by him,
with the rising of the sun into the morrow. Would that I were
immortal and ageless all my days,
and honoured as are honoured Apollo and Athena,   540
as surely as this day now bears evil for the Argives!"

        Thus Hector spoke to the assembly, and the Trojans shouted their
    applause.
And they released their dripping horses from under the harness,
and tethered them with reins, each by his own chariot;
and they fetched from the city oxen and fat sheep
with all speed, and got honey-hearted wine
and grain from the houses, and collected a mass of firewood besides;   547
and the winds bore the smoke from the plain into heaven.   549

And they in high confidence between the lines of battle   553
sat down the night long, and their many fires blazed.
As when in heaven, stars about the bright moon
shine conspicuous when the upper air turns windless,
and all the peaks and jutting cliffs are shown,
and valleys, and from heaven above the boundless bright air is rent with
    light
and all the stars are seen, and the shepherd's heart rejoices,
so between the ships and streams of Xanthos   560
in such multitude shone the watchfires of the Trojans' burning, before
    Ilion.
A thousand fires were burning on the plain, and by each one
sat fifty men in the glow of fire's gleaming;
and the horses munched their white barley and their grain
standing beside their chariots as they awaited Dawn on her fair throne.

So the Trojans held their guard; but preternatural Panic,
handmaid of cold Flight, held the Achaeans,
and all the best of them were stricken with grief too great to bear.
As dual winds rouse the fish-filled sea,
Northern Boreas and Zephyros from the West, both blowing from
    Thrace,
coming on a sudden; and the wave massed to darkness
rises in a crest, and far along the salt sea it scatters seaweed—
so was the spirit rent in the breasts of the Achaeans.

          And the son of Atreus, stricken at heart with great grief,
went back and forth commanding the clear-voiced heralds   10
to summon by name each man to the assembly,
but with no hue and cry, and he himself went to work with the foremost.
They took their seat in the assembly, stricken; and Agamemnon
stood up, streaming tears like a dark-water spring,
which down sheer rock streams sombre water;
so groaning deeply he addressed his words to the Argives:
"O friends, leaders and protectors of the Argives—
greatly has Zeus the son of Cronus bound me in grievous deception,
hard he is, who at one time promised me and gave assurance
that I would return home after sacking well-walled Troy.   20
Now he has devised an evil deceit and bids me
go back to Argos dishonoured, since I have destroyed a multitude of men.
This, it seems, must please Zeus, supreme in might,

who has brought to ruin the citadels of many cities,

and will destroy yet more; for his is the greatest power.

But come—let us all be persuaded to do as I say;

let us flee with our ships to our beloved homeland,

for we will not ever take Troy of the wide ways."

So he spoke, and all the men were hushed in silence;

for a long time the sons of the Achaeans were quiet with sorrow.   30

At length Diomedes of the war cry addressed him:

"Son of Atreus, I will first combat your folly,

which is one's right, my lord, in the assembly; and do you not be angered.

You first reviled my courage before the Danaans,

you said that I was unwarlike and a coward; all these things

the Argives know, both young and old.

To you the son of devious Cronus gave half measure;

he granted that by your sceptre you would be honoured beyond all men,

but courage he did not give you, which is the greatest power.

What possesses you? Do you really suppose that the sons of Achaeans

    are so   40

unwarlike and cowardly, as you declare?

But if your own spirit is set on departing,

go—the way lies open, your ships stand by the sea,

those so many ships that followed you from Mycenae;

but the rest of the long-haired Achaeans will remain,

until we sack Troy. Come! Let even they

flee in their ships to the beloved fatherland,

we two, I and Sthenelos, will fight until we learn first-hand

the fated end of Ilion; for it was with god we came."

So he spoke; and all the sons of the Achaeans shouted assent,   50

in admiration of the word of Diomedes breaker of horses.

And standing among them the horseman Nestor addressed them:

"Son of Tydeus, in war you are strong beyond all,

and in counsel you are best among all your age.

No man of all the Achaeans will slight your word,

nor speak against it; but your words have not reached a conclusion.

How young you are yet—you might even be my son,

the youngest by birth—but you talk good sense to

the Argive kings, for what you say is proper.

But come, I who claim to be older than you,   60

I will speak plainly and thoroughly. No man can

discredit my word, not even lord Agamemnon;

without tribe, lawless, without home is that man,

who desires cold-blooded war among his own people.

Let us yield now to night's darkness

and prepare our meals; let the guards each

camp out along the ditch dug outside the wall.

On the young men I lay all these charges. And then,

son of Atreus, do you take the lead; for you are the most kingly;

make a banquet for the senior leaders. It is fitting for you, it is not

    unseemly;   70

your shelters are full of wine that Achaean ships

bring every day from Thrace across the broad high sea.

All hospitality is yours—you are lord of many—

and when a multitude is assembled, listen to that man who gives the best

counsel. Very great is the need of all Achaeans

for good and shrewd counsel, when close by their ships the enemy

burn their many watchfires; who could take joy in this?

This is the night that will either destroy the army or save it."

          So he spoke; and they listened closely and obeyed.

Forth the guards hastened under arms   80

mustered about Nestor's son Thrasymedes, shepherd of the people,

and about Askalaphos and Ialmenos, sons of Ares,

and about Meriones and Aphareus and Deïpyros and

about the son of Kreion, shining Lykomedes.

Seven leaders of the guards there were, and with each a hundred

young men proceeded grasping long spears in their hands.

On arrival, they settled in the space between the ditch and rampart, and there they kindled fires, and each prepared his meal.

And the son of Atreus led the Achaeans' senior leaders in a body
into his shelter, and before them set a hearty feast;   90
and they reached out their hands to the good things set ready before them.
And when they had put away desire for eating and drinking,
the old man taking the lead began to weave his plan to them,
Nestor, whose counsel in time past had proved best,
he in his wisdom spoke and addressed them:
"Most glorious son of Atreus, lord of men Agamemnon,
with you I will end, with you begin, since over many
men are you lord and Zeus has put into your hand
both sceptre and tradition, that you might take counsel in their interest.
Therefore you beyond others should speak out what you have to say, and
    also listen,   100
and even fulfil the advice of another, when the spirit moves him
to speak some word for good; for whatever he may begin will depend
    on you.
So then, I will speak as it seems best to me.
Nor shall any other man have in mind counsel better than this,
such as I have turned in mind both in the past and still now—
turned since that time when you, O descended from Zeus, went and took
the girl Briseïs from the shelter of Achilles, for all his anger,
not at all in accordance with our counsel; for I did indeed
strongly dissuade you; but you, yielding to your great-hearted fury,
dishonoured the best of men, one whom the very gods esteem;   110
for you have taken and hold his prize. Still, even now
let us consider how we might, making atonement, win him over
with propitiatory gifts and gentle words."

Then answered him the lord of men, Agamemnon:
"Old one, not at all falsely have you recounted my delusion—
I was struck with delusion, I myself make no denial. Worth many
warriors is the man whom Zeus loves in his heart,
as now he honours this one, and brings defeat to the Achaean people.

But since I was struck with delusion, guided by my wretched sense,
I am willing to make amends and to offer untold recompense.   120
To all of you I will enumerate the illustrious gifts:
seven tripods untouched by fire, ten talents of gold,
twenty gleaming cauldrons, twelve horses—
muscular, bearers of prizes, who won contests with their speed of feet.
A man would not be bereft of possessions,
nor lacking in valuable gold, who owned as much
as the single-hoofed horses have won for me in prizes.
And I will give seven women, skilled in flawless works of hand,
women of Lesbos, whom, when he himself took strong-founded Lesbos,
I selected, who in beauty surpass all tribes of women;   130
these I will give to him, and among them will be the one I took away,
the daughter of Briseus. And more—I will swear a great oath
that I never mounted her bed and lay with her,
which is the custom of humankind, of men and of women.
These things, all of them, will be his at once; and if later
the gods grant us to sack the great city of Priam,
let him heap his ship with gold and bronze in abundance,
coming in when we Achaeans divide among ourselves the spoils;
and let him himself choose twenty Trojan women,
who, after Helen of Argos, are most beautiful.   140
And if we return to Achaean Argos, nurturer of tilled fields,
he will be my son-in-law, and I will honour him equally with Orestes,
who, late-born to me, was raised in great luxury.
I have three daughters in my well-built halls,
Chrysothemis and Laodike and Iphianassa;
of these, let him take which he will as his own, without bride-price,
to the house of Peleus; and I will give bride-gifts with her,
a great many, such as no man has yet bestowed upon his daughter.
Seven citadels I will give to him, well-inhabited,
Kardamyle and Enope and grassy Hire,   150
sacred Pherai and Antheia of the deep meadows

and lovely Aipeia and Pedasos with its vines.
All are near the sea, on the border of sandy Pylos,
and in them dwell men who are rich in sheep and rich in cattle,
who will honour him with gifts as they would a god,
and who under sceptre of his rule will fulfil his prospering laws.
These things I will accomplish for him if he gives over his anger.
Let him give way—Hades is implacable and unyielding;
and therefore is for mortal men most hateful of all the gods—
let him submit to me, since I am the greater king   160
and since I claim myself to be in age the elder."

        Then answered him the Gerenian horseman Nestor:
"Most glorious son of Atreus, lord of men Agamemnon,
the gifts you offer lord Achilles cannot now be slighted;
come, let us dispatch chosen men, who with all swiftness
will go to the shelter of Peleus' son Achilles.
Come now, those men I select, let them do as I say.
Let Phoinix beloved of Zeus lead first of all,
and then great Ajax and godlike Odysseus;
and let the heralds Odios and Eurybates follow with them.   170
Bring water for their hands, bid them speak no word of ill omen,
so that we may conciliate Zeus son of Cronus, that he might take pity."

        So he spoke, and what he said found favour with all,
and without delay the heralds streamed the water over their hands,
the young men filled mixing bowls brimful with wine,
and after preparing libations in each cup, distributed it to all.
Then when they had poured offering and drunk as much as their spirit
    desired,
they set out from the shelter of Agamemnon son of Atreus.
And to them the Gerenian horseman Nestor gave many instructions
looking encouragingly at each, but most of all at Odysseus,   180
to endeavour to win over the blameless son of Peleus.

        And the two groups went along the shore of the tumultuous sea,
making many prayers to the god who holds the earth

that they might readily persuade the proud heart of Aeacides.
And so they came to the shelters and ships of the Myrmidons,
and found him delighting his heart in a pure-toned lyre,
exquisitely wrought, with a bridge of silver upon it,
which he won from spoils when he laid waste the city of Eëtion.
With this he was delighting his spirit, and singing of the glorious deeds
    of men;
Patroclus by himself was sitting opposite in silence,   190
watchfully awaiting Aeacides, for when he would break off his singing.
And they came forward, godlike Odysseus leading the way,
and stood before him. In amazement Achilles sprang up,
lyre in hand, leaving the place where he was sitting;
so likewise Patroclus rose, when he saw the men.
And greeting them Achilles of the swift feet spoke:
"Welcome; surely you come as dear friends—indeed there is great need—
who are dearest to me, even in anger, of the Achaeans."
So speaking godlike Achilles led them closer,
and seated them on divans and shimmering carpets.   200
And at once he addressed Patroclus who was standing near:
"Set up a larger mixing bowl, son of Menoetius,
and mix stronger wine, and prepare a cup for each man;
for these beneath my roof are my dearest friends."
        So he spoke, and Patroclus obeyed his beloved companion.
He threw down a great meat-block by the light of the fire,
and placed on it the back of a sheep and of a fat goat,
and the chine of a fattened pig rich with lard;
Automedon held the board for him, and godlike Achilles carved.
And these he deftly cut up and pierced through on spits,   210
and the son of Menoetius, a man like a god, made the fire burn big.
Then when the fire had burned down and its flame was extinguished,
spreading the embers, he arranged the spits above them,
lifting and placing them upon the andirons, and sprinkled holy salt.
And when he had roasted the meat and heaped it on chargers,

Patroclus took bread to distribute around the table
in fine baskets, but Achilles distributed the meat.
And he himself sat facing godlike Odysseus
by the opposite wall, and to the gods he bade
Patroclus, his companion, make offering; and he into the fire cast the
    first cuts.   220
Then they reached out their hands to the good things set ready before
    them.
        And when they had put away desire for eating and drinking,
Ajax nodded to Phoinix; and godlike Odysseus perceived him,
and filling a cup with wine he pledged Achilles:
"To your happiness, Achilles; we do not lack fair share of feasting,
both in the shelter of Agamemnon son of Atreus,
and now even here; there is abundance to satisfy the spirit
for us to dine on. But our work of concern is not fair feasts,
but destruction too great to behold, beloved of Zeus,
is what we fear; it is in doubt whether we will save our well-benched
    ships,   230
or they will be destroyed, if you do not arm yourself in might.
Hard by the ships and defensive wall they have pitched camp,
the high-spirited Trojans and their far-renowned allies,
blazing many fires throughout the army, and no longer, they say,
will they be restrained, but will fall upon our black ships.
Zeus the son of Cronus shows them favourable omens
of lightning; Hector in the great exultation of his strength
rages uncontrollably—trusting in Zeus, he respects neither
man nor god, but overpowering fury has entered in him.
He prays that shining dawn will show forth swiftly;   240
for he threatens to hack the stern-posts from the ships
and destroy them in ravenous fire, and slaughter
the Achaeans beside the ships when they are roused by smoke.
These things I fear terribly in my heart, lest the gods
accomplish these threats for him, and then our fate would be

to perish in Troy, far from the horse-grazed pastures of Argos.
Rise up! if you are minded even at this late hour to save
Achaea's sons in their extremity from the Trojan onslaught.
For you too there will be grief in time after, nor is there any means
to find remedy once evil is accomplished; before that take thought   250
how you might ward off from the Danaans their day of evil.

      "O my friend, surely your father Peleus gave you instruction
on that day, when he sent you from Phthia to Agamemnon;
'My child, strength of body Athena and Hera will give you,
if that is their will, but your great-hearted spirit is for you
to restrain within your breast; friendship is far better;
desist from strife that creates only evil, and they will honour you more,
youths and elders of the Argives alike.'
So the old man instructed you, and you have forgotten. But even now
stop, give up this heart-grieving anger; and Agamemnon   260
will give you gifts in compensation, if you desist from this anger;
come now, hear me, and I will enumerate for you
all the gifts in his shelter Agamemnon promises to you;
seven tripods untouched by fire, ten talents of gold,
twenty gleaming cauldrons, twelve horses—
muscular, bearers of prizes, who won contests with speed of their feet.
A man would not lack possessions,
nor would he be lacking in valuable gold, who owned as much
as Agamemnon's horses have won in prizes with their feet.
He will give seven women, skilled in flawless works of hand,   270
women of Lesbos, whom, when you took strong-founded Lesbos,
he selected, who in beauty then surpassed all tribes of women;
these he will give to you, and among them will be the one he took away
    before,
the daughter of Briseus. And more—he will swear a great oath,
that he never mounted her bed and lay with her,
which is the custom, my lord, both of men and of women;
these things, all of them, will be yours at once; and if later

the gods grant us to sack the great city of Priam,
heap your ship with gold and bronze in abundance,
coming in when we Achaeans divide among ourselves the spoils;   280
and choose for yourself twenty Trojan women,
who, after Helen of Argos, are most beautiful.
And if we return to Achaean Argos, nurturer of tilled fields,
you can be his son-in-law, and he will honour you equally with Orestes,
who, late-born to him, was raised in great luxury.
He has three daughters in his well-built halls,
Chrysothemis and Laodike and Iphianassa;
of these, take which you will as your own, without bride-price,
to the house of Peleus; and he will give bride-gifts with her,
a great many, such as no man has yet bestowed upon his daughter.   290
Seven citadels he will give to you, well-inhabited,
Kardamyle and Enope and grassy Hire,
sacred Pherai and Antheia of the deep meadows
and lovely Aipeia and Pedasos with its vines.
All are near the sea, on the border of sandy Pylos,
and in them dwell men who are rich in sheep and rich in cattle,
who will honour you with gifts as they would a god,
and who under sceptre of your rule will fulfil your prospering laws.
These things he will accomplish for you if you give over your anger.

        "But if the son of Atreus has become more hateful, even to the
    bottom of your heart,   300
he and his gifts, then on all the other Achaean forces
have pity, those worn to extremity throughout the army, who honour you
like a god; surely in their eyes you would win very great glory.
For you might kill even Hector, since he would close upon you
in the grip of his deadly madness, seeing that he claims there is no man
    his equal
of Danaans whom our ships brought to this place."

        Then answering him spoke Achilles of the swift feet;
"Zeus-descended son of Laertes, Odysseus of many stratagems,

I must speak out what I have to say without care for consequence,
how I will now decide and thus how it will be accomplished,   310
so that you do not sit around me murmuring now from one side, now
    from another;
for hateful to me as the gates of Hades is that man,
who hides one thing in his mind, but says another;
and it is I who will say how it seems best to me.
I think neither Atreus' son Agamemnon will persuade me,
nor the other Danaans, since it seems there is no thanks
for doing battle against enemy men without respite, forever;
the fate is the same if a man hangs back, and if he battles greatly,
in equal honour are both coward and warrior;
and they die alike, both the man who has done nothing and he who has
    accomplished many things.   320
Nor is there any profit for me, because I have endured affliction at heart,
ever staking my life to do combat.
As a bird to her unfledged young brings
in her mouth whatever she catches, but for herself it goes badly,
so I too have passed many sleepless nights,
and come through many blood-soaked days of fighting,
doing battle with men who fight for their own wives.
Twelve cities of men I have sacked from my ships,
and eleven, I say, on foot throughout Troy's rich-soiled land;
and from all these I carried off as spoil many treasures, valuable
    treasures,   330
and would take and give them all to Agamemnon
the son of Atreus; and he hanging back beside his swift ships
accepted them, and would distribute little, and hold on to much.
Other prizes of honour he doled out to the noble men and to the kings;
theirs remain unplundered; mine alone of the Achaeans
he took away, and holds the bride fitted to my heart. Let him lie with her
and take his pleasure. But why must the Argives be at war with
the Trojans? Why did the son of Atreus assemble and lead

an army here? Was it not for Helen of the lovely hair?

Do the sons of Atreus alone of mortal men love their wives?   340

No, for any man who is decent and wise

loves her who is his own and cares for her, as I too loved

this one from my heart, spear-won though she be.

And now since he has taken my prize from my hands and cheated me,

let him not test me who know him too well—he will not persuade me—

but, Odysseus, let him ponder with you and the other kings

how to stave off from his ships consuming fire.

To be sure, he has done a great deal of work without me;

he has now even built a wall, and driven a trench around it,

broad and long, and planted stakes inside;   350

but not even so will he be able to withstand the strength

of man-slaying Hector; but so long as I was fighting among the Achaeans,

Hector was not minded to stir up battle beyond the wall,

but used to come only so far as the Scaean gates and oak tree.

There once he stood up to me alone, and barely escaped my onslaught.

          "Now, since I am not willing to do battle with shining Hector,

tomorrow having made holy sacrifice to Zeus and all the gods,

and heaping full my ships, after I have drawn them down to the salt sea—

you will see for yourself, if you should wish to and if these things interest

     you,

at very early morn, riding the fish-filled Hellespont,   360

my ships, and in them men eager to row;

and if the illustrious Earth-Shaker should grant fair passage,

on the third day I shall arrive at Phthia of the rich soil.

A great many possessions are there for me, which I left behind when I

     came on this ruinous journey,

and from here I shall lead away more gold and ruddy bronze

and fair-belted women, and grey iron,

as much as was assigned to me; but the prize of honour, though he gave me,

that lord Agamemnon in his towering outrage has taken back,

the son of Atreus. State all these things to him, as I direct, openly, so that other Achaeans too will scorn him 370

if, as I have no doubt, he still hopes to cheat some one of the Danaans,

ever covered as he is in shamelessness; nor would he,

dog though he is, dare to look me in the face.

I will no longer join him in counsel, nor in deed;

for he has cheated me outright and sinned against me; let him not ever
    again

deceive me with words; enough for him. Let him go his cursed way

without hindrance; for Zeus all-devising has snatched his wits from him.

      "His gifts are hateful to me. I hold him at the value of a splinter.

Not if he gave me ten and twenty times as much

as he now owns, and if more were to come from other quarters, 380

not as much as is brought into Orchomenos, or Egyptian

Thebes, where the greatest abundance of wealth lies stored in houses,

and which has a hundred gates, and through each two hundred

men march forth with horse and chariot,

not if he were to give me as many gifts as there are grains of dust or sand,

not even then would Agamemnon persuade my heart,

before he pays me back all this heart-grieving outrage.

I will not marry a daughter of Agamemnon son of Atreus,

not if she rivals golden Aphrodite in beauty,

and in skill matches Athena the gleaming-eyed; 390

not even so will I marry her. Let him acquire another one of the Achaeans,

someone who is befitting him and is more kingly.

For if the gods preserve me so long and I reach my home,

then Peleus himself will seek out a woman for me;

there are many Achaean women throughout Hellas and Phthia,

daughters of noble men, who defend high cities;

of these whichever I like I will make my beloved wife.

There time and again my strong spirit was set upon

a wife, wooed and wedded, a wife suited to me,

to enjoy the wealth that aged Peleus acquired. 400

For not worth my life is all they say

Ilion used to possess, the well-settled high city,

in those days before, in peacetime, before there came the sons of the
     Achaeans,

not all that Phoebus Apollo the archer's

stone threshold contains in rocky Pytho.

Cattle and fat sheep are carried off as plunder,

tripods are for the getting and tawny high-headed horses;

but the life of a man does not come back, not by plunder,

not by possession, once it passes the barrier of his teeth.

For my mother tells me, the goddess Thetis of the silver feet,   410

that two fates carry me to death's end;

if I remain here to fight around the city of the Trojans,

my return home is lost, but my glory will be undying;

but if I go home to the beloved land of my father,

outstanding glory will be lost to me, but my life will be long,

nor will death's end come on me swiftly.

And I would advise the rest of you

to make sail for home, since you will never see the fated end

of lofty Ilion; for sure it is that over it far-thundering Zeus

stretches his protective hand, and its people are now bold.   420

     "But you go to the Achaean nobles

and openly declare my message, for this is the privilege of counsellors,

so they will think out in their minds some other better plan,

which might save their ships and the army of the Achaeans

by their hollow ships, since this plan of theirs is not feasible

that they have now devised while my wrath raged.

Let Phoinix remain here and sleep with us,

so that he may come with my ships to our beloved fatherland

tomorrow, if he wishes; I will not take him by force."

     So he spoke, and all the men were hushed in silence   430

amazed at his words; for he had spoken very powerfully.

At length Phoinix the aged horseman addressed him,

bursting forth in tears; for he feared greatly for the ships of the Achaeans:

"If now you ponder going home, shining Achilles,

and you do not intend in any way at all to defend the swift ships

from obliterating fire, because rage has assailed your heart,

how, then, apart from you, dear child, could I be left here

on my own? With you the aged horseman Peleus dispatched me

on that day when he sent you from Phthia to Agamemnon,

a child, knowing nothing of indiscriminate war,   440

nor of speaking in assembly, where men develop distinction;

for that reason he sent me out to teach you all these things,

to be both a speaker of words and a performer of deeds.

So therefore, dear child, I would not willingly be left behind

away from you, not if a very god should give me promise

to scrape old age away and render me fresh flourishing with youth,

as I was when I first left Hellas, the land of lovely women,

fleeing the hostility of my father, Amyntor son of Ormenos,

who was enraged with me on account of his mistress, she of the fine hair,

whom he lay with in love, and dishonoured his wife,   450

my mother; she constantly begged me, at my knees,

to have intercourse with the mistress, so that she would hate the old man.

I obeyed her and did this; my father immediately suspecting

prayed and prayed for a curse upon me, and called upon the loathsome

    Furies,

that he might never set upon his knees any dear child

born of me; and the gods fulfiled his curse,

both Zeus of the underworld and dread Persephone.

I was ready to kill him with a sharp bronze sword;

but some one of the immortal gods turned my wits, who put me in mind

of people's opinion and the censure of mankind,   460

that among the Achaeans I might not be called a parricide.

Then no longer at all could the spirit in my chest be restrained

to wander along our halls, with my father angered;

true it is that many times kinsmen and cousins living around

restrained me with their pleas there in the halls;

many fat sheep and shambling twist-horned cattle
they slaughtered, many pigs luxuriant with fat
were singed and stretched across the fire of Hephaestus,
and much wine was drunk from the vats of the old man;
nine nights they kept watch close about me,   470
and taking turns they held guard, nor ever did the fires go out—
one beneath the entrance of the well-guarded courtyard,
the other in the alcove before my bedroom doors.
But when the tenth night came upon me with its murky darkness,
then I smashed the close-fitted doors of my chamber,
went out, and leapt over the courtyard wall
easily, escaping notice of the men on guard and household women.
Then I fled far away, through Hellas' wide country,
and arrived at Phthia of the rich soil, mother of flocks,
into the house of lord Peleus; and he willingly received me   480
and loved me, as a father loves his child,
his only child late-born to many properties;
and he made me rich, and gave me as a gift the rule of many people,
and I lived on the border of Phthia, ruling the Dolopes.
And you I made as great as you are, godlike Achilles,
loving you from my heart, for with no other man were you willing
to go out to the feast, nor would you eat in your own halls
before I settled you on my knees,
and cutting the meat first, gave you your fill and held the wine to your lips.
Many times you soaked through the tunic on my breast   490
spewing forth wine in your troublesome childish way.
So I suffered much for you and laboured much,
with this in mind—that the gods would not create any offspring for me
of my own; but you, godlike Achilles, I tried to make my son,
so that you might one day defend me from abject ruin.

          "Come, Achilles, master your great spirit; you must not keep
your heart without pity. And even the gods themselves can be turned,
although their majesty and honour and strength are even greater;

but with burnt sacrifices and prayers of propitiation
and libation and the savour of burnt offerings men turn them around   500
by praying, whenever some man has transgressed and strayed.
For Prayers of Penitence exist, daughters of great Zeus,
halting and grimacing and with squinting eyes,
their concern is to follow blind Delusion.
Delusion—she is strong and swift of foot, and thus
far outstrips all Prayers, and over every land she gets ahead
to trip up men; but Prayers of Penitence make amends thereafter.
The man who respects these daughters of Zeus when they approach,
him they greatly help and heed him as he prays;
but the man who spurns and rigidly rejects them,   510
then they go and pray to Zeus the son of Cronus
that Delusion follow him, so that thwarted by his blindness, he is punished.
Come, Achilles, you too grant that honour come to Zeus' daughters,
honour that bends the will of other, even noble, men.
If the son of Atreus were not bringing gifts, and naming gifts to follow,
but continued to make violent outrage,
I would not bid you cast off your wrath
to defend the Argives, despite their need.
But now he both offers many things forthwith, and promises more later,
and has dispatched the best men to make supplication   520
chosen throughout the Achaean army, men who to you yourself
are dearest of the Argives; do not slight their word,
nor their journey; before, your anger was not blameworthy.

    "Thus also in days of old, we have heard the famous deeds of
    warrior men
when swelling anger seized them;
they were open to gifts and were moved by words.
I myself remember this deed of long ago, it is nothing new,
it was like this, I will tell it among you, all my friends;
the Curetes and the Aetolians, steadfast in battle, were fighting
around the city of Calydon, and killing each other,   530

the Aetolians defending lovely Calydon, Oineus' city,

the Curetes straining to sack it in war.

For it happened that Artemis of the golden throne had stirred up evil
     among them

in anger, as Oineus made no offering of first fruits to her

on the high ground of his orchard—the other gods shared in sacrificial
     hecatombs,

but to her alone, the daughter of great Zeus, he had not offered sacrifice.

Either he had forgotten, or he had not thought of it, in the great delusion
     of his heart.

In her anger, she, child of Zeus who showers arrows,

incited a wild boar, foaming mad, with flashing tusks,

who did much evil to Oineus' orchard, as boars do;   540

many the tree he hurled to the ground, trunks and all, great trees

with their very roots and the blossoms of their fruit.

Meleager the son of Oineus killed it,

having gathered the hunting men of many cities

and their dogs; for in truth he could not have killed it with few;

so great it was, it brought many to the sorrow of the funeral pyre.

And then over its body, the goddess incited much uproar and cry for battle,

concerning the head of the boar and its bristled hide,

between the Curetes and the great-hearted Aetolians.

          Then so long as Meleager beloved of Ares went to battle,   550

so long things went badly for the Curetes, nor could they

stand their ground outside the wall, for all their numbers;

but when anger entered Meleager, anger that also swells

in the breasts of other men, even those of good understanding and
     shrewd mind,

why then, angered in his heart at his own mother Althaia

he lay apart with his wedded wife, beautiful Cleopatra,

the daughter of Marpessa—she of the slender ankles, the child of Euenos

and of Idas, who was the strongest of men upon earth

at that time, and even raised his bow against lord

Phoebus Apollo for the sake of this maiden with slender ankles—   560
after that, within their home her father and lady mother
used to call her name Halcyon, for her
mother shared the halcyon's fate, the sorrowing sea bird,
weeping, because Phoebus Apollo who works from afar had snatched her
    daughter away;
it was with this Cleopatra that Meleager lay brooding on his heart-grieving
    rage,
raging at his mother's curses, because she
in anguish over his slaying of her brother, made prayer again and again to
    the gods,
again and again beating the nourishing earth with her hands,
calling on Hades and dread Persephone,
sitting bent-kneed, her bosom soaked with tears,   570
to send death to her child; and Erinys who walks in darkness
heard her from the nether dark of Erebus, and her heart is implacable.

      "And soon around the gates arose the roar of the Curetes, the din
of towers being assailed; and the Aetolian elders beseeched Meleager,
and sent the gods' noblest priests,
to come out and defend them, pledging a great reward:
wherever lay the richest field in lovely Calydon,
there they urged him to take for himself a piece of land, of surpassing
    beauty,
and mark off from the common lot fifty acres,
one half for vineyards, one half open field for ploughing.   580
Again and again the aged horseman Oineus entreated him,
standing on the threshold of his high-roofed chamber,
shaking the fitted doors, pleading with his son,
time and again his sisters and lady mother
entreated him; but he denied them vehemently; time and again did his
    companions,
who were the most devoted and dearest to him of all men;
but not even so did they win over the heart in his breast,

until that moment when his chamber was hammered with close blows,
   and the Curetes
were scaling the walls and setting fire to the great city.
And then his fine-belted wife supplicated Meleager   590
as she wept, and went through everything for him,
all the sufferings that come to those whose city is taken;
they kill the men and fire reduces the city to dust,
strangers lead off the children and slender-waisted women.
And as Meleager heard tell of these evil deeds, his heart was stirred,
and he went and clad his body in his glittering armour.
So he beat back from the Aetolians their day of evil,
yielding to his own heart; but they never paid him the gifts,
the many splendid and welcome gifts—and he averted the evil to no end.

      "But you Achilles, do not think such things in your mind, nor let
   some dark spirit   600
turn you that way, dear one; it would be less worthy
to defend the ships once they are burning. But come while there are gifts;
the Achaeans will honour you like a god.
But if without gifts you enter the man-destroying battle,
you will no longer be so honoured, for all you beat back the war."

      Then answering him, Achilles of the swift feet spoke:
"Phoinix, old father, cherished by Zeus, in no way do I have need
of such honour—I think I am honoured by the just measure of Zeus
which would keep me by the curved ships, as long as life's breath
remains in my breast and my knees have motion.   610
And I will tell you something else and put it away in your mind;
do not confound my heart with your weeping and groaning,
currying favour for the warrior son of Atreus; you should not
hold him so dear, lest you become hateful to me who love you.
It is fitting for you to join me to trouble him who troubles me.
Rule equally with me, and share half my honour.
These men will take my message, but you stay and take your rest
on a soft bed here; when the dawn shows forth

we will consider whether we will return with our men or stay."

      He spoke, and he motioned silently with his brows to
  Patroclus   620
to smooth the snug bed for Phoinix, so that with all speed
the others would think of going back from his shelter. And Ajax
the godlike son of Telamon spoke his word among them:
"Zeus-descended son of Laertes, Odysseus of many stratagems,
let us go; for it does not seem to me that fulfilment of our mandate
will be accomplished on this journey. We must report his word without
  delay
unfavourable even as it is, to the Danaans,
who surely await us now. But Achilles
has made savage the great-hearted spirit in his breast,
he is hard, and turns his back on that friendship of companions   630
for which we honoured him beyond all others by the ships,
pitiless; a man will accept payment even from his brother's killer
or for his dead child,
and the man who has paid much in penalty remains there, in his country,
and the heart and the proud spirit of the other is checked,
by accepting recompense. But in your breast the gods have placed
an implacable, a baneful spirit, for the sake of a single
girl; and now we offer you seven, exceptional, the best,
and many other things besides. Gentle your heart,
respect your house; we are under your roof   640
from all the multitude of the Danaans, and beyond all others,
as many as the Achaeans are, yearn to be closest and dearest to you."

      And answering him Achilles of the swift feet spoke:
"Ajax, son of Telamon descended from Zeus, leader of the people,
you seem in a way to speak everything after my mind,
but my heart swells with rage, when I recall those things—
how in the presence of the Argives he degraded me,
the son of Atreus, as if I were some worthless vagabond.
But all of you go and speak my message openly—

that I shall have no thought again of bloodstained war   650
until the son of brilliant Priam, shining Hector,
reaches the ships and shelters of the Myrmidons,
killing Argives, and smokes the ships with smoldering fire;
about my shelter and dark ship
I think, Hector, eager though he be for war, will be stopped."

       So he spoke. And the men each having taken up a double-handled
    cup
and having poured libations beside the ships went back, and Odysseus led.
And Patroclus bade the companions and servant women
lay out a snug bed for Phoinix forthwith;
and they in obedience laid out the bed as he commanded,   660
with fleeces and a covering cloth and fine nubbed linen.
There the old man lay down and awaited the shining dawn;
but Achilles slept in the inner recess of his well-built shelter,
and with him lay a woman, one he had taken from Lesbos,
the daughter of Phorbas, Diomede of the lovely cheeks;
and on the other side lay Patroclus, and by him
fair-belted Iphis, whom godlike Achilles gave him
when he took steep Seyros, the high city of Enyeus.

       And when the others appeared inside the son of Atreus' shelter,
then with cups of gold uplifted the sons of the Achaeans pledged
    them   670
rising to their feet, one after the other, and made interrogation.
And first to make inquiry was the lord of men Agamemnon:
"Come, tell me, O illustrious Odysseus, great pride of the Achaeans,
will he beat back the blazing fire from our ships,
or did he refuse, and does rage still have hold of his great-hearted spirit?"

       Then in turn much-enduring, godlike Odysseus addressed him:
"Most glorious son of Atreus, lord of men Agamemnon;
the man is unwilling to quench his rage, but is all the more
filled with wrath, and rejects you and your gifts.
And he urges you yourself to consult among the Argives   680

how you might save your ships and the army of the Achaeans.
He himself threatened when dawn shows forth
to haul his well-benched double-ended ships to the sea;
and he said he would advise the rest of us
to make sail for home, 'since you will never see the fated end
of lofty Ilion; for sure it is that over it far-thundering Zeus
stretches his protective hand, and its people are now bold.'
Thus he spoke; and these men are here to confirm this, who came with me,
Ajax and the two heralds, both men of good sense.
But Phoinix the old man sleeps there, as he urges,   690
in order that he may follow with him in his ships to their beloved fatherland
tomorrow, if he chooses; for he will not take him by force."

       So he spoke, and all the men were hushed in silence
amazed at his words; for he had spoken very powerfully.
For a long time the sons of the Achaeans were quiet with sorrow.
At length Diomedes of the war cry addressed them:
"Most glorious son of Atreus, lord of men Agamemnon;
you should not have beseeched the blameless son of Peleus
offering endless gifts. He is a proud man as it is;
but now you have inclined him all the more to pride.   700
Come, let him be, either he will go
or he will stay. Then he will fight again, whenever
the spirit in his own breast bids him and god urges.
But come, for so I speak, and let us all be persuaded;
let us now take rest in sleep having satisfied our hearts with
food and wine, for this is our strength and courage;
but when Dawn the beautiful shows forth a finger of rosy light,
swiftly array men and horses before the ships,
urging them on, and yourself fight in the front lines."
So he spoke, and all the princes assented,   710
in admiration of the word of Diomedes breaker of horses.
Then when they had poured libations, each man went to his shelter
where they laid themselves to rest and took the gift of sleep.

10. ILIÁDOS K

Then beside their ships the other nobles of the grand Achaean army
slept the whole night long, overcome by sinking sleep;
but sweet sleep did not hold Agamemnon, son of Atreus
shepherd of the people, as he churned in his mind many things.
As when the husband of Hera of the lovely hair flashes lightning forth,
conjuring a great monstrous rain, or hail,
or fall of snow, so that snowflakes powder the ploughed fields,
or somewhere makes rise the massive jaws of piercing war—
so again and again within his breast did Agamemnon groan aloud
from the depths of his heart, and the wits within him were seized with
    trembling.   10
Whenever he looked towards the Trojan plain,
he was astonished at the many fires that burned in front of Ilion,
at the sound of hollow flutes and din of men;
and then when he beheld the ships and army of Achaeans,
he tore clumps of hair by the roots from his head,
looking to Zeus on high, and his noble heart was full to bursting.
        And this plan appeared best to his mind,
to go to Nestor, Neleus' son, first among men,
that he might put together with him some perfect scheme
that would somehow avert destruction from all Danaans.   20
Standing up, he put a tunic about him,
and beneath his smooth feet he bound his splendid sandals;

then he put about him the tawny skin of a gleaming
huge lion that reached to his feet, and took up his spear.

     And in the same way trembling took hold of Menelaos—for sleep
was not settling on his eyelids either—lest the Argives suffer,
they who for his sake had come over the vast sea
to Troy to stir up ferocious war.
First he covered his broad back with a dappled
leopard skin; then taking his bronze helmet   30
he placed it on his head; and his spear he took in his massive hand.
So he set out to go to rouse his brother, who ruled greatly
over all the Argives, and like a god was honoured by his people.

     He found him putting his splendid armour about his shoulders
by the stern of his ship; and his coming was welcome to his brother.
Menelaos of the war cry addressed him first:
"Why do you arm in this way, my brother? Will you dispatch
some companion of ours as spy against the Trojans? But I do greatly
fear that no one will undertake this task for you,
going alone to spy on enemy men   40
through the ambrosial night; surely, that man will be bold of heart."

     Then answering him lord Agamemnon spoke:
"You and I have need of a plan, Zeus-cherished Menelaos,
a shrewd plan, if anyone is to defend and save
the Argives and their ships, for Zeus' heart has turned against us.
It is to Hector's sacrifices he has paid more heed.
For I have never seen, nor heard tell
of one man, on one day, contriving so much evil,
as Hector beloved of Zeus has wrought upon the sons of the Achaeans
on his own, he the beloved son of neither god, nor goddess.   50
Such deeds he has committed as I think will weigh on Argives
for a long time to come; such evils he has devised for the Achaeans.
But come now—run beside the ships and summon
Ajax and Idomeneus; I am going to illustrious Nestor

to urge him to rise from sleep, and see if e he is willing
to go to the sacred post of guards and give them orders.
Him they would obey above all; for his son
commands the watch guards with Meriones,
companion of Idomeneus; to these men above all others we entrusted the
     duty."
Then Menelaos of the war cry answered him: 60
"How would you charge me with your order?
Shall I remain there keeping watch with them until you come,
or shall I run after you, when I have clearly instructed them?"
Then answered him Agamemnon lord of men:
"Remain there, lest we somehow miss each other
as we come and go; for there are many byways throughout this camp.
Call out, wherever you go, and bid them stay awake,
naming each man by his paternal family name,
showing respect to all, and do not let your heart be haughty,
but let us do this work ourselves. For on us, it seems,   70
at our very birth Zeus cast burdensome ill fortune."

          So speaking he dispatched his brother, having given clear
     instructions.
Then he set out for Nestor, shepherd of the people;
he found him beside his shelters and dark ships
in a soft bed; and beside him lay elaborate armour,
his shield and two spears and gleaming helmet;
and by him his war-belt lay all-shimmering, with which the old man
would gird himself when he armed for man-destroying war
to lead his people, since he had not yielded to distressful age.
Then raising himself upon his elbow, lifting his head,   80
he addressed the son of Atreus and questioned him with a word:
"Who here goes alone among the ships and army
through the murk of night, when other mortal men are sleeping—
are you seeking some lost mule, or one of your companions?

Speak up, do not come to me in silence. What is your need?"

    Then answered him Agamemnon lord of men:

"O Nestor, son of Neleus, great pride of the Achaeans,

you will recognise Agamemnon son of Atreus, whom beyond all men

Zeus has enmeshed in toil unceasing, as long as life's breath

remains in my breast and my knees have motion.   90

I wandered here, since soft sleep does not settle

on my eyes, but war and cares for the Achaeans are my concern.

For terribly do I fear for the Danaans; my strength is not

steady, I am distraught, my heart seems to leap through

my breast, my shining limbs shake beneath me.

But if you wish to act, since sleep has not reached you,

come, let us go down to the watches, so that we can see

whether, worn out with exhaustion and lack of sleep,

they are drowsing and have forgotten wholly their watch duty;

enemy men are camped nearby; nor do we know   100

whether even in the night they might be minded to do battle."

    Then answered him the Gerenian horseman Nestor:

"Most glorious son of Atreus, lord of men Agamemnon,

surely all-devising Zeus will not fulfil everything that Hector

purposes, all he now dreams; indeed I think that he

will be afflicted with yet more cares, if Achilles should

turn his heart back from his grievous anger.

I will indeed follow you; and let us again arouse the others,

both the spear-famed son of Tydeus and Odysseus,

and swift Ajax and the brave son of Phyleus.   110

And perhaps someone would also go and summon these men—

Ajax, like a god, and lord Idomeneus;

for their ships are at the farthest point, not at all near.

And dear though he is, and respected, I will reproach

Menelaos—even if you should be indignant with me, I will not

    conceal it,

since he sleeps, and has left it to you to toil alone.
Now he ought to be at work going among all our best men
in supplication; for a need has come that no longer can be borne."

   Then in turn Agamemnon lord of men addressed him:
"Old father, another time I even encourage you to blame him; 120
for often he holds back and is reluctant to go to work,
not withdrawing because of shirking, or thoughtlessness of mind,
but looking to me and waiting for my urging;
but this time he woke well before me and came to me.
I sent him to call out those men you asked after.
Come, let us go; we will catch up with them before the gates
with the watch guards, where I directed them to gather."

   Then answered him the Gerenian horseman Nestor:
"So no one of the Argives can rebuke him
nor disobey him, when he urges and stirs another man to action." 130

   So speaking he put a tunic about him,
and beneath his smooth feet he bound his splendid sandals,
then he buckled round himself a cloak of crimson,
with sweeping double folds, flushed with thick wool.
He took up his sturdy spear pointed with sharp bronze,
and set out to go among the ships of the bronze-clad Achaeans.

   Then first it was Odysseus, like Zeus in wiles,
whom Nestor, the Gerenian horseman, roused from sleep
calling aloud; and the sound of his voice swept around Odysseus'
 sleeping spirit,
and he came out of his shelter and cried to them: 140
"Why do you wander thus, alone among the ships and army
through the ambrosial night—what need so great has come upon you?"

   Then answered him the Gerenian horseman Nestor:
"Zeus-descended son of Laertes, Odysseus of many stratagems,
do not be angry; for such distress assails the Achaeans.
Come with us to rouse yet another man, who should rightly

join our counsel, as to whether we flee, or fight."

So he spoke; and going into his shelter resourceful Odysseus
threw over his shoulders his patterned shield, and set out with them.
They made their way to Diomedes son of Tydeus; and found him   150
outside his shelter with his weapons; around him his companions
slept, their shields beneath their heads; their spears
had been driven upright on their butt-ends in the ground, and far into the
    distance their bronze heads
flashed like Zeus the father's lightning. But the warrior himself
slept, the hide of a field ox spread beneath him,
and under his head was laid a lustrous blanket.
Approaching, the Gerenian horseman Nestor roused him up,
shaking him with his foot, and urged and rebuked him to his face:
"Rise up, son of Tydeus; why do you slumber in night-long sleep?
Have you not seen the Trojans, encamped on the rise of the plain,   160
close by the ships, and little land yet separates them?"

So he spoke; and Diomedes abruptly rose from sleep,
and raising his voice addressed Nestor with winged words:
"You are hard, old man; you never give over your toil.
Are there not other sons of the Achaeans, younger men,
then, who could wake each leader
ranging back and forth in all directions? You are impossible, old man."

Then in turn the Gerenian horseman Nestor addressed him:
"Yes, all such things, my boy, you rightly state;
I have blameless sons, I have my people,   170
many of them, any one of whom might go around and make the
    summons.
But great indeed is the need that assails the Achaeans.
For now, for all of us, it stands upon the razor's edge
whether there will be abject destruction for the Achaeans, or life.
Come now, rouse swift Ajax and the son of Phyleus,
if you truly pity me, since you are younger."

So he spoke; and the other put about his shoulders the skin

of a gleaming huge lion that reached to his feet, took up his spear,
and set out; and having roused his men from sleep the warrior led them
   forth.
         And when they joined with the assembled guards,   180
they did not find the watch commanders sleeping,
but all were sitting on alert with their weapons.
As dogs keep painful lookout around their flocks in the fold
when they hear a bold and fearless beast, who goes down through the
   woods
across the mountains, and much tumult of men and dogs
accompanies it, and sleep is banished from them,
so the grace of sleep was banished from their eyes
as they kept watch throughout the baneful night; for always
they were turned toward the plain, waiting to hear the Trojans coming.
And seeing them the old man rejoiced and encouraged them with
   a word
and lifting his voice he addressed them with winged words: 190
"In this way now, dear boys, continue your watch, nor let sleep
catch any man, that we not become a source of joy to our enemies."
         So speaking he passed swiftly through the trench; and with him
   followed
the Argive leaders, those who had been summoned to the council.
With them went Meriones and the splendid son of Nestor;
for the leaders themselves had called them to join in the council.
When they had gone across the trench that had been dug, they
   were seated
in a clear space, where the ground showed through the bodies
that had fallen, the place from where mighty Hector had turned back   200
from killing Argives, when night closed around him.
There they sat and spoke plain words to one another.
         And to them the Gerenian horseman Nestor began to speak:
"O friends, is there not some man who, trusting in his own
enduring courage, would go among the great-hearted Trojans,

in the hope that he might with luck catch some enemy straggler,

he might with luck even hear of any talk among the Trojans,

whatever they deliberate among themselves, whether they intend

to remain afield here by the ships, or withdraw

back to their city, since they have defeated the Achaeans?   210

He could learn all such things and could come back to us

unharmed; great would be his glory under heaven

among all mankind, and his reward would be outstanding.

For as many nobles as hold sway among the ships,

each one of these will give him a black sheep,

a female with young beneath her; no possession vies with it—

he will ever be included in the feasts and festivals."

       So he spoke, and all the men were hushed in silence.

Then Diomedes of the war cry spoke among them:

"Nestor, my heart and my strong spirit urge me   220

to make my way into the host of enemy men nearby,

into the Trojans; but I would that some other man came with me,

it would be more heartening and give more confidence—

with two going out together one notices before the other

where advantage lies; a man alone, even if he is observant,

all the same his mind has shorter reach, and his judgement is narrow."

       So he spoke, and many were willing to accompany Diomedes.

The two Aiantes were willing, henchmen of Ares,

Meriones was willing, and the son of Nestor was very willing,

and Atreus' son spear-famed Menelaos was willing,   230

and enduring Odysseus was willing to enter in the throng

of Trojans, for the spirit in his breast was ever bold with resolve.

      And these Agamemnon lord of men addressed:

"Son of Tydeus, Diomedes, delighting my heart,

you will choose as companion whom you wish,

the best of those who have declared themselves, since many are ready.

But do not out of feelings of respect leave behind

the better man, and take the lesser with you, yielding to decorum,

looking to his birth, not even if he is more kingly."
So he spoke, and was afraid for fair-haired Menelaos.   240
And in turn Diomedes of the war cry addressed them:
"If you bid me choose my own companion,
how could I, then, not think of godlike Odysseus,
whose heart is so very willing and whose spirit is strong
in every kind of labour, and whom Pallas Athena loves?
With this one along, even out of blazing fire
we two would return, since beyond others he knows how to use his wits."
Then in turn, much enduring godlike Odysseus addressed him:
"Son of Tydeus, there is no more need of praise than of blame,
for you speak among Argives who know these things.   250
Come, let us go; for the night draws to an end, and dawn is near.
The stars have advanced in their course, and the greater part of night has
    passed—
two of the watches—but the third watch still is left."
            So speaking the two stepped into their dread armour.
And to the son of Tydeus steadfast Thrasymedes gave
a double-edged sword (his own was left beside his ship)
and shield; and round Diomedes' head he placed his bull-hide
helmet, without ridge or plume, which is called a
skull cap, and guards the head of hot-blooded young men.
And to Odysseus Meriones gave quiver, bow   260
and sword; and round his head he placed his helmet
made of hide, stretched tight inside with many
thongs, while outside the white-shining teeth
of a bright-tusked boar ran close-set round and round
well and skilfully applied, and felt was fitted in the centre;
this in time before Autolykos had carried out of Eleon,
after breaking into the snug house of Amyntor son of Ormenos,
and Autolykos then gave it to Amphidamas of Cythera to take to Skandeia,
and Amphidamas gave it to Molos as a guest-gift,
and he gave it to his son Meriones to carry with him.   270

And now it was put around and protected Odysseus' head.

      Then the two stepped into their dread armour,
and went their way, and left behind there all the other nobles.
And to them, on the right hand near the path,
Pallas Athena sent a night heron; they did not see it with their eyes
through the murk of night, but heard its ringing cry.
And Odysseus rejoiced in the bird sign, and made prayer to Athena:
"Hear me, daughter of Zeus who wields the aegis, who ever
is my aid in all adversity, nor do I escape your notice
as I set out; now again especially be my friend, Athena,   280
and grant that we come back in honour to the ships,
having performed a great deed, which will be trouble for the Trojans."
Then after him prayed Diomedes of the war cry:
"Hear me now also, child of Zeus, Weariless One,
accompany me as when you accompanied my father godlike Tydeus
into Thebes, when he was going as messenger on behalf of the
    Achaeans,
the bronze-clad Achaeans whom he left at the river Asopos,
and carried conciliatory words for the Cadmeians
thither; but going back he devised dark deeds
with you, goddess of Zeus, since in solicitude you supported him.   290
So now be willing to stand by and protect me;
to you in return I will sacrifice a broad-browed yearling heifer,
unbroken, which no man has ever led beneath the yoke;
this I will sacrifice to you, after sheathing its horns with gold."
Thus they spoke praying, and Pallas Athena heard them.

      And when they had made prayer to the daughter of great Zeus,
they set out like two lions into the black night,
through the carnage, through the corpses, through the war-gear and dark
    blood.

      But nor did Hector allow the high-hearted Trojans
to sleep either, but he summoned in a body all the nobles,   300

those who were leaders and counsellors of the Trojans.
Having called these all together, he laid out his shrewd plan:
"What man would undertake this work for me and bring it to fulfilment
for a great reward? The return to him will be certain;
for I will give him a chariot and two high-necked horses,
whichever are best by the swift ships of the Achaeans,
whoever dares this—and he will win himself glory—
to go close to the fast-running ships and find out
whether the swift ships are guarded, as before,
or now broken under our hands   310
they are making plans among themselves for flight, and are not minded
to stand guard the night, worn out with fatigue beyond endurance."
So he spoke; and all the men were hushed in silence.

   Now there was among the Trojans a certain Dolon, the son of
  Eumedes—
a sacred herald, a man of much gold and much bronze—
who was, to be sure, mean in appearance, but swift of foot;
and he was the only son among five sisters.
He it was who then made speech to Hector and the Trojans:
"Hector, my heart and my strong spirit urge me
to go close to the fast-running ships and find this out;   320
but come, and hold up this sceptre for me and swear to me,
that you will give me the horses and the chariot wrought with bronze
that carry the blameless son of Peleus.
I will be no idle scout for you, nor short of expectation;
for I am going to their army, right through until I come
to Agamemnon's ship, where I think the nobles likely
are taking counsel, whether to flee or whether to fight."

   So he spoke, and Hector took the sceptre in his hand and swore
  an oath to him:
"Let Zeus himself now be witness, Hera's far-thundering husband;
on these horses no other man of all the Trojans will be carried,   330

but you, I say, will forever glory in them."
So he spoke, and swore an empty oath, and urged the other on.
At once Dolon cast across his shoulders his curved bow,
and put about him as an outer cover a grey wolfhide,
and on his head a cap of weasel skin, and took his sharp throwing-spear.
He set out toward the ships from his army; nor was he destined
to come back from the ships and bring report to Hector.

But when at last he left behind the throng of horses and men,
he went along the way eagerly; and as he came Zeus-descended
Odysseus marked him, and spoke to Diomedes: 340
"Here is some man, Diomedes, who comes from the army,
I do not know whether he is a spy on our ships,
or is stripping one of the corpses of those who died.
But let us allow him first to pass by us out upon the plain
a little way, then rushing at him we could grab him
quickly. And if he should get ahead of us with speed of feet,
keep driving him toward the ships away from his army,
rushing at him with your spear, that he not somehow escape to the city."

Having so spoken, the two lay down off the path
among the corpses; and the other ran swiftly by in heedlessness.   350
And when he was as far away as the width of a day's ploughing
by mules—for they are better than oxen
in dragging a wrought plough through the deep fallow land—
the two men ran at him, and hearing the thud of their feet he came to
    a halt;
for in his heart he hoped that comrades were coming
from the Trojans to turn him back, Hector having summoned him again.
But when then they were as far as the cast of a spear, or even less,
he saw that they were enemy men, and made his swift knees move
to flee; and at once they made a rush to chase him.
As when two jagged-toothed dogs spy their quarry,   360
pressing hard upon a fawn or hare without respite
all through the wooded country, and it flees crying before them,

so did the son of Tydeus and Odysseus sacker of cities
make pursuit, continuously cutting Dolon from his people.

       But when he was about to reach the watch posts
as he fled toward the ships, then Athena cast strength in
Tydeus' son, so that no bronze-clad Achaean
should boast that he struck Dolon first, and Diomedes come second
    place.
And rushing toward him with his spear, powerful Diomedes addressed
    him:
"Stay, or I shall catch you with my spear; nor do I think that you   370
will long ward off your sheer destruction under my hand."
He spoke, and let fly his spear, but missed the man on purpose,
and flying over his right shoulder the point of the well-honed shaft
fixed in the ground. And Dolon stopped in terror
jabbering—the clattering of teeth came from his mouth—
green with fear. And the two men, breathing hard, caught up,
and seized him with their hands; and in tears he spoke a word:
"Take me alive, and I will redeem myself; for in my home is
bronze and gold and well-worked iron,
and from this my father would freely give you untold ransom,   380
were he to learn that I was alive by the ships of the Achaeans."
Then in answer spoke resourceful Odysseus:
"Take courage, let no thought of death be on your heart.
But come tell me this and explain exactly;
where do you go alone like this towards the ships from your army
through the murk of night, when other mortal men are sleeping?
Are you stripping one of the corpses of those who died,
or did Hector send you to spy out everything
by our hollow ships, or did your own spirit urge you?"
Then Dolon answered him, and his limbs shook beneath him: 390
"With many delusions, beyond sense, Hector led me on,
who promised to give me the single-hoofed horses of the glorious son of
    Peleus

and his chariot wrought with bronze,
and urged me to make my way through the fast-moving black night
and go close to the enemy men and find out
whether the swift ships are guarded, as before,
or now broken under our hands
you are making plans among yourselves for flight, and are not minded
to stand guard the night, worn out with fatigue beyond endurance."
      Then smiling at him resourceful Odysseus addressed him: 400
"Surely now it is on big rewards your heart was set,
the horses of brilliant Aeacides! They are difficult
for mortal men to control and drive,
for any other man than Achilles, whom an immortal mother bore.
But come, tell me this and explain exactly;
where now, when you came here, did you leave Hector shepherd of the
    people?
Where does his war-gear lie, where are his horses?
And of the other Trojans, how stand the guards and sleepers?
What do they deliberate among themselves? Do they intend
to remain afield here by the ships, or withdraw   410
back to their city, since they have defeated the Achaeans?"
      Then again Dolon the son of Eumedes addressed him:
"So, I will state these things to you very exactly.
Hector is with all those who are counsellors,
he holds council by the tomb of godlike Ilos,
away from the clamour; the guards you ask of, sir,
none have been detailed to protect nor guard the army.
As many as have hearths at Troy, those on whom there is necessity,
they keep themselves awake and exhort one another
to stay on guard; but as for our far-flung allies,   420
they sleep; for they leave it to the Trojans to watch over them;
for their children do not lie near by, nor their wives."
      Then in turn resourceful Odysseus addressed him:

"Yes, but how do they sleep—mixed with the horse-breaking Trojans
or apart? Tell me in detail, so that I may know."
And then answered him Dolon son of Eumedes:
"So, I will go through these things too very accurately.
On the side toward the sea are the Carians and Paeonians armed with
    curved bows,
and the Leleges and Kaukones and illustrious Pelasgians.
The side toward Thymbre fell to the Lycians and noble Mysians   430
and horse-breaking Phrygians and the Maeonians, masters of the chariot.
But why do you interrogate me about each of these things?
For if you two desire to make your way into the host of Trojans,
over there are the Thracians, newly arrived and on their own, on the
    outskirts of everyone;
and in the middle is Rhesos the king, son of Eïoneus.
His are the most beautiful horses I have beheld and the most
    magnificent;
they are whiter than snow, they run like the wind.
His chariot is finely wrought with silver and with gold;
he came bearing golden armour, astounding,
a wonder to behold; this is not like anything for mortal   440
men to wear, but is something rather for the deathless gods.
But now then, take me to the fast-running ships,
or leave me here, tied in hard bonds,
so that you can go on your way and make trial of me,
as to whether I informed you correctly, or did not."
       Then looking from beneath his brows powerful Diomedes
    addressed him:
"Do not before me, Dolon, make dreams of escape,
excellent though your news be, seeing that you have come into our hands.
For if we were to release you now, or let you go,
you would surely come again another time to the swift ships of the
    Achaeans,   450

either spying about or fighting against us;
but if you should lose your life killed beneath my hands,
then you will never be a cause of pain to the Argives."
He spoke, and the other was about to supplicate him,
to grasp his chin with his stout hand, but Diomedes struck the middle of
    his neck,
flashing out with his sword, and cut through both tendons,
and the head of the man as he was speaking was jumbled in the dust.
Then they took from his head the cap of weasel skin,
and his wolfhide and back-curved bow and his long spear.
And these to Athena of the Spoils godlike Odysseus   460
held high in his hand and spoke a word in prayer:
"Rejoice, goddess, in these things; for upon you first of all the immortals
on Olympus we will call for aid; and even as before
conduct us to the horses and sleeping places of the Thracian men."
Thus he spoke, and lifting the spoils high, away from him,
he placed them upon a tamarisk tree, and made a plain sign upon it,
bundling reeds and luxuriant boughs of the tamarisk,
so that it would not escape their notice as they returned through the
    fast-moving black night.
And the two men made their way forward through the war-gear and
    dark blood,
and going onward they soon found themselves at the Thracian
    camp.   470
The men were sleeping, worn out with exhaustion, their splendid
    war-gear
lying well ordered beside them on the ground,
in three rows; and beside each man stood a pair of horses.
Rhesos slept in the middle, and beside him his swift horses
were tethered by reins to the outer chariot rail.
As first to see him, Odysseus signed to Diomedes:
"This is the man, Diomedes, and these to be sure are the horses
that Dolon described to us, Dolon whom we killed.

But come, and show your great strength; there is no need for you
to stand by idly with your weapons—come, release the horses;   480
or you kill the men, and the horses will be my care."

      So he spoke; and gleaming-eyed Athena breathed strength into
   Diomedes,
and he began to kill, turning this side and that; and abject groaning rose
   from the men
struck by his sword, and the ground was made red with blood.
As a lion advances on unguarded flocks,
goats or sheep, leaping on them with evil intent,
so the son of Tydeus ranged among the Thracians,
until he had slain twelve men; and whomever the son of Tydeus stood
   over
and struck with his sword, that man would resourceful Odysseus
drag out of the way, taking hold of his foot from behind,   490
thinking to himself that now the horses with their fine manes
might easily pass through, and their hearts not shake with fear
as they trod upon the dead, unused as they still were to such things.
But when the son of Tydeus came upon the king,
the thirteenth man, he robbed him of his honey-sweet life
as he lay breathing heavily; for an evil dream stood by his head
that night—Diomedes, seed of Oineus, through the contrivance of Athena.

      And all the while steadfast Odysseus untied the single-hoofed
   horses,
and roped them together with their reins and drove them from the mass
   of men,
striking them with his bow, since he had not thought to take   500
the shining whip in his hands from the elaborate chariot.
Then he whistled, signaling to godlike Diomedes;
but Diomedes lingered, weighing in his mind the most shaming thing
   that he could do—
whether to seize the chariot, where the elaborate armour lay,
pulling it by the pole or lifting up and carrying it away,

or whether he should take the life of still more Thracians.
As he was turning these things in his mind, Athena
drew up near him and spoke to godlike Diomedes:
"Think now of returning, son of great-hearted Tydeus,
to the hollow ships, lest you return in full flight;   510
and lest by chance some other god awake the Trojans."
So she spoke; and he recognised the voice of the goddess speaking,
and swiftly mounted the horses, and Odysseus smote them
with his bow; and they flew toward the swift ships of the Achaeans.

      But Apollo of the silver bow did not keep blind watch,
when he saw Athena attending the son of Tydeus.
Raging at her, he descended into the great host of Trojans,
and aroused Hippokoön, a leading counsellor of the Thracians,
and noble kin of Rhesos; starting up from sleep,
when he saw the empty space, where the swift horses had stood,   520
and the men gasping amid the brutal carnage,
he cried out and called by name his beloved companion.
Clamour and unbounded uproar rose from the Trojans,
who came running as one; and they in amazement looked on the
    harrowing deeds,
all that was done by the men who were now on their way to the hollow
    ships.

      And when they arrived at the place where they had slain Hector's
    spy,
there Odysseus beloved of Zeus held the swift horses,
and the son of Tydeus leaping to the ground placed the bloody war-spoils
in the hands of Odysseus, and mounted the horses,
and put whip to them, and they two not unwilling flew on   520
to the hollow ships; for there their hearts tended.

      And Nestor was first to hear their thunder and spoke out:
"O friends, leaders and protectors of the Argives,
shall I be wrong or right in what I shall say? My heart directs me.
The thunder of swift-footed horses pounds my ears.

Would that Odysseus and powerful Diomedes were even now
driving here single-hoofed horses from the Trojans—
but dreadfully I fear in my heart lest they have met some misfortune,
these best of Argives, from the mob of Trojans."
He had not yet spoken all he was saying, when the men themselves
    arrived;   540
and they descended to the ground, and rejoicing the others
greeted them with clasped hands and warm words.

        And first to make inquiry was the Gerenian horseman Nestor:
"Come, tell me, O illustrious Odysseus, great pride of the Achaeans,
how you got hold of these horses; by making your way into the throng
of Trojans, or did some god you fell in with present them to you?
Like rays of the sun are they!
I am always encountering the Trojans, nor, I say, am I one
to loiter by the ships, old warrior though I am,
but I have never seen nor imagined such horses.   550
I suspect some god you encountered gave them to you;
For Zeus who gathers the clouds loves you both,
and the daughter of Zeus who wields the aegis, gleaming-eyed Athena."
Then answering him resourceful Odysseus addressed him:
"O Nestor, son of Neleus, great pride of the Achaeans,
easily could a god if he so wished give even better
horses than these, since the gods are far mightier than men.
But these horses, old sir, of which you speak, are newly arrived
from Thrace; their master brave Diomedes
killed, and twelve comrades beside him, nobles all.   560
The thirteenth was a scout we captured by the ships,
who was dispatched to spy upon our army
by Hector and the other noble Trojans."

        So speaking he drove the single-hoofed horses across the ditch
laughing gleefully; and with him went the other Achaeans rejoicing.
And when they arrived at the well-made shelter of Tydeus' son,
they secured the horses with fine-cut leather thongs

to the horse manger, where Diomedes' own swift-footed horses
stood, munching wheat sweet as honey.
And on his ship's stern Odysseus laid Dolon's bloodstained war-gear,   570
until they could prepare their dedication to Athena.
They themselves wading into the sea washed away the copious sweat
from their shins and neck and thighs.
And when the sea's swell had washed the dense sweat
from their skin and their very spirits were refreshed,
then stepping into well-polished baths they bathed;
and when both had been bathed and anointed luxuriantly with oil
they sat down to a feast, and drawing from the full mixing bowl
they poured libation of honey-sweet wine to Athena.

Dawn from her bed arose by the side of good Tithonos,
to bring light of day to deathless gods and mortal men,
and to the swift ships of the Achaeans Zeus sent Strife forth,
the baneful one, who carried in her hands the monstrous battle emblem.
She took her stand upon Odysseus' dark, great-bellied ship,
which was in the middle so as to call in both directions—
to the shelters of Telamonian Ajax,
and to those of Achilles, for these had drawn their balanced ships
at the ends of the line, confident in their might of hands and manly
 prowess;
standing there, the goddess shrieked her great and terrible cry,   10
and flung great strength in each Achaean's
heart, to fight on without respite and to do battle;
and suddenly war became more sweet to them than going home
in hollow ships to their beloved fatherland.

      And the son of Atreus cried aloud and bade the Argives
gird for action; and he himself put on his glittering bronze among them.
First he strapped the splendid greaves around his shins,
fitted with silver bindings around his ankles;
next he girt about his chest a breastplate,
which in time before Kinyras gave him to be a guest-gift,   20
for the great rumour had been heard in Cyprus that the Achaeans
were about to sail out in their ships to Troy;
for this reason Kinyras gave it to him, seeking favour with the king.

And on it were ten bands of dark enamelled blue,
twelve of gold and twenty bands of tin;
snakes of blue enamel reared toward his throat,
three on either side, like bands of a rainbow that the son of Cronus
has propped upon a cloud, a portent in the eyes of mortal men.
And over his shoulders he slung his sword; and on it glittered
studs of gold, and the scabbard round was   30
silver, fitted with straps of gold.
Then he took up his man-surrounding, much-emblazoned forceful shield,
a thing of beauty, around which ran ten rings of bronze,
and on it twenty pale-shining discs of tin,
and in the very centre was one of dark enamelled blue.
And crowning this the grim-faced Gorgon
stared out with dreadful glare, Terror and Rout about her;
and the shield's baldric was of silver, and on it
a blue-dark serpent writhed, with three heads
turned in all directions, growing from a single neck.   40
Then on his head he placed his helmet, ridged on both sides, with four
    bosses,
plumed with horsehair; and the crest nodded terribly above.
He took two strong spears, tipped in bronze,
and sharp; and the bronze flashed far from him into heaven;
and in response Hera and Athena thundered,
giving honour to the king of gold-great Mycenae.

       Then each man gave orders to his charioteer
to draw his horses up in good array there at the ditch,
and the men themselves on foot and armed with weapons
hurried forward; a quenchless cry of battle rose before the face of
    morning;   50
they marshalled well ahead of the horsemen at the ditch,
but the horsemen followed closely. And the son of Cronus
brought evil tumult on them, and down from on high out of clear air
he rained drops that dripped with blood, since he was about

to hurl many a strong man to Hades.

       The Trojans there on the other side, where the plain rose,
were marshalled about great Hector and blameless Poulydamas
and Aeneas, who was honoured like a god by the Trojans in their land,
and three sons of Antenor, Polybos and shining Agenor
and youthful Akamas, like to the immortal gods.   60
And Hector bore the circle of his shield among the front ranks;
as Aulios, the shining star of shepherds, appears from clouds,
then ducks again into the clouded shadows,
so Hector would appear now among the front ranks,
and now urging on the rear; and all in bronze
he shone like a lightning bolt of father Zeus who wields the aegis.

       And the men, like reapers who face each other
as they work their lines down a rich man's field
of wheat or barley, and the swathes fall and fall in succession,
so the Trojans and Achaeans, surging toward each other,   70
cut their enemy down, nor did either have thought of disastrous flight,
but head to head the combat gripped them; they lunged like wolves;
and Strife who causes groaning sorrow rejoiced as she looked on,
for she alone of gods was present at their fighting,
the other gods were not there with her, but uninvolved
sat idly in their own homes, where for each
beautiful houses had been built along the folds of Olympus;
and all gave blame to the dark-clouded son of Cronus,
because he planned to make a gift of glory to the Trojans.
But the father had no regard for them; and having slipped away at a
   distance from   80
the others, he sat apart exulting in his glory,
looking down upon the city of the Trojans and the ships of the Achaeans
and the flash of bronze and on men killing and men being killed.
As long as it was dawn and the heaven-sent day was rising,
so long the missiles of both sides reached their marks, and the people fell;
but at the time when a woodcutting man prepares his morning meal

in the wooded hollows of a mountain, when his arms have grown weary
from felling great trees, and his heart is filled with weariness,
and the longing for food and its pleasure grips him round his senses,
then did the Danaans in their valour smash through the lines,   90
calling to each other across the ranks. And Agamemnon,
first to rush into their midst, killed a man, Bienor shepherd of his people,
and then his companion Oïleus, driver of horses.
For, leaping from the chariot, he had stood to face him,
but Agamemnon struck him in the face, as he charged straight for him
    with his sharp spear;
and his helmet did not hold off the bronze-weighted spear,
but through it and through bone it went, and the brains
were all spattered within it; so Agamemnon beat him down for all his fury.
            And Agamemnon lord of men left them there,
their bare chests gleaming, since he had stripped the tunics round them,   100
and he went to kill and strip Isos and Antiphos,
two sons of Priam, bastard and lawful son both
in one chariot; the bastard was charioteer,
and illustrious Antiphos in his turn was the chariot fighter; these two
    Achilles,
in the foothills of Ida, once bound with willow shoots
after seizing them as they shepherded their sheep, but he released them
    for ransom;
but now this time Atreus's son wide-ruling Agamemnon,
struck the one with his spear on the chest above his breast,
and smote Antiphos with his sword beside his ear, and sent him flying
    from his chariot.
And with no loss of time he stripped them of their splendid armour,   110
recognising them; for he had seen them that time before, beside the fast
    ships,
when swift-footed Achilles had led them down from Ida.
And as a lion easily rips to shreds the tender offspring of a swift deer,
taking hold of them with its powerful teeth,

coming into their place of hiding, and strips from them their tender life;

and the mother even should she be close by is not able to defend them,

for a dreadful trembling comes upon even her,

and with all speed she flies through dense thickets and the woods,

striving, sweating before the onslaught of the powerful beast;

so then no one of the Trojans was able to ward off destruction   120

from them, but they too were fleeing before the Argives.

      Then Agamemnon slew Peisandros and battle-steady Hippolochos,

sons of skilled Antimachos, who expectant of gold,

of splendid gifts, from Alexandros,

loudly spoke against handing Helen to fair-haired Menelaos—

now his two sons it was lord Agamemnon slew

as they were in a single chariot; together they were trying to hold their swift horses;

for the shining reins had slipped their hands,

and the horses were thrown into panic. And like a lion the son of Atreus

sprang to face them; and they two from the chariot made supplication: 130

"Take us alive, son of Atreus, take the worthy ransom!

Many valuables lie in the house of Antimachos,

bronze and gold and iron wrought with labour;

from these our father would satisfy you with priceless ransom,

were he to know that we two were alive by the ships of the Achaeans."

So weeping they addressed the king

with placating words; but the voice they heard was implacable:

"If indeed you are sons of skilled Antimachos,

who once in assembly of the Trojans urged them to kill Menelaos,

who had come as ambassador with godlike Odysseus,   140

on the spot, nor let him go back to the Achaeans,

you now will pay for your father's indecent outrage."

He spoke, and shoved Peisandros from his chariot to the ground

with a spear stroke to the chest; and he was thrust on his back to the bare
    earth;
Hippolochos sprang down; but Agamemnon slew him on the ground,
smiting away his hands with his sword and cleaving off his neck;
then like a log sent him rolling through the throng.
He left them, and where the most battle ranks were roiled,
there he charged, along with the other strong-greaved Achaeans.
And soldiers on foot killed those compelled to flee on foot,   150
and horsemen killed horsemen—dust rose beneath them
from the plain, which the far-thundering feet of the horses raised—
cutting them down with bronze. But powerful Agamemnon,
killing always, followed with the Argives, urging them on.
As when obliterating fire falls on a thick-wooded forest,
and the wind carries it barrelling along in every direction, and the small
    trees
fall uprooted, assailed by the blast of fire,
so then at the hands of Atreus' son Agamemnon the heads fell
of fleeing Trojans; and many high-necked horses
rattled empty chariots after them between the lines of battle,   160
at a loss without their blameless charioteers; for they upon the earth
were lying, far dearer to the vultures than to their wives.
But Zeus led Hector out from under the flying shafts and dust,
out of the man-slaughtering and the blood and out of the throng of battle;
and the son of Atreus followed, strenuously urging the Danaans.
       Past the tomb of Ilos, son of Dardanos long ago,
right across the plain, past the wild fig tree, the Trojans sped
intent on getting to the city; but he, the son of Atreus, screaming,
    followed always,
and his invincible hands were spattered with gore.
And when they reached the Scaean gates and oak tree,   170
there both sides stood their ground and awaited each the other.
And those Trojans who still fled across the open plain like cattle
that a lion scatters coming in the milky murk of night,

all of them, but on one alone there comes her sheer destruction—
her neck he shatters utterly taking her in his powerful teeth
first, then her blood and entrails he devours entirely;
so the son of Atreus lord Agamemnon drove the Trojans before him,
killing always the hindmost man; and they fled.
And face down and on their backs they were hurled in numbers from
     their chariots
at the hands of Atreus' son; for he raged ever onward with his spear.   180

          But when he was about to reach the sheer city and its wall,
then it was that the father of men and gods
coming down from heaven, seated himself on the peaks of Ida
with its many springs; and in his hands he held his lightning bolt.
And he summoned Iris of the golden wings to take a message:
"Come here, swift Iris, tell this word to Hector;
so long as he sees Agamemnon shepherd of the people
running in the front lines, killing ranks of men,
so long let him draw back, and urge the rest of his people
to engage the enemy throughout the mighty combat;   190
but when, struck by a spear or wounded by an arrow,
Agamemnon leaps into his chariot, then to Hector will be handed the power
to kill, until that time he arrives at the well-benched ships
and the sun goes down and night's holy shadow comes upon him."

          So he spoke, and swift Iris with feet like the wind did not
     disobey,
and went down from the peaks of Ida into sacred Ilion.
She found the son of wise Priam, shining Hector,
standing amid his horses and bolted chariots,
and standing close, Iris of the swift feet addressed him:
"Hector, son of Priam, Zeus' match in counsel,   200
Zeus the father sent me to speak these words to you:
as long as you see Agamemnon shepherd of the people
running in the front lines, killing ranks of men,
so long you must withdraw from battle, and urge the rest of your people

to engage the enemy throughout the mighty combat;
but when, struck by a spear or wounded by an arrow,
Agamemnon leaps into his chariot, then to you will be handed the power
to kill, until that time you arrive at the well-benched ships
and the sun goes down and night's holy shadow comes upon you."
Then having so spoken, Iris of the swift feet departed,   210
and Hector sprang from his chariot in his armour to the ground,
and brandishing his sharp spears he made his way to every place
    throughout the army,
rallying the men to fight, and he stirred up the dread battle.
They wheeled around and stood facing the Achaeans;
on the other side the Argives pulled their ranks together,
and the battle was prepared, and face to face they took their stand; and in
    their midst Agamemnon
was first to attack, since he desired to advance far beyond all others.
        Tell me now Muses, who have your homes on Olympus
what man came first against Agamemnon
of either Trojans, or their famous allies.   220
Iphidamas the great and good son of Antenor,
who was raised in Thrace where the soil is rich, the mother of flocks.
Kisseus raised him in his house when he was a child,
the father of his mother Theano of the lovely cheeks;
and when he achieved the measure of glorious young manhood,
then Kisseus tried to detain him, making offer to him of his own
    daughter;
But once wed he set out from the marriage chamber following the news
    of the Achaeans
with twelve curved ships that accompanied him.
These balanced ships he then left in Percote,
and going on foot he came to Ilion;   230
then it was he came face to face with Agamemnon son of Atreus.
When they both had advanced almost upon each other,
the son of Atreus missed his throw, and his spear was turned aside;

then Iphidamas struck his blow down across the belt beneath
   Agamemnon's breast plate
and put his strength behind it, trusting his mighty hand;
he did not pierce the shimmering war-belt, but long before
the spear-point, as it met the silver, was bent back like lead.
And seizing the spear in his hand, wide-ruling Agamemnon
drew it toward him like a lion in fury, then from the hand of the other
wrenched it, and with his sword struck him on the neck, and unstrung
   his limbs.   240
And so falling there Iphidamas took his rest in brazen sleep,
poor wretch, far from his wedded wife, aiding his countrymen,
far from his lawful bride, and had known no delight from her; although
   he had given much for her;
he had given first a hundred cattle, and promised a thousand
goats and sheep alike, which in countless number roamed his pastures.
But before that time Agamemnon son of Atreus killed and stripped him,
and departed through the throng of Achaeans bearing his splendid armour.
      Now when Koön, outstanding of men, saw him,
he the eldest born of Antenor, overwhelming grief
for his fallen brother shrouded his eyes;   250
he took a stand on one side with his spear unobserved by shining
   Agamemnon,
and struck him down across the middle of his arm below the elbow,
and the point of the gleaming spear passed right through.
Then the lord of men Agamemnon shuddered,
but even so did not relinquish the battle and the fighting,
but gripping his spear of wind-strengthened wood, he rushed at Koön.
Koön was trying to drag his brother Iphidamas, born of the same father,
by the foot, and was calling to all the leading men;
and as he was dragging him through the battle throng, Agamemnon
   struck him
with his honed bronze-headed spear, under Koön's bossed shield, and
   unstrung his limbs,   260

and coming close, struck off his head on the body of his brother.
There the sons of Antenor at the hand of the kingly son of Atreus,
fulfilling their destiny, sank into the house of Hades.

　　　　　But Agamemnon ranged around the ranks of other men
with his spear and sword and massive rocks for throwing,
while the blood welled still warm from his wound;
but when the wound began to dry, and the blood was stopped,
sharp pains entered the son of Atreus' spirit.
As when a sharp arrow of pain strikes a woman in the agony of childbirth,
piercing pain, which the spirits attending birth-pain send,   270
daughters of Hera, who hold the bitter pangs of birth,
so sharp pain entered the son of Atreus' spirit.
He started up into his chariot, and to the charioteer gave orders
to drive to the hollow ships; for he felt heavy of heart.
But he cried out in a piercing voice so as to be heard by the Danaans:
"O friends, leaders and counsellors of the Argives,
it is you now who must defend our seagoing ships
from disastrous battle, since all-devising Zeus has not allowed me
to war with Trojans the whole day long."
So he spoke; and the charioteer lashed the beautiful-maned horses   280
toward the hollow ships, and they two not unwilling flew on.
Their chests were covered with foam, and they were spattered with dust
　　　below,
as they bore the stricken king away from battle.

　　　　　And as Hector saw Agamemnon departing,
he called to the Trojans and Lycians, shouting in a voice that carried far:
"Trojans and Lycians and Dardanian spearmen,
be men, my friends, and recollect your fierce courage.
Their best man has gone, and to me Zeus the son of Cronus has given
a great triumph. Come, drive your single-hoofed horses straight
for the strong Danaans, so that you may seize a victorious triumph."   290
So speaking he incited the strength and spirit of every man.

As when some hunter lets loose his gleaming-toothed dogs
upon a wild boar or lion,
so Hector the son of Priam, like to man-destroying Ares,
let loose the great-hearted Trojans upon the Achaeans.
And he himself, with high resolve, was moving among the front fighters,
and he fell upon the fray like a whirling storm wind,
which rushing downward churns the dark-faced ocean.

      Then who was the first and who the last he killed,
Hector son of Priam, when Zeus granted glory to him?   300
Asaios was first, and Autonoös and Opites
and Dolops the son of Klytos and Opheltios and Agelaos
and Aisymnos and Oros and Hipponoös steadfast in battle.
He killed these Danaan leaders, and then
turned on the masses, as when the West Wind drives shining clouds
that the South Wind carried, battering them in a towering storm,
and wave after swollen wave is rolled before it, and the foam
is scattered high by the blast of veering wind;
so the massed ranks of men were routed by Hector.

      Then there would have been ruin and deeds without remedy,   310
and the fleeing Achaeans would surely have fallen into their own ships,
had not Odysseus called out to Diomedes the son of Tydeus:
"Son of Tydeus, what has happened that we have forgotten our fierce
    courage?
But come here, old friend, and take your stand by me; for it will
be disgrace if Hector of the shimmering helm should take the ships."
Then in turn powerful Diomedes addressed him:
"To be sure I will stand my ground and keep my spirits; but only for a
    little while
will we have profit of this, since Zeus who gathers the clouds
chooses to give victory to the Trojans, rather than to us."
He spoke, and thrust Thymbraios from the chariot to the ground,   320
striking with his spear down through the left breast; and Odysseus

killed Molion, the godlike henchman of his lord.
Then they left them where they were, since they had stopped their
     fighting;
and setting out the two made havoc through the battle throng, as when
     two boars
fall on hunting dogs, in their high confidence.
So rousing themselves again they slew the Trojans; and the Achaeans
gratefully caught their breath, after taking flight from Hector.

          Then they seized a chariot and slew two of the best men in the
     country,
the two sons of Merops from Percote, who beyond all men
was skilled in divination, and kept trying to dissuade his sons   330
from going to man-destroying war; but they did not
heed him; for the spirits of dark death were leading them on.
After depriving them of life and spirit, Diomedes the spear-famed
son of Tydeus deprived them of their splendid armour;
and Odysseus killed Hippodamos and Hypeirochos.
Then the son of Cronus drew the lines of battle tight and equal
looking down from Ida; and the men kept killing one another.
And the son of Tydeus with his spear wounded Agastrophos,
the warrior son of Paion, through the hip joint; his horses were not
at hand for his escape; great was his recklessness of spirit;   340
for his attendant was holding the horses a distance away, while he on foot
kept running through the front lines, until he lost his life.

          And Hector marked them through the lines of battle, and sprang
     for them
crying aloud; and ranks of Trojans followed with him.
And seeing him Diomedes of the war cry shuddered,
and straightway he called to Odysseus who was nearby:
"This curse comes rolling for us both, Hector the mighty;
come, let us stand our ground and defend ourselves as we await him."
He spoke, and weighing his long-shadowed spear, he let it fly
and hit—he did not miss—aiming at Hector's head,   350

the top of his helmet; but bronze was beaten back by bronze,
nor did it reach Hector's fair skin; for the helmet
triple-layered and hollow-eyed, checked it, the helmet that Phoebus
    Apollo gave him.
And Hector at once retired a great distance, and joined his company,
and fell on his knees and remained there and leaned with his massive hand
upon the earth; and around his eyes the black night closed.
And while the son of Tydeus made his way after his thrown spear
a very long way from the front fighters, where it had sped down upon the
    earth,
then Hector caught his breath, and springing back into his chariot
drove off into the army, and eluded the dark spirits of death.   360
And rushing at him with his spear powerful Diomedes spoke:
"You escaped death once again now, dog; yet very close it was the evil
came to you; now once more Phoebus Apollo saved you,
to whom no doubt you make prayer when you approach the thud of spears.
Meeting again, I will surely finish you,
if one of the gods should be ally to me too.
Now I will go after the other Trojans, whomever I catch."
            He spoke and proceeded to strip the body of Paion famed for his
    spear;
but Alexandros, husband of Helen of the lovely hair,
drew his bow upon the son of Tydeus, shepherd of the people,   370
leaning against a column on the tomb that men had built
for Ilos, son of Dardanos, elder of his people long ago.
Diomedes was removing the gleaming breastplate of strong Agastrophos
from his chest, and the shield from his shoulders,
and his weighty helmet; and Alexandros, raising his bow by the grip,
let fly, nor did the shaft escape his hands in vain,
but struck the flat of Diomedes' right foot; and passing clean through the
    arrow
fixed in the ground; and laughing heartily Alexandros
sprang from his hiding place and shouted, exulting:

"You have been struck, my arrow did not escape my hand in vain;
would that   380
it had snatched away your life, striking deep into the hollow of your flank!
So would the Trojans have caught their breath from suffering,
who shudder at you as bleating goats shudder at a lion."
Then without fear did powerful Diomedes address him:
"Loud-mouthed archer, splendid in your crown of curls, ogler of girls,
if you made trial of me with real weapons,
your bow and arrow flurries would be of no use to you.
Now having scratched the flat of my foot you boast like this!
I care as little as if a woman struck me, or a foolish child.
For this is the dull shaft of a cowardly man, a nonentity.   390
Very differently, even if it grazes only a little,
does a spear prove its edge in my hands, and quickly lays a man lifeless.
His wife's cheeks are torn in mourning,
his children are without father; and he reddening the earth with his blood
rots, and more birds than women swarm about him."
So Diomedes spoke, and coming from close by spear-famed Odysseus
took his stand before him; then sitting down behind him Diomedes
dragged the sharp arrow
from his foot; and a hard pang of pain passed through his skin.
He started up into his chariot, and to the charioteer gave orders
to drive to the hollow ships; for he felt heavy of heart.   400

And spear-famed Odysseus was left on his own, nor did any one
of the Argives stay with him, since fear had seized them all.
Then troubled he spoke to his own great-spirited heart:
"Ah me, what will become of me? Great is the evil if I should take flight
in fear of this outnumbering; but more dreaded is this, if I should be caught
on my own; the son of Cronus has put to flight the other Danaans.
But why does my heart debate these things?
For I know that cowards shrink from war,
and he who would be best in battle, he must
strongly stand his ground, whether he is killed, or kills another."   410

While he churned these things through his heart and mind,
all the while the ranks of shield-bearing Trojans drew near,
and penned him in their midst, bringing on themselves great calamity.
As when around a wild boar the dogs and sturdy youths
circle, and the boar comes out of his deep thicket
honing his white tusks to sharpness between his supple jaws,
and they dart about him, and at that there comes a grinding of his teeth,
and they must await his coming, dread though he be,
so all around Odysseus beloved by Zeus rushed
the Trojans. And the first man he struck was blameless Deïopites   420
above the shoulder, lunging with his sharp spear,
and then he killed Thoön and Ennomos;
and then Chersidamas as he was leaping from his chariot
he pierced with his spear in the navel beneath his bossed shield;
and he, falling in the dust, clutched the earth with his clenched hand.

       These he left, and he then struck Charops the son of Hippasos
   with his spear,
the full brother of well-born Sokos.
And Sokos, a man like a god, went to protect him,
and coming up he took his stand hard by Odysseus and spoke a word to
   him:
"Hail illustrious Odysseus, insatiable in cunning and in the toil of war,   430
this day either you will vaunt over two sons of Hippasos,
having killed two such men and stripped their armour—
or struck down under my spear you will lose your own life."
So speaking he thrust at the circle of Odysseus' shield;
and through the shield's bright surface went the heavy spear,
and through his elaborate breastplate it forced its way,
and severed all the skin from his ribs; yet
Pallas Athena did not allow it to reach the man's entrails.
And Odysseus knew that the weapon had not reached a mortal spot,
and drawing back he spoke his word to Sokos: 440
"Poor wretch, surely now sheer destruction draws upon you.

Indeed, you have stopped me doing battle with the Trojans,
but I say to you here that slaughter and dark death
will come this day and broken by my spear
you will give glory to me, and your soul to Hades of famed horses."
He spoke, and the other having turned back was in the act of taking flight,
when Odysseus fixed his spear in his back as he was turning,
between the shoulders, and drove it through his chest,
and he fell with a thud. And godlike Odysseus vaunted:
"O Sokos, son of Hippasos, skilled breaker of horses,   450
death's end has found you first, and you have not escaped.
Poor wretch, nor will your father and lady mother
close the lids of your eyes in death, but the birds,
eaters of raw flesh, will tear at you, beating about you their frenzy of wings;
but when I die, the shining Achaeans will honour me with funeral rites."
So speaking he pulled the heavy spear of skilled Sokos
out of his own flesh and out of his bossed shield;
and when it was drawn, his blood spurted up, and he was sick at heart.

    And when the great-hearted Trojans saw Odysseus' blood,
cheering along the throng of battle they all ran for him;   460
and backward he withdrew, and shouted to his comrades.
Three times he shouted to them, in as loud a voice as a man's head could
    hold,
and three times Menelaos beloved by Ares heard his shouting,
and straightway he spoke to Ajax who was close by him:
"Zeus-descended son of Telamon, Ajax, leader of the people,
the voice of steadfast Odysseus reaches all around me,
a voice as if the Trojans do him violence, having cut him off
on his own in the mighty combat.
Come, let us go through the throng; for it is better to defend him.
I fear lest he suffer some harm left alone among the Trojans,   470
good soldier as he is, and become a great cause of regret to the Danaans."
So speaking he led on, and Ajax followed with him, a man like a god.
Then they found Odysseus beloved by Zeus; and round about him

the Trojans pressed, like bloodstained jackals in the mountains
about a wounded stag that a man has struck
with an arrow from his bowstring; he escapes the man fleeing
with the swiftness of his feet while the blood flows warm and his knees
    are light,
but when at last the sharp arrow has broken him,
the jackals, eaters of raw meat, there in the mountains devour him
in the shadows of a glade; and to this place some god leads a lion,   480
ravening; and the jackals scatter, and the lion it is who devours it;
so around skilled Odysseus of the many wiles
the Trojans pressed in their multitude and strength, but the warrior,
lunging with his spear, warded off the pitiless day of death;
and Ajax drew near bearing his shield like a tower,
and took his stand beside him; and the Trojans scattered, every man in
    every direction.

     And Menelaos the warlike led Odysseus from of the throng,
taking his hand, while his henchman drove the horses near;
and Ajax, springing upon the Trojans, killed Doryklos,
a bastard son of Priam, and then struck Pandokos,   490
and struck Lysandros and Pyrasos and Pylartes.
As when a river in flood descends to the plain,
winter-flowing down the mountains, driven hard by the rain from Zeus,
and draws into itself and carries along dry oaks in multitude, pines
in multitude, and hurls the mass of flotsam into the salt sea,
so glorious Ajax swept the plain, wreaking havoc,
slaying men and horses. Hector did not
know, since he fought on the far left of the battle,
by the banks of the Scamander river, where in greatest numbers
the heads of men were falling, and where quenchless cry of battle rose 500
around great Nestor and Idomeneus the warlike.
Amid these was Hector doing battle, performing deeds of devastation
with spear and horsemanship, laying waste the ranks of young men.

     But still the illustrious Achaeans would not have yielded passage,

had not Alexandros, husband of Helen of the lovely hair,
stopped Machaon shepherd of the people doing feats of valour,
striking him with a three-barbed arrow in the right shoulder.
Then were the Achaeans, breathing fury, greatly afraid for him,
lest by chance, the tide of battle turning, the Trojans seize him,
and at once Idomeneus addressed godlike Nestor: 510
"O Nestor, son of Neleus, great pride of the Achaeans,
come, mount your chariot, let Machaon
mount beside you, and to the ships with all speed drive the single-hoofed
    horses.
For a healer is a man worth many other men,
in cutting out arrows and sprinkling on the soothing medicines."
So he spoke, and the Gerenian horseman Nestor did not disobey;
straightway he mounted his chariot, and beside him mounted Machaon
the son of Asclepius the blameless healer.
He lashed his whip to start the horses, and they two not unwilling flew on
to the hollow ships; for there their hearts tended.   520

            And Kebriones saw that the Trojans were routed
and standing by Hector, he addressed him with a word:
"Hector, we two engage with the Danaans here
on the fringe of grievous battle; but other
Trojans are in a mob of panic, horses and men alike.
Telamonian Ajax is wreaking havoc; well do I know him;
for he holds his broad shield about his shoulders. Come, let us too
drive the chariot and horses straight there, where most of all
horsemen and infantry hurling forth their evil strife
are destroying one another, and quenchless cry of battle rises." 530
So speaking Kebriones lashed the splendid-maned horses
with his whistling whip; and hearing the crack they
lightly bore the swift chariot among the Trojans and Achaeans,
trampling underfoot the dead and their shields; and the axle beneath
was all spattered with blood and the rails which ran around the chariot,
struck by droplets from the hooves of the horses

and from the rims of the wheels; and Hector strained to plunge into the
    throng
of men, rushing to crush them; and he flung upon the Danaans
shameful panic, and it was but a little while he held off from his spear's
    work.
He ranged around the ranks of the other men   540
with his spear and sword and massive rocks for throwing,
yet avoided battle with Ajax son of Telamon.   542

      But Zeus the father seated on high stirred fear in Ajax,   544
and he stood stunned, and behind him swung his shield of seven-fold
    oxhide,
and drew back, glancing about him, towards his company of men, like a
    beast,
turning about him, little by little exchanging knee for knee.
As when a tawny lion from the midst of a pen of cattle
is chased by dogs and rustic men,
who do not suffer him to seize the cream of their herd,   550
on alert the whole night long; and he in his lust for meat
makes straight for them, but achieves nothing; for showers of spears
fly against him from the men's strong hands
and burning torches, which he shrinks from for all his desire,
and at dawn he departs far away, his spirit aggrieved;
so Ajax then aggrieved in heart kept retreating
from the Trojans, much against his will; for he feared greatly for the ships
    of the Achaeans.
As when a donkey being led beside a field breaks free of young boys,
unhurried, a donkey about whose flanks many sticks have already broken,
and going into a deep stand of corn he starts eating; and the boys   560
beat him with their sticks, but their strength is as a child's,
and with much exertion they drive him out only when he has had his fill
    of feed;
so did the high-spirited Trojans and their far-flung allies
keep after great Ajax the son of Telamon,

striking with their wooden spears at the middle of his shield.
And now Ajax would recollect his fierce courage,
turning himself about again, and would restrain the ranks
of horse-breaking Trojans; now again he would swerve around to flee.
But he blocked them all from making passage to the swift ships,
he, by himself, running between Trojans and Achaeans   570
to take his stand; some spears flung forwards
by strong hands stuck in his great shield,
many also falling short, before grazing his white skin,
came to a stop in the earth, straining to have their fill of his flesh.

    Then as Euaimon's splendid son Eurypylos saw him
assailed by the flurry of missiles,
he went and took his stand beside him and took aim with his bright spear,
and struck Apisaon, son of Phausios, shepherd of the people,
in the liver, below the midriff, and at once his knees buckled beneath him.
Eurypylos rushed forward and began to strip the armour from his
    shoulders;   580
and then Alexandros, godlike in beauty, saw him as
he was stripping away Apisaon's armour, and straightway he drew
his bow on Eurypylos, and struck him in the right thigh
with his arrow; and the arrow shaft was broken off, and weighted his leg
    with pain,
and he drew back into the band of his companions, shunning death,
and cried out in a piercing voice so as to be heard by the Danaans:
"O friends, leaders and counsellors of the Argives,
turn around and take your stand and defend from pitiless fate
Ajax, who is assailed with spears, and I say he will not
escape from this grievous war. Come, take up position facing the foe   590
around Ajax the great son of Telamon."
So spoke Eurypylos, wounded; and the men took their stand by him
in a body, inclining their shields against their shoulders,
holding aloft their spears; and Ajax came to join them;
and wheeled around and took his stand, since he had reached the band of

his companions.

　　So they fought like blazing fire;
and from out of the battle the sweating horses of Neleus
were carrying Nestor, and bringing Machaon the shepherd of the people.
And swift-footed brilliant Achilles took notice as he saw him;
for he stood upon the stern of his cavernous ship   600
looking upon the sheer toil of war and heartbreaking rout.
And at once he addressed his companion Patroclus,
calling from the ship; and the other hearing from within the shelter
came out, like to the war god; and this was for him the beginning of evil.
And the brave son of Menoetius addressed him first:
"Why have you called for me, Achilles? What is your need of me?"
Then answering him spoke Achilles of the swift feet:
"Illustrious son of Menoetius, you who please my heart,
now I think the Achaeans will stand about my knees
in supplication; for a need has come that can no longer be borne.   610
Come, go now, Patroclus beloved of Zeus, ask of Nestor
who is that man he brings wounded from battle.
Surely, from behind he is like Machaon in all respects,
the son of Asclepius, but I did not see the face of the man;
for the horses flew past me, speeding forward."
So he spoke; and Patroclus obeyed his beloved companion,
and set out running along the shelters and tents of the Achaeans.

　　Now when the others reached the son of Neleus' shelter,
they descended to the nourishing earth,
and his henchman Eurymedon released the old man's horses   620
from the chariot; and the men dried the sweat from their tunics,
standing to face the breath of wind by the shore of the salt sea;
then going into the shelter they seated themselves on divans;
and for them Hekamede with the lovely hair made a porridge,
Hekamede whom the old man got from Tenedos, when Achilles
　　sacked it,
the daughter of great-hearted Arsinoös, she whom the Achaeans

picked out for him, because he surpassed all men in counsel;
she first pushed forward a table for them
a beautiful one, well polished with legs of blue enamel, then on it
a bronze basket for bread, and also an onion as relish for the drink   630
and pale yellow honey, beside sacred barley meal,
and near it a cup of surpassing beauty, which the old man had taken from
     his home,
studded with gold rivets; it had four handles,
and on either side of each two doves
of gold were feeding, and below them were two flanges.
Any other man would labour to lift it from the table
when it was full, but Nestor, the old man, raised it with ease.
It was in this the woman resembling goddesses made a mix for them
with Pramnian wine, and on it grated goat-milk cheese
with a bronze grater, and sprinkled gleaming barley over;   640
and she summoned them to drink, when she had prepared the porridge.

          Then when they had both drunk and slaked their parching thirst,
they took pleasure in words, talking each to the other;
and Patroclus came and stood in the entrance, a man like a god.
And seeing him, the old man rose from his shining chair,
and led the other in, taking his hand, and urged him to be seated;
but Patroclus standing opposite declined and spoke a word:
"There is no sitting for me, old one, Zeus-cherished, you will not
     persuade me.
Honoured, quick to anger, is he who sent me to find out,
who that man was you brought back wounded; but I myself   650
know, for I see Machaon shepherd of the people.
And now I go back to make report as messenger to Achilles.
Well do you know, old one, Zeus-cherished, the kind of man that one is;
a man to be dreaded; swift would he be to blame even the blameless."

          Then answered him the Gerenian horseman Nestor:
"Why now does Achilles so pity the sons of the Achaeans,
all those who have been wounded by hurled arrows and spears? He

    knows nothing
of grief, such grief as has risen throughout the army; for our best men
are lying in the ships wounded by arrows and cut by spears.
The son of Tydeus, powerful Diomedes, is wounded,   660
Odysseus has been struck by a spear, and spear-famed Agamemnon;
and Eurypylos has been wounded in the thigh by an arrow;
this other one I just now brought from battle,
struck with an arrow from a bowstring; but Achilles,
noble as he is, does not trouble himself for the Danaans nor pity them.
Is he waiting until that moment when the swift ships near the sea,
despite the Argives' efforts, are burned with consuming fire,
and we ourselves slain, one by one? Well, my strength is not
as once it used to be in my supple limbs.

        "Would that I were young as then, and my strength unfailing,   670
as when dispute broke out between me and the Eleans
concerning raiding of cattle, when I killed Itymoneus,
the noble son of Hypeirochos, who used to live in Elis,
when I was driving cattle in reprisal; protecting his herd
he was struck at the front of the fray by a spear from my hands,
and he dropped; his men, rustics, fled on all sides.
We collected our booty from the plain, a great deal of it,
fifty herds of cattle, as many flocks of sheep,
as many droves of pigs, as many wide-ranging herds of goats,
and a hundred and fifty tawny horses,   680
all mares, with foals under many.
And these we drove into Neleian Pylos
during the night, to the city; and the heart of Neleus was rejoiced,
because so much had fallen to me, young as I was going to war.

        "With the showing of dawn the heralds sang out
for those to come, to whom debt was owed in shining Elis;
and the leading men of Pylos assembled
to make division of the spoils. For the Epeans of Elis owed debt to many,
and we few in Pylos had suffered outrage;

for coming here mighty Heracles had committed outrages   690
years before, and all who were our best men had been killed;
we were twelve sons of blameless Neleus,
of whom I alone was left, and the others, all of them, were destroyed.
Made arrogant by these events, the bronze-clad Epeans
with wanton aggression had contrived against us reckless deeds.
So now the old Neleus chose a herd of cattle and a great flock of sheep,
selecting three hundred of them and their shepherds.
For a great debt was owed to him in shining Elis, one for
four prizewinning horses with their chariot,
setting out to join the races; for they were to run   700
for a tripod; but Augeias, lord of men, seized them there,
and sent away their charioteer in anguish for his horses.
So old Neleus angered over those things said and done
now chose for himself an immense amount; and the rest he gave to his
     people
to divide, lest anyone leave deprived of his fair portion.

          "We then were settling all of these things, and round about the
     city
were making sacrifices to the gods; and on the third day the Epeans all
came, many men and single-hoofed horses alike
in full force. And with them the two Moliones came under arms,
still boys, not yet experienced at all in furious deeds of war.   710
There is a town, Thryoessa, a steep hill town,
far off beside the Alpheus river, on the boundary of sandy Pylos;
this they besieged, eager to smash it,
and in addition they had scoured the whole plain; but Athena
came as messenger to us, racing from Olympus in the night
with word to arm; nor was it an unwilling host she raised in Pylos,
but rather men urgent to go to war. Neleus did not
permit me to arm myself, and he hid away my horses;
for he said that I knew nothing at all of the work of war;
but even so I distinguished myself among our horsemen,   720

on foot though I was, since this was how Athena led the battle.

   "There is a river Minyeïos, emptying into the sea
near to Arene, where we horsemen of Pylos
awaited the shining dawn, and bands of soldiers on foot kept streaming up;
then after arming ourselves with our weapons with all haste,
in full light we arrived at the sacred waters of Alpheus.
There, after offering splendid sacrifices to almighty Zeus,
and a bull to Alpheus, a bull to Poseidon,
and to Athena of the gleaming eyes a cow from the herd,
then through the host we took our evening meal at our posts, 730
and lay down to sleep, each man in his armour
about the flowing waters of the river. And the great-hearted Epeans
took their stand around the city, spoiling to sack it.
But before that came to be, a mighty work of war loomed for them,
for when the shining sun held himself above the earth,
we joined in battle, making prayers to Zeus and to Athena.
And when the battle came about of Pylians and Epeans,
I was first to kill a man—and carried off his single-hoofed horses—
Moulios the spearman; he was the son-in-law of king Augeias,
and had wed his eldest daughter, fair-haired Agamede, 740
who knew as many healing herbs as the broad earth brings forth.
I struck him as he came for me with my bronze-tipped spear,
and he fell in the dust; and I springing into his chariot
took my place among the front fighters; and the great-hearted Epeans
fled from fear this way and that when they saw the man fall,
the leader of their horsemen, who used to be the best in waging battle.
Then I sprang upon them like a dark windstorm,
and I seized fifty chariots, and from each
two men caught the earth in their teeth, broken by my spear.
And now I would have slain the Moliones boys from the line of Aktor, 750
had not their father, the wide-ruling Earth-Shaker Poseidon,
saved them from battle, enfolding them in dense mist.
Then Zeus put great power into the hands of the Pylians;

for I declare we chased the Epeans across the broad plain,
killing them and picking up their fine armour,
till we brought our steeds to a stand in Bouprasion, fertile in wheat,
at the Olenian Rock, where is the hill called Alesion;
from there Athena turned our people back.
And there having killed my last man, I left; and the Achaeans
drove their swift horses back from Bouprasion towards Pylos.   760
And all men gave glory to Zeus among the gods, but among men to Nestor.

          "Thus was I among men, if this ever happened. But Achilles
alone will have benefit of his prowess; although I think that he
will weep much after, when his people have perished.
O my friend, surely Menoetius so instructed you
on that day, when he sent you forth from Phthia to Agamemnon;
for we two were inside, myself and brilliant Odysseus,
and we heard everything in those halls, as he instructed;
for we had come to the well-placed house of Peleus
gathering the army throughout all-nourishing Achaea,   770
and there we found the warrior Menoetius inside
and you, by Achilles' side; and the aged horseman Peleus
was burning the fat-rich thighbones of an ox to Zeus who hurls the
     thunderbolt,
in an enclosure of his courtyard; and he was holding a golden goblet,
making libations of fire-bright wine on the fiery sacrifices;
you two were busy with the meat of the ox, when we two
stood in the entrance. In amazement Achilles sprang up,
and led us in, taking us by the hand, and urged us to be seated;
and duly set before us tokens of hospitality, which are the right of strangers;
then when we were satisfied with eating and drinking,   780
I began my speech, urging you to come with us;
both of you were very eager, both of them gave many instructions;
old Peleus enjoined his son Achilles
always to be best and to be better than all others,
and right there and then Menoetius, son of Aktor, enjoined you thus:

'My son, in birth Achilles is your superior,
but you are older; in strength he is far the better;
but speak you well to him and put in his mind close counsel
and point the way; he will listen for his own good end.'
So the old man instructed, but you have forgotten. Yet even now   790
you might speak these things to brilliant Achilles, in the hope that he
    might yet be persuaded.
Who knows, if with help from some god you might stir his heart,
winning him over? For the persuasion of a comrade is a worthy thing.
       "But if in his heart he shrinks from some divine prophecy
and his lady mother has revealed something to him from Zeus,
come, let him send you at least forth, and let the rest of the host follow
    with you,
the Myrmidons, so that you might be salvation's light to the Danaans.
And let him give you his splendid armour to wear to war,
with the hope that likening you to him the Trojans will back off
from fighting, and the warrior sons of the Achaeans draw breath   800
in their extremity; for respite in war is brief.
Fresh forces would easily push battle-weary men
to their city away from the ships and our shelters."
       So he spoke, and stirred the heart in the other's breast;
and he set out running along the ships to Achilles Aeacides.
But when in his running Patroclus came to the ships
of godlike Odysseus, where was the place of assembly and tribunal,
and where also stood their altars to the gods,
there Eurypylos encountered him, the son of Zeus-descended
Euaimon, who had been wounded in his thigh by an arrow,   810
hobbling out of battle; running sweat streamed down
his head and shoulders, and from his grievous wound
dark blood gushed; but still his wits were unshaken.
Seeing him the valiant son of Menoetius was filled with pity,
and in sorrow he spoke winged words:
"Poor wretches, leaders and counsellors of the Danaans,

so it is then that far from your dear ones and fatherland you were destined
to glut the running dogs in Troy with your white flesh.
But come, tell me this, Eurypylos, cherished by Zeus, brother warrior,
somehow, yet, will the Achaeans sustain monstrous Hector   820
or will they be destroyed before this at his hand, broken with his spear?"
Then in turn Eurypylos with wise understanding addressed him in reply:
"No longer, Patroclus, Zeus-descended, will there be defence
of the Achaeans, but into their dark ships will they fall.
All those now, whoever before were our best men,
lie in the ships wounded by spear or arrow
at the hands of the Trojans; and Hector's strength rises always.
Come, you at least save me, taking me to my dark ship,
and cut the arrow from my thigh, and from it wash the dark blood
with warm water, and sprinkle on soothing herbs,   830
good ones, which they say you learned of from Achilles,
which Chiron taught him, the most honourable of the Centaurs.
As for the healers Podaleirios and Machaon,
Machaon I suspect lies in his shelter wounded,
himself in need of a blameless healer;
the other on the Trojan plain still withstands the piercing war."
Then in turn the valiant son of Menoetius addressed him:
"How can these things be? What shall we do, Eurypylos, brother warrior?
I am on my way to tell brilliant Achilles of the counsel
that Gerenian Nestor watchman of the Achaeans charged me.   840
Nevertheless I will not neglect you in your affliction."
He spoke, and taking hold of Eurypylos beneath his chest he led the
    shepherd of the people
to his shelter; and seeing him his henchman put oxhides under him.
Stretching him out there, Patroclus with his knife cut from his thigh
the piercing, sharp arrow, and washed the dark blood from him
with warm water, and applied a bitter root,
crumbling it with his hands, one that stills pain, which stopped all his
pangs of pain. And the wound dried up, and the blood ceased to flow.

So the valiant son of Menoetius tended wounded Eurypylos
in his shelter; and in massed throngs the men fought on,
Argives and Trojans. Nor was the ditch of the Danaans destined
to survive hereafter, nor the broad wall above it,
which they built in defence of the ships and drove around the ditch,
without giving to the gods glorious sacrifice of hecatombs,
to protect the swift ships and vast plunder
enclosed within. For the wall had been built against the will of the
    immortal
gods; and therefore it stood firm for no great time.
As long as Hector was alive and Achilles filled with wrath   10
and the city of lord Priam was not sacked,
so long the great wall of the Achaeans stood firm.
But when all the best of the Trojans were dead,
and many of the Argives killed, while some survived,
and the city of Priam had been sacked in the tenth year,
and the Argives had set out in their ships to their beloved fatherland,
then did Poseidon and Apollo devise a plan
to level the wall, channelling the might of the rivers,
all the rivers that stream from the hills of Ida to the sea—
Rhesos and Heptaporos and Karesos and Rhodios   20
and Granicus and Aisepos and shining Scamander
and Simoeis, beside which many oxhide shields and crested helmets
had fallen in the dust, along with the race of almost divine men.

And Phoebus Apollo diverted the mouths of all the rivers to one place,
and for nine days he hurled their rolling waters against the wall; and Zeus
    rained
without respite, so as more rapidly to render the defences seaborne
    flotsam;
and the Earth-Shaker himself, trident in hand,
took the lead, and with the waves dislodged all foundations
of wood and stone, which the toiling Achaeans had set.
And he made all smooth along the powerfully flowing Hellespont,   30
and covered back again the great shore with sand,
having destroyed the wall; and he turned the rivers to run
along their beds, where before their lovely flowing water used to roll.

These things Poseidon and Apollo intended in time to come;
but for now battle and the din of war blazed round
the well-built wall, and the timbers of the ramparts resounded
as they were struck; Argives broken under the lash of Zeus,
cowering in the hollow ships, were stayed
in dread of Hector, violent master of the rout;
he, as before, fought on, like a whirling storm wind.   40
As when in the midst of dogs and hunting men
a wild boar or lion wheels about, revelling in his strength,
and the men arraying themselves like a wall of defence
stand to face him and hurl from their hands
volleys of spears; but never does his noble heart
feel fear, nor does he flee—and his courage will kill him—
and relentlessly he wheels about testing the ranks of men,
and wherever he charges, there the ranks of men give way;
so Hector going along the battle throng turned and twisted
exhorting his companions to cross the ditch; yet his   50
own swift-footed horses had not the courage to dare, but whinnying
drew up to the edge of the trench lip; for they were in terror of the wide
    ditch,
for it was neither easy to overleap from up close

nor to pass through, for around the whole ditch steep overhanging
  banks
reared on either side, crowned with stakes,
sharp-pointed, that the sons of the Achaeans had fixed
close-set and massive, as a deterrent to enemy men.
A horse straining with a well-wheeled chariot there could not easily
get within, and the Trojans were pressing to see whether they could
   accomplish this on foot.

      Then Poulydamas standing beside bold Hector spoke: 60
"Hector and you other leaders of the Trojans and allies,
we would be reckless to drive the swift horses through the ditch.
Surely it is disastrous to try; sharp-pointed stakes have been set upon it,
and next to them is the wall of the Achaeans.
It is not possible to dismount and fight between them
with the chariots; it is narrow, there where I think we will come to harm.
If Zeus the high-thunderer, intent on baneful deeds, destroys them
utterly, and is eager to aid the Trojans,
then assuredly I wish this would happen at once,
and the Achaeans die here, nameless, far from Argos.   70
But if they should rally round, and there should be counterattack
from the ships, we would be entangled in the trench they dug—
then I think not even a returning messenger would
get back to the city under attack of the Achaeans when they have rallied.
Come, do as I say, let us all be persuaded;
assemble the horses and their attendants at the ditch,
and let us ourselves on foot, under arms with our weapons,
all follow Hector in a body; then the Achaeans
will not stand, if the shackles of destruction are fastened on them."

      So spoke Poulydamas, and his words of caution found favour
   with Hector.   80
At once he sprang from his chariot in his armour to the ground;
nor did the rest of the Trojans stay up upon their chariots,
but all sprang away, when they saw shining Hector.

Then each man gave orders to his charioteer
to draw his horses up in good array there at the ditch;
and having divided up, arrayed themselves in order,
marshalled into five divisions, the men followed their leaders.
Those who went with Hector and blameless Poulydamas,
they were the most numerous and the best, and most determined
to shatter the wall and battle by the hollow ships;   90
and Kebriones was third to follow with them; for by his chariot
Hector left another man, inferior to Kebriones his charioteer.
Paris was leader of the second body along with Alkathoös and Agenor;
Helenos and godlike Deïphobos led the third,
two sons of Priam; and with them was Asios the warrior,
Asios son of Hyrtakos, whose great blazing
horses carried him from Arisbe, away from the river Selleeïs.
And of the fourth company Anchises' brave son was leader,
Aeneas, and with him were two sons of Antenor,
Archelochos and Akamas, both skilled in all forms of fighting.   100
Sarpedon was leader of the glorious allies,
and chose in addition Glaukos and warlike Asteropaios;
for these men seemed to him far and away the best
of the others after himself; for Sarpedon was pre-eminent over all.

　　　　And when they joined together, wrought shield to shield,
then in impatient speed they charged straight for the Danaans, and they
　　　thought
the Achaeans would no longer hold their ground, but would fall back
　　　upon their dark ships.
The rest of the Trojans and far-renowned allies
trusted in the plan of blameless Poulydamas;
but not Asios the son of Hyrtakos, leader of men, who was not willing   110
to leave his horses there and his attending charioteer,
but approached the swift ships, horses and all—
the fool, he was not destined to elude evil death
as he gloried in his chariot and horses by the ships,

nor to return back home to windy Ilion;

before that accursed fate enveloped him

on the spear of Idomeneus, noble son of Deucalion.

Asios charged to the left of the ships, the very place where the Achaeans

would return with their horses and chariots from the plain;

there he drove his horses and chariot across, nor did he find   120

the gates shut, nor the long bolt drawn,

but men opening it wide, in the hope that they might give safe passage to any

of their companions fleeing to the ships from the war.

Aiming straight to this place Asios held his horses, and his men followed

shouting their piercing cries; for they thought the Achaeans would not

hold their ground, but would fall back on their dark ships—

the fools; for at the gates they found two outstanding men,

the high-hearted sons of Lapith spearmen,

one the son of Peirithoös, powerful Polypoites,

the other Leonteus, like to man-destroying Ares.   130

These two, there before the towering gates,

stood firm, like high-headed oaks in the mountains,

which withstand wind and driving rain all their days,

made fast by their great, far-reaching roots;

so they two trusting in their strength of hand and might

awaited the coming of great Asios, nor fled.

And the Trojan men went straight for the well-built wall, holding high

their shields of tanned oxhide, with a great war-shout

all around lord Asios and Iamenos and Orestes

and Adamas the son of Asios, and Thoön, and Oinomaos.   140

For some time the Lapiths inside the wall were urging the strong-greaved
    Achaeans

to fight in defence of the ships;

but when they saw the Trojans charging

the wall, then was there uproar and panic among the Danaans,

and the two Lapiths flew out of the gates and began to fight before them,

like two wild boars that in the mountains

await an approaching band of dogs and men,
and slicing slantwise smash the woods around them
felling trees by the roots, amid the grinding clatter of their teeth,
until someone striking at them takes their lives.   150
So the bronze shining armour ground and clattered on the chests
of the men, struck as they faced their foe; for they were fighting violently,
trusting in their strength and in their people above them.
And those above were letting fly with boulders from the well-built
    ramparts,
fighting for themselves, their shelters,
and the fast-running ships; the boulders fell to the ground like snow
that a furious wind, convulsing mottled clouds,
pours down in drifts upon the nourishing earth.
So the missiles rained from the hands of both Trojans
and Achaeans; and the helmets rang hollow around them,   160
and the bossed shields, struck by boulders like millstones.

        Then Asios the son of Hyrtakos cried aloud and struck his thighs,
and in distress he spoke a word:
"Father Zeus, so now even you turn out to be a liar
through and through; I did not think the Argive warriors
would withstand our might and unassailable strength of hands.
But they, like flickering-waisted wasps or bees,
who have made their hives by the rugged roadside,
and do not leave their hollow home, but staying their ground
for the sake of their children fight off the men who hunt their honey,   170
so these men, although only two, refuse to withdraw
from the gates, until either they have killed or been killed."
So he spoke, but uttering these things he did not persuade the mind of
    Zeus;
for Zeus' heart desired to give Hector glory.

        And other men battled about the other gates—
heavy work it is for me, as if a god, to relate all things;
for everywhere demonic fire reared about the wall

of stone; and the Argives, stricken though they were, by necessity

battled for their ships. And the gods grieved in their hearts,

all who were allies in war of the Danaans.   180

And the Lapiths kept clashing in warfare and battle.

      There the son of Peirithoös, powerful Polypoites,

with his spear struck Damasos through his bronze-cheeked helm;

nor did the bronze helmet withstand it, but right through

the brazen point crushed bone, and the brains

were all spattered within it; so he destroyed him for all his fury.

And then he killed Pylon and Ormenos.

Then Leonteus, follower of Ares, struck the son of Antimachos,

Hippomachos, with his spear, hitting down across his war-belt.

Then drawing his sharp sword from its sheath,   190

darting forward from the throng, he first struck Antiphates

at close quarters; and on his back Antiphates lay stretched upon the gound;

and then Menon and Iamenos and Orestes—

all of them, one after the other, Leonteus brought low to the nourishing

    earth.

      While the Lapiths were stripping the fallen of their glittering

    armour,

all the while the young warriors who followed Poulydamas and Hector,

those who were most numerous and best, and most determined

to shatter the wall and destroy the ships with fire,

still stood hesitating by the ditch.

For a bird came to them as they were readying to cross,   200

a high-flying eagle skirting the host, going left,

carrying in its talons a crimson snake, portentous,

still alive, breathing, and not forgetful of its fighting spirit;

and in its turn it struck the eagle holding it across the breast, by the throat,

twisting itself back; and the eagle, smarting with pain, let it fall from its

    grasp

to the earth, dropping it in the midst of the battle-throng,

and with a piercing cry flew off with a blast of the wind.

The Trojans shuddered when they saw the writhing snake
lying in their midst, a portent of Zeus who wields the aegis.
Then Poulydamas spoke to bold Hector, standing close: 210
"Hector, always somehow you fault me in assembly
when I point out things that are best, since it seems it is not fitting
that a mere citizen speak against you, not in council,
nor ever in war, but only ever to increase your might;
now, however, I will speak out, as it seems best to me.
Let us not go forth fighting the Danaans for the sake of the ships.
For thus I think it will be accomplished, if truly
this bird came for the Trojans, just as we were intent on crossing,   218
bearing a blood-coloured serpent in its talons, a portent,
alive; but he let it fall before he reached his beloved home,
and did not succeed in carrying it to give to his children.
So we, even if we shatter both the gates and wall of the Achaeans
with our strength, and the Achaeans withdraw,
we will not travel the same road back from the ships in good order;
we will leave behind many of the Trojans, those whom the Achaeans
will slay with bronze as they fight on behalf of their ships.
So would a diviner interpret this, one who in his heart clearly
knew portents, and one whom the people trust."

          Then looking at him from beneath his brows spoke Hector of the
     shimmering helm: 230
"Poulydamas, these things you declare are no longer pleasing to me.
You know how to think up some other speech better than this one.
But if you now make this declaration truly, in earnest,
then the gods themselves have utterly deprived you of your wits,
you who bid me forget the counsel of far-thundering Zeus,
which he himself promised to undertake and granted,
and you now bid me put my faith in long-winged birds;
for them I care nothing, nor am concerned
whether they go right towards the light and sun,
or go left towards the misted darkness.   240

Let us have faith in the will of great Zeus,

who is lord of all mortal beings and all immortals.

Only one omen is best—to defend the fatherland.

Why do you fear war and battle?

Even if all the rest of us are killed about you

beside the ships of the Argives, for you there is no reason to fear dying;

for your heart is not battle-hardy, nor warlike.

But if you hang back from battle, or with persuasion of words

you cause another to turn back from war,

straightway struck down under my spear you will lose your own life." 250

   Then so speaking he led on, and the men followed

with unearthly din; and Zeus who wields the lightning bolt

caused a rush of wind to rise from the peaks of Ida,

which bore a cloud of dust straight for the ships; and he bewitched

the wits of the Achaeans, and gave glory to the Trojans and to Hector.

Then trusting in portents of Zeus and in their own strength

they endeavoured to shatter the great wall of the Achaeans.

They tore at the towers' outworks, and tried to throw down the ramparts,

and to dislodge the retaining struts, which the Achaeans

placed first in the earth to buttress the towers.   260

These they were trying to pull up, hoping to shatter the Achaean

wall; but the Danaans did not at all give way,

and hedging the ramparts round with their oxhide-shields,

from these they hurled their missiles at the enemy as they came below

 the wall.

   And both Aiantes, urging the men always, ranged in every

 direction

on the ramparts, rousing the spirit of the Achaeans,

with words of gentle persuasion for one man, another they

reproached with words of harshness, whomever they saw hanging back

 from the fight:

"O friends, you of the Argives who are outstanding, who are middling,

you who are less skilful—since men are by no means alike   270

in war—now the work is for us all;
and you yourselves mark this. Let no man turn himself back
towards the ships when he hears Hector's shouting,
but face forward and urge each other on—
if only Olympian Zeus of the lightning bolt
grant that we turn the tide of battle back and chase the enemy to the city!"
So shouting aloud the two rallied the fighting throng of Achaeans;
as flakes of snow pour down in drifts
on a winter's day, when all-devising Zeus begins
to snow, showing to mankind these the shafts of his artillery,   280
and hushing the winds to sleep, he heaps the snow steadily, so that it
    shrouds
the heights of high mountains and peaks of cliffs,
and blossoming lowlands and the rich-worked lands of men;
and the snow drifts the bays and beaches of the grey salt sea,
and the sea swell splashing it is stilled; and all else
is cloaked from above, when the snows of Zeus weigh down;
just so did the stones fly thick from both sides,
some at the Trojans, some from the Trojans at the Achaeans,
as they bombarded each other; and thundering rose above all the wall.

          Not even then would the Trojans and shining Hector   290
have shattered the walls and the long door-bolts,
had all-devising Zeus not driven his own son Sarpedon
upon the Argives, like a lion on twist-horned cattle.
Straightway he held before him the circle of his shield,
splendid, of beaten bronze, which the bronze-smith
hammered, and inside had stitched layers of oxhide
with golden wires right round the circle.
Holding this before him, brandishing two spears,
he set out like a mountain-raised lion, who has been without
meat for a long time, whose bold spirit drives him   300
to try for the flocks and to enter into their close-fenced fold;
and even if he should find herdsmen there

standing guard with dogs and spears about the flocks,
he is not minded to be driven from the fold without a try,
but either springing forth he snatches one away, or he
is struck in the forefront of fighting by a spear from a swift hand;
so his spirit drove godlike Sarpedon
to rush at the wall and to smash the ramparts.

      And straightway he spoke to Glaukos the son of Hippolochos:
"Glaukos, why are we two esteemed beyond all   310
with seats of honour in Lycia, with cuts of meat and goblets filled
and all men looking on us as if on gods,
and why were we allotted a great plot of land by the banks of Xanthos,
a beautiful plot, with an orchard and wheat-bearing field?
So we must now take our stand among the foremost
of the Lycians and engage in searing battle,
so that any of the close-armoured Lycians may say,
'Not inglorious are they, our kings who hold sway
over Lycia, and consume fat-rich sheep
and choice honey-sweet wine; but, mark you! their strength is   320
outstanding, since they fight with the front rank of Lycian men.'
O old friend, if we two escaping this war
were destined to be ageless and deathless always,
I myself would not fight in the frontlines,
nor would I send you into battle where men win glory;
but now, since the fates of death stand by us
in their thousands, which a mortal man cannot escape nor flee,
let us go—either we will give the right to vaunt to someone else or he to us."
So he spoke, and Glaukos did not turn back, nor did he disobey;
and straight on they both advanced, leading the great host of Lycians.   330

      And seeing them Menestheus, the son of Peteos, shuddered;
for it was to his sector of the wall they were coming, bringing ruin with
    them;
he peered along the wall of the Achaeans in the hope that he might see one
of the leaders, someone who could ward off disaster from his comrades.

Then he marked the two Aiantes, insatiable in war,
holding position, and Teucer just coming from his shelter
nearby; but not by shouting could he reach them,
so great was the clamour—battle cries reached heaven—
of shields and horsehair-crested helmets
and the very gates being struck; for all the gates were shut, and the
    Trojans   340
positioning themselves about them were trying to break through by force
    and enter.
And quickly he dispatched the herald Thoötes to Ajax:
"Go, illustrious Thoötes, run to summon Ajax,
both men would be better; indeed that would be by far the best of all,
since here will soon be wrought sheer destruction;
so heavily do the Lycian leaders bear upon us, who even before, as now,
showed themselves to be ferocious throughout the mighty combat.
But if the toil of war and battle has arisen there for them too,
at least let strong Telamonian Ajax come alone,
and let Teucer follow with him, well skilled in bows."   350

      So he spoke, nor did the herald hearing him disobey,
and he left on the run along the wall of the bronze-clad Achaeans,
and coming up he stood beside the two Aiantes, and straightway he spoke:
"Aiantes, you leaders of the bronze-clad Argives,
the beloved son of Peteos, cherished by Zeus, bids
you go there so that if only for a little you share the toil of fighting,
both of you would be better; indeed that would be by far the best of all,
since there soon will be wrought sheer destruction;
so heavily do the Lycian leaders bear upon us, who even before, as now,
showed themselves to be ferocious throughout the mighty combat.   360
But if here too war and battle has arisen,
at least let strong Telamonian Ajax come alone,
and let Teucer follow with him, well skilled in bows."

      So he spoke, nor did great Telamonian Ajax refuse.
At once he spoke winged words to the son of Oïleus;

"Ajax, and powerful Lykomedes—you two

remain here and urge the Danaans to battle strongly;

I am going there and will meet the fighting.

I will come back quickly, when I have defended them."

Then so speaking Telamonian Ajax departed,   370

and Teucer went with him, the brother of Ajax by the same father.

And following with them Pandion carried Teucer's curved bow.

When they arrived at the rampart of great-hearted Menestheus,

keeping inside the wall they came to hard-pressed men,

for the Lycians' powerful leaders and commanders

were mounting the ramparts like a whirling storm wind,

and face-to-face the Achaeans joined with them in battle, and the war

shouts rose.

And Telamonian Ajax first killed a man,

the companion of Sarpedon, Epikles the great-hearted,

striking him with a jagged glittering stone, which lay inside the wall,   380

huge, on the top of the heap beside the rampart; nor could a man easily

hold it with both hands, not even in his youthful prime,

such as mortal men are now; but Ajax lifting it high hurled it on the

Lycian,

and smashed the four-horned helmet, and shattered his skull utterly

all in a mass; and he then like a diver

plunged from the towering rampart, and his spirit left his bones.

And Teucer struck Glaukos the powerful son of Hippolochos

with an arrow as he rushed against the towering wall,

there where he saw his arm was bare of armour, and so he stopped his

fighting spirit.

At once Glaukos leapt from the wall, in stealth, lest one of the

Achaeans   390

see that he was wounded and exult over him with words.

And grief descended on Sarpedon as Glaukos departed,

since he marked it at once; nevertheless he did not forget his fighting

spirit,

but with sure aim he struck Alkmaon son of Thestor

with his spear, and wrenched out the shaft; and following with the spear
    Alkmaon

fell face forward, and round him clashed his armour elaborate with
    bronze.

Then Sarpedon, seizing the breastwork with strong hands,

pulled, and the whole of it gave way all along the wall; above

the rampart was laid bare, and he had made a passage for many.

       And Ajax and Teucer both failed to hit Sarpedon—Teucer with an
    arrow   400

struck the shining baldric around his chest

that held his man-surrounding shield; but Zeus warded off death from

his son, so that he not be broken by the ships' sterns;

springing forward Ajax thrust at Sarpedon's shield; his spear did not

go right through, but he battered at Sarpedon as he came in fury.

Sarpedon gave way a little from the battlement; but he did not withdraw

entirely, since his spirit was hoping to win glory.

And turning himself about, he called to the godlike Lycians:

"O Lycians, why do you relax your fierce courage?

Hard it is for me, strong though I am,   410

to break this alone and make a way to the ships.

Come, join with me; for the work of many men is better."

So he spoke, and in dread of their lord's rebuke

they pressed all the more around the lord who bore their counsels;

but the Argives from the other side strengthened their ranks

from inside the wall; and great was the task set before them all;

for neither were the powerful Lycians able to break the wall

of the Danaans and make a way to the ships,

nor were the Danaan spearmen ever able to thrust

the Lycians from the wall, when once they had made their position,   420

but as two men fall out over boundaries,

measuring rods in hand in a common-worked field,

who wrangle in the tiny spot for equal share,

so then did the narrow ramparts separate them; and above them the men
kept tearing at the oxhide shields about each other's chests,
well-rounded shields and bristling hides fluttering with tassels.
And many men were wounded down through their flesh with pitiless
    bronze,
both the fighter whose back was exposed by his turning,
and many right through their very shields.
And everywhere the towers and ramparts were spattered   430
with the blood of men from both sides, Trojans and Achaeans.
Yet still the Trojans were not able to make a rout of the Achaeans,
but they held on, as a woman careful in her poverty holds her scales,
and holding a weight and her wool, one on each side, she raises them
to balance equally, so as to gain for her children a meagre pittance.

      So their fighting and the line of war were pulled tight and equal,
until the time when Zeus gave victorious glory to Hector
son of Priam, who was first to rush within the wall of the Achaeans.
With a piercing voice he shouted so as to be heard by the Trojans:
"Rise up, Trojans, breakers of horses, shatter the wall   440
of the Argives, hurl into their ships the demonic fire."
So he spoke inciting them; and all gave ear to him,
and made straight for the wall in a mob. They
scaled the outworks, pointed spears in hand,
while Hector seizing a rock carried it with him, a rock that
stood before the gates, blunt at the bottom,
but sharp it was on top; a rock that the two best men of the country
could not without effort heave from the earth to a wagon
such as mortal men are now; but he with ease brandished it, and on
   . his own.
the son of devious Cronus made it light for him;   450
as when a shepherd easily carries the fleece of a ram,
picking it up with his left hand, and the burden weighs little on him,
so Hector lifting the stone bore it straight for the doors,
which close-guarded the gates, tightly fitted,

a towering pair; two bars inside,

crossing each other, held it, and a single bolt was fitted on.

He went and stood close, and taking a firm stance, he struck them in the
   middle,

his legs straddled wide, so that his blow lose no force,

and shattered both hinges; the stone fell inside

under its own weight. The gates groaned loud on either side, the bolts   460

did not hold, the doors were sundered in every direction

by the blow of the stone. Glorious Hector sprang at them,

his face dark like the rushing night; he shone with the dreadful

gleam of bronze that he had put about his body; in his hands he held

two spears. No one coming against him could have restrained him,

except the gods, when he leapt through the gates; and his eyes blazed
   with fire.

Whirling around he called to the Trojans through the battle-throng

to scale the wall; they obeyed his urging,

and at once stormed over the wall, and some through the well-wrought

gates themselves rushed in; the Danaans fled   470

to the hollow ships; and there arose tumult unceasing.

Now when Zeus had brought Hector and the Trojans to the ships,
he left both the armies beside them to endure toil and hardship
without respite, and he himself turned his shining eyes away
into the distance, looking down to the land of the horse-tending
    Thracians
and the close-fighting Mysians and the proud Hippemolgoi,
who live on milk, and the Abioi, most upright of men.
Toward Troy he turned no more at all his shining eyes;
for in his heart he did not imagine any of the immortals
would go to aid the Trojans or Danaans.

        But the lord Earth-Shaker kept no blind watch;   10
for he too sat marvelling at the war and battle,
high up on the topmost crown of wooded Samothrace;
from there was displayed the whole of Ida,
the city of Priam was displayed and the ships of the Achaeans.
There, coming out of the sea, he sat and he pitied the Achaeans
beaten down at the hands of the Trojans, and he reproached Zeus
    violently.
In a moment he descended from the rugged mountain,
swiftly striding forward on his feet; and the great mountains and
    woodlands shook
beneath the immortal feet of Poseidon as he proceeded.
Three strides he made, and on the fourth he reached his goal—   20

Aigai; where his illustrious house was built in the depths of the sea,
gleaming golden, imperishable for ever.
Arriving there he yoked to his chariot a pair of horses shod with bronze,
swift-flying, with luxuriant manes of gold,
and he clad himself in gold, and grasped his golden
well-wrought whip, and stepped into his chariot.
And he set out to drive across the waves; and the creatures of the sea
    gambolled at his coming
out of their deep places from every side, nor did they fail to recognise
    their lord,
and the sea parted in joy; and the horses flew on
lightly, nor was the bronze axle beneath even moistened;   30
so the swift-springing horses carried him to the ships of the Achaeans.

        There is a certain broad deep cave in the depths of ocean
between the islands Tenedos and rugged Imbros;
there Poseidon the Earth-Shaker drew up his horses
releasing them from the chariot, and cast before them ambrosial
    fodder
to eat; and around their feet he threw golden fetters,
infrangible, not to be loosened, so they would steadfastly await
their lord's return; and he proceeded to the Achaean army.

        And like fire or whirling wind the thronging Trojans
followed Hector son of Priam, battle-hungry always,   40
united in their loud shouts and cries; they thought they would seize the
    ships of the Achaeans,
and kill all their best men beside them.
But Poseidon, the earth-shaking holder of the earth,
rallied the Argives, emerging from the deep salt sea,
likening himself in form and tireless voice to Calchas.
He addressed the two Aiantes first, zealous though they were already:
"Aiantes, you must save—both of you—the Achaean people
being mindful of your valour, and not of shivering flight.
In any other place I do not fear the unassailable might of hand

of the Trojans who have scaled in a body up and over our great wall;   50
the strong-greaved Achaeans will hold them off;
but I most terribly, greatly fear lest we suffer in that place
where this fiery madman leads—
Hector, who boasts to be the son of mighty Zeus.
May one of the gods so put it in your hearts
to stand your ground strongly yourselves, and to exhort the others.
Then you might drive him back, for all his rushing speed, from the swift-
     sailing ships,
though the Olympian himself stir him to battle."

      He spoke, and with his staff the Earth-Shaker who holds the
     earth
struck them, filling both with mighty courage,   60
and he made their limbs light, their feet and their arms.
And he himself rose to fly like a swift-winged hawk,
which borne aloft from a sheer rock
swoops to pursue some other bird across the plain;
so Poseidon who shakes the earth shot away from them.
And of the two, swift Ajax son of Oïleus first understood,
and straightway he addressed Ajax son of Telamon:
"Ajax, since one of the gods who hold Olympus
bids us, in the likeness of our seer, to do battle by the ships—
for he is not Calchas, the augur of birds who prays to god;   70
the stride of his feet and legs from behind
I quickly recognised as he was going; gods though they be they are easily
     known;
and the spirit in my own breast
has been stirred the more to fight and to do battle,
my feet beneath me strain for action as do my hands above."

      And answering him spoke Telamonian Ajax:
"So now too my hands, invincible, strain about my spear shaft,
and my spirit stirs, and by the feet beneath me
I am rushed along; I yearn, even on my own,

to fight with Hector son of Priam, who is battle-hungry always."   80
        So they spoke such things to one another,
exulting in their resolve for battle, which the god had placed within their
    hearts.
Meanwhile the Earth-Holder rallied other Achaeans behind them,
who were reviving their spirits beside the swift ships.
For their very limbs were undone by grievous toil,
and anguish pierced their hearts as they beheld
the Trojans, who in a body had scaled up and over their great wall;
as they looked on them they wept tears beneath their brows;
for they did not think they would escape clear of destruction; but the
    Earth-Shaker,
moving easily among them, pressed them into strong formations.   90
He came first to Teucer and Leïtos, urging them on,
and to Peneleos the warrior and to Thoas and Deïpyros and
Meriones and also Antilochos, raisers of the battle cry.
Urging them he spoke winged words:
"For shame, Argives, young boys; I trusted your
fighting to save our ships.
But if you hang back from baleful war,
then now appears the day we will be broken by the Trojans.
O shame! This is a great wonder I see with my eyes,
a terrible thing, which I never thought would be accomplished—   100
that Trojans reach our ships—Trojans, who just before
were like skittish deer, which flittering through the woods
are so much food for jackals, leopards, wolves,
useless, incapable of defence, nor is there fire of fighting in them.
So the Trojans in time before used to be unwilling
to stand face to face against Achaean might or strength of hand, not even
    for a little while;
now far from the city, they fight beside the hollow ships,
through the cowardice of our leader and the slackness of our people,

who angered with him are not willing to ward off the Trojans
from the swift-voyaging ships, but are killed among them.   110
And if in truth he is wholly guilty,
the warrior son of Atreus, wide-ruling Agamemnon,
because he outraged Peleus' swift-footed son,
still we cannot hang back from our fighting.
Come, let us quickly mend our ways, for the hearts of noble men can be
    amended.
You are not right to slacken your fierce courage,
you, all the best men in the army; I would not
quarrel with a man who hung back from fighting
because he was worthless, but with you I am angry with all my heart.
Weaklings! You will soon bring about some even greater evil   120
by this slackness. Each one of you put in your mind
a sense of shame and righteous censure, for now a great battle stirs;
Hector of the war cry is fighting by our ships
in his might, and has smashed our gates and the long door-bolt."

        Taking the lead this way the Earth-Holder spurred on the
    Achaeans.
And about the two Aiantes the powerful ranks
took position, ranks that Ares would not have slighted on inspection,
nor Athena who drives the army into battle for they, the best men,
the chosen, awaited the Trojans and shining Hector,
and spear was locked with spear, one shield upon another,   130
buckler weighed on buckler, helmet on helmet, man on man,
and the helmets plumed with horsehair touched with shining crests
when the men nodded; so tight did they stand beside each other.
Spears brandished in their emboldened hands
made layered ranks; their minds were fixed ahead and they were hungry
    to do battle.

        The Trojans pressed forward in a body, and Hector led them
straight on, raging, like a boulder rolling from a cliff

that a river in winter flood has forced from the brow of a hill,
having torn its foundation of remorseless rock with an immense
    downpour,
and leaping high the boulder flies along, and the forest crashes
    beneath it;   140
straight on it runs without wavering, until it reaches
level ground; then it rolls no more, for all its urgency.
So for a while Hector threatened to sweep through
the tents and ships of the Achaeans to the sea
as he slaughtered; but when he ran into their close-pressed ranks,
he came to a stop, so close he brushed against them. And facing him the
    sons of Achaeans,
stabbing with their swords and two-edged spears,
drove him from them; and he retreated, staggering.
With a piercing voice he shouted so as to be heard by the Trojans:
"Trojans and Lycians and close-fighting Dardanians,   150
stay by me; not for long will the Achaeans withstand me,
for all they array themselves in a wall of defence,
but, I suspect, they will give way under my spear, if truly
it is the highest of gods who drives me, the far-thundering husband of
    Hera."
            So speaking he rallied the spirit and heart of each man.
And among them Deïphobos had stepped forth, intent on a great deed,
the son of Priam, and held before him the circle of his shield,
advancing with light strides and edging forward behind his shield.
Meriones took aim at him with his shining spear,
and did not miss him, but struck across the circle of the   160
oxhide shield; but it did not drive through, for far before
the long spear shattered at the shaft-head socket; and Deïphobos
held the oxhide shield away from him, and feared in his heart
the spear of warlike Meriones. And Meriones the warrior
drew back into the band of his companions, greatly angered
on two counts—he had lost the victory and shattered his spear;

he went beside the shelters and the ships of the Achaeans
to bring his long spear, which he had left behind in his shelters.

      And the rest fought on, with quenchless cry of battle rising.
Teucer son of Telamon first killed a man,   170
Imbrios the spear-fighter, son of Mentor of many horses;
he dwelt in Pedaios, until the coming of the sons of the Achaeans,
and wed a bastard daughter of Priam, Medesikaste.
But when the double-ended ships of the Danaans came,
he returned to Ilion, and distinguished himself among the Trojans,
and made his home near Priam; and Priam honoured him like his sons.
This man the son of Telamon stabbed with his long spear beneath the ears,
then wrenched the spear out; and Imbrios fell back like an ash tree,
which, on the peak of a mountain conspicuous from far around,
felled by a bronze axe brings its tender leaves to touch the ground.   180
So he fell, and his armour, elaborate with bronze, clashed about him.
Teucer made a rush, intent on stripping his armour;
and Hector took aim with his shining spear as he did,
but Teucer watching straight ahead evaded the bronze spear
barely, and Hector struck Amphimachos, son of Kteatos, who was the son
    of Aktor,
across the chest with his spear as he was returning to the fighting;
he fell with a thud, and his armour clashed upon him.
And Hector rushed to snatch from his head the helmet,
close fitted to the brows of great-hearted Amphimachos;
but Ajax thrust out with his shining spear as Hector   190
charged; but Hector's flesh was nowhere visible, he was entirely
covered with dreadful bronze; so Ajax struck the boss of his shield,
and with his great strength forced him back; and Hector withdrew
from both corpses, and the Achaeans dragged them away.
And Stichios and noble Menestheus, leaders of the Athenians,
carried Amphimachos back among the Achaean host,
but the two Aiantes carried Imbrios away, intent on displaying their fierce
    courage;

as two lions having snatched a goat from saw-toothed dogs
bear it through dense underbrush
holding it high above the ground in their jaws,   200
so the two Aiantes holding Imbrios high stripped his helmet
and his armour; and from his soft neck the son of Oïleus
cut off his head, in his rage for the death of Amphimachos,
and swinging it round, he hurled it like a ball through the throng; and
    it fell
in the dust before the feet of Hector.

                Then Poseidon, his heart consumed with rage
at the falling of his grandson in dread combat,
set out to go to the shelters and ships of the Achaeans
to rouse the Danaans, and to wreak heartache for the Trojans.
But spear-famed Idomeneus chanced upon him,   210
as he made his way from a companion who had just come to him
    from the
fighting, having been wounded behind the knee by sharp bronze.
His companions had carried the wounded man, and having given orders
    to the healers
he was going to his shelter; for he was still minded to take part in battle.
And the lord Earth-Shaker addressed him,
assuming the voice of Andraimon's son Thoas,
who in all Pleuron and steep Calydon
ruled the Aetolians, and was honoured like a god by the people:
"Idomeneus, leader of the Cretan council, where then are the threats
that the sons of Achaeans made to the Trojans?"   220

                In turn Idomeneus, leader of the Cretans, answered him:
"O Thoas, no man is to be blamed now, as far as I myself
know; for all of us know how to fight.
No slack fear constrains any man, nor yielding to doubt
does anyone shirk the evil fighting; but this way
it seems is pleasing to the almighty son of Cronus,
that the Achaeans die here, nameless, far from Argos.

Come Thoas, for before this you were battle-steady,

and rallied another whenever you saw him hanging back;

therefore do not be reluctant now and give every man his order."   230

　　　　　Then Poseidon who shakes the earth answered him:

"Idomeneus, may that man never yet return

home from Troy, but become here a plaything of dogs,

who on this day would willingly hang back from doing battle.

But come, taking your armour follow this way; we must hurry

　　　matters on

together, to see if we may be of use in any way, though we are but two.

United, there is valour in even worthless men;

and we two know how to fight—even against good warriors."

　　　　　　So speaking Poseidon set out again, a god among the fighting

　　　throng of men;

and when Idomeneus arrived at his well-built shelter,   240

he put his splendid armour about his body, and grasped two spears.

And set out like a bolt of lightning that the son of Cronus

taking hold of in his hand brandishes from radiant Olympus

to declare a sign to mortal men, and its flashings outshine everything in

　　　heaven;

so the bronze armour shone about his chest as he was running.

Then his good henchman Meriones encountered him

while he was still near the shelter. For he had come after to fetch a bronze

　　　spear.

And strong Idomeneus spoke to him:

"Meriones, swift-footed son of Molos, most beloved of companions,

why have you come here leaving the strife and battle?   250

Have you been hit somewhere, and a spear-point afflicts you—

or do you come to me as a messenger? As for myself, I have no

desire to sit about the shelters, but to fight."

Then wise Meriones addressed him in reply: 254

"I come to see if by chance some spear of yours was left inside the

　　　shelters,   256

for me to carry; for we broke the one that I used to bear before,
striking the shield of arrogant Deïphobos."

       Then in turn Idomeneus leader of the Cretans addressed him:
"You will find one spear or twenty, if you wish,   260
standing in my shelter against the shining inner wall,
Trojan spears, which I took from men who have been killed; for I do not
    expect
to fight standing at a distance from my enemies.
Therefore my spears and bossed shields are there,
and helmets and war-belts gleaming brightly."

       Then again wise Meriones answered him:
"I too, by my shelters and dark ship, have
much Trojan spoil; but it is not close at hand to take.
And indeed I think I am not careless of my courage,
but among the front ranks throughout the field of battle where men
    win glory   270
I take my stand, whenever the conflict of war arises.
Let my fighting slip the notice of some other
of the bronze-clad Achaeans, but I think that you yourself know of it."

       Then in turn Idomeneus leader of the Cretans answered him:
"I know your courage, what manner of man you are; why must you
    recount these things?
If all the best of us should now be gathered by the ships
for an ambush, where more than anywhere men learn the value of their
    courage—
there the man who is cowardly and he who is brave is exposed for what he is,
for the complexion of the coward changes colour this way and that,
nor can he restrain the spirit in his breast to sit without moving,   280
but fidgeting, he shifts from one leg to the other,
and in his breast his heart pounds violently
as he thinks of death, and there is a chattering of his teeth;
but the complexion of the brave man does not change, nor is he
greatly afraid, once he takes his place among the ambush of men,

and his prayer is that with all speed he may join the distress of battle—
there no man would slight your spirit and strength of hands.
Even if you were wounded by a spear thrown or struck by a sword in the
    toil of battle,
the blow would not land upon your neck from behind, nor in your back,
but would meet your breast or your belly   290
as you press forward among the clutch of frontline fighters.
But come, let us not discuss these things longer like children
standing around, lest someone high-handedly rebuke us,
but go to my tent and get a heavy spear."

          So he spoke; and Meriones a match for swift Ares
at once took up a bronze spear and went from the shelter,
with Idomeneus, his mind set firmly on battle.
As Ares ruinous to mortals sets out to war,
and Rout follows with him, his beloved son, powerful and fearless,
who puts to flight even the steadfast warrior;   300
they two go armed from Thrace to join with the Ephyroi
or the great-hearted Phlegyes; and they do not
heed the prayers of both sides, but grant glory to one or to the other—
such were Meriones and Idomeneus, leaders of men,
as they were setting out for war, helmeted in gleaming bronze.

          And Meriones spoke a word to the other first:
"Son of Deucalion, at what place do you intend to enter the battle-
    throng?
On the left of the whole army, or in the middle,
or on the right? For nowhere else do I think the long-haired Achaeans
so unequal to the combat."   310
Then Idomeneus leader of the Cretans answered him:
"There are others in the centre to defend the ships,
the two Aiantes and Teucer, who is best of the Achaeans
with the bow, and good in close combat;
they will drive that one to have his fill of war, for all his eagerness,
this Hector, son of Priam, even if he is very powerful.

A hard climb it will be for him, for all his great hunger to do battle,
to best their spirit and invincible strength of hands,
and bring fire to the ships, unless the son of Cronus himself
should throw a burning firebrand onto the swift ships.   320
Great Telamonian Ajax will yield to no man
who is mortal and eats the grain of Demeter,
and can be torn by bronze or by great boulders thrown;
nor would he give way to man-shattering Achilles
in close combat; though in swiftness of feet it is not possible to contend
    with Achilles.
As for us, hold this course to the left of the army, so that we swiftly see
whether we will give the right to vaunt to someone else, or he to us."

        So he spoke; and Meriones a match for swift Ares
led the way, until they arrived at the army, where he had urged.
And when the Trojans saw Idomeneus, firelike in spirit,   330
him and his retainer in their elaborate armour,
then calling along the throng of battle they all ran for him;
The fray of massed men rose by the sterns of the ships;
as when under a shrill wind whirling gales rush
on a day when the dust is thickest on the roadsides,
and converging they raise a great hazy cloud of dust,
so the fighting men converged on the same spot, and their hearts were
    intent
on killing each other with sharp bronze throughout the throng of battle.
The man-destroying battle bristled with long, flesh-tearing spears
that the men held; it dazed their eyes—   340
the bronze light from the glittering armour
and from the breastplates new-burnished and the shining shields,
as the men converged. Strong-hearted indeed would that man be
who could rejoice on looking at the battle toil, and not grieve.

        So two powerful sons of Cronus, Poseidon and Zeus, disposed to
    both sides,
wrought painful hardship for the fighting men.

Zeus was planning victory for Hector and the Trojans,
to glorify swift-footed Achilles (nor did he wish
wholly to destroy the Achaean army in front of Ilion,
but only to glorify Thetis and her strong-hearted son);   350
Poseidon had aroused the Argives, entering among them
in secret, emerging out of the grey salt sea; for he was oppressed with grief
because the Argives were being defeated by the Trojans, and violently did
    he reproach Zeus.
To be sure the same generation and same parentage belonged to both,
but Zeus had been born first and knew more.
Therefore while Poseidon shrank from defending the Achaeans openly,
in secret he ever stirred them to action throughout the army, but in the
    likeness of a man.
So the two gods stretched the rope of violent strife and of war that levels all
    alike
back and forth across both sides.
unbreakable, not to be undone, a rope that made slack the strength of
    knees of many men.   360

        And greying though he was, Idomeneus in command of the
    Danaans
rushed upon the Trojans and incited panic in them.
He slew Othryoneus, who was with them from Kabesos,
who had come recently after report of the war,
and had asked for the hand of the most beautiful of Priam's daughters,
Cassandra, without bride-price, and promised a great deed—
to drive away from Troy by force the sons of the Achaeans.
And old Priam nodded assent and promised to give her to him;
and Othryoneus fought trusting in his promises.
At this man Idomeneus took aim with his shining spear   370
and cast, striking him in mid high-stepping stride; nor did his breastplate
    protect him,
bronze though it was, which he was wont to wear, but it fixed in the
    middle of his stomach,

and he fell with a thud. And Idomeneus vaunted over him in a loud
   voice:
"Othryoneus, I compliment you beyond all men,
if you are really to accomplish all you promised
to Dardanian Priam; and he promised you his daughter.
We too would promise to fulfil the same terms for you,
and give you the son of Atreus' most beautiful daughter,
bringing her out from Argos to marry, if joining with us
you would sack the well-settled city of Ilion.   380
Come, follow me, so that we may come to agreement by our seagoing ships
about your marriage, since we are not greedy about marriage gifts."

       So speaking the warrior Idomeneus dragged Othryoneus by the
   foot
through the mighty combat. But Asios came up to defend him,
dismounted ahead of his horses; his retainer and charioteer
held them close in check as they breathed upon his shoulders; and he
   longed with all his heart
to strike Idomeneus; but it was Idomeneus who first struck him with his
   spear
in the throat beneath his chin, and the bronze drove straight through;
he fell as when an oak falls, or white poplar,
or stately pine that in the mountains timbering men   390
fell with fresh-whetted axes to make a ship;
so he lay stretched out before his chariot and horses,
roaring, clutching at the bloodied dust.
His charioteer was struck out of such wits as he possessed before,
and had not courage to turn the horses back,
to escape from out of enemy hands; and so battle-staunch Antilochos
striking with his spear impaled him in the middle; nor did his breastplate
   protect him,
bronze though it was, which he was wont to wear, but the spear fixed in
   the middle of his stomach.
Then, gasping, he dropped from the well-wrought chariot,

and Antilochos, son of great-hearted Nestor, drove off the horses   400
from the Trojans toward the strong-greaved Achaeans.

      And Deïphobos came up very close to Idomeneus
stricken with grief over Asios, and took aim with his shining spear-shaft.
But watching straight ahead, Idomeneus evaded the bronze point;
for he was sheltered under the round shield
that he carried, adorned as it was with rings of oxhide
and gleaming bronze, fitted with two struts inside it.
Beneath this he crouched his whole body, and the bronze spear flew
    over,
and his shield rang harshly as the spear brushed by.
Yet Deïphobos did not hurl it from his powerful hand in vain,   410
but he struck Hypsenor, son of Hippasos, shepherd of the people,
in the liver, under the midriff, and in an instant unstrung his knees.
And Deïphobos exulted wildly, shouting loud:
"Asios then does not lie unavenged, but I think that
even on his way to Hades, the mighty keeper of the gates,
he will rejoice in his heart, since I have given him an escort."
So he spoke; and grief descended on the Argives at his crowing,
and most of all he stirred the spirit of wise Antilochos.
And though grieving, he was not heedless of his comrade,
but running up stood astride and put his shield to cover Hypsenor.   420
Then getting their shoulders under him, two faithful companions,
Mekisteus the son of Echios and godlike Alastor,
bore him, groaning heavily, to the hollow ships.

      And Idomeneus did not check his great fury, but ever strove
to bury some Trojan in death's dark night,
or to fall himself, warding off destruction from the Achaeans.
The beloved son of Aisyetes, cherished by Zeus
the warrior Alkathoös—he was Anchises' son-in-law,
and had married the eldest of his daughters, Hippodameia,
whom her father and lady mother loved with all their hearts   430
in their home; for she surpassed all her age

in beauty and handiwork and good sense; and for this reason
the best man in Troy's broad land had married her—
this man Poseidon broke at the hands of Idomeneus,
bewitching his shining eyes, shackling his bright limbs.
And he was neither able to flee back, nor to escape,
but while he stood without moving, like a pillar or a high-leafed tree,
the warrior Idomeneus stabbed him in the middle of his chest
with his spear, and he laid open the bronze armour about him,
which before had protected his body from death.   440
Now, though, it rasped loud as it was rent about the spear,
and Alkathoös fell with a thud, and the spear-shaft plunged into his
      heart,
and his heart as it laboured shook the butt-end of the spear;
then mighty Ares dispatched its vital force.
And Idomeneus exulted wildly, shouting loud:
"Deïphobos, do we reckon that it is fair exchange,
that three men were slain for one? Since you it was who boasted this way.
Madman, come yourself and take your stand face to face against me,
so you may see what son of Zeus has come here,
Zeus who first begat Minos the guardian of Crete,   450
Minos then begat his blameless son Deucalion,
and Deucalion begat me, lord of many men
throughout wide Crete; now I have carried my ships here
as evil to you and your father and to all Trojans."
         So he spoke; and Deïphobos weighed in his mind two ways,
whether he should find some one of the great-hearted Trojans as a
      comrade
after drawing back, or should take a chance on his own.
And this seemed to him as he considered to be best—
to go to Aeneas; and he found him standing at the back of the throng;
for he was ever wrathful with godlike Priam,   460
because noble though he was among men, Priam held him in no honour.
Standing close to him he spoke winged words:

"Aeneas, leader of the Trojan council, now there is need for you
to protect your brother-in-law, if any care for family comes to you.
Come, follow me, let us fight for Alkathoös, who in time before
as your sister's husband raised you in his house when you were young;
the famed spearman Idomeneus has killed him."

So he spoke; and stirred the heart in Aeneas's breast to confusion;
and Aeneas strode after Idomeneus, his mind resolutely set on battle.
But no thought of flight gripped Idomeneus like some untested child,   470
but he remained, like a wild boar in the mountains confident in his
    courage,
who awaits a great approaching band of men
in a desolate place, and his back bristles above,
and his eyes glitter with fire; then he sharpens his tusks,
straining to defend himself against both dogs and men;
so spear-famed Idomeneus awaited, nor did he retreat,
as Aeneas, swift to defend, approached; but Idomeneus called to his
    companions,
looking to Askalaphos and Aphareus and Deïpyros and
Meriones and Antilochos too, masters of the battle cry;
rallying these he addressed them with winged words: 480
"Come, friends, and stand by me, who am alone; for terribly I fear
Aeneas, drawing near, swift of foot, who advances on me,
who is powerful indeed in slaying men in battle;
and he has also the bloom of youth, which is the greatest strength.
For if we were of the same age with this same spirit,
at once either he would carry away a great victory, or would I."

So he spoke; and as one in spirit they all
stood in a body, inclining their shields against their shoulders.
But on the other side Aeneas called to his companions,
looking to Deïphobos and Paris and brilliant Agenor,   490
who with him were leaders of the Trojans; and
the host followed, as flocks follow after a ram
when they go to drink from their place of pasture, and the shepherd rejoices;

so the heart in the breast of Aeneas rejoiced,

as he saw the host following in company with him.

These men charged in close combat around the body of Alkathoös at
     close range

with their long spears; and the clash of bronze around their chests

was terrible to hear through the throng of battle as they hurled spears

at one another. Two warlike men pre-eminent beyond others,

Aeneas and Idomeneus, both a match for Ares,   500

strained to cut each other's flesh with pitiless bronze.

          And Aeneas was first to cast at Idomeneus;

but he, watching straight ahead, evaded the bronze spear,

and the point went quivering down into the ground,

for it sprang in vain from the strong hand of Aeneas.

Then Idomeneus struck Oinomaos in the pit of the stomach,

and shattered the hollow of his breastplate; and the bronze made his
     entrails

gush through, and falling in the dust he clutched the earth with his
     clenched hand.

And from the corpse Idomeneus wrenched his long-shadowed spear,

but was not able to strip the rest of the splendid armour   510

from the dead man's shoulders; for he was assailed by spears and arrows.

His feet were no longer steady when he attacked,

not for darting forward after his thrown spear, not for fleeing from harm;

so in close-standing combat he fought off the pitiless day of death,

and his feet no longer carried him for speedy flight from fighting.

Step by step Idomeneus retreated, as Deïphobos took aim at him with his

shining spear; for the bitterness he held for him was undying.

But even then he missed, and struck Askalaphos with his spear,

the son of Ares Enyalios, the god of war; through his shoulder the heavy
     spear

held its way; and falling in the dust he clutched the earth with his
     clenched hand.   520

Nor had mighty roaring Ares heard a thing

of his son falling in the mighty conflict,

but he sat beneath golden clouds on the height of Olympus,

held by the will of Zeus, there with the rest of the

immortals gods, debarred from battle.

And around the body of Askalaphos the men charged in close

combat.

And Deïphobos seized the shining helmet from Askalaphos;

then Meriones, match of the swift war god,

leaping forward struck Deïphobos' arm with his spear, and from his hand

the hollow-eyed helmet resounded as it fell on the ground.   530

Meriones swiftly swooping like a vulture

wrenched the heavy spear from the top of his arm,

and withdrew back into the band of his companions. But Polites,

brother of Deïphobos, reaching both arms about his brother's waist,

led him back from the grievous fighting, until he reached his swift

horses, who behind the line of battle and the fighting

stood waiting for him, holding their charioteer and patterned chariot;

and they carried him to the city groaning heavily

in his distress; and blood poured from his new-wounded arm.

And the rest fought on, with quenchless cry of battle rising.   540

Aeneas rushing at Kaletor's son Aphareus

struck him in the throat with his sharp spear as he was turned toward him;

his head lolled to one side, back fell his shield

and helmet; and death which shatters the spirit seeped around him.

Antilochus, eyeing Thoön as he turned away,

charged and stabbed him and severed the whole vein

that runs the length of the back to reach the neck;

he severed the whole of it away, and the other dropped on his back

in the dust, spreading both arms wide to his dear companions.

Antilochos rushing up stripped the armour from his shoulders,   550

glancing about him; Trojans standing round from every side

stabbed his broad all-gleaming shield; but they could not

get within it even to scratch with pitiless bronze the tender skin

of Antilochos, for earth-shaking Poseidon fiercely
protected Nestor's son, even amid the multitude of blows.
Never was he clear of his enemies, but kept wheeling
among them; nor did he hold his spear still, but it was ever
shaken, brandished, and with all his heart he aimed
to make a spearcast or attack at close quarters.

But Antilochos did not escape the notice of Adamas as he took
   aim through the fighting throng,   560
he the son of Asios, who struck the middle of his shield with sharp bronze,
attacking from close at hand; but dark-haired Poseidon,
grudging him Antilochos' life, deprived his spear of power.
Half of it remained in the shield of Antilochos,
like a fire-hardened spike, and half hung to the ground;
and Adamas withdrew into the band of his companions, shunning death.
But following after, Meriones struck Adamas as he was departing with
   his spear
between genitals and navel, where more than anywhere
wounds in war are grievous hard for pitiful mortal men.
There the spear stuck; and with the spear inside him   570
he gasped his last, like a wild ox that in the mountains herdsmen
have hobbled with twisted rope and drive by force against its will;
so wounded by the blow he gasped his last, albeit for a short time, not
   long at all,
until the warrior Meriones, looming close, dragged the spear back
from his flesh; and then darkness covered over his eyes.

And Helenos smote Deïpyros at close quarters on the temple
   with his
great Thracian sword, and smashed away his crested helmet.
Struck off, it fell on the ground, and one of the Achaeans
took possession of it where it rolled among the feet of the fighting men;
and down over his eyes black night covered Deïpyros.   580

Then grief seized the son of Atreus, Menelaos of the war cry,
and he approached menacing the warrior lord Helenos,

shaking his sharp spear; but Helenos raised the grip of his bow.
At the same moment both men let fly—one aimed
with his ash-wood spear, the other with an arrow from his bowstring.
The son of Priam struck Menelaos in the chest with his arrow,
in the hollow of his breastplate—but the bitter arrow flew back;
as when across a great threshing floor black-skinned beans and
   chickpeas
rebound away from the broad winnowing-fan
thrown by the whistling wind and the draught of the winnower's swing,   590
so from the breastplate of glorious Menelaos
rebounding hard, the bitter arrow flew to a distance.
But the son of Atreus, Menelaos of the war cry,
struck Helenos on the hand with which he held his polished bow; and
   straight through
his hand into the bow he drove the bronze spear.
And Helenos shrank into the band of his companions, shunning death,
dangling his hand by his side; and trailing the ash-wood spear.
And great-hearted Agenor pulled it from his hand,
which he bound with sheep's fleece skilfully twisted
that his retainers kept for him, the shepherd of his people, to make a
   sling.   600

      Then Peisandros came straight at glorious Menelaos;
but an evil fate led him to the moment of his death,
to be broken by you, Menelaos, in dread combat.
And when they had advanced almost upon each other,
the son of Atreus threw and missed, and his spear was turned aside;
but Peisandros stabbed the shield of glorious Menelaos;
nor was he able to drive his bronze spear through,
for the broad shield stopped it, and the spear was snapped
at the socket. And at this the son of Atreus rejoiced in his heart and
hoped for victory, and drawing his silver-studded sword   610
he sprang for Peisandros; but behind the cover of his shield Peisandros
   grasped

his splendid axe, well wrought in bronze, set on a handle of long,
   well-polished
olive-wood; and at the same moment they bludgeoned one another.
Peisandros struck the ridge of the other's horsehair-crested helmet
on the very peak below the crest, but Meneleaos struck Peisandros on the
   brow as he drew near,
over the base of the nose; the bones cracked, and his two eyes
dropped to the ground by his feet, bloodied, in the dust.
He fell, curled in pain. And Menelaos placing his foot upon his chest
stripped the dead man's armour and spoke in exultation:
"This is the way you will leave the ships of the Danaans of swift
   horses,

620

you Trojans of reckless deeds, never sated with dread battle.
Nor are you deficient in other outrage and insult,
with which you insulted me, cowardly bitches, nor do you at all fear
in your heart the harsh wrath of far-thundering Zeus
protector of hospitality, who in days to come will sack utterly your high
   city;
you who went away taking my lawful wife and my many possessions
against decency, when you had been treated hospitably by her;
now, this time, it was on our seagoing ships you were set
to hurl deadly fire, and to kill Achaean warriors.
But you will be checked somewhere, for all your rushing haste
   for war.

630

Father Zeus—for you, they say, surpass the wisdom of all other
men and gods; yet all these matters are your doing—
how you favour indecent men—
the Trojans, whose spirit is ever reckless, nor can they
have enough of the din of all-leveling war!
There is satiety in all things, even sleep and even love,
and in sweet song and blameless dance;
surely a man hopes for satisfaction from those things more than
from war. But the Trojans are insatiate of battle."

So speaking, blameless Menelaos stripped the bloody armour   640
from the corpse and gave it to his comrades,
and he going back again took his place among the frontline fighters.
      But then there sprang at him King Pylaimenes' son
Harpalion, who followed his beloved father to take part in the fight
at Troy, nor did he again reach his fatherland;
Harpalion stabbed the shield of the son of Atreus, in the middle,
at close quarters with his spear; but he was not able to drive his bronze
      spear through,
and withdrew back into the band of his companions shunning death,
darting glances all around him, lest someone graze him with their
      spear.
But as he was departing Meriones let fly an arrow tipped with
      bronze,   650
and struck him on the right buttock; and the arrow
made its way straight on through beneath the bone, down through the
      bladder.
Sitting there, in the arms of his beloved companions
breathing his life forth, like a worm he lay outstretched
upon the ground; and the dark blood flowed forth, and soaked the earth.
And the great-hearted Paphlagonians attended upon him,
and setting him in a chariot they led him to sacred Ilion
grieving. And among them went his father, pouring tears;
nor was there any recompense for his son's dying.
      But Paris was greatly angered in his heart that Harpalion was
      killed;   660
for he used to be his guest friend among the many Paphlagonians;
and angered for his sake he let fly a bronze-tipped arrow.
And there was a certain Euchenor, the son of the seer Polyidos,
a rich man and a brave man, who had his home in Corinth,
and who embarked upon his ship well knowing his deadly fate;
for many times the old man, brave Polyidos, told him
that he would waste away with painful disease in his own halls,

or be broken under Trojan hands among the ships of the Achaeans.
Thus he chose to avoid both the Achaeans' harsh fine for deserters
and hateful disease, so that his spirit not endure such sufferings.   670
This was the man Paris struck under the jaw and ear; in an instant his
  spirit
was gone from his limbs, and the hateful darkness took him.

            So they fought like blazing fire.
And Hector beloved of Zeus had not heard, nor did he know
that on the left of the ships his people were being killed
by the Argives—and an Achaean victory would soon have
come about; for such a one as the earth-holding Shaker of the Earth
rallied the Argives, and defended them too with his own strength.
But Hector held steady to where he first attacked the gates and wall
after shattering the close-set ranks of Danaan spearmen.   680
There the ships of Ajax and Protesilaos were
drawn up on the shore of the grey salt sea; and above these
the wall stood lowest; there more than anywhere
the men and even horses were the most formidable in the fighting.
And there the Boeotians and Ionians with their trailing robes,
the Locrians and Phthians and the glorious Epeans
with difficulty held him from the ships as he sprang forward— they were
  not able
to force brilliant flamelike Hector from them—
nor could the Athenians' chosen men, among whom
Menestheus the son of Peteos was leader, and with him followed   690
Pheidas and Stichios and goodly Bias; and the leaders of the Epeans
were Meges the son of Phyleus and Amphion and Drakios;
and at the head of the Phthians were steadfast Medon and Podarkes.
Now Medon was the bastard son of godlike Oïleus,
and a brother of Ajax, but he was living
in Phylake, away from his fatherland, having killed a man there,
the kinsman of his stepmother Eriopis, she whom Oïleus married;
but Podarkes was the child of Iphiklos, son of Phylakos.

These under arms at the head of the great-hearted Phthians
fought alongside the Boeotians defending the ships.   700

          And Ajax the swift son of Oïleus would never, not at all,
take his stand apart from Telamonian Ajax, not even a little,
but as in a fallow field two dark-faced oxen pull a sturdy plough,
equal in spirit, and around the base of their horns
heavy sweat streams forth—
only the well-polished yoke keeps the two apart
as they strain along the furrow, and reach the edge of the field—
so the two men stood firm side by side with each other.
And many men indeed, and noble men, followed the son of Telamon
as companions, who relieved him of his shield,   710
whenever sweat and fatigue gripped his knees;
but the great-hearted Locrians did not accompany the son of Oïleus;
for they had not the strength to stand firm in close combat.
They did not possess bronze-fitted helmets crested with horsehair,
nor did they have well-rounded shields and ash-wood spears,
but trusting in bows and in twisted woollen slings
they had followed along to Ilion, and with these,
volleying thick and fast, they shattered the ranks of Trojans.
So now others in their elaborate war-gear fought at the front
with the Trojans and Hector of the brazen helm,   720
while the Locrians were concealed as they volleyed from behind; and the
     Trojans forgot
their will to fight, roiled by the arrows.

          Then would the Trojans shamefully have withdrawn
from the ships and from the shelters to windswept Ilion,
had not Poulydamas come up to address bold Hector:
"Hector, it is impossible to guide you with words of persuasion.
Because god gave you feats of war in abundance,
do you therefore also seek to surpass others in skill of counsel?
You cannot take for yourself all gifts together;
god granted to one man feats of war,   730

to another skill in dance, to another the lyre and song,
and in the breast of another far-thundering Zeus placed
outstanding judgement, and many are the men who profit from it,
since he saves many, and he himself knows this most of all.
So then I will speak as it seems best to me.
On all sides the circle of war blazes round you;
the great-hearted Trojans—since they came over the wall,
some stand aloof and idle in their armour, others are doing battle
as fewer men against greater numbers, having been dispersed among the
    ships.
So draw back and summon all the best men here;   740
from this point we might devise a comprehensive plan—
either we could fall upon the many-oared ships,
if god should choose to give us strength, or thereafter
we might depart from the ships unscathed. For indeed I
fear lest the Achaeans pay back the debt of yesterday,
since beside their ships there still remains a man insatiate
of war, whom I think will not hold back much longer from the fighting."

         So spoke Poulydamas, and his words of caution found favour
    with Hector.
At once he sprang from his chariot in his armour to the ground.
And lifting his voice addressed him with winged words: 750
"Poulydamas, you keep all the best men assembled here,
and I am going over there and will meet the fighting.
I will come back quickly, when I have well instructed them."

         He spoke, and set out like a dazzling snow-clad mountain,
shouting, and swept through the Trojans and their allies.
All the rest hurried toward Poulydamas, the gracious son of Panthoös,
since they heeded Hector's words.
But Hector made his way through the front ranks seeking
Deïphobos and mighty lord Helenos
and Adamas son of Asios and Asios son of Hyrtakos, in the hope that he
    would come upon them.   760

And he found them no longer unharmed, in no way unscathed,
but some lay by the stern of the Achaean ships
having lost their lives at Argive hands,
others were inside the city wall wounded by spear and sword.
At the left wing of this woeful battle he soon found
Alexandros the godlike, husband of Helen of the lovely hair,
encouraging his companions and stirring them on to battle.
And standing close Hector addressed him with slighting words:
"Accursed Paris, outstanding only in beauty, woman crazed, seducer,
where is Deïphobos and mighty lord Helenos   770
and Adamas son of Asios and Asios son of Hyrtakos,
where is Othryoneus? Now headlong the whole
of lofty Ilion is destroyed; now is your own sheer destruction certain."

        Then in turn Alexandros godlike in beauty answered him:
"Hector, since it is your desire to blame the blameless—
at another time before I may have held back more from fighting,
but mother did not bear me to be an utter coward.
For from the moment you stirred your comrades to do battle by the
    ships,
from that time we remaining here have been fighting the Danaans
without ceasing. Some companions have died, of those you ask;   780
only Deïphobos and mighty lord Helenos
have left the field, wounded by long spears,
both on the arm; the son of Cronus warded off their deaths.
Now lead on, wherever your heart and spirit bid.
We eagerly will follow with you, nor do I think
we lack courage, as far as our strength goes;
beyond his strength not even a zealous man can fight."

        So speaking the warrior won over his brother's heart;
and setting out they went, where the fighting and outcry were greatest,
around Kebriones and blameless Poulydamas,   790
Phalkes and Orthaios and godlike Polyphetes
and Palmys and Askanios and Morys, sons of Hippotion,

who had both come as reserves from rich-soiled Askania
only the morning before, and now Zeus roused them to do battle.

They went like a stormy blast of baneful wind
that with the thunder of father Zeus descends to earth,
and amid sublime uproar hits the ocean, where curl the endless
seething waves of the tumultuous deep,
whitened to foam, waves in front, then ranks of waves behind;
so the Trojans, closely ranged in ranks in front, then ranks behind,   800
glittering with bronze, followed with their leaders.
And Hector son of Priam led them, equal of man-destroying Ares,
and held before him the circle of his shield,
dense-layered with skins and generous bronze hammered on it;
and his shining helmet shook about his temples.
In every point, from either side, he kept testing the ranks as he advanced,
to see if they might give way to him as he strode forward under cover of
    his shield;
but he did not perturb the spirit in the breasts of the Achaeans.

And Ajax was first to challenge him, advancing with long strides:
"Madman, come close; why do you vainly try to fright the Argives?   810
It is not that we lack skill in battle,
but by the harsh lash of Zeus the Achaeans have been broken.
Doubtless your heart hopes to destroy our ships
utterly; but we too have ready strength of hand to defend them.
Sooner by far will your fair-settled city
be seized and sacked under our hands;
and to you yourself I say that time is near, when fleeing in fear
you will pray to father Zeus and the rest of the immortals
that your horses with their beautiful manes be swifter than falcons,
when they carry you to your city, raising dust across the plain."   820

Then as he spoke a bird flew towards him on the right,
a high-flying eagle; and as it did the host of the Achaeans shouted loud,
emboldened by the omen. But shining Hector answered him:
"Ajax, clumsy in speech, plough-ox, what have you said?

I wish I were as surely the son of Zeus who wields the aegis
for all my days, and that lady Hera bore me,
and I were honoured as Athena is honoured, and Apollo,
as surely as this day now brings evil to the Argives,
every one of them, and you shall be struck among them, should you dare
to await my long spear, which will rend your lily-soft skin,   830
and you will glut the dogs and birds of Troy
with your fat and flesh, when you fall beside the ships of the Achaeans."
So speaking he led on, and the leaders followed
with unearthly din, and the host behind them shouted:
the Argives shouted from the other side, nor did they forget
their courage, but waited as Troy's best men approached;
and the crying out of both reached to the high clear air and the radiance
    of Zeus.

Now the shouting did not escape the notice of Nestor, although he was
    drinking,
and to the son of Asclepius he addressed winged words:
"Take thought, noble Machaon, how these matters will be;
the battle shouts of our sturdy young men grow greater by the ships.
You now sit and drink the dark-gleaming wine,
until Hekamede of the lovely hair has heated warm water to bathe
and washed away your clotted blood,
and I will go to a watch place and quickly look around."
       So speaking he took up the wrought shield of his son
Thrasymedes breaker of horses, which was lying in his shelter   10
shining with bronze—for Thrasymedes was carrying his father's shield—
and took up a strong spear pointed with sharp bronze.
But outside his shelter he halted, and saw at once the shameful work of war,
men fleeing in rout and, driving them to panic from behind,
the prideful Trojans; and the wall of the Achaeans fallen.
As when the great deep sea shimmers dark with silent swell
foreboding the swift passage of shrill winds
but does not break, rolling neither forward nor aside,
until some fair deciding wind descends from Zeus above,
so the old man deliberated, his heart torn   20
two ways, whether to go to the throng of Danaans of swift horses,
or to Agamemnon, son of Atreus and shepherd of the people.
And this to him as he pondered seemed to be best,

to go to the son of Atreus. The fighting men continued to kill
each other; the unwearying bronze rang about their bodies
as they stabbed at one another with their swords and double-edged spears.

      Then as they came up from the ships, the kings cherished by
   Zeus fell in with Nestor,
they who had been wounded by bronze weapons—
the son of Tydeus, Odysseus and Agamemnon, son of Atreus;
far from the fighting their ships had been hauled up   30
on the shore of the grey salt sea; for they had drawn up the first ships
towards the plain, and built the wall by their sterns.
And indeed wide though it was, the beach could not contain
all the ships, and the host was constrained.
Therefore they had hauled the ships up in ranks, and occupied
the whole of the seashore along the deep bay, all that the headlands
   enclosed.
So these kings having learned late of the battle crying and fighting
came all together leaning on spears, and the heart in the breast of every
   man
was anguished; and the old man Nestor fell in with them,
and made the hearts of the Achaeans quail in their breasts.   40
And lifting his voice lord Agamemnon addressed him:
"O Nestor, son of Neleus, great pride of the Achaeans,
why have you left the fighting that destroys men and made your way here?
I fear lest mighty Hector may fulfil his word against me,
as he once threatened, speaking to the Trojans in assembly,
that he would not go back to Ilion from the ships,
until he had destroyed our ships with fire, and killed the men themselves.
So he spoke in the assembly; now all this has been accomplished.
Alas! Sure it is the other strong-greaved Achaeans too
have set down anger in their heart against me, like Achilles,   50
and are not willing to fight by our ships' sterns."

      Then answered him the Gerenian horseman Nestor:
"These things have been prepared ere this, nor

could Zeus the high-thunderer himself work them differently.
For the wall is now fallen, which we trusted
would be unbreachable defence for our ships, and for ourselves,
and by the swift ships our men sustain relentless battle,
without respite; nor would you now know, though looking hard,
from which side the Achaeans in their panic are driven in rout;
they are being killed in such confusion, and the outcry reaches heaven. 60
Let us consider how these matters will be,
if a plan can accomplish anything. But I do not recommend that we
enter the fighting; for it is not possible for a wounded man to do battle."

    Then in turn the lord of men Agamemnon addressed him:
"Nestor, since the men are fighting by the sterns of the ships
and the wall that was built was no help, nor in any way the ditch,
for which the Danaans suffered much, and hoped in their hearts
would be unbreachable defence for our ships and for ourselves—
this it seems must please Zeus, supreme in might.   69
For I knew it, even when he willingly defended the Danaans,   71
and I know it now that he exalts these Trojans like the blessed gods,
and has bound and tied our power and strength of hands.
But come, and let us all be persuaded as I say;
those ships that were first drawn up close by the water,
let us haul them down, and we will launch all these into the shining salt sea,
and when they're afloat, we'll bring them to anchor until divine night
comes, if at that point the Trojans hold back from fighting;
then we might launch the whole fleet.
For there is no blame in fleeing evil, even at night;   80
it is better that a fleeing man escape evil than is captured."

    Then looking at him beneath his brows resourceful Odysseus
    addressed him:
"Son of Atreus, what sort of word has escaped the barrier of your teeth?
Ruinous one—would that you commanded some other worthless army,
and were not lord of us, whom Zeus
has assigned, from youth to old age, to keep winding up the

hard threads of wars, to the bitter end, until we perish to a man.
So then, do you now intend to abandon the wide-wayed city of Troy,
for which we have suffered much hardship?
Be silent, lest some other Achaean hear such an utterance,   90
which no man would let pass through his mouth,
no man who knows in his heart how to speak what is fit,
and who bears a sceptre, and whom his people trust
in such numbers as those of the Argives among whom you rule.
And now I utterly scorn your judgement, the things you have said—
you, who even as war and battle is joined, urge
us to drag our well-benched ships to the sea, so that the Trojans
have yet more reason to boast, victorious as they already are,
and sheer destruction weighs upon us! For the Achaeans
will not hold the battle while the ships are being hauled to the sea,   100
but will look anxiously about them, and hold back their fighting spirit.
Then will your plan bring harm, O leader of the people."

  Then answered him the lord of men Agamemnon:
"O Odysseus, you have touched my heart close with this hard
rebuke; indeed I do not order the sons of the Achaeans against their will
to haul the well-benched ships down to the sea.
May there be someone now who tells a better plan than this,
be he young or old; it would be welcome to me."

  And among them now spoke Diomedes of the war cry:
"That man is near, nor will we search for long, if you are willing   110
to be persuaded, and each of you not in anger grudge me
because by birth I am youngest among you.
I too claim to be the child of a noble father,
Tydeus, whom the heaped earth covers over in Thebes.
For to Portheus were born three blameless sons,
and they dwelt in Pleuron and rugged Calydon,
Agrios, Melas, and third was the horseman Oineus,
the father of my father; and in valour he stood above them.
But while he remained there, my father made his home in Argos,

after wandering; for so I suppose Zeus and the other gods wished it. 120
And he married one of the daughters of Adrastos, and lived in a house
rich in substance, and possessed in abundance worked fields
bearing wheat, and there were many orchards of fruit around them,
and he had many herds of cattle; and he surpassed all Achaeans
with the spear. These things you have likely heard, if they are true;
therefore not by saying that I was base in birth and courage could you
slight the words I speak, should I state them well.
Come, let us go to the fighting, wounded though we are, out of necessity;
there let us keep ourselves clear of the spears and arrows
of the fighting throng, lest someone suffer wound on wound, 130
but, rallying the others, we will send those in who, although before
doing loyal service in their heart, stood apart and did not go to battle."
So he spoke; and the others listened closely and obeyed,
and they set out to go, and the lord of men Agamemnon led them.

But the glorious Earth-Shaker kept no blind watch,
but went among them in the likeness of an old man,
and took hold of the right hand of Atreus' son Agamemnon,
and speaking addressed him with winged words:
"Son of Atreus, now I think that Achilles' ruinous heart
rejoices in his breast, as he looks upon the rout and slaughter 140
of the Achaeans, since there is no feeling in him, not a little.
Let him perish so, may god blight him.
But with you the blessed gods are not yet wholly angry,
and I think the leaders and counsellors of the Trojans
will yet fill the broad plain with their dust; and you yourself will see
them fleeing to their city from the ships and shelters."
So speaking he shouted in a great voice as he swept across the plain,
as loud as nine thousand men cry in battle, or ten thousand
men joining in the strife of war;
so great was the voice the lord Earth-Shaker launched from his chest, 150
and he cast great strength in each Achaean's heart,
to fight and do battle unceasing.

Now Hera of the golden throne looked with her eyes upon him

from Olympus, from the pinnacle where she stood; and immediately she
    recognised

him as he busied himself with the battle where men win glory,

her own brother and her husband's brother, and she rejoiced in her heart;

then she looked towards Zeus sitting on the highest peak of Ida

of the many springs, and hatred grew in her heart.

And then ox-eyed lady Hera strategised,

how she might beguile the wits of Zeus who wields the aegis.   160

And this plan seemed to her heart to be best,

that she herself go to Ida, well equipped,

to see if he might perchance desire to lie beside her skin

in love-making, and she might pour harmless, balmy sleep

upon his eyelids, and sharp wits.

And setting forth she went to her chamber, which her dear son
    Hephaestus had built for her,

and who had fitted the snug doors to doorposts

with a secret bolt; this no other god could open;

and entering there she shut the shining doors.

Then first with ambrosia she cleansed from her lovely body   170

all impurities, and anointed herself with lush oil,

ambrosial sweet, which had been scented for her;

and when it was stirred, the fragrant breath all through the bronze-
    floored house of Zeus,

spread alike to earth and heaven.

Then having anointed her beautiful skin and hair with this,

and combed it, with her hands she braided the shining

beautiful, ambrosial locks flowing from her immortal head.

And she put about her an ambrosial robe that Athena

had brushed smooth and skilfully finished for her, and set on it many
    intricate decorations;

and with golden brooches she fastened this across her breast;   180

and she girded herself about with a belt fitted with a hundred tassels;

then in her carefully pierced ears she placed earrings,
with three drops, like mulberries, and their rich beauty shone forth;
shining among goddesses she covered herself above with a flowing
    headdress,
fresh and fine—white shining like the sun;
and beneath her smooth feet she bound her splendid sandals.
        Then when she had placed everything about her body in strategic
    order,
she set out from her chamber, and summoning Aphrodite
apart from the rest of the gods, she spoke a word to her:
"Could you listen, dear child, to something that I would say,   190
or would you refuse me, resentful in your heart
because I aid the Danaans, and you the Trojans?"
Then Aphrodite the daughter of Zeus answered her:
"Hera, eldest goddess, daughter of mighty Cronus,
speak what you will; my heart compels me to accomplish it,
if I am able to accomplish it, and if it can be accomplished."
Then with calculated guile lady Hera addressed her:
"Grant me now your power of love and desire, with which you
subdue all immortal gods and mortal men.
For I am going to the end of the nourishing earth to visit   200
Ocean, the source of the gods, and mother Tethys,
who in their house nurtured me well and raised me,
after receiving me from Rhea, when far-thundering Zeus set
Cronus down beneath the earth and murmuring sea.
I am going to see them, and I will resolve their unending quarrels;
for a long time now they have held back from each other
in love and in bed, since bitterness has entered their desire.
If winning over their dear hearts with words I could restore them
to their bed to be united in lovemaking,
I would ever be called dear to them and even honoured."   210
Then laughter-loving Aphrodite answered her:
"It is not possible, nor is it seemly to refuse your request;

for you sleep in the arms of almighty Zeus."
She spoke, and from her breast unbound a band pricked out with
curious design; and there all her charms were wrought.
And on it was lovemaking, and desire was on it, and on it was the
    language of love
and its persuasion, which steals the sharp wits of even thinking men.
This it was she dropped in Hera's hands, and spoke to her and said her
    name:
"There now, between your breasts place this band
of curious design, on which all things have been devised; nor do I think   220
that you will return unsuccessful, whatever your heart desires."
So she spoke, and ox-eyed lady Hera smiled,
and smiling then she placed it between her breasts.
            Aphrodite the daughter of Zeus went to her home;
but Hera in a flash left the peak of Olympus,
crossing Pieria and lovely Emathia,
pressing on over the snowcapped mountains of the horse-tending
    Thracians,
over their highest peaks, nor touched them with her feet;
from Athos she strode to the heaving sea,
and arrived at Lemnos, the city of divine Thoas.   230
There she fell in with Sleep, the brother of Death,
and clung to his hand, and spoke to him and said his name:
"Sleep, lord of all, both gods and men,
as once before you heard my plea, so now too once more
hear me; I would know gratitude to you all my days.
For my sake, lull to sleep those two bright eyes beneath the brows of Zeus,
immediately after I have lain beside him in making love.
I will give you gifts, a gorgeous throne, imperishable forever,
made of gold; Hephaestus, my crook-legged son,
will make it, fashioning it with art, and will set a stool beneath
    your feet,   240
on which you can rest your shining feet while at your revels."

Then answering her spoke gentle Sleep:
"Hera, eldest goddess, daughter of mighty Cronus,
any other of the everlasting gods I would
readily put to sleep, even the waters of the river
Ocean, who is the source of all things;
but Zeus, the son of Cronus, I would not come near,
nor put to sleep, unless he himself should bid me.
For another time before this your command goaded me on,
that day when Heracles, that overbearing son of Zeus   250
sailed from Ilion, having utterly sacked the city of the Trojans;
I did indeed lull to sleep the mind of Zeus who wields the aegis,
my sweetness poured about him, but in your heart you planned evils for
    his son.
You stirred blasts of stiff winds across the sea,
and caused him to be carried away to fair-settled Kos,
apart from all his friends. And awakening Zeus raged violently,
hurling us gods through his halls, and seeking me above all others;
and he would have cast me never to be seen again from the sheer clear air
    into the sea,
had Night, subduer of gods and men, not saved me.
Fleeing, I came to her as suppliant, and Zeus checked himself, angry
    though he was;   260
for he shrank from committing deeds hateful to swift Night.
Now again you bid me accomplish this other impossible thing."
        Then in turn ox-eyed lady Hera addressed him:
"Sleep, why do you fret in your mind about these things?
Or do you think that far-thundering Zeus will aid the Trojans
as greatly as he was angered over Heracles, his own son?
But come, and I will give you one of the younger Graces
to wed and to call your wife."   268
So she spoke and Sleep rejoiced, and addressed her in answer: 270
"So come, now swear oath to me on the inviolate water of the Styx,
and with one hand grasp the nourishing earth,

and with the other the shining salt sea, so that all
the lower gods round Cronus be witness to us,
swear that you will give me one of the younger Graces,
Pasithea, whom I have longed for all my days."

So he spoke, nor did the goddess white-armed Hera disobey,
and she swore the oath as he bid, and called by name upon all gods
who are down in Tartaros, and who are called the Titans.
And when she had sworn and concluded the oath,   280
the two set out from Lemnos, leaving the city of Imbros,
mantled in mist, and lightly they made their passage.
They arrived at Ida of the many springs, the mother of wild creatures,
and at Lekton, where they first left the sea; then they made their way
upon dry land, and beneath their feet the topmost forest quivered.
There Sleep remained before Zeus' eyes beheld him,
ascending a towering fir tree, which on Ida at that time
grew tallest, reaching through the mist to clear high air;
there he sat concealed within the fir tree branches,
in the likeness of a clear-voiced bird, which in the mountains   290
the gods call *chalkis*, but men *kymindis*.

But Hera swiftly proceeded to Gargaros, the peak
of lofty Ida; and Zeus who gathers the clouds beheld her.
And as he saw her, desire wrapped his sharp wits round,
just as when they first mingled in lovemaking,
rocking back and forth in bed, in secret from their beloved parents.
And he stood before her, and spoke out and said her name:
"Hera, where do you hasten, coming down from Olympus to this place?
You have no horses or chariot, in which you could have ridden."
Then with calculated guile lady Hera gave him answer: 300
"I am going to the end of the nourishing earth to see
Ocean, the source of the gods, and mother Tethys,
who in their house nurtured me well and raised me.
I am going to see them, and I will resolve their unending quarrels;
for a long time now they have held back from each other

in love and in bed, since bitterness has entered their desire.
My horses are tethered at the foot of Ida of the many springs,
who will carry me over the dry land and wet sea.
But now for your sake I have come here down from Olympus to this place,
lest somehow you be angry with me afterwards, if without speaking   310
I should have gone to the house of deep-flowing Ocean."

   Then answering her spoke Zeus who gathers the clouds:
"Hera, you can make your way there later just as well.
Come, let us both go to bed and find pleasure in the making of love.
For never ever has desire for goddess or woman
so overcome me, flooding my senses,
not when I desired the wife of Ixion,
who bore me Peirithoös, equal to the gods as counsellor;
nor when I desired Danaë of the shapely ankles, daughter of Akrisios,
who bore Perseus, conspicuous among all men;   320
not when I desired the daughter of far-famed Phoinix,
who bore me Minos and godlike Rhadamanthys too;
not when I desired even Semele, nor Alkmene in Thebes,
who gave birth to a strong-willed son, Heracles,
and Semele bore Dionysus, a source of joy for mortal men;
nor when I desired lady Demeter of the lovely locks,
nor when I desired glorious Leto, nor you yourself,
as now I desire you and sweet longing captures me."

   Then with calculated guile lady Hera addressed him:
"Most dread son of Cronus, what kind of thing have you said?   330
If now you desire to go to bed in lovemaking
on the heights of Ida, everything can be seen!
How would it be, if one of the ever-living gods
should see us in bed, and go and point us out
to all the rest? I could not simply rise from bed
and return to your house; it would be cause for outrage!
But if you desire this right now and longing fills your heart,
there is your chamber, which your dear son Hephaestus built for you,

and fitted snug doors to the doorposts;

let us go to lie there, since bed is now your pleasure."   340

      Then answering her spoke Zeus who gathers the clouds:

"Hera, have no fear in this regard that god or any man will see;

for I will cover such a cloud around you,

one of gold; Helios the sun himself could not see through it,

though the light of his eyes sees sharpest."

He spoke, and the son of Cronus caught up his wife in his arms.

And the divine earth beneath them put forth new-burgeoning grass,

dewy clover, crocuses and hyacinth

so thick and soft it held them from the ground.

On this they lay, and were blanketed around by a cloud   350

of golden beauty, and from it the bright dew fell.

      So the father slept without stirring on the peak of Gargaros,

broken by sleep and desire, and held his wife in his arms.

And gentle Sleep set out on the run for the ships of the Achaeans,

to give a message to the earth-holding Shaker of the Earth.

And standing close to him he spoke winged words:

"Now with good heart, Poseidon, fight for the Danaans,

and give them glory if only for a little, while Zeus still

sleeps, since I have covered soft slumber about him;

Hera tricked him to go to bed in lovemaking."   360

      So speaking he departed for the well-known tribes of men,

but incited Poseidon all the more to fight for the Danaans.

And immediately, with a great leap forward to the front ranks, he urged
    them on:

"Argives, do we once again yield victory to Hector,

son of Priam, so that he can seize our ships and win him glory?

For this is what he thinks and boasts, since Achilles

remains by the hollow ships angered at heart.

But our longing for Achilles will not be so great if the rest

of us stir ourselves to defend one another.

Come, let us all be persuaded as I say;   370

put on your shields, whichever are the best and greatest in the army,
cover your heads with all-blazing helmets,
take in your hands your longest spears,
and let us go; and I myself will lead, nor do I think Hector
son of Priam will still stand his ground, for all his fury.
And that man who is staunch in battle, but bears a small shield on his
    shoulders,
let him give it to one less warlike, and let him wear the greater shield."

      So he spoke; and they eagerly heeded him and obeyed.
And the kings themselves drew up their men, wounded though they were,
the son of Tydeus and Odysseus and Atreus' son Agamemnon,   380
visiting all the divisions, and made the exchange of battle armour;
and the best warriors donned the best armour, and gave the lesser
    armour to the lesser man.
Then when each had put the gleaming armour around his body,
they set out; and leading them was Poseidon who shakes the earth,
wielding a terrible fine-pointed sword in his mighty hand,
like a lightning bolt; against it no mortal man can join battle
in baleful war, but fear holds back all men.
From the other side shining Hector ranked the Trojans.
And now they stretched the strife of battle tight beyond endurance,
dark-haired Poseidon and shining Hector,   390
the one defender of the Argives, the other of the Trojans.
And the sea surged against the shelters and the ships
of the Argives; and the men clashed with a great war cry.
No wave of the sea thunders so loud against the shore
when roused in every direction by the hard North Wind,
no roar of fire blazing is so great
in the narrow valleys of the mountain, when it springs up to consume the
    forest,
no wind howls so loud about the high-crowned oaks,
when it roars greatest in its raging,
as was the sound of Trojans and Achaeans   400

fearfully shouting, as they urged each other on.

      And shining Hector first took aim at Ajax
with his spear, since he had turned to face him, nor did he miss,
but hit him where the two straps were stretched across his chest,
one for his shield, the other for his silver-studded sword;
these protected his tender skin. And Hector was angered
because his swift spear had escaped from his hand in vain,
and he drew back into the band of his companions, shunning death.
Then as Hector was retreating, great Telamonian Ajax
lifted a boulder—one of many propping the swift ships,   410
which rolled among the fighters' feet—with one of these
he struck Hector in the chest above his shield rim, near the throat;
and with the blow sent him spinning like a top, and Hector whirled
    entirely around.
As when by the force of a bolt from father Zeus an oak tree falls,
roots and all, and a dreadful scent of sulphur rises
from it, and it is not courage that grips the man who sees it
from close by—for hard to bear is the thunderbolt of mighty Zeus—
so did Hector in his might drop straightway to the ground in the dust;
and from his hand he let fall his spear, and his shield fell in upon him
and his helmet, and around him rang his armour ornate with bronze.   420
And screaming loud the sons of the Achaeans ran towards him,
hoping to drag Hector away, and hurled their spears in droves;
but none was able to wound or stab
the shepherd of the people; for before that the best warriors ringed him
    round,
Poulydamas and Aeneas and godlike Agenor
and Sarpedon, leader of the Lycians, and blameless Glaukos;
nor did any of the others forsake him, but they held
their circled shields before him. Then his companions
lifting him in their arms carried him from the battle toil, until they came
    to his swift
horses, who behind the line of battle and the fighting   430

stood waiting for him, holding their patterned chariot and charioteer;
and they carried him, groaning heavily, to the city.
But when they reached the crossing of the fair-flowing stream
of whirling Xanthos, which is born of immortal Zeus,
there they lowered him from the horses to the ground, and over him
splashed water; and Hector came to his senses and looked up with his eyes,
then, kneeling, vomited dark-clouded blood.
And back again he sank upon the ground, and over his eyes
the dark night closed; the blow still overwhelmed his strength.

And the Argives, when then they saw Hector going to a distance
  from them,   440
lunged for the Trojans all the more, and recollected their fighting spirit.
There ahead of them all swift Ajax son of Oïleus
stabbed Satnios son of Enops, lunging with his sharp spear
for him, whom a blameless nymph of the river had borne
to Enops, as he was tending cattle by the banks of the river Satnioeis.
This man the spear-famed son of Oïleus, drawing near,
stabbed down through his flank; and Satnios fell back, and about him
the Trojans and Danaans swarmed in powerful combat.
And Poulydamas the spear-wielder, son of Panthoös,
came to his defence, and struck Prothoënor, son of Areïlykos   450
on the right shoulder; through his shoulder the heavy spear
held its way; and falling in the dust he clutched the earth with his
  clenched hand.
And Poulydamas exulted wildly, shouting aloud:
"I, Panthoös' great-hearted son, do not think this spear of mine
leapt in its turn from my mighty hand in vain,
but some one of the Argives safeguards it in his flesh, and I think that
propped on this staff he will descend into the house of Hades."
So he spoke, and grief descended on the Argives at his vaunting.

And most of all he stirred the heart of Ajax,
son of Telamon; for the man fell very close to him;   460
and swiftly he took aim with his shining spear as Poulydamas departed.

But Poulydamas himself avoided the dark fate of death,
leaping aside, and the son of Antenor, Archelochos,
caught the throw; since the gods purposed his destruction.
The spear struck him at the joint of the head and neck,
at the last vertebra, and cut through both tendons.
His head and mouth and nose hit the ground
before his legs and knees as he fell.
Now in his turn Ajax shouted so as to be heard by blameless Poulydamas:
"Think hard, Poulydamas, and tell me truly;   470
was the killing of this man not fair exchange for Prothoënor?
He does not seem base-born to me, nor from mean stock,
but a brother of Antenor breaker of horses,
or perhaps his son; for he seemed most like him in the face."
He spoke though knowing the answer well, and grief clutched the
    Trojans around the heart.

        Then astride his fallen brother, Akamas struck Boeotian
    Promachos
with his spear, since the other was trying to drag the body by the feet.
And over him Akamas exulted wildly, shouting aloud:
"Argive arrow-throwers, insatiable braggarts,
toil and hardship are not ours alone,   480
but someday you too will so die.
Take thought how Promachos sleeps among you, broken
by my spear, so that recompense for my brother's death not go
long unpaid; hence it is a man prays
that a brother be left in his halls as his defender against destruction."
So he spoke, and grief descended on the Argives at his vaunting.

        And he stirred the heart of skilful Peneleos most of all,
who rushed for Akamas; but Akamas did not await the onslaught
of lord Peneleos, who instead stabbed Ilioneus,
the son of Phorbas of the many flocks, whom Hermes loved   490
best of all Trojans and to whom he granted many possessions;
but to Phorbas his mother bore only Ilioneus.

This man Peneleos struck below the brow at the base of the eye,
and thrust out the eyeball; the spear drove straight through the eye
and through the tendon at the back of his neck, and he collapsed, both
    arms
spread wide; and Peneleos drawing his sharp sword
drove it through the middle of his neck, and struck to the ground
his head with its helmet; and still the heavy spear
was fixed in his eye. And holding it up like the head of a poppy
he flaunted it before the Trojans and spoke, vaunting: 500
"From me, O Trojans, tell the beloved father
and the mother of haughty Ilioneus to wail in their halls;
for the wife of Promachos, son of Alegenor, will not
rejoice in the coming home of her beloved husband, at that time when
we lords of the Achaeans depart from Troy with our ships."
So he spoke; and a trembling seized them all beneath their limbs,
and each man looked about him, to see how he might escape sheer
    destruction.

        Tell me now Muses, who have your homes on Olympus,
who was first of the Achaeans to win bloodied spoils,
when the illustrious Earth-Shaker turned the tide of battle.   510
First Telamonian Ajax struck Hyrtios,
the son of Gyrtios, leader of the strong-spirited Mysians;
and Antilochos slew and stripped Phalkes and Mermeros;
and Meriones killed Morys and Hippotion;
and Teucer destroyed Prothoön and Periphetes.
Then the son of Atreus stabbed Hyperenor, shepherd of the people,
down across his flank, and the bronze spear poured the entrails out
as it tore through; and down through the wound that had been stabbed
    his life
rushed in urgent haste, and darkness covered his eyes.
And Ajax the swift son of Oïleus killed the most men;   520
for no man was his match in speed of feet to run down
men when they were fleeing, once Zeus drove panic upon them.

And as they fled through the palisade and ditch,
many were laid low by Danaan hands,
and the rest were checked beside the chariots, and there stood their
    ground,
green with fear, driven to flight; then Zeus awoke
on the heights of Ida beside Hera of the golden throne.
He stood, starting up, and beheld the Trojans and Achaeans,
the first fleeing in rout and driving them to panic from behind,
the Argives, and lord Poseidon among them;
and he saw Hector lying on the plain, his companions sitting
round him—racked with painful gasping, dazed at heart,   10
vomiting blood, since not the weakest of Achaeans had struck him.
And seeing him the father of gods and men was filled with pity,
and looking terribly from beneath his brows he spoke a word to Hera:
"Now your evil-making, hopeless one, your deception, Hera,
has put a stop to shining Hector's fighting, and driven his men to flight.
I rather think that, once again, you may be first to reap the profit of
your grievous evil scheming, and will I lash you with strokes of
    lightning.
Or do you not recollect that time you were hung on high, and from your
    feet
I let two anvils drop, and around your hands I threw fetters
of infrangible gold? And you hung in the clear sky above and in the
    clouds below;   20

and the gods across high Olympus could not bear this,

yet they stood around powerless to set you free; and if I caught hold of
     anyone,

I would seize him and hurl him from the threshold of Olympus, so that
     he came to

earth with little strength to move; and not even so did unceasing grief

for godlike Heracles let my spirit go—

but you, winning over the storm gales with the aid of the North Wind,

had swept him into the murmuring sea, plotting your evil schemes,

and then carried him away to well-settled Kos.

And there I rescued him myself and at once led him up

into the horse-grazed pastures of Argos, him who had endured many
     struggles as it was.   30

I will remind you of these things again, so that you give over your
     deceptions,

and see if they will protect you, your lovemaking and bed—

the bed where you lay, coming from the gods to deceive me."

          So he spoke and ox-eyed lady Hera shuddered,

and she spoke and addressed him with winged words:

"Let Earth now be witness to this and wide Heaven above,

and the down-flowing water of the Styx, which is the greatest

oath for the blessed gods and most dread,

and by your sacred head and by our own bed

of marriage—on which I would not ever swear in vain;   40

not through my doing did Poseidon who shakes the earth

distress the Trojans and Hector, and help the others,

but it seems his own spirit stirred him and urged him,

when he saw the Achaeans worn to extremity by the ships and pitied them.

But I would advise him also

to go to the place where you lead, O Lord of the Dark Clouds."

          So she spoke; and the father of gods and men smiled,

and answering her he spoke winged words:

"If now then, lady Hera of the melting eyes, you indeed

were to take your seat among the immortals sharing my view,   50
then would Poseidon, even if he strongly wished it otherwise,
soon turn the direction of his mind to follow your heart and mine.
And if now you are speaking truly, accurately,
then go among the tribe of gods, and summon Iris
and Apollo famed for his bow to come here,
so that she can go among the host of bronze-clad Achaeans
and tell lord Poseidon
to cease his fighting and return to his own home;
and let Phoebus Apollo rally Hector for battle,
and breathe strength in him at once, and make him forget the pains   60
that now bear hard upon him through his lungs, and
let him roll the Achaeans back again after stirring abject panic,
so that they fall fleeing into the many-benched ships
of Peleus' son Achilles. And he, Achilles, will rouse his companion
Patroclus, whom shining Hector with his spear will kill
in front of Ilion, after Patroclus has destroyed a multitude
of other young men, among them my own son, godlike Sarpedon;
and enraged at Patroclus dying, godlike Achilles will kill Hector.
And from that point, then, without respite, I will effect a retreat
from the ships, all the way until that time the Achaeans   70
capture steep Ilion through the designs of Athena.
Before that I neither stop my anger nor will I permit any other
of the immortals to defend the Danaans here at Troy,
not before the wish of the son of Peleus is fulfilled,
as I first promised him, nodding my head in assent,
on that day when the goddess Thetis clasped my knees
entreating me to honour Achilles, sacker of cities."

          So he spoke; nor did Hera the white-armed goddess disobey,
but made her way down from the peaks of Ida to high Olympus.
As when a man's thought flashes, after he has travelled   80
much land, and in his sharp mind he thinks:
"Would that I were in this place or that," and he wishes for many things,

so swiftly did lady Hera fly in anxious haste.
She arrived at steep Olympus, and came up to the immortal gods
assembled in the house of Zeus; and seeing her
all sprang up and greeted her with upraised goblets.
She ignored the rest, but from Themis of the lovely cheeks
she accepted a cup; for she was first to come running to meet her,
and speaking she addressed her with winged words:
"Hera, why have you come? You are like one distraught.   90
To be sure, the son of Cronus has routed you, he who is your husband."

      Then answered her the goddess white-armed Hera:
"Do not, divine Themis, ask me about these things; you know yourself
what sort of arrogant, unyielding heart he has.
Come, begin the fair feast in the halls of the gods;
and you will hear of these things with the other immortals,
of the wicked deeds that Zeus reveals. And I do not think
that the heart of everyone will rejoice alike, be he mortal
or god, even though he might now feast in good cheer."

      So spoke lady Hera and sat down,   100
and throughout the house of Zeus the gods were shaken. Hera smiled
with her lips, but her forehead by her dark brows
did not soften; and she spoke among them all in anger:
"We are fools, who struggle against Zeus so senselessly.
Are we still set on stopping him, approaching him
with words or force? He sits apart and has no regard for us,
he does not worry about us; he says that among immortal gods
he is incontestably pre-eminent in power and strength.
So therefore accept it, since he might send misfortune to each of you.
Already I suspect he has now wrought pain for Ares;   110
for his son is dead in battle, dearest of men,
Askalaphos, whom mighty Ares says is his son."

      So she spoke, and Ares struck his burly thighs
with the flat of his hand, and spoke in grief:
"Do not blame me now, all you who hold Olympus,

that I go to avenge the murder of my son at the ships of the Achaeans,
even if it is my fate to lie struck by Zeus' bolt
amid blood and dust together with the corpses."
So he spoke, and called for Panic and Rout to yoke his horses;
and himself put on his all-shining armour.   120
And there would have come some even greater and more grievous
rage and wrath at Zeus' hands against the immortals,
had not Athena, greatly fearing for all the gods,
sprung through the doorway, left her chair where she was sitting,
and snatched the helmet from his head and the shield from his shoulders,
and stood his bronze spear against a wall, seizing it from his massive
    hands.
Then she accosted furious Ares with her words:
"Raving madman, deranged, you have lost your wits! To no purpose
do you have ears to hear—your mind is gone, and your sense of shame.
Do you not hear what the goddess white-armed Hera said,   130
who just this minute now has come from Olympian Zeus?
Or do you wish to take your fill of trouble,
and come back to Olympus by force, for all your grieving,
and to plant a seed of great evil for all the rest of us?
Zeus will straightway leave the high-hearted Trojans and Achaeans,
and come to Olympus to wreak havoc among us,
and will lay hold of us, one after another, guilty or not.
Therefore I now bid you again let go the anger for your son;
already someone better than he in might and strength of hands
either has been killed, or will be. It is hard   140
to rescue the race and offspring of all men."

    So speaking she sat furious Ares in his chair.
And outside the hall Hera summoned Apollo
and Iris, who is messenger for gods and men,
and raising her voice she addressed them with winged words:
"Zeus commands you both to go to Ida with all speed;
and when you get there and look upon the face of Zeus,

do whatever he urges and commands."

      So speaking the lady Hera went back

and took her seat; and accordingly the two gods, darting away,
    flew off.   150

And they arrived at Ida of the many springs, mother of wild creatures,

and found the far-thundering son of Cronus sitting on the topmost peak
    of Gargaros,

encircled by a fragrant cloud.

Then on arriving they stood before Zeus who gathers the clouds;

and when he saw them, he was not angered in his heart,

because they obeyed so swiftly the words of his beloved wife.

And to Iris first he addressed his winged words:

"Go now, swift Iris, and to lord Poseidon

bear this message in its entirety, nor be false messenger.

Order him to desist from war and battle   160

and to go among the tribe of gods, or into the bright salt sea.

And if he does not obey my words, but ignores them,

let him then consider in his mind and in his very heart,

that, mighty though he be, he might not have the fortitude

to withstand me coming against him, since I think I am more powerful
    by far than him in strength

and am in birth the elder, yet he it is whose heart does not shrink

from deeming himself my equal—I whom even the other gods dread."

      So he spoke, nor did swift Iris with feet like the wind disobey,

but made her way down from the peaks of Ida to sacred Ilion.

As when from clouds there flies snow or icy hail   170

by the blast of Boreas, the North Wind born of the high clear sky,

so did fleet Iris swiftly fly in eager haste.

And standing close she addressed the illustrious Earth-Shaker:

"I came here bearing a message for you, dark-haired

holder of the earth, from Zeus who wields the aegis.

He commands you to desist from war and battle

and to go among the tribe of gods, or into the bright salt sea.

And if you do not obey his words, but ignore them,
he threatens that he too will come here
to do battle, face to face; and he bids you avoid   180
his hands, since he says he is more powerful by far than you in strength
and in birth is elder. Yet your own heart does not shrink
from deeming yourself his equal—he whom even the other gods dread."

      Then greatly troubled the famous Earth-Shaker addressed her:
"Oh for shame! Great though he is, what he says is insolent,
if he will hold me down, his equal in honour, against my will by force!
For we are three brothers, whom Rhea bore to Cronus,
Zeus and I, and third is Hades who rules the dead.
And everything was divided into three parts, and we each had a share of
    honour;
and when we shook the lots, it fell to me to dwell forever   190
in the grey salt sea, and Hades drew the misted realm of darkness,
and Zeus the broad heavens in the high clear sky and clouds,
but earth is yet common to us all, and high Olympus;
therefore I shall not live at the will of Zeus, but untroubled
and mighty though he is, let him stick with his third share.
Let him not try to frighten me with threat of hands as if I were someone
    altogether worthless;
it would be better for him to rebuke with his violent words
his daughters and his sons, those whom he begot,
who will listen to his summoning by necessity."

      Then swift Iris with feet like the wind answered him: 200
"Is it in this way, then, dark-haired holder of the earth,
I should bear this harsh and powerful word to Zeus,
or will you change your mind at all? The minds of the great are yielding.
And you know the Furies always attend the elder born."

      Then in turn Poseidon who shakes the earth addressed her:
"Immortal Iris, indeed it was proper you spoke this word;
it is a good thing, when a messenger knows what is right.
But this is a bitter pain that comes upon my heart and spirit,

when he should choose to abuse with words of anger
one of equal rank and one allotted equal fate.   210
But for now, although angered, I will withdraw,
but I will tell you something else, and I make this threat from the bottom
    of my heart;
if against my goodwill, and that of Athena who carries the spoils of war
and Hera and Hermes and lord Hephaestus,
he spares steep Ilion, and is not willing
to sack it and give great power to the Argives,
let him know this, that the anger between us will be not be healed."
So speaking the Earth-Shaker left the Achaean army,
and leaving, plunged into the open sea; and the Achaean warriors felt his
    loss.

  And then Zeus who gathers the clouds spoke to Apollo: 220
"Go now, beloved Phoebus, to Hector of the brazen helm;
for the Earth-Shaker who hold the earth has already now
departed for the bright salt sea, shrinking from my towering anger.
For others too would have heard of our battle,
the gods who are below, the Titans around Cronus.
This is far the best outcome both for me and for him,
since before it came to that, although displeased, he yielded
to my strength of hands, otherwise nothing would have been brought to
    pass without the sweat of conflict.
But take in your hands the tasselled aegis,
and shake it to rout the Achaean warriors.   230
And let shining Hector be your own care, Far-Shooter;
rouse the great strength in him all the while, until the Achaeans
flee in panic to the ships and Hellespont.
From that point I myself will consider word and action,
to ensure that the Achaeans too have respite again from battle."

  So he spoke; and nor did Apollo fail to heed his father,
but made his way down the peaks of Ida in the likeness of a swift

dove-killing hawk, lightest of all things on wings.
He found the son of wise Priam, shining Hector,
sitting up—he was not still lying, but was just gathering his strength,   240
and recognising his companions about him, and his hard breathing and
    sweat
were abating, since the will of Zeus who wields the aegis had roused him.
And standing close Apollo who strikes from afar addressed him:
"Hector son of Priam, why do you sit apart from all the others
scarcely stirring? Or has some trouble come upon you?"

         Then with little strength Hector of the shimmering helm
    addressed him:
"Which god are you, most powerful one, who speaks to me face to face?
Did you not hear, how by the sterns of the Achaean ships
Ajax of the great war cry struck me, as I was slaying his companions,
with a boulder to the chest, and put a stop to my fierce courage?   250
And I thought this day I would look upon the dead
and halls of Hades, when I had breathed my life out."

         Then in turn lord Apollo who shoots from afar addressed him:
"Have courage now; such an ally has the son of Cronus
sent to you from Ida to stand by and defend you—
Phoebus Apollo of the golden sword, I who even before
watched over you, both you and your steep city.
But come, now rouse your many chariot-fighting men
to drive their swift horses to the hollow ships;
and going before you I will smooth the whole way   260
for the horses, and will turn back the Achaean warriors."

         So speaking he breathed great strength into the shepherd of the
    people.
As when a horse confined to a stall, fed on barley at the manger,
breaking his tether runs with pounding feet across the plain,
to immerse himself in the fair-flowing waters of his accustomed river,
triumphant, and he holds his head high, his mane

streaming about his shoulders; emboldened by his beauty,
his knees bear him lightly to the pasture and places horses love;
so did Hector lightly move his feet and knees,
urging on the horsemen, since he heeded the god's voice.   270
And as dogs and rustic men give chase
to a horned stag or wild goat—
one that the wild rock-cliff or dusky forest
protects, which, after all, it was not their destiny to catch—
and drawn by their shouting a full-maned lion appears
in their path, and immediately he turns the pack of them around, for all
    their eagerness;
so the Danaans for a while followed, always in a body,
striking wounds with their swords and two-edged spears,
but when they saw Hector ranging through the ranks of his men,
they were filled with terror, and the heart in all sank to their feet.   280

       Then spoke up among them Thoas son of Andraimon,
far the best of the Aetolians, skilled in the work of spear,
outstanding in close combat; in assembly few Achaeans
could best him, when young warriors would contend with words;
with keen understanding he spoke up and addressed them:
"Oh shame! This is a great wonder I see with my eyes,
how once again Hector is back on his feet, having eluded death.
Each of us was surely hoping in his heart that he
had died at the hands of Telamonian Ajax;
but once more one of the gods protected and rescued   290
Hector, who has already unstrung the knees of many Danaans,
as I think he will again now; for it is not without
far-thundering Zeus he stands forth as champion like this in his
    determination.
Come, let us all be persuaded as I say;
let us command the troops to return to the ships,
and ourselves, those of us who claim to be the army's best,
let us take our stand, to see if we can hold them off as they first

encounter us,
with spears raised. And I think that for all his zeal
he will in his heart shrink from entering the throng of Danaans."

     So he spoke; and they listened closely and obeyed him.   300
And those around Ajax and lord Idomeneus—
Teucer and Meriones and Meges, Ares' equal—
closed the line of battle, having called the best men forth
to face Hector and the Trojans; and behind them
the troops made their way back to the Achaean ships.

     But the Trojans pressed forward in a body, and Hector led
with his long strides; and in front of him went Phoebus Apollo,
his shoulders cloaked in cloud, holding the furious aegis,
a thing of dread, thick-fringed all around, dazzling, which the bronze-
    smith
Hephaestus gave to Zeus for putting men to flight.   310
Holding this in his hands, Apollo led the army;
but the Argives awaited in a body, and from both sides
piercing cries arose, and arrows sprang from their bowstrings,
and spears in multitude from men's bold hands
were driven in the flesh of vigorous young warriors,
and many, too, fell short, before they grazed white skin,
standing fast in the ground, longing to glut themselves on flesh.

     And so long as in his hands Phoebus Apollo held the aegis steady,
the missiles of both sides reached their mark, and the people fell;
but when, looking straight into the face of the Danaans of
    swift horses,   320
he shook it, and howled at them aloud, then he bewitched
the spirit in them, and they forgot their furious courage.
And as a herd of cattle or great flock of sheep
is struck to panic by two wild beasts in the milky murk of a black night,
coming on a sudden when no herdsman is by,
so the Achaeans fled in helpless terror; for Apollo
hurled the panic in them, and gave glory to the Trojans and to Hector.

Then man killed man as the ranks were shattered.
Hector slew Stichios and Arkesilaos,
one the leaders of the bronze-clad Boeotians,   330
the other the trusted companion of great-hearted Menestheus.
And Aeneas killed Medon and Iasos;
Medon had been the bastard son of godlike Oïleus,
the brother of Ajax, although he had lived
in Phylake, far from the land of his fathers, having killed a man,
a kinsmen of his stepmother Eriopis, whom Oïleus married;
and Iasos was a commander of the Athenians,
and was called the son of Sphelos, son in turn of Boukolos.
And Poulydamas killed Mekisteus, and Polites killed Echios
in the forefront of battle, and godlike Agenor killed Klonios.   340
And Paris struck Deïochos in the lower back from behind
as he was fleeing among the frontline fighters, and drove the bronze
    spearhead right through.

And while these stripped the fallen of their armour, the Achaeans,
thrashing in the trench and palisade,
fled here and there and made their way into the ramparts from sheer
    necessity.
And shouting loud, Hector gave orders to the Trojans,
to make a rush for the ships, and to leave the bloodied spoils:
"That man whom I see away from the ships on the other side,
there and then I will find a way to bring about his death, nor
will his kin, male or female, give him his portion of fire when he has
    died,   350
but the dogs will tear him in the sight of our city."
So speaking, down from his shoulder he brought his whip to drive the
    horses,
calling to the Trojans across the ranks; and they with him,
shouting all together, held their chariot-drawing horses
amid the inhuman roar; and at the front Phoebus Apollo,
without effort, dashed the sides of the deep trench with his foot

and threw them down in the middle, and made a long causeway for
    passage,
in width as far as a spear is cast
when a man makes trial of his strength.
There the Trojans poured forth in battle ranks, Apollo at the front   360
holding the prized aegis; he threw down the wall of the Achaeans
without effort at all, as a child tumbles sand by the sea,
who when in his childish way has made his play-castle,
sweeps it away again with his feet and hands, still playing—
so then you, Apollo to whom we cry aloud, destroyed the work of much
    toil and hardship
of the Argives, and aroused the terror of panic upon them.
       When they were checked beside the ships, there they stood their
    ground,
and calling out to one another and lifting their hands
to all the gods, each man prayed aloud.
And Gerenian Nestor, watchman of the Achaeans,   370
prayed hardest, reaching his hands toward the starry heaven:
"Father Zeus, if ever in Argos rich in wheat,
burning the fat-rich thighs of an ox or a sheep,
some one of us made prayer for safe return, and you promised and gave
    assent,
be mindful of this, O Olympian, and ward off the pitiless day of death,
do not let the Achaeans be broken this way by the Trojans."
So he spoke praying, and Zeus the all-devising thundered loud,
heeding the prayers of the old man, Neleus' son.
But when the Trojans heard the thunder-stroke of Zeus who wields the
    aegis,
they lunged for the Argives all the more, and recollected their fighting
    spirit.   380
       And as a great wave of the wide-ranging sea descends
over the sides of a ship, when the strength of the wind bears down—
for this it is that swells the waves the most—

so the Trojans with a great cry kept coming down through the wall
and driving their horses in they fought by the ship sterns
at close quarters with their two-edged spears, they from their chariots,
and the Achaeans, having climbed aloft, from the black ships
with long pikes that were lying upon their ships,
jointed together for sea battles, their points encased with bronze.

      And so long as the Achaeans and Trojans   390
fought for the wall beyond the line of swift ships,
Patroclus sat in the shelter of generous Eurypylos
and cheered him with his words, and on his baneful wound
he sprinkled healing herbs as remedies for the dark pangs of pain;
but when he saw the Trojans surging over the rampart,
and the uproar and panic among the Danaans,
then he groaned and struck his thighs
with the flat of his hand, and spoke in grief:
"Eurypylos, despite your need, I can no longer
linger with you here; for now a great battle has arisen.   400
Let your retainer continue to attend you, but I
am going to hasten to Achilles, so as to urge him to fight.
Who knows, if with help from some god I might stir his heart,
winning him over? For the persuasion of a comrade is a worthy thing."

      And his feet were carrying him as he spoke; meanwhile the
  Achaeans
steadily awaited the attacking Trojans. They were not able
to thrust them, although fewer, back from the ships;
nor were the Trojans ever able to break the Danaan lines
and get into the midst of the ships and shelters;
but as measuring cord makes straight a ship timber   410
in the hands of an experienced carpenter who,
with the inspiration of Athena, knows all skills well,
so their fighting and the line of war were pulled tight and equal.

      And while others fought the battle about one ship or the other,
Hector made straight against glorious Ajax.

And around a single ship the two fought their fight, but neither could
   succeed,
not Hector to drive the other off and set the ship ablaze,
nor Ajax to force Hector back, since divine power drove him.
And then shining Ajax struck Kaletor the son of Klytios
in the chest with his spear as he brought fire to the ship;   420
he fell with a thud, and the firebrand dropped from his hand.
And as Hector with his own eyes saw his cousin
falling in the dust in front of the black ship,
he called on the Trojans and Lycians, shouting loud:
"Trojans and Lycians and Dardanians who fight at close quarters,
do not draw back from battle anywhere in this narrow passage,
but rescue the son of Klytios, nor let the Achaeans
strip the armour from him, fallen in the gathering place of ships."

     So speaking he cast at Ajax with his shining spear;
but missed him, and struck Lykophron the son of Mastor,   430
the henchman of Ajax from Cythera, who lived near him,
since he had killed a man in holy Cythera—
this man he struck on the head above the ear with his sharp sword,
as he stood close to Ajax; he fell backwards from the stern of the ship
to the ground in the dust, and the strength of his limbs was undone.
And Ajax shuddered, and addressed his brother:
"Teucer old man, now our trusted comrade has been killed,
Mastor's son, whom after coming to our home from Cythera
we esteemed equal to our parents in our halls;
great-hearted Hector has killed him. Where now are your arrows   440
that bring swift death, and the bow that Phoebus Apollo gave you?"

     So he spoke; and the other heard, and running up stood close
   beside him,
his back-curved bow in his hand and his quiver of arrows.
And swift were the shafts he began to let fly at the Trojans;
he struck Kleitos, the splendid son of Peisenor,
companion of Poulydamas, son of noble Panthoös,

as he held reins in his hand. For he was struggling with his horses;
he was holding his course to the very place, where the most ranks were
    in disordered panic,
as service to Hector and the Trojans; but evil came to him
swiftly, nor did any of them for all their desire ward it off from him,   450
for into the back of his neck there struck a sorrow-bearing arrow—
he fell from the chariot and the horses started,
rattling the empty car. At once lord Poulydamas
marked this, and was first to intercept the horses.
He gave them to Astynoös son of Protiaon,
and pressed him urgently to hold the horses close while keeping lookout;
then he himself went back to the frontline fighters.

        And Teucer took up another arrow, this one for Hector
of the brazen helm; and would have stopped his fighting by the ships of
    the Achaeans,
if he had snatched Hector's life away, by striking him as he excelled in
    valour;   460
but he could not slip by the sharp mind of Zeus, who kept watch over
Hector, and who deprived Teucer son of Telamon of glory—
he broke a bowstring—one strong made and on a blameless bow—
as he drew it on Hector; and the bronze-weighted arrow
was knocked wide, and the bow fell from his hand.
And Teucer shuddered, and spoke to his brother:
"See! Some god now wholly thwarts our plans
for battle, and has struck the bow from my hand,
snapped a new-strung bowstring, one which I bent on
this early morning, so that it could withstand the constant springing
    arrows."   470
        Then answered him great Telamonian Ajax:
"Come, old man, let the bow and the flurrying arrows
lie, as some god confounds them, grudging the Danaans;
rather take your long-shadowed spear in your hands and your shield upon
    your shoulder,

to do battle with the Trojans and rally the rest of our people.
Although they have beaten us, let them not without struggle take
our well-benched ships, and let us recollect our fighting spirit."

            So he spoke; and the other put his bow in his shelter,
and about his shoulders he put his four-layered oxhide shield,
and over his powerful head he placed his well-forged helmet   480
with flowing horsehair, and terribly the crest nodded over it,
and he took his strong spear fitted with sharp bronze,
and set out, and running fast he came to stand by Ajax.

            And as Hector saw that the shafts had been thwarted,
he called out to the Trojans and Lycians, shouting loud:
"Trojans and Lycians and Dardanians who fight at close quarters,
be men, my friends, and recollect your fierce courage
among the hollow ships; for I now have seen with my own eyes
the shafts of their best archer thwarted by the hand of Zeus.
Easily seen is Zeus' help to men,   490
either those in whose cupped hands he places victory's glory,
and those whom he lays low and is not minded to defend;
as now he lays low the might of Argives, and stands by us.
Come, fight to the ships together; and he of us who,
struck or stabbed, meets his fated death,
let him so die; there is no shame for a man to die fighting to defend
his fatherland; but his wife is safe and his children after him,
and his home and property are undefiled, if the Achaeans
depart with their ships for their own fatherland."
So speaking he stirred the courage and spirit of each man.   500

            Then Ajax in turn on the other side called out to his companions:
"For shame, you Argives; now it is certain we either die,
or are saved and ward off evil destruction from the ships.
Or do you think if Hector of the shimmering helm should seize the ships
that each of you will return on foot to his fatherland?
Did you not hear Hector as he rallied all his people,
Hector who burns to set our ships ablaze?

He does not summon you to come to dance, but to do battle.
For us there is no better plan than this, and no strategy—
to join our strength of hands and courage in close combat.   510
Better either to die once for all, or live,
than to be wrung to exhaustion in dread combat
like this, by our ships, to no avail, at the hands of lesser men."
So speaking he stirred the courage and spirit of each man.

          Then Hector slew Schedios, the son of Perimedes,
leader of the Phocians; and Ajax slew Laodamas
leader of the infantry, the outstanding son of Antenor;
and Poulydamas slew and stripped Otos of Kyllene,
companion of Meges, son of Phyleus, leader of the great-hearted Epeans.
And seeing this Meges charged at him, but Poulydamas ducked and
     slipped   520
out of reach; and Meges missed, for Apollo
did not suffer the son of Panthoös to die among the frontline fighters;
but Meges then struck Kroismos in the middle of the chest with his spear,
and he fell with a thud. And he stripped the armour from his shoulders.
And as he did, Dolops, son of Lampos, the skilled spearman charged at
     him,
Dolops, whom Lampos son of Laomedon
bore to be best of his sons, well skilled in deeds of fierce courage;
he then struck Meges' shield in the middle with his spear
attacking from close in. But Meges' tight-made breastplate saved him,
which he wore with fitted plates; this breastplate Meges' father Phyleus
     once   530
carried out of Ephyra, away from the river Selleëis;
for a guest friend, Euphetes lord of men, gave it to him
to wear to war, as a defence against his enemies;
and now it warded off death from the body of his son.
But Meges with his sharp spear struck the curved crown of Dolops' helmet,
bronze-strengthened and crested with horsehair, on the very peak,
and tore the horsehair crest from it; the whole plume fell to the ground

in the dust, resplendent with freshly crimsoned dye.
But as Dolops stood his ground and battled with him, and still hoped for
    victory,
warlike Menelaos came as defender to Meges,   540
sidling up unobserved, and took his stand with his spear and struck
    Dolops in the shoulder from behind;
the spear-point sped eagerly through his chest,
straining forward; then he slumped and fell face down.
The two men went to strip the bronze-strengthened armour
from his shoulders; and Hector called out to all his kinsmen
loudly, but first rebuked the son of Hiketaon,
strong Melanippos; he at one time pastured his shambling cattle
in Percote, when the enemy men were far away;
but when the double-ended ships of the Danaans came,
he returned to Ilion, and distinguished himself among the Trojans,   550
and made his home near Priam; and Priam honoured him like his sons.
This man Hector rebuked and called out by name:
"In this way, Melanippos, shall we now hang back? Does your heart
have no care for the killing of your cousin?
Do you not see how diligent they are about the arms of Dolops?
Come, follow me; we can no longer avoid close combat
with the Argives—either we kill them, or top to bottom,
they take sheer Ilion and her people are killed."
So speaking he led on, and the other followed with him, a man like a god.
        And great Telamonian Ajax rallied the Argives: 560
"O friends, be men, and let shame be in your heart;
fear shame before each other throughout the mighty combat;
when men fear shame, more are safe than slain,
but when men flee, neither glory nor any victory is seen."
So he spoke, and the men themselves burned to defend themselves,
and took his words to heart, and secured their ships
with a fence of bronze; but Zeus stirred on the Trojans.
        And Menelaos of the war cry urged Antilochos:

"Antilochos, no other of the Achaeans is younger than you,
nor swifter in feet, nor as brave in waging battle;   570
if you were to jump forth you could strike one of the Trojan men."
So speaking he hastened back again, but stirred the other;
and Antilochos leapt out from the frontline fighters and menaced with his
    shining spear,
looking close about him; the Trojans gave way before
him as he cast his spear. And not in vain did he throw the shaft,
but struck the son of Hiketaon, great-hearted Melanippos,
on the chest beside the nipple as he made his way to battle;
he fell with a thud, and darkness covered his eyes.
And Antilochos rushed towards him, like a dog that springs for
a wounded fawn that as it flies from its covert   580
a hunter strikes with a cast of his spear, and undoes the strength of its
    limbs.
So towards you, Melanippos, steadfast Antilochos leapt
to strip your armour. But he did not escape the notice of shining Hector,
who came running through the fighting throng to face him.
And Antilochos, quick to fight though he was, did not await him,
but shrank in fear like a wild beast who has committed violence,
who having killed a dog, or a herdsman among his cattle
takes flight, before a mob of men has been assembled;
so the son of Nestor fled in fear, and Hector and the Trojans
with unearthly din poured their doleful spears and arrows after him;   590
then wheeling about, Antilochos took his stand when he reached the
    band of his companions.

          And the Trojans like flesh-eating lions
surged towards the ships, fulfilling the plans of Zeus,
who roused in them always their great spirit, and bewitched the senses
of the Argives and deprived them of glory, but spurred the others on.
For Zeus' heart desired to give glory to Hector
son of Priam, so that he would hurl upon the curved ships demonic
and unwearying fire, and bring to fulfilment the whole extravagant

prayer of Thetis. So all-devising Zeus awaited this—
to see with his own eyes the blaze of one ship burning;   600
from that point he intended to effect in turn retreat
of the Trojans from the ships, and give glory to the Danaans.
With these things in mind he urged on Hector son of Priam
toward the hollow ships, eager as he already was.

       And Hector raged like spear-wielding Ares, or as baneful fire
rages in the mountains, in the thickets of deep woods;
there was foam about his mouth, his eyes
glittered beneath his savage brows; the helmet around
his temples was shaken terribly as he
fought; for Zeus himself from out of the clear sky was ally to him,   610
Zeus who honoured him alone among so many men
and gave him glory; for Hector was to be
short-lived; already Pallas Athena was stirring against him
his fated day of death through the might of the son of Peleus.
And Hector sought to break apart the ranks of men, testing them,
there where he saw the fighting throng was greatest and armaments best;
yet he was not able, for all his great raging, to break them apart.
For the men stood firm against him, closely ranged together like a wall,
   like a massive
wild rock close to the grey salt sea,
which withstands the rushing passage of the shrieking winds   620
and the swelling waves that spit and roar against the headland;
so the Danaans withstood the Trojans steadfastly nor did they flee.
But glittering in the firelight, Hector leapt everywhere into the fighting
   throng,
and fell on them, as when upon a fast ship there falls a furious wave
that reaches to clouds born of the winds, and the whole of the ship is
buried under foam, and the dreadful blast of wind
roars against the sail, and the sailors' wits are shaken
in their terror; for only by a little are they carried out from under death;
so was the heart rent in the breast of each Achaean.

Then Hector came like a baleful lion upon cattle,   630
which in the lowland of a great marsh-meadow graze
in their great number, the herdsman among them wholly unskilled
in battling a wild beast about the carcass of his twist-horned cow—
always he walks with the first cow, or with the last,
but the lion attacks the middle
and devours his cow, and all the herd flees before him; so the Achaeans
fled in holy terror before Hector and father Zeus,
all of them; yet Hector only killed Periphetes of Mycenae,
the beloved son of Kopreus, who as messenger of lord Eurystheus
went often to strong Heracles.   640
He was born a better son of a far lesser father
in respect to every kind of skill, both speed of feet and waging battle,
and for judgement he was in the first ranks of Mycenaeans.
He, then, now handed Hector triumphant glory;
for having turned his back he was caught on the rim of his shield,
which he carried extending to his feet, as a barrier for spears;
tangled on this he fell face up, and the helmet around his brows
clashed terribly around him as he fell.
And Hector took sharp notice, and running up stood close beside him,
and fixed his spear into his chest, and hard by Periphetes' own comrades,
    killed   650
him; and they were not able, for all their anguish for their comrade,
to be of help, for they themselves feared greatly shining Hector.

        And the Achaeans got among the ships, and the ends
of those ships drawn inland first gave them protection; but the Trojans
    poured in.
Then back from the frontline ships the Argives fell
by force, and there beside the shelters stood their ground
together, and did not scatter through the camp; for shame held them
and fear; and they called to one another continuously.

        Now again Gerenian Nestor, the Achaeans' defence, more than
    all

beseeched each man, imploring him in the name of his parents: 660
"O friends, be men, and in your heart put a sense of shame
before your fellow man, and remember too, each of you,
your children and wives and property and parents,
you whose parents are living and you whose parents have died.
And for the sake of those who are not here I implore you
to take a strong stand, and do not be turned to flight."
So speaking he roused the courage and spirit of each man.
Then from their eyes Athena drove the clouded mist
of divine enchantment, and a great light came on them from either side,
from the ships and from the field of battle that levels all,   670
they made out Hector of the war cry and his companions,
both those standing back in the rear who did not fight,
and those battling by the swift ships.

          And it no longer pleased Ajax's great-hearted spirit
to stand there where the other sons of the Achaeans hung back,
but he ranged the ships' raised decks with his long strides,
wielding in his hands a great polished sea-fighting pike,
jointed with bolts, twenty-two cubits long.
As when a man who is skilled in the riding of horses
has harnessed four horses together, chosen from many,   680
and speeds out of the plain toward a great city, racing
along a public road, and many watch him in wonder,
men and women; and without hesitation and always sure-footed
he changes, leaping, from one to the other, and the horses fly along;
so Ajax ranged upon deck after deck of the swift ships
with his long strides; and his voice reached the clear sky of heaven,
and shouting always in a voice of terror he urged the Danaans
to defend the ships and the shelters. Nor did Hector
await in the noisy throng of close-armoured Trojans,
but as a flame-bright eagle swoops upon a flock of winged birds   690
as they feed beside a river,
geese or cranes or long-necked swans,

so Hector made directly for a dark-prowed ship
flying straight towards it; and from behind Zeus drove him
with his mighty hand, and drove his army with him.

      Once more there was fierce fighting by the ships.
You would have thought the men tireless, unwearying,
as they faced off in the battle; so vehemently they fought.
And this is how those fighting thought: the Achaeans
did not imagine they would escape from evil, but would be
    destroyed,   700
and the heart in each Trojan's breast hoped
to set the ships ablaze and kill the Achaean warriors.

      And with these thoughts in mind they took their stand against
    each other;
Hector laid hold of the stern of a sea-going ship,
a splendid one, swift at sea, that bore Protesilaos
to Troy, but did not bring him back to his fatherland.
Around his ship Achaeans and Trojans
slew one another at close quarters; they did not now
await the rush of bowmen's arrows at long range, nor the rush of spears,
but standing close, all of one mind,   710
they fought with hatchets and axes
and great swords and two-edged spears.
Many swords, splendid ones, hilted and bound with black leather,
fell to the ground from the hands and shoulders
of the fighting men; and the dark earth flowed with blood.

      And when Hector seized the stern, he did not relax his grip at all,
but holding the stern-post with his hands, he called to the Trojans:
"Bring fire, all of you together, raise the battle!
Now Zeus has given us one day worth all the others,
to seize the ships, the ships that coming here against the gods' will   720
have laid much suffering on us, through the cowardice of our elder
    counsellors,
who kept me from fighting when I wished to

by the ships' sterns and checked our army.

But if at that time far-thundering Zeus caused our wits to fail,

now he himself urges and commands us."

So he spoke, and his men attacked the Argives all the harder.

And Ajax no longer withstood their attack, for he was battered by spears
    and arrows,

yet he withdrew only a little, expecting to die,

onto the seven-foot thwart, and left the high deck of the balanced ship.

There he took his stand, on the lookout, and always with his spear   730

he fended from the ships any Trojan who carried unwearying fire.

And shouting always in a fearsome voice he urged the Danaans:

"O friends, Danaan warriors, henchmen of Ares,

be men, my friends, and recollect your fierce courage.

Or do we think there are allies behind us,

or some wall better than this, which might ward off disaster from our
    men?

There is no nearby city fitted with ramparts,

harbouring a people with strength in reserve, in which we could defend
    ourselves,

but on the plain of the close-armoured Trojans,

our backs against the sea, we sit a long way from our native land.   740

Therefore salvation's light is in our strength of hands, not in soft
    platitudes of war."

He spoke, and in fury laid on with his sharp spear.

Any Trojan who moved to the hollow ships

with fire for burning, in obedience to Hector's order,

Ajax would stab, at the ready with his long spear;

and twelve men he struck before the ships, at close quarters.

So they fought around the well-benched ship;
but Patroclus was drawing close to Achilles, shepherd of his people,
streaming hot tears like a dark-water spring,
which down sheer rock streams sombre water.
And seeing him swift-footed godlike Achilles pitied him,
and speaking out, he addressed him with winged words:
"Why are you tearful, Patroclus, like a foolish
girl, who runs after her mother demanding to be picked up,
grasping her dress, and holds her back as she hurries,
and looks at her weeping, until she is picked up?   10
Like her, Patroclus, you let your soft tears fall.
Have you something to proclaim to the Myrmidons or me,
some message from Phthia you alone have heard?
But they say Menoetius still lives, Aktor's son,
and Peleus, son of Aeacus, is alive among the Myrmidons;
should both of those die we would surely be grieved—
or do you weep in pity for the Argives, because they perish
by the hollow ships on account of their arrogance?
Speak out, don't hide it, so that we both know."
          Then groaning deeply you addressed him, rider Patroclus: 20
"O Achilles, son of Peleus, far greatest of the Achaeans,
do not be angry; for such distress assails the Achaeans.
Now all who were before our best men
are lying in the ships wounded by arrows and cut by spears.

The son of Tydeus, powerful Diomedes, is wounded,
Odysseus has been struck by a spear, as has spear-famed Agamemnon;
and Eurypylos has been wounded in the thigh by an arrow;
the physicians with their many drugs attend them,
healing their wounds; but it is you cannot be treated, Achilles.
May it never take hold of me, this anger that you harbour.   30
Cursed in valour! Yet how will other men born hereafter profit
    from you,
if you do not ward off shameful destruction from the Argives?
Pitiless one: your father was not the horseman Peleus,
nor Thetis your mother, but the grey sea bore you
and the wild cliffs, since your mind is unbending.
But if in your heart you shrink from some divine prophecy
and your lady mother has revealed something to you from Zeus,
send me forth at least without delay, and let the rest of the host of
    Myrmidons
follow with me, that I might be salvation's light to the Danaans.
And give me your arms to wear upon my shoulders,   40
with the hope that likening myself to you the Trojans will hold off
from fighting, and the warrior sons of the Achaeans draw breath
in their extremity; for respite in war is brief.
Fresh forces would easily push battle-weary men
to their city, from the ships and from our shelters."

        So he spoke beseeching, the great fool; for he was to
beseech his own evil death and destruction.
Then greatly troubled swift-footed Achilles answered him:
"O Zeus-descended Patroclus, what a thing you have said!
I have no concern for any prophecy I know,   50
nor has my lady mother revealed anything to me from Zeus,
but terrible anguish comes upon my heart and spirit
when a man seeks to rob one equal to him
and to take back his prize of honour because he is pre-eminent in power;
mine is a terrible anguish, because I have undergone sufferings at heart.

The girl, whom the sons of the Achaeans picked out as prize for me,
acquired by my spear, after I sacked her strong-walled city,
she it was, from my hands, lord Agamemnon took back,
the son of Atreus, as if I were some worthless vagabond.
But let us leave these things in the past; for it was not, after all, possible   60
for my heart to be angered forever. But assuredly I did say
I would not make an end of my wrath, except when
the battle and the fighting reached my own ships.
You then put on your shoulders my illustrious armour,
and lead the war-loving Myrmidons to battle,
if in truth a dark cloud of Trojans now closes round
the ships in overwhelming might, and the Argives are backed against
the breakers of the sea, having little portion left of land.
The entire city of the Trojans has come out
emboldened; for they do not see the brow of my helmet   70
glittering near. They would swiftly in their flight fill the gullies with
their dead, if lord Agamemnon were
solicitous of me; but as it is they fight about his very camp.
For no spear rages in the hands of Diomedes son of Tydeus
to ward off from the Danaans their destruction,
never yet have I heard the voice of the son of Atreus shouting
from his hated head, but the voice of man-slaying Hector
calling to the Trojans breaks all round, and they with their war shout
pour down upon the whole plain, as they overcome Achaeans in battle.
But even so, Patroclus, ward off disaster from the ships,   80
fall upon them with overwhelming might, lest with blazing fire
they burn our ships, and take away our cherished journey home.

"But hear me, as I lay in your mind the sum of my instruction,
so that you win great honour and victorious glory for me
from the Danaans, who will then send
the beautiful girl back again, and hand over glorious gifts in addition.
After you have driven the Trojans from the ships, come back; and if
Hera's far-thundering husband should grant you to win glory,

you must not, without me, strive to battle
the war-loving Trojans; you will render me less honoured;   90
do not—as you exult in the war and throng of fighting,
as you kill Trojans—lead on to Ilion,
lest one of the ever-living gods of Olympus
intervene—Apollo who shoots from afar loves these people greatly—
but turn back, after you have brought the light of safety to the ships,
and let the others struggle on across the plain.
Father Zeus and Athena and Apollo!—Would that
not one of the Trojans escape death, as many as they be,
not one of the Argives, but we two emerge from the destruction,
so that we alone strip the sacred veil from Ilion."   100

      Thus they were speaking such things to one another,
but Ajax no longer stood his ground; for he was battered by spears and
   arrows;
the plan of Zeus overpowered him and the noble Trojans
hurling spears. The shining helmet around his temples
rang dreadfully when struck, and it was struck continually
upon its strong-made plates; his left shoulder was wearied,
always holding steady his glancing shield; nor could the Trojans
shake it from its position around him as they pressed in with their missiles;
and always he was gripped with painful breathing, and down from his
   limbs
sweat streamed on every side, nor was he able by any means   110
to draw breath; and on every side evil was piled upon evil.

      Tell me now Muses who have homes on Olympus,
how fire first fell upon the ships of the Achaeans.
Hector taking a stand close by smote Ajax's ashen spear
with his great sword behind the spearhead near its socket,
and struck it off completely; and Telamonian Ajax
brandished this, the lopped spear, vainly in his hands, while far from him
its bronze point resounded as it fell to the ground.
And Ajax understood within his blameless heart and shuddered

at the workings of the gods, seeing that Zeus who thunders on high   120
wholly cut across his plans for battle, and desired victory for the
    Trojans;
he retreated out from the missiles; and the Trojans hurled unwearying
    fire
on the swift ship; and at once the quenchless flame of fire poured down
    upon it.
        And as the fire lapped the stern, Achilles
struck his thighs and addressed Patroclus:
"Rise up god-cherished Patroclus, rider of horses;
I see the blast of enemy fire about the ships;
I fear lest they will take the ships and there be no escape.
Put on the armour quickly, I will muster the men."
        So he spoke, and Patroclus began to arm himself with gleaming
    bronze.   130
First he strapped the splendid greaves around his shins,
fitted with silver bindings around his ankles;
next he girt about his chest the breastplate—
elaborate, star-strewn—of swift-footed Aeacides;
across his shoulders he slung his bronze sword
studded with silver; and then the great strong shield;
over his powerful head he placed the well-forged helmet
with its flowing horsehair; and terribly the crest nodded on it.
He took strong spears, fitted to his hand.
Only the spear of blameless Aeacides he did not take up,   140
heavy, massive, powerful; this no other of the Achaeans could
wield, but only Achilles knew how to wield it,
the spear of Pelian ash, which Chiron gave to his beloved father
from the heights of Mount Pelion to be death to warriors.
        And Patroclus bade Automedon yoke the horses swiftly,
Automedon whom he honoured most after man-shattering Achilles,
and most trusted to await his called command in battle.
Automedon led the swift horses under the yoke for him,

Xanthos and Balios, who could fly with the wind,
they whom Podarge, mare of windstorms, bore to the West Wind,   150
as she grazed in a meadow beside the stream of Ocean.
And in harness alongside he put blameless Pedasos,
who in time before Achilles took as prize after sacking the city of Eëtion.
He, mortal though he was, kept pace with the immortal horses.

      And Achilles armed the Myrmidons with their weapons, ranging
everywhere among the shelters; and they streamed in, like raw flesh-
   devouring wolves,
whose hearts are filled around with boundless courage,
who having slaughtered a great horned stag in the mountains
devour it, and the jaws of each are red with blood,
and in a pack they go, lapping from a dark-water spring   160
with narrow tongues the dark surface of the water,
disgorging clots of blood; and the heart
within them is not shaken, and the pinched belly of each growls;
so the leaders and counsellors of the Myrmidons
around swift-footed Achilles' noble henchman
streamed in; and in their midst like the war god stood Achilles,
rallying the horses and shield-bearing men.

      Fifty were the swift ships that Achilles
beloved of Zeus led to Troy and in each
were fifty men, his companions, at the rowlocks;   170
he made five of these leaders, whom he trusted
to give orders; and he himself ruling powerfully was commander.
One detachment Menesthios of the shimmering war-belt led,
the son of the river Spercheios, rain-filled from Zeus above,
whom the daughter of Peleus bore, beautiful Polydora,
to tireless Spercheios, the woman having lain with the god,
but in name the child was born to Boros, son of Perieres,
who wed her openly, after giving bride-gifts without number.
Warlike Eudoros was leader of the next,
born of an unwed maiden, Polymele, the daughter of Phylas,   180

lovely in dance; mighty Hermes Argeiphontes loved her
when his eyes fell on her among the singers
on the dancing floor of Artemis, goddess of the golden arrow and din of
    hunt;
swiftly climbing to her upper chamber, Hermes the healer lay in secret
with her; and she gave a glorious son to him,
Eudoros, swift beyond measure in running, and a warrior.
But when Eileithyia, the goddess who causes pain in birth,
brought him forth to the light of day and he beheld the rays of the sun,
then powerful Echekles, the strong son of Aktor,
led Polymele in marriage to his home, after giving countless bride-gifts
    for her,   190
and the old man Phylas nurtured the boy well and reared him,
embracing him round with love as if he were his own son.
Of the third detachment warlike Peisandros was leader,
the son of Maimalos, who was finest among all Myrmidons
in fighting with the spear, after Patroclus, companion of the son of Peleus.
The fourth the aged horseman Phoinix led;
Alkimedon led the fifth, the blameless son of Laerkes.

      Then when Achilles had drawn them up marshalled in good order
with their leaders, he laid a strong injunction on them:
"Myrmidons, let no one forget the threats   200
that you made by our fast ships against the Trojans
during all the time of my wrath, when each of you blamed me:
'Cruel son of Peleus, your mother nursed you on bile,
pitiless one, who hold your companions against their will beside the ships.
Let us go back home again in our sea-going ships
since bitter anger has so fallen on your heart.'
In your gatherings you often said such things to me; but now looms
the great task of battle, for which before you longed.
Therefore each one of you with brave heart go to battle with the Trojans."

      So speaking he roused the fury and spirit of each man;   210
and the ranks, when they hearkened to their king, pressed more closely.

As when a man puts in place the wall of a high-roofed house
with close-fitting stones, to escape the force of the winds,
so helmets joined together and shields with their bosses.
Buckler weighed on buckler, helmet on helmet, man on man,
and the helmets plumed with horsehair touched with shining crests
when the men nodded; so close did they stand beside each other.
And out before them all two men were armed,
Patroclus and Automedon, one in spirit,
to go to battle at the forefront of the Myrmidons. But Achilles   220
went to his shelter, and removed the cover from a chest,
beautiful, ornamented, that silver-footed Thetis
put on the ship for him to take, having packed it carefully with tunics
and cloaks to protect him from the wind, and thick fleecy blankets;
here he kept his fine-wrought cup nor did any other
man drink gleaming wine from it,
nor did he make libation to any of the gods but Zeus the father.
Taking this from the chest he purified it with sulphur
first, then washed it with bright streams of water,
and washed his own hands, and drew off gleaming wine.   230
Then standing in the middle of the courtyard he prayed and poured wine
     in libation,
looking up into the sky, and Zeus who strikes with the thunderbolt
     saw him:
"Lord Zeus of Pelasgian Dodona, dwelling far away,
ruler of Dodona of the bitter winter, around you dwell the Selloi
your interpreters, sleepers on the ground with unwashed feet;
surely once before this you heard me when I prayed;
honouring me you smote hard the host of the Achaeans;
now, as once before, fulfil this wish for me;
for I will remain amid my gathered ships,
but I am sending my companion with the many Myrmidons   240
to combat; send glory forth with him, Zeus far-thunderer;
make brave the heart within his breast, so that even Hector

comes to know whether my henchman on his own will prove skilled
in fighting, or his hands rage invincible only at that time
when I myself go to join war's struggle.
Then when he has driven the din of battle and the fighting from the ships,
unharmed let him return to my swift ships
with all his armour and his close-fighting comrades."
So he spoke in prayer, and Zeus all-devising heard him;
and the father granted one thing to him, but the other he refused him;   250
that his companion would drive the war and the fighting from the ships
he granted him, but he refused his safe return from battle.

   And when Achilles had made libation and prayed to father Zeus
he went into his shelter again, and put the cup back in the chest.
Then he went to stand before his shelter; for in his heart he still wished
to look upon the dread combat of the Trojans and Achaeans.

   And the Myrmidons with Patroclus the great-hearted set out
  under arms,
then charged with high resolve against the Trojans.
Straightway they poured forth like wasps by the wayside,
which children are wont to enrage,   260
provoking them continually, as they live in their nests by the road,
children only; but they create trouble shared by many;
if some wayfaring man as he passes
unwittingly stirs them, the wasps with bold spirit
each and all fly straight out and defend their young.
With such heart and fury, then, the Myrmidons
poured from the ships; and quenchless cry of battle rose.

   And Patroclus shouting loud called to his companions:
"Myrmidons, companions of Achilles, son of Peleus,
be men, my friends, and recollect your fierce courage,   270
so that we give honour to the son of Peleus, who is far best
of the Achaeans by the ships and we his close-fighting henchmen far the
  best,
and the son of Atreus will know, wide-ruling Agamemnon,

his delusion, when he paid no honour to the best of the Achaeans."
So speaking he roused the fury and spirit of each man;
and in a pack they fell upon the Trojans; and the ships around them
echoed terribly with the force of the Achaeans' shouting.

And the Trojans when they saw the brave son of Menoetius,
him and his henchman, glittering in their armour,
the heart in every man was thrown into confusion, the ranks were
    shaken,   280
supposing that from beside the ships the swift-footed son of Peleus
had cast off his anger, and come to friendship;
each man looked about him for where he could flee the sheer destruction.

And Patroclus was first to take aim with his shining spear
straight down through the middle, where the tumult was greatest,
beside the stern of the ship of great-hearted Protesilaos,
and he struck Pyraichmes, who led the Paeonians, marshallers of the
    chariots,
out of Amydon, away from the wide-flowing river Axios;
he struck him on the right shoulder, and he fell on his back in the dust
crying aloud. And his Paeonian comrades about him   290
scattered in flight; for Patroclus drove panic upon them all
when he killed their leader, who used to be their best in battle.
And from the ships he drove them, and extinguished the blazing fire,
and the half-burned ship was left as it was; with inhuman roar
the Trojans fled in fear. Danaans streamed
over the hollow ships; and there arose tumult unceasing.
As when from the high peak of a great mountain
Zeus who gathers the lightning sets the thick cloud moving,
and all the peaks and jutting cliffs are shown,
and the valleys, and from heaven above the boundless bright air is rent
    with light,   300
so the Danaans having driven the enemy fire from their ships
caught their breath for a moment; but there was no respite from fighting;

for the Trojans did not yet flee before the war-loving Achaens
from the black ships in headlong flight,
but still they took their stand before them; and withdrew only by necessity.

Then man slew man as the ranks of leaders
were shattered. And the bold son of Menoetius first
hit Areïlykos in the thigh as he was turning
with his sharp spear, and the bronze drove straight through;
and the spear shattered bone, and face down he fell upon the earth.   310
Then warlike Menelaos stabbed Thoas
in the chest where he was exposed beside his shield, and unstrung his
    limbs.
And Meges son of Phyleus, his eye on Amphiklos as he attacked,
got to the Trojan first, striking at the top of the thigh, where a man's
muscle is thickest, and round the spear-point
the tendons severed; and darkness covered his eyes.
Then one of Nestor's sons, Antilochos, stabbed Atymnios with his sharp
    spear,
and drove the bronze spear through his flank,
and he fell forward; but from close at hand, his brother Maris
lunged with his spear at Antilochos in anger for his brother's death,   320
standing guard before his body; but Thrasymedes, like a god, another
    son of Nestor,
got to him first, before he stabbed, nor did he miss,
striking his shoulder hard; and the head of the spear rent
the top of the arm from its muscles, and shattered utterly the bone;
he fell with a thud, and darkness covered over his eyes.
So the two men broken by two brothers
entered Erebos, noble companions of Sarpedon—
the spear-skilled sons of Amisodaros, who
reared the raging Chimaera to be a bane to many men.
And Ajax son of Oïleus, lunging forward, took Kleoboulos   330
alive, tripped up in the rout; and on the spot

unstrung his strength, striking his neck with his hilted sword,
and all the sword was made hot with blood; and over his eyes
crimson death and powerful fate took him.
And Peneleos and Lykon charged together; for with spear-casts
they had missed each other, and both had made their cast in vain;
and so they charged at each other again with swords. Then Lykon
smote the ridge of the other's horsehair-crested helmet; but his splendid
sword shattered about it; and Peneleos slashed the other's neck below
   the ears,
his whole sword plunged in, and only his skin held,   340
and his head dangled to the side; and his limbs were made slack.
Then Meriones catching Akamas with the swiftness of his feet
stabbed him down through his right shoulder as he was about to mount
   behind his horses;
he fell from his chariot, and down upon his eyes spread the mist of death.
And Idomeneus stabbed Erymas in his mouth with the pitiless bronze;
the bronze spearhead made its way right on through
below the brain, then shivered the white bones,
and his teeth were shaken out; both his eyes
filled with blood, so through his mouth and down through his nose
he spouted blood as he gaped for breath, and the black cloud of death
   folded round him.   350

     So these Danaan leaders were killing each their man.
As ravaging wolves beset lambs or kids,
seizing them out from under the flocks that in the mountains
have been separated through the folly of their shepherd,
and swiftly the wolves with bold heart snatch them as prey,
so the Danaans beset the Trojans; and they recalled only
shameful flight, and forgot their fighting courage.

     And great Ajax aimed always to hurl his spear at Hector
of the brazen helm; but with his skill in warfare Hector,
his broad shoulders protected with his bullhide shield,   360
kept watch for the hiss of arrows and thud of spears.

Well he marked the turn of victory's tide,
but even so he stood his ground, standing by his loyal companions.
        As when from Olympus a thundercloud rises into heaven
from out of the bright upper air, when Zeus pulls tight the violent
    winds,
so out from the ships arose a storm of shouting and confusion,
and the Trojans in disorder crossed the ditch again. Swift-footed horses
carried Hector off, armour and all, and he left behind the Trojan
host, whom the deep ditch checked against their will;
and many swift chariot-drawing horses, snapping their yoke-poles   370
in the ditch, left their masters' chariots behind.
And Patroclus followed calling to the Danaans,
his mind set on evil for the Trojans; they in shouting and confusion of
    flight
filled all the byways, for their ranks were cut to pieces. The swirl
    of dust
billowed to the clouds, and the single-hoofed horses ran at full stretch
back to the city from the ships and shelters.
        And Patroclus—where he saw the Trojan host most struck with
    panic,
there he drove, shouting his commands; men pitched headlong
from their chariots beneath his axles, the chariots crashed and rattled;
then straight over the ditch his swift horses leapt,   380
straining forward; and his heart pressed him to speed against
    Hector,   382
for he longed to strike him; but Hector's swift horses carried him away.
As beneath a tempest the whole black-clouded earth is made heavy
on an autumn's day, when Zeus pours his most violent deluge,
when he rages in his anger at mankind,
who in the place of assembly impose by force their crooked judgements,
and drive out Justice, heedless of the gaze of gods,
and all their running rivers are filled to flooding,
then the torrents cut away the many hillsides,   390

and the running water thunders loud into the dark, tumultuous sea
headlong from the mountains, and the worked fields of men are washed
      away,
so the Trojan horses thundered loud as they raced on.

           And Patroclus, when he had cut off the front ranks of the Trojans,
turning back, he penned them against the ships, nor
for all their desire did he allow them to set foot within their city, but
      between
the ships and the river and their city's high walls
he rushed among and he killed them, and exacted vengeance for many.
First he struck Pronoös with his shining spear
in the chest where he was exposed beside his shield, and unstrung his
      limbs;   400
and he fell with a thud. Then Thestor, son of Enops,
he next attacked—Thestor in his well-polished chariot
sat crouching, struck out of his wits, the reins slipped
from his hands, and Patroclus approaching with his spear struck
his right jaw, and drove the spear through his teeth.
And catching him by the spear he dragged him over the chariot rail, as
      when a man
sitting on a jutting rock hauls a lively fish
out from the sea with his line and hook of bright bronze;
so he hauled Thestor out of his chariot gaping on his shining spear,
then shoved him down upon his face; and his spirit left him as he was
      falling.   410
Then with a stone he struck Erylaos as he was rushing for him
down through the middle of his head; and the whole of his head within
      its strong helmet
was cleaved in two; and he dropped face forward
on the ground, and death which shatters the spirit seeped around him.
Then Erymas and Amphoteros and Epaltes
and Tlepolemos, Damastor's son, and Echios and Pyris
and Ipheus and Euippos and Polymelos son of Argeas—

all of them, one after the other, he brought low to the nourishing earth.

And when Sarpedon saw his loose-robed Lycian comrades
broken at the hands of Patroclus, son of Menoetius,   420
he called out, addressing the godlike Lycians:
"For shame, O Lycians! Whither do you flee? Now be swift to fight.
For I will go forth to meet this man, so that I may learn
who this is who holds sway over us and has worked so much evil
on the Trojans, since the knees of many men, brave men, he has
    unstrung."

He spoke and leapt from his chariot in his armour to the ground;
and from the other side Patroclus leapt from his chariot, when he saw him.
And they, as great birds of prey, hook-clawed, bent-beaked,
screaming loud on a high rock go to battle,
so these, screaming, charged at one another.   430

And seeing them the son of devious Cronus pitied them,
and he spoke to Hera, his sister and his wife:
"Alas for me that Sarpedon, dearest of men to me,
is destined to be broken by the hand of Patroclus son of Menoetius.
My heart is inclined two ways in my breast as I debate this,
whether snatching him alive from tearful battle
I should set him down in the rich country of Lycia,
or now beat him down at the hands of Menoetius' son."

Then answered him ox-eyed lady Hera:
"Most dread son of Cronus, what kind of word have you spoken?   440
This mortal man, long ago consigned to his allotted fate—
you wish to release him from the hard-sorrow death?
Do so; but not all the other gods will approve.
And something else I will tell you, and you put it away in your mind—
if you should send Sarpedon to his home alive,
take care, lest some other of the gods should also wish
to send his beloved son away from the ferocious combat.
For around the great city of Priam there are fighting many
sons of the immortals; you will arouse a terrible rancour in them.

But if he is dear to you, and your heart feels pity,   450
then let him in this ferocious combat
be killed at the hands of Menoetius' son Patroclus,
but when his soul and his life force have left him,
send Death and gentle Sleep to carry him
until they come to the country of broad Lycia,
where his brothers and his kinsmen will bury him
with a tomb and marking stone, for this is the honour of the dead."

      So she spoke; and the father of gods and of men did not disobey.
But to the earth he rained drops of blood
honouring his beloved son, whom Patroclus was to   460
destroy in Troy's rich soil, far from the land of his father.

      And when they had advanced almost upon each other,
then Patroclus struck illustrious Thrasydemos,
who was the good henchmen of his lord Sarpedon,
in the lower belly, and unstrung his limbs.
And Sarpedon attacking second missed Patroclus
with his shining spear, but struck the horse Pedasos
on the right shoulder with the spear; and he crashed down, gasping out
   his life,
and collapsed in the dust screaming, and his life-spirit flew away.
And the paired horses wheeled apart, the yoke groaned, their reins   470
were tangled, since their trace horse lay in the dust.
But spear-famed Automedon found an end to this;
drawing his fine-edged sword from beside his sturdy thigh,
darting forward with swift skill, he cut away the trace;
and the two horses righted themselves, and were pulled on course by the
   reins.

      And again the two men came together in heart-devouring strife.
And again Sarpedon missed with his shining spear,
and over Patroclus' left shoulder the spear-point
passed, nor struck him. But then Patroclus attacked with his bronze-
   headed spear;

and from his hand the shaft did not fly in vain,   480
but struck, there where the lungs close in around the beating heart;
Sarpedon fell as when an oak falls, or white poplar,
or stately pine that in the mountains timbering men
fell with fresh-whetted axes to make a ship;
so he lay stretched out before his chariot and horses,
roaring, clutching at the bloodied dust.
As when a lion coming among a herd slaughters a fiery, great-hearted
bull among the shambling cattle,
and it dies groaning under the lions' jaws,
so at the hands of Patroclus did the leader of the shield-bearing   490
   Lycians
rage as he lay dying, and called by name his beloved comrade:
"Glaukos old friend, warrior among men, now you must
be a spearman and brave warrior;
if you are quick, let bitter war be your desire.
Before all else, range everywhere to rouse the Lycian leaders
to go to battle round Sarpedon;
and then you yourself fight for me with your bronze spear.
For I will be a disgrace and a rebuke for you
all your days through if the Achaeans
strip the armour from me, fallen among the gathering of their ships.   500
Hold on strongly, and rally all the people."
      Then as he was so speaking, the end that is death covered
his nose and eyes. Patroclus stepping with his heel upon his chest
yanked his spear from the flesh, and the lungs followed with it;
so he drew forth the man's soul and his spear-point together.
And the Myrmidons kept hold of Sarpedon's panting horses,
as they strained for flight, free of their master's chariot.
      But a dreadful grief descended on Glaukos as he heard Sarpedon's
   voice,
and his heart was stirred, because he was not able to defend him.
Taking his own arm with his hand he pressed it; for his wound bore

    hard
upon him where Teucer, warding off harm from his companions,
had struck him with his arrow as he rushed the high rampart.
And praying, Glaukos addressed Apollo who shoots from afar:
"Hear me, lord, you who are somewhere in the rich land of Lycia,
or in Troy; for you are able, wherever you are, to hear
a man in distress, as distress comes to me now.
For I have this mighty wound, and my arm
is pierced around with sharp pain, nor can I staunch the blood,
and my shoulder is heavy beneath it;
I cannot hold my spear steady, nor can I join in battle   520
going among my enemies. And the best of men has perished,
Sarpedon, son of Zeus—who did not defend his own son.
But you, lord, heal this powerful wound for me,
calm the pains, and give me strength, so that
summoning my Lycian companions I stir them to do battle,
and myself fight about the body of the man who has died."

        So he spoke praying, and Phoebus Apollo heard him;
at once he stopped the pains, and from the grievous wound
he staunched the dark blood, and cast strength in his spirit.
And Glaukos knew this within his heart and he rejoiced,   530
because the great god had heard his praying at once.
First, ranging everywhere he roused the Lycian leaders
to go to battle round Sarpedon;
and then with long strides he went among the Trojans,
to Poulydamas the son of Panthoös, and shining Agenor,
then to Aeneas and to Hector of the brazen helm.
And standing close to him he spoke winged words:
"Hector, now do you take no thought at all of your allies,
who for your sake, far from their friends and fatherland,
waste away their lives, but you are unwilling to fight for them.   540
Sarpedon lies dead, lord of the spear-bearing Lycians,
who protected broad Lycia with his just judgement and strength;

brazen Ares has broken him with his spear at the hands of Patroclus.
Come friends, take your stand by him, feel shame in your heart
lest they strip his armour away, and maltreat his body,
they the Myrmidons, in anger that so many Danaans have died,
those whom we killed by their swift ships with our spears."

So he spoke, and there swept the Trojans, head to foot, a wave of
    grief,
uncontainable, unrelenting, since Sarpedon had been a support of their
    city,
outlander though he was; for with him many   550
troops had followed, and he had been pre-eminent in waging battle.
And in pressing haste they made straight for the Danaans; and leading
    them
was Hector, angered for Sarpedon. But the Achaeans
were rallied by Patroclus, the rugged-hearted son of Menoetius;
and he first addressed the two Aiantes, both already burning to do battle:
"Aiantes, now let it be your desire to fight,
as such as you were among men before, or yet better.
The man lies dead who first leapt upon the Achaean's rampants,
Sarpedon. Come, let us see if we can mutilate and shame him and seize
the armour from his shoulders to bear away; and any one of his
    companions   560
defending the body, let us beat him down with our pitiless bronze."
So he spoke, but they already burned to make defence.

And when the men on both sides had strengthened their ranks,
Trojans and Lycians and Myrmidons and Achaeans
met to fight about the body of the man who died,
shouting fearfully; and the arms of the men rang loud.
And Zeus spread a deadly darkness on the ferocious combat,
so that over his beloved son there would be deadly toil of fighting.

The Trojans first pushed back the dark-eyed Achaeans;
then not the worst among the Myrmidons was struck—   570
shining Epeigeus, the son of great-hearted Agakles,

who ruled in well-settled Boudeion
in time before; but after slaying his noble cousin
he had come as suppliant to Peleus and Thetis of the silver feet;
and they sent him to accompany Achilles, breaker of men,
to Ilion of the horses, to wage battle with the Trojans.
This man shining Hector struck, as he took hold of Sarpedon's body,
on the head with a boulder; and the whole of his head within its strong
    helmet
was cleaved in two; and he dropped face forward
upon the corpse, and death which shatters the spirit seeped
    around him.   580

          And grief descended on Patroclus for his dead companion,
and he made straight through the frontlines like a swift hawk,
who sets to scattered flight the daws and starlings;
so rider Patroclus, straight for the Lycians
you rushed, and for the Trojans, your heart enraged over your companion.
And he struck Sthenelaos, the dear son of Ithaimenes,
on his neck with a boulder, and smashed the tendons from it.
Then the frontline fighters and illustrious Hector fell back;
as far as a cast is made of a long hunting javelin,
which a man hurls forth making trial of his strength, either in contest 590
or also in war when his life-shattering enemies press close,
so far did the Trojans give way, and the Achaeans push them.

          Then Glaukos, leader of the shield-bearing Lycians, was first
to turn, and he killed great-hearted Bathykles,
the beloved son of Chalkon, who making his home in Hellas
was outstanding in prosperity and wealth among the Myrmidons;
this man Glaukos, turning suddenly, stabbed with his spear in the middle
of his chest, just as the other in pursuit was catching him,
and he fell with a thud. Crushing grief took hold of the Achaeans,
as the brave man fell; but the Trojans rejoiced greatly,   600
and running up they stood about him in a throng; nor did the Achaeans
forget their courage, but bore their fury straight towards them.

Then in turn Meriones slew a Trojan commander,
Laogonos, the bold son of Onetor, who was priest of Idaean
Zeus, and was honoured like a god by the people;
this man Meriones struck below the jaw and ear, and swiftly his spirit
left his limbs, and the hateful darkness took him.
And Aeneas let fly a bronze-tipped spear at Meriones,
for he hoped to strike him as he strode forward under cover of his shield;
but Meriones looking straight ahead dodged the bronze spear-point,   610
for he ducked forward, and the long spear-shaft
was fixed in the earth behind him, the butt-end quivering;
then mighty Ares took away its force.   613
And Aeneas was angered in heart and called out: 616
"Meriones, my spear would surely have put swift end to you for good,
dancer though you be, had I only hit you."
Then spear-famed Meriones answered him in return:
"Aeneas, hard it is for you, for all your strength,   620
to quench the life of every man who comes against you
to defend himself; yes, even you are mortal.
And if I too should chance to strike you dead centre with sharp bronze,
even strong as you are and trusting in your strength of hand,
you would soon give glory to me and your soul to Hades."
So he spoke; but the brave son of Menoetius rebuked him:
"Meriones, why do you, a good warrior, utter these things?
Old friend, it is not by abusive words the Trojans
will give way from the corpse; the earth will bury many a man before that.
For the sum of war lies in strength of hands, the sum of words in
     council;   630
therefore there is no need to pile up words, but to do battle."
So speaking he led on, and the other followed with him, a man like a god.

          And as the clangour of woodcutting men is raised
in the glens of a mountain, and is heard from far away,
so from the wide-wayed earth arose the pounding of men's
bronze and strong-made ox-hide shields,

as they stabbed at one another with their swords and double-edged spears.
Nor would even a clear-sighted man still recognise godlike Sarpedon,
since with blood and dust and missile shafts
he was covered from his head right down to the bottom of his feet;   640
and always the men thronged about his corpse, as when flies
in a sheepfold buzz about pails over-full of milk
in the season of spring, when milk soaks the buckets;
so they thronged about the corpse; nor ever did Zeus
turn his shining eyes from the ferocious combat,
but ever gazed down upon them, and pondered in his heart
many things as he brooded on the slaying of Patroclus,
whether now in the ferocious combat,
right there about godlike Sarpedon, shining Hector
should kill Patroclus with his bronze spear and take the armour from his
    shoulders,   650
or whether for yet more men he should increase the hard toil of war.
And this seemed to him as he considered, to be best—
that the good henchmen of Peleus' son Achilles
one more time should force the Trojans and bronze-helmed Hector
to their city, and snatch the lives of many.
And in Hector first he inspired a coward's spirit:
mounting his chariot, Hector turned his team for flight, and bade the
    other
Trojans flee; for he saw how the holy scales of Zeus were balanced.
Then the strong Lycians did not stand firm, but fled,
all of them, when they saw their king struck in the heart   660
lying in a heap of corpses; for many men had dropped upon him,
when the son of Cronus stretched tight the mighty strife of battle.
Then from the shoulders of Sarpedon the Achaeans seized his armour,
bronze, glittering; and this to the hollow ships
the brave son of Menoetius gave his companions to carry.
        And then Zeus who gathers the clouds addressed Apollo:
"Come now, beloved Phoebus, take Sarpedon out of range of the flying

weapons and cleanse him of his dark-clouded blood, and
conveying him far away, bathe him in the flowing of a river
and anoint him with ambrosia, and put ambrosial clothing
   round him.   670
And send him forth to be conveyed with swift guards of honour,
Sleep and Death, the twins, who will soon
lay him in broad Lycia's rich country;
there his brothers and his kinsmen will bury him
with a tomb and marking stone, for this is the honour of the dead."

   So he spoke, nor did Apollo fail to hearken to his father;
down from the Idaean mountains he descended into the dread field of
   battle,
and straightway lifting godlike Sarpedon out of range of flying weapons,
conveying him far away, he bathed him in the flowing of a river
and anointed him with ambrosia, and put ambrosial clothing round
   him.   680
And he sent him forth to be conveyed with swift guards of honour,
Sleep and Death, the twins, who soon
set him down in broad Lycia's rich country;

   But Patroclus shouting to Automedon to follow with the horses,
made for the Lycians and Trojans, blinded to his great folly—
fool; if only he had observed the son of Peleus' command,
he might yet have escaped from the fated evil of dark death.
But the mind of Zeus is ever mightier than the mind of man;
Zeus who puts even a brave man to flight and takes away his victory
easily, but at another time urges him on to battle;   690
Zeus who now put fury in the breast of Patroclus.

   Then who was the first, who was the last you slew,
Patroclus, when the gods summoned you deathward?
Adrestos first, and Autonoös, and Echeklos,
and Perimos the son of Megas, and Epistor, and Melanippos,
and then Elasos and Moulios and Pylartes;
these he killed, and the rest turned their thoughts to flight, every man of

them.

Then would the sons of the Achaeans have taken high-gated Troy

under the hands of Patroclus, as he raged ever forward with his spear,

had not Phoebus Apollo on the strong-built tower   700

taken his stand, with deadly deeds in mind for him, but help for the

    Trojans.

Three times to the angled joint of the high wall went

Patroclus, and three times Apollo smote him back,

batting with immortal hands the shining shield.

But when for the fourth time Patroclus charged like something more

    than human,

the god calling out in a voice of dread spoke winged words:

"Give way Patroclus, seed of Zeus; it is not fated

that the city of the noble Trojans be sacked under your spear,

nor under that of Achilles, he who is greater by far than you."

So he spoke; and Patroclus withdrew a great way back,   710

shunning the wrath of far-shooting Apollo.

       And at the Scaean gates Hector pulled up his single-hoofed

    horses;

he debated whether, driving through the tumult, he should go to battle

    once again,

or should call for his men to mass within the walls.

And as he thought these things there came up to him Phoebus Apollo,

in the likeness of a young and powerful man,

Asios, who was the maternal uncle of horse-breaking Hector,

brother of Hecuba, and son of Dymas,

who dwelt in Phrygia, by the flowing waters of Sangarios.

In likeness to him Apollo son of Zeus addressed him: 720

"Hector, why do you give over fighting? You should not.

Would I were stronger than you by as much as I am weaker!

Then you would soon regret holding back from war.

But come, drive your strong-hoofed horses against Patroclus,

in hope you might kill him, and Apollo give you great glory."

        So speaking he set out again, a god among the fighting throng
    of men,
and shining Hector called to skilled Kebriones
to whip the horses into battle; and Apollo
set out and made his way into the throng, and against the Argives
he launched evil rout, and to the Trojans and to Hector he gave
        glory.   730
And Hector let the other Danaans go, and did not kill them,
but it was against Patroclus he drove his strong-hoofed horses.
And Patroclus from his side jumped from behind his horses to the
    ground,
holding his spear in his left hand, and with the other he seized a rock
glittering and jagged, which his hand covered over,
and with his strength behind it he hurled; he did not long stand in awe of
    the man,
nor was his cast in vain, but he struck Hector's charioteer
Kebriones, a bastard son of worthy Priam,
between his eyes with the sharp rock as he held the horses' reins.
The stone shattered his brows, the bone did not hold,   740
his eyes fell to the ground in the dust
before his feet; and he, like a diver,
dropped from the strong-made chariot, and his spirit left his bones.
And mocking, you addressed him, rider Patroclus:
"How now, truly a most nimble man; how easily he somersaults!
No doubt were he also in the fish-filled sea,
this man would fill the bellies of many as he groped for molluscs,
leaping from a ship, even in rough seas;
as now on land he somersaults lightly from his chariot.
To be sure, there are divers among the Trojans too."   750
So speaking he made for the warrior Kebriones
with the spring of a lion, who ravaging a sheepfold
is struck on the chest, and it is his courage that destroys him;
so at Kebriones, Patroclus, did you leap in your fury.

>   And from the other side Hector sprang from behind his horses to
>   the ground.
> They two around Kebriones contended like lions
> who in mountain heights fight over a slain deer,
> both hungry, both with high resolve,
> so over Kebriones the two masters of battle,
> Patroclus son of Menoetius and shining Hector,   760
> strained to cut the flesh of one another with pitiless bronze.
> When Hector caught Kebriones by the head, nor would let go,
> Patroclus from the other side took hold of his feet; and the rest of the
> Trojans and Danaans joined in the ferocious combat.
> As the East and South Winds vie with each other
> in a mountain glen to set the deep woods shaking,
> oak and ash and fine-barked cornel
> that hurl at each other sharp-pointed boughs
> with inhuman roar, crashing as they shatter,
> so the Trojans and Achaeans surging towards each other   770
> cut their enemy down, nor did either have thought of disastrous flight.
> And around Kebriones many sharp spears stuck fast
> and feathered arrows springing from their bowstrings,
> and many great boulders battered the shields
> of the men fighting round him. But Kebriones lay in the whirling dust,
> a great man in his greatness, unmindful of his horsemanship.
>   As long as the sun stood astride the middle heaven,
> so long the shafts of both sides found their mark, and the people fell;
> but when the sun passed over to the time for unyoking of oxen,
> then even beyond fate the Achaeans were the stronger.   780
> Away from the flying weapons they dragged the warrior Kebriones,
> away from the shouting of the Trojans, and from his shoulders took his
>   armour,
> and Patroclus with evil intent sprang for the Trojans.
>   Three times then he charged at them, swift Ares' equal,

shouting his terrifying cry, and three times he slew nine men;
but when for the fourth time he swept against them, like something more
    than human,
then for you, Patroclus, was shown the end of life;
for meeting you in the ferocious combat was Apollo
the dread. Patroclus did not see him as he closed in through the tumult;
for cloaked in thick mist Apollo met him,   790
then stood behind, and struck the back and broad shoulders of Patroclus
with the flat of his hand, so that his eyes spun.
From his head Phoebus Apollo struck the helmet;
and rolling beneath the horses' hooves it rang resounding,
four-horned, hollow-eyed, the horsehair crest defiled
with blood and dust. Before this it was forbidden that
the horsehair-crested helmet be defiled by dust,
for it had protected the handsome head and brow of the godlike man
Achilles; but now Zeus gave it to Hector
to wear on his head; but his own death was very near.   800
In Patroclus' hands the long-shadowed spear was wholly shattered,
heavy, massive, powerful, pointed with bronze; from his shoulders
his bordered shield and belt dropped to the ground;
then lord Apollo, son of Zeus, undid his breastplate.

      Confusion seized his wits, his shining limbs were loosed beneath
    him,
Patroclus stood stunned. Behind him, in his back, between his shoulders,
a Dardanian man struck with a sharp spear at close range,
Euphorbos son of Panthoös, who surpassed the youths of his own age
in work of spear and horsemanship and speed of feet;
already he had brought down twenty men from behind their horses   810
since first coming with his chariot, to learn the art of war;
he first let fly his spear at you, rider Patroclus,
but did not kill you. And back he ran again, and mingled in the crowd,
snatching from your flesh his ash-wood spear, and did not stand to wait

Patroclus, naked though he was among the fighters.
And Patroclus, broken by the blow of the god and by the spear,
tried to retreat into the band of his companions and shun death.

But Hector, when he saw great-hearted Patroclus
drawing back, when he saw him wounded with sharp bronze,
then through the ranks he closed upon him, and stabbed with
   his spear   820
into his lower flank, and drove the bronze point through;
with a thud Patroclus fell, and his falling brought great anguish on the
   Achaean army.
As when a lion overpowers a tireless boar in spirited combat,
they who on the mountain heights go to battle with high resolve
over a small spring, and both desire to drink,
and as the boar gasps hard for breath, the lion beats him down with
   violent strength—
so, having slain so many, the brave son of Menoetius
was stripped of his life by Hector son of Priam at close quarters with his
   spear.
And vaunting over him Hector spoke out winged words:
"Patroclus, surely you thought you would cut down our city,   830
and stripping the Trojan women of their day of freedom
would carry them in ships to your beloved fatherland,
you fool; for in front of them the swift horses of Hector
galloped with outstretched legs to battle, and I with my spear myself
outshone the battle-loving Trojans, I who warded off from them
the day of slavery; you the vultures will devour here.
Poor wretch, nor, great though he is, did Achilles rescue you,
who, I suppose, laid many injunctions on you, while he remained and you
   departed:
'Do not return to me, Patroclus, master of horses,
by the hollow ships, before you have ripped man-slaying Hector's   840
bloodied tunic around his breast.'
Thus I suppose he spoke to you, and persuaded your fool's wits."

Then with little strength you answered him, rider Patroclus:
"Make your great boast now, Hector; for Zeus the son of Cronus
has given you victory and Apollo, they who easily broke me;
for they took the armour from my shoulders.
But if twenty such as you had encountered me,
all would have died here broken beneath my spear;
deadly Fate and the son of Leto killed me,
and of men it was Euphorbos; you were third to kill me.   850
And something else I will tell you, and you put it away in your mind—
you yourself will not live long, but already
death and powerful fate stand close beside you,
to be broken at the hands of blameless Achilles Aeacides."
Then the closure of death enveloped him as he was speaking
and his soul flying from his limbs started for Hades,
lamenting her fate, abandoning manhood and all its young vigour.
      And shining Hector addressed him, dead though he was:
"Patroclus, why do you now prophesy sheer destruction for me?
Who knows whether Achilles, son of Thetis of the lovely hair,   860
might be stabbed first by my spear, and lose his life?"
So speaking he drew his bronze-pointed spear from the wound,
stepping on Patroclus with his heel, and shoved him on his back away
    from his spear.
      And straightway he went with his spear after Automedon,
the godlike henchman of swift-footed Aeacides,
and took aim to strike him; but the swift horses bore Automedon away,
the immortal horses that the gods gave as glorious gifts to Peleus.

And the felling of Patroclus at the hands of the Trojans in the fighting
did not go unnoticed by warlike Menelaos,
and he set out through the frontline warriors armoured in gleaming
     bronze,
and stood astride the body, as a mother cow lows
over her firstborn, knowing nothing before this of bearing young;
so fair-haired Menelaos stood over Patroclus;
he held before him his spear and the circle of his shield,
straining to kill any man who might come against him.

      And Euphorbos son of Panthoös of the strong ash-spear
did not lose sight of blameless Patroclus as he felled him; but took a stand
     close by him,   10
and called out to Menelaos beloved by Ares;
"Son of Atreus, Menelaos cherished by Zeus, leader of the people,
give way—leave the corpse, and let the bloodied spoils be,
for none of the Trojans or our illustrious allies
struck Patroclus with his spear before me in the ferocious combat;
therefore let me win outstanding glory among the Trojans,
lest I strike you, and strip you of the life you hold as sweet as honey."

      Then greatly troubled fair Menelaos answered:
"Father Zeus! It is no good thing to brag vaingloriously.
The pride of the leopard is not so great, nor of the lion,   20
nor of the wild baneful boar—in whose breast the heart is mightiest
in vaunting of his strength—

as the pride carried by the sons of Panthoös of the strong ash-spear!
And yet Panthoös' son strong Hyperenor, breaker of horses,
had no enjoyment of his youth when he made light of me and stood up
    to me
and said that I was most shameful of warriors;
and I do not think he returned on his own feet
to delight his dear wife and doting parents.
And so I say I will undo your strength too, should you stand
against me. So I urge you to retreat back   30
into your host, and not stand against me,
before you suffer some harm; even a fool learns after the event."

       So he spoke; but he did not persuade Euphorbos, who spoke in
    answer:
"Now, Menelaos cherished by Zeus, you will surely pay for
my brother, whom you killed, and boast of,
and made his wife a widow in the inmost part of her new bridal chamber,
and upon his parents laid accursed grief and lamentation.
Yet I might stop the lamentation of those unhappy wretches,
were I to carry your head and armour
and drop them into the hands of my father Panthoös and my mother
    shining Phrontis.   40
Come! This trial will not be long untested
nor unfought, this trial of either prowess or of flight."

       So speaking Euphorbos stabbed the circle of Menelaos' shield;
the bronze did not smash through, but the spear-point was bent back
in the mighty shield; then Menelaos son of Atreus rose up
with his bronze spear, having made prayer to Zeus the father;
and struck Euphorbos at the base of his throat as he was retreating
    backward,
and trusting in his strength of hand he leaned his weight into the blow;
the spear-point drove straight through the soft neck,
and Euphorbos fell with a thud, and his armour clashed upon him. 50
His hair, like the hair of the Graces, was made wet with blood,

his locks, which were pinched in like a wasp's waist by clasps of silver and
     gold.
Like a flourishing young olive tree that a man nurtures
in a sequestered place, where abundant water soaks it,
conspicuous in beauty, and which the breath of winds from all directions
sets aquiver, and it is thick with white flowers,
and of a sudden the wind coming with a great storm-blast
uproots it from its hollow and lays it out upon the earth,
such was Euphorbos of the strong-ash spear, son of Panthoös,
who fell at the hand of Menelaos, son of Atreus, who began stripping
     his armour.   60
As when a lion raised in the mountains, trusting his prowess,
snatches a cow from a grazing herd, choosing whichever is best—
her neck he shatters utterly taking her in his powerful teeth
first, then her blood and entrails he devours entirely;
and around him the dogs and men and herders
howl a great deal from a distance, but are not willing
to approach him, for great is the sickly fear that seizes them;
so the heart in the breast of no man dared
to come against glorious Menelaos.
          Then would the son of Atreus easily have carried off the
     splendid armour   70
of Panthoös' son, had not Phoebus Apollos grudged him,
Apollo who stirred up Hector, swift Ares' equal,
likening himself to a man, Mentes, leader of the Ciconians.
And speaking winged words Apollo addressed him:
"Hector, now do you run about chasing after what cannot be won,
the horses of brilliant Aeacides; they are difficult
for mortal men to control and drive,
for any other man than Achilles, whom an immortal mother bore.
And all the while Atreus' warlike son Menelaos,
standing guard over Patroclus, has slain the best of Trojans,   80
Euphorbos son of Panthoös, and stopped him of his fierce courage."

So speaking he set out again, a god among the fighting throng of men,
and dreadful grief covered Hector's dark heart round.
And then when he glanced across the ranks, at once he saw
the one man taking away the illustrious armour, the other lying
upon the earth; and blood streaming from the wound that had been struck.
And Hector set out through the frontline warriors armoured in gleaming
    bronze,
crying a piercing cry, like to the inextinguishable flame of
Hephaestus. And the son of Atreus marked his sharp crying,
and troubled he took counsel with his own great-hearted spirit: 90
"Oh me, if I should abandon the splendid armour
and Patroclus, who lies here dead for the sake of my honour,
I fear that should one of the Danaans see me he would reproach me.
But if I should battle on my own with Hector and with the Trojans
out of shame, I fear they would in their multitude surround me, who am
    but one.
Hector of the shimmering helm leads all the Trojans to this spot.
But why does my heart debate these things?
When a man seeks to go to battle against the will of a god
with a man whom some god honours, swift and great will disaster's wave
    roll upon him.
Therefore no Danaan would reproach me, who might see me   100
retreating before Hector, since Hector fights with help from god.
If only I could somewhere hear word of Ajax of the great war-cry,
we two returning could recollect our fighting spirit
and against even divine power we might somehow drag away the body
for Peleus' son Achilles; this would be least of evils."

            While he churned these things through his heart and mind,
all the while the ranks of Trojans came on, Hector at the lead.
Then Menelaos withdrew back, and left the body,
turning always around, like a thick-maned lion
that dogs and men pursue away from a farmstead   110
with spears and shouting, and the brave heart in his breast

is chilled, and he goes unwillingly from the fold;
so away from Patroclus fair Menelaos went,
then wheeling about he took his stand when he reached the band of his
    companions,
glancing around for great Ajax, the son of Telamon;
and he soon saw him on the left wing of all the fighting
encouraging his companions and stirring them on to battle,
for Phoebus Apollo had cast unearthly fear in them.
Straightway he went on the run, and coming up to him spoke out:
"Ajax, come, old friend, let us rush to Patroclus,   120
who has died, and see if we can carry his body at least to Achilles,
naked as it is; for Hector of the shimmering helm has his armour."

      So he spoke; and stirred the spirit of brilliant Ajax,
and he set out through the front ranks, together with fair Menelaos.
And when Hector had taken the illustrious armour,
he began to drag at Patroclus, so as to cut his head from his shoulders
    with his sharp bronze sword,
after hauling the corpse away, to give it to the Trojan dogs;
but Ajax drew near, bearing his shield like a tower,
and Hector, turning back, withdrew into the throng of his companions,
and sprang up into his chariot; and he gave the splendid armour   130
to the Trojans to carry to the city, to be his own great glory.

      And Ajax putting his broad shield as covering about the son of
    Menoetius
took his stand, as a lion stands over its young,
a lion that hunting men encounter as it leads its little ones
in the woods; and the lion is confident in his strength,
and draws down all folds of his forehead to veil his scowling eyes;
so Ajax stood astride the warrior Patroclus,
and on the other side Menelaos the son of Atreus, beloved by Ares,
took his stand, and great was the grief swelling in his breast.

      Then Glaukos the son of Hippolochos, leader of the Lycian
    men   140

looking at Hector from beneath his brows, rebuked him with harsh
    words:
"Hector, best in beauty, so it turns out you fall far short in battle;
rumour has you excellent for this—for being a runner.
Take thought now for how you might save your home and city
on your own, with the people who live in Ilion;
for there is no Lycian who will go to battle with the Danaans
for the sake of your town, since it seems there is no thanks
for doing battle against enemy men without respite, forever.
How would you save some lesser man from among the throng of battle,
you of iron heart? Since Sarpedon, your guest friend and your
    comrade,   150
you left as prey for Argives, a thing to scavenge,
him who was of great service to you and to your city,
when he was living; but now you have not courage to ward off the dogs
  from him.
Now, therefore, if any of the Lycian men obeys me
we will go home, and Troy's sheer destruction will be certain.
For if the Trojans now had any spirit of great confidence,
something unshakeable, such as enters men who on behalf of their
    fatherland
inflict the toil of war and battle on their enemies,
we would soon drag Patroclus inside the walls of Ilion.
If he arrived at the great city of lord Priam   160
dead, when we dragged him from the heat of battle,
then would the Argives quickly ransom the splendid armour
of Sarpedon, and we would bring him into Ilion;
for so great is the man whose henchman has been killed, best by far
of the Argives by the ships, as are his close-fighting comrades.
But you, you did not dare to stand against
great-hearted Ajax, looking him in the eyes amid the war cries of your
    enemies,
nor fight him face to face, because he is your better."

Then looking at him from under his brows Hector of the
   shimmering helm addressed him:
"Glaukos, why, being the man you are, do you speak so brazenly?   170
Old friend—and yet I used to think that with regard to wits you were
   above the others,
all those who dwell in Lycia of the rich soil;
but now I utterly scorn your judgement, what a thing you have said—
you who say that I do not stand up to monstrous Ajax.
I dread neither combat nor the thunder of horses;
but the mind of Zeus who wields the aegis is ever mightier;
Zeus who puts even a brave man to flight and takes away his victory
easily, but at another time urges him on to battle.
But come here, old man, stand by me and watch my work of war—
either I will be a coward the whole day long, as you declare,   180
or I will put a stop to some Danaan, for all his high desire for deeds of
   prowess,
from defending dead Patroclus."
     So speaking he called to the Trojans, shouting loud:
"Trojans and Lycians and Dardanians who fight at close quarters,
be men, my friends, and recollect your fierce courage,
while I put on the armour of noble Achilles,
the splendid armour, which I stripped after slaying strong Patroclus."
Having spoken so, Hector of the shimmering helm then departed
from the deadly battle; and running, overtook his comrades
quickly, at no great distance, catching them with his swiftness of feet   190
as they carried to the city the famous armour of the son of Peleus.
And standing apart from the sorrowful fighting he exchanged his armour;
and his own he gave to be carried to sacred Ilion
by the war-loving Trojans, and he put on the immortal armour
of Peleus' son Achilles, which the heavenly gods
gave to his beloved father, and he then gave it to his son
when he grew old; but the son would not grow old in the armour of his
   father.

And as from afar Zeus who gathers the clouds saw him
arrayed in the armour of the godlike son of Peleus,
shaking his head he addressed his own heart: 200
"Ah, poor wretch, death troubles your heart not at all,
death which is now close by you; you are putting on the immortal armour
of a noble man, before whom all others tremble.
His companion whom you have slain was both strong and gentle,
and you were not right to take the armour from his head and shoulders.
But yet I will hand you now great victory,
compensation for this—that Andromache will not receive
you safe-returned from fighting, nor the famous armour of the son of
    Peleus."

He spoke, and the son of Cronus nodded with his blue-black
    brows;
he fitted the armour upon Hector's body, and the terrible battle spirit   210
of Ares entered him, and Hector's limbs were filled inside
with strength and courage. And he went toward his illustrious allies
crying aloud, and appeared to them all
made bright by the armour of the great-hearted son of Peleus.
And going among them he stirred the spirit of each with his words,
Mesthles and Glaukos and Medon and Thersilochos,
Asteropaios and Deisenor and Hippothoös and
Phorkys and Chromios and Ennomos the augur of birds: 218
"Hear me, you myriad tribes of allies who dwell around us.   220
It was not to solicit and seek mere numbers
I gathered each of you here from your cities,
but so that with willing heart you might save for me
Troy's wives and children from warmongering Achaeans;
with these things in mind I wear down my own people with demands
for food and gifts, to raise the courage of each of you.
Therefore let each man now turn to face straight forwards, either to
    perish
or survive; for this is the communion of war.

Whoever should drag Patroclus, dead as he is,
among the horse-breaking Trojans, the man to whom Ajax yields,   230
to him I shall give over half the spoils, and half I myself
shall have; and his glory shall be as great as even mine."
So he spoke, and they set out in full force straight for the Danaans,
with uplifted spears; and greatly did their hearts hope
to drag the corpse from the grip of Telamonian Ajax,
the fools; for over it Ajax would rob the life of many.

     And then Ajax spoke to Menelaos of the war cry:
"Old man, Menelaos cherished by Zeus, I no longer think we two
ourselves will return home from this battle.
I do not so much fear for the body of Patroclus,   240
which will soon glut the dogs and birds of Troy,
as I fear for my own head, lest something befall me,
and for yours, since this cloud of war smothers all things round,
this Hector, and sheer destruction comes once more upon us.
But come, call the best of the Danaans, perhaps someone may hear."

     So he spoke; nor did Menelaos of the war cry disobey,
and he cried out in a piercing voice so as to be heard by the Danaans:
"O friends, leaders and counsellors of the Danaans,
who in the house of the sons of Atreus, Agamemnon and Menelaos,
drink the public's wine, and who each commands   250
his people, whose honour and glory is granted from Zeus—
hard it is for me to distinguish each
of the leaders, so great the strife of war has blazed—
but let each man of his own will set out, let each be angered in his heart
that Patroclus become a thing of play for the dogs of Troy."
So he spoke; and swift Ajax son of Oïleus was sharp to hear,
and came first to join him, running through the fighting throng;
and after him came Idomeneus and Idomeneus' henchman
Meriones, equal to the man-slaughtering war god Enyalios;
but who, from his own wits, could name the others,   260
all those who, coming after, stirred the Achaeans' fighting?

And the Trojans surged forward in a throng; and Hector gave
   lead.
As when at the outpouring of a river rain-filled from Zeus above,
a great sea swell roars against the running current, and the capes
boom around as the surf splatters seawards,
so then did the Trojans advance with a roar; and the Achaeans
took their stand around the son of Menoetius united in spirit,
fenced about with their shields of bronze. And around their
gleaming helmets the son of Cronus poured
thick mist, since before this he had no hatred for Menoetius' son,   270
while he was living and was henchman to Achilles,
and he abhorred that he should become prey for the dogs of the Trojan
enemy; therefore Zeus roused the companions of Patroclus to defend
   him.

And first the Trojans forced the dark-eyed Achaeans back;
abandoning the body they fled; but not one of them
did the high-hearted Trojans kill with spears, for all their desire,
but they began to drag the body. Yet for a short while only were the
   Achaeans
to desert it; Ajax swiftly wheeled them hard around,
Ajax who in stature and deeds exceeded
the other Danaans after blameless Achilles.   280
He charged through the frontlines with the courage of a wild boar
that in the mountains easily scatters the dogs and sturdy youths
as it wheels through the narrow valleys;
so did the son of noble Telamon, glorious Ajax,
easily scatter the ranks of Trojans as he sped towards them,
those who stood astride Patroclus, and were most intent on
dragging him to their city and claiming glory.
And already the glorious son of Pelasgian Lethos,
Hippothoös, was dragging Patroclus by the foot through the powerful
   combat,

having tied it near the ankle with his sword strap, around the
   tendons,   290
seeking the favour of Hector and the Trojans; but evil came to him
swiftly, nor did any of them ward it off from him, for all they desired.
The son of Telamon, springing through the throng of battle,
struck him at close quarters through his helmet with its cheeks of bronze;
the crested helmet split apart about the spear-point,
smashed by the great spear and his weighty hand,
and his brains spurted from the wound along the spearhead socket,
mingled with his blood. And there, at once, his life force was undone, and
   from his hands
he let drop the foot of great-hearted Patroclus to lie upon the ground,
and he close by it fell face-first upon the body,   300
a long way from the rich soil of Larisa, nor did he repay his beloved
parents for his nurture, and short was the life allotted to him,
who was broken under the spear of great-hearted Ajax.

      And once again Hector took aim at Ajax with his shining spear;
but watching straight in front he evaded the bronze point,
barely, and Hector struck Schedios the son of great-hearted Iphitos,
by far the best of the Phocians, who used to live in a house
in famous Panopeus, ruling over many men—
this man he struck squarely below the collarbone, and all the way through
the sharp spear-point of bronze projected, at the base of his shoulder;   310
he fell with a thud and his armour clashed upon him.

      And Ajax then struck Phorkys, the brilliant son of Phainops,
in the middle of his stomach, as he stood astride Hippothoös,
and shattered the hollow of his breastplate; and the bronze spear made
his entrails gush through, and falling in the dust he clutched the earth
   with his clenched hand.
Then the front ranks fell back, even shining Hector;
and the Argives gave a great cry and dragged off the dead men,
Phorkys and Hippothoös, and undid the armour from their shoulders.

Then would the Trojans once more have gone up into Ilion,
broken by their cowardice before the warlike Achaeans,   320
and the Argives would have won glory even beyond the fate decreed by
    Zeus
with their strength and power; but Apollo himself
roused up Aeneas, likening himself in form to Periphas,
the herald, son of Epytos, who at the side of Aeneas' old father
had grown old as a herald, and had kindly thoughts in his mind for him;
likening himself to this man Apollo, son of Zeus, addressed him:
"Aeneas, how would you and your men defend sheer Ilion
if a god were against you? In truth I have seen other men
trusting in their might, their strength, their manhood,
their own numbers, although fewer, protect their country!   330
Zeus desires victory for us more than the Danaans;
but you and your men are struck with unspeakable panic and do not fight."

So he spoke; and Aeneas looking him in the face recognised
    Apollo
who shoots from afar, and calling loud he spoke to Hector:
"Hector and you other leaders of the Trojans and their allies,
for shame now, that under the hands of the warlike Achaeans
you go up into Ilion, broken by your cowardice.
But come, for one of the gods standing close to me has said
that Zeus the supreme master of battle still supports us;
therefore let us go straight against the Danaans, and do not let them   340
bring Patroclus at their leisure to the ships now he has died."

So he spoke, and leaping out far beyond the front fighters he took
    his stand;
and the others wheeled about and took up position facing the Achaeans.
And then Aeneas stabbed Leokritos with his spear,
the son of Arisbas, the noble companion of Lykomedes.
And as he fell Lykomedes, dear to Ares, pitied him,
and coming up he stood very close and took aim with his shining spear;
and struck Apisaon son of Hippasos, shepherd of his people,

in the liver beneath the midriff, and straightway his limbs were loosed
   beneath him,
he who had come from Paeonia of the rich soil   350
and had also been, after Asteropaios, best in waging battle.
And as he fell warlike Asteropaios pitied him,
and he advanced straight forwards determined to go to battle with the
   Danaans;
but it was no longer possible, for on every side they made a barrier with
   their shields,
as they stood around Patroclus, holding their spears before them.
And Ajax ranged among them all, giving his many orders;
no man, he commanded, was to retreat from the body,
nor was any man to fight in front beyond the other Achaeans,
but to stand close around the body and fight at close quarters.
Thus towering Ajax enjoined them; and the earth was soaked   360
with crimson blood, and one upon the other fell the bodies
of both Trojans and their enduring allies,
and of the Danaans; for they too did not fight without bloodshed,
although far fewer died, for always they were mindful
to defend one another throughout their company from sheer slaughter.

     So they fought in the likeness of fire; nor could you have said
the sun or moon was ever safe in the sky,
for they were shrouded in mist at the place of battle where all the bravest
stood around the fallen son of Menoetius.
But the rest of the Trojans and strong-greaved Achaeans   370
fought untroubled beneath the clear high air, and the piercing rays
of the sun were spread, and no cloud appeared over all
the earth or mountains. They fought with pause for rest,
evading one another's arrows and the groaning pain they bring,
standing off at a good distance; but those in the middle of the mist
and fighting suffered painfully, worn down by pitiless bronze,
all who were bravest. But two men,
two men of renown, Thrasymedes and Antilochos, had not yet learned

of the falling of blameless Patroclus, but still thought
that he was alive in the front of the throng, waging battle.   380
These two, watchful for the death and flight of their comrades,
battled on by themselves, since so Nestor had enjoined them,
urging them away from the black ships toward the place of battle.

But for the others the great strife of hard contention rose
the whole day long; and always, relentlessly, the sweat of toil
stained the knees and shins and feet of each man under him,
and the hands and eyes of those who fought
about the noble henchman of swift-footed Aeacides.
As when a man gives the hide of a great ox bull
dripping with fat to his servants to stretch,   390
and taking it they stretch it, standing about
in a circle, and soon its own moisture goes, and the fat soaks in
with so many pulling, and the whole of it is stretched to its whole extent—
so there and there, in little space,
they pulled the body on either side; and great was their hearts' hope—
the Trojans to drag it to the city, and the Achaeans
to drag it to the hollow ships; and about it a savage contest
rose; nor would Ares who drives the army into battle, nor Athena
have made light of it had they seen, not even if war-rage gripped them
     strongly.

Such was the evil toil of men and even horses that Zeus
     strained tight   400
this day above Patroclus; but godlike Achilles did not yet
know that Patroclus was dead.
For the men were fighting at great distance from the swift ships,
beneath the wall of Troy; so Achilles did not ever in his heart
imagine he had died, but believed that having come right up to the city
     gates,
Patroclus would return alive, since Achilles did not in any way imagine
he would try to sack the citadel without him—nor even with him.
For many a time, listening in private, he had heard this from his mother,

who always would make report to him of the design of mighty Zeus;
but this time his mother did not tell him of such great evil as had
    happened,   410
that his dearest companion had died.

        And always around the body of Patroclus, gripping their pointed
    spears, the men
relentlessly pressed hard upon and killed each other.
And thus would one of the bronze-clad Achaeans speak:
"O friends, it will be no distinction to return for us
to the hollow ships, but right here may the black earth open
for us all; this would be far better for us
than if we yield this man to the horse-breaking Trojans
to drag to their city and to claim the glory."
And in turn one of the great-hearted Trojans would cry out: 420
"O friends, even if fate has us all die together
beside this man, let no one draw back from this battle."
Thus would a man speak, and rally the strength of each.

        So they fought, and the unyielding tumult
reached through the murmuring high clear air to the brazen sky.
And at a distance from the battle the horses of Aeacides
had been mourning from the time they first learned of the falling of their
    charioteer
in the dust at the hands of man-slaying Hector.
Indeed Automedon, the courageous son of Diores,
struck them again and again, lashing with his swift whip,   430
again and again he spoke to them with soothing words, again and again
    he threatened;
but they were neither willing to go back to the ships by the broad
    Hellespont,
nor into the fighting with the Achaeans,
but remained unmovable as a marker of stone that stands upon the burial
    mound
of a man who has died, or of a woman.

So they remained motionless, holding the splendid chariot in place,
hanging their heads upon the earth, and hot tears
from their lids flowed down to the ground as they wept
with longing for their charioteer; and their luxuriant manes were soiled
   as they streamed down
from under their yoke-pad on either side.   440

      And seeing them as they wept the son of Cronus pitied them,
and shaking his head he addressed his own heart;
"Ah, poor wretches, why did we give you to lord Peleus,
a mortal man, you who are ageless and immortal?
Was it so you might suffer grief among unhappy men?
For there is nothing more wretched than mankind
of all things that breathe and creep upon the earth.
But verily, not on you, nor your elaborate chariot
will Hector son of Priam ride; for I will not allow it.
Is it not enough, that he has the armour and so exults?   450
I shall cast strength in your knees, and in your heart,
so that you bring Automedon safe from fighting
to the hollow ships. And I shall still give the Trojans the glory
of killing, until that time they come to the well-benched ships."   454

      So speaking he breathed new strength into the horses;   456
and they tossing the dust from their manes to the earth,
lightly carried the swift chariot among the Trojans and Achaeans,
and on them Automedon went to battle, grieving though he was for his
   companion,
charging with the horses like an eagle among geese.   460
Out from the Trojan tumult he would adroitly flee,
then adroitly would rush in, pressing hard through the throng of battle.
But he killed no men, as he charged in pursuit, for alone in the divine
   chariot
it was not possible
both to attack with his spear and to manage the flying horses.
      But at length a comrade set eyes upon him,

Alkimedon, the son of Laerkes, son of Haimon.
And he took position behind the chariot and spoke to Automedon:
"Automedon, which of the gods now put this useless plan
in your heart, and took away your good wits—   470
how will you fight against the Trojans at the head of the battle
on your own—your companion slain, and Hector exulting
with the arms of Aeacides on his own shoulders?"

        And in turn Automedon the son of Diores answered him:
"Alkimedon, who else of the Achaeans is your equal
to control and hold the strength of these immortal horses?
If only Patroclus, the gods' equal in skill,
were alive; but now death and fate have swallowed him.
Come now, take the whip and glossy reins,
and I will dismount the chariot, to fight.   480

        So he spoke, and Alkimedon, leaping at once into the swift-
    fighting,
chariot, seized the whip and reins into his hands,
and Automedon leapt down. And shining Hector marked him,
and at once spoke to Aeneas from close by:
"Aeneas, leader in counsel of the bronze-clad Trojans,
I see the two horses of swift-footed Achilles
making appearance in the fighting with unworthy charioteers.
I could hope to capture them, if you were willing in your
heart to join with me, since they would not endure our onslaught,
standing up to go to war against us."   490

        So he spoke; nor did the good son of Anchises disobey.
And the two men set out directly, their shoulders covered by their
    shields
of tough oxhide hammered with much bronze.
And going with them were both Chromios and godlike Aretos;
and greatly did their hearts hope
to kill the two men and seize the high-necked horses;
fools, who were not destined to return without the spilling of blood

by Automedon; for he, making prayer to Zeus the father,
was filled round his dark heart with strength and courage.
And forthwith he spoke to Alkimedon, his trusted comrade: 500
"Alkimedon, do not hold the horses at a distance from me,
but have them breathing hard upon my back; for I do not think
that Hector son of Priam will check his fury,
until he has mounted behind the fine-maned horses of Achilles,
killing us both, and put to flight the ranks of Argive men,
or himself is taken among the frontline fighters."

          So speaking he called to the two Aiantes and to Menelaos:
"Aiantes and Menelaos, leaders of the Argives,
leave the body to those who can best
stand over it and ward off the ranks of men,   510
and you ward off death's pitiless day from those who are living;
for bearing hard for this place through the battle and its tears
are Hector and Aeneas, who are the best men of the Trojans.
But these things surely lie in the lap of the gods;
I will make my throw, and all that follows will be Zeus' care."

          He spoke, and balancing the long-shadowed spear he hurled it,
and struck the circle of the shield of Aretos;
and it did not protect him from the spear, but the bronze passed straight
    through,
and piercing his war-belt, into the pit of his stomach it drove.
And as when a sturdy young man wielding his sharp axe   520
smites behind the horns of a field-ranging ox
so as to cut all the way through; and it falls lurching forward,
so Aretos lurched, then fell on his back; and in his belly
the shaking spear, keenly sharp, unstrung his limbs.
And Hector took aim at Automedon with his shining spear;
but he, looking straight ahead, dodged the bronze spear-point,
for he ducked forward, and the long spear-shaft
was fixed in the earth behind him, the butt-end quivering;
then mighty Ares took away its force.

And surely now with swords they would have been stabbing at
  close quarters,   530
had not the two Aiantes driven them apart as they raged,
coming through the battle throng when their companion called.
Struck with dread before them,
Hector and Aeneas and godlike Chromios retreated back again,
and left Aretos there, lying, his life ripped out.
And Automedon, swift Ares' equal,
stripped his armour, and spoke vaunting:
"Now I have indeed lightened my heart of a little grief for the dying of
the son of Menoetius, although I have killed a lesser man."
So speaking, he seized the bloody spoils and placed them in the chariot,   540
and himself climbed up, covered from his feet to his hands above
with blood, like a lion that has feasted on a bull.

      And once again the powerful combat was drawn tight across
  Patroclus,
hard to bear, full of tears; and thereon Athena stirred the struggle,
coming down from heaven; far-thundering Zeus sent her
to rally the Danaans, for now his intent had changed.
As when for mortal men Zeus bends the livid rainbow
from the heavens to be war's portent,
or portent of a chilling storm that stops men from their working
of the earth, and afflicts the flocks,   550
so Athena, having concealed herself in a livid cloud,
plunged into the host of the Achaeans, and stirred each man.

      And first she addressed the son of Atreus strong Menelaos,
  rousing him,
since he was close by her,
having likened herself to Phoinix in body and unwearying voice:
"For you, Menelaos, it will surely be a disgrace and a rebuke
should the trusted companion of illustrious Achilles
be dragged by swift dogs beneath the wall of Troy.
Come, stand strong, rally the whole of your army."

Then in turn Menelaos of the war cry addressed her: 560
"Phoinix, old father born long ago, if only Athena
would give me strength, and keep off the rush of flying spears and arrows!
Then would I have heart to stand beside and protect
Patroclus; for his dying has touched my heart to the quick.
But Hector has the dread strength of fire, nor does he cease
rampaging with his bronze spear; for to him Zeus gives glory."
       So he spoke, and the gleaming-eyed goddess Athena rejoiced,
that to her of all the gods he had prayed first.
And she placed strength in his shoulders and in his knees,
and threw into his breast the boldness of a horsefly,   570
that though driven repeatedly away from a man's skin,
craves to bite, so delectable is human blood to it.
With such boldness did Athena fill him round his dark heart,
and he made his way to Patroclus, and took aim with his shining spear.
And there was among the Trojans a certain Podes, the son of Eëtion,
a rich man and a good man, and Hector honoured him above all others
in his realm, since he was his own companion at the feasts;
this man fair Menelaos struck down across his war-belt
as he was darting for flight, and the bronze point drove right through,
and he fell with a thud. Then Menelaos son of Atreus   580
dragged the body out of the Trojans' reach into the band of his own
       companions.
       And Apollo, standing close, goaded Hector
in the likeness of Phainops, the son of Asios, who of all
Hector's guest friends was dearest to him, and had his home in
       Abydos: 584
"Hector, what other Achaean shall ever have fear of you,   586
who flee before such a one as Menelaos, who was before
a feeble spearman? And now he departs carrying, on his own,
a dead body out from under the Trojans; he killed your trusted comrade,
a noble man among the front fighters, Podes the son of Eëtion."   590
So he spoke; and a dark cloud of grief enveloped Hector,

and he set out through the frontline fighters armoured in gleaming bronze.
And as he did the son of Cronus took up the tasselled
glinting aegis, and drew the clouds down over Ida;
flashing lightning forth he thundered fearfully, and shook the aegis,
giving victory to the Trojans, and the Achaeans he put to flight.

      And Peneleos the Boeotian first began the rout;
for he was struck on the shoulder by a spear as he turned to face ahead,
the tip grazing him; the spear-point of Poulydamas just scratched
the bone, for he came up close to make his throw.   600
In turn Hector stabbed Leïtos from close quarters on the wrist of his hand,
Leïtos son of great-hearted Alektryon, and put a stop to his fighting;
glancing all about him, he retired in fear, since in his heart he could no
    longer hope
to do battle, spear in hand, with the Trojans.
And as Hector was rushing after Leïtos, Idomeneus
struck him on the breastplate across his chest, beside the nipple;
but the long spear shattered at the shaft-head socket, and the Trojans
shouted aloud. Then Hector took aim at Idomeneus, Deucalian's son,
as he stood in his chariot; he missed him by a little,
but struck the henchman and charioteer of Meriones,   610
Koiranos, who had followed with him from strong-built Lyktos—
for Idomeneus first set out on foot when he left the double-sided ships,
and would have handed a great victory to the Trojans,
had not Koiranos sharply driven the swift-footed horses,
and come as salvation's light to him, and warded off the pitiless day of
    death,
but he lost his own life at the hands of man-slaying Hector—
for Hector struck him below the jaw and ear, and the spear shoved his
    teeth out
at the root, and cut his tongue in two.
Koiranos fell from the chariot, and the reins streamed to earth.
And Meriones, stooping, took them with his own hands   620
from the ground, and spoke to Idomeneus:

"Lash on, now, until you come to the swift ships;
you know yourself, the Achaeans' strength is gone."
So he spoke, and Idomeneus lashed his fine-maned horses
toward the hollow ships; for fear had fallen on his heart.

And it did not escape great-hearted Ajax and Menelaos
that Zeus was giving to the Trojans the turn of victory's tide.
And great Telamonian Ajax was first of them to speak:
"Alas, by now even a great fool can see
that father Zeus himself stands by the Trojans;   630
all their weapons find their mark, whoever throws them,
good warrior or bad, Zeus directs them all alike,
but all ours fall like this, useless to the ground.
But come, let us consider the best plan,
and how we will drag this body away, and how we ourselves
returning home can bring joy to our own companions,
who as they look this way are doubtless filled with grief, nor still
    believe
that man-slaying Hector's might and invincible strength of hand
can be restrained, but that he will fall upon our black ships.
If only there were some companion who could swiftly bring a
    message   640
to the son of Peleus, since I do not think that he has learned
of this disastrous news, that the companion dear to him has died.
And yet nowhere can I see such a one of the Achaeans;
for they and the horses are alike engulfed in mist.
Father Zeus, come—save the sons of the Achaeans from this mist,
make clear the air, grant our eyes to see,
and destroy us in the light of day, since thus it pleases you."
So he spoke; and as he wept his tears Zeus the father pitied him,
and scattered the mist forthwith and thrust back the murk;
the sun shone out, and thereupon the whole field of battle was
    revealed.   650

Then Ajax spoke to Menelaos of the war cry:

"Look about now, god-cherished Menelaos, if you can see
Antilochos still living, great-hearted Nestor's son;
despatch him to go with all speed to brilliant Achilles
to tell him that his far dearest companion has died."
So he spoke, nor did Menelaos of the war cry disobey,
but set out like a lion from a cattle fold,
when he has worn himself out harrying dogs and men,
who do not suffer him to seize the cream of their herd,
on alert the whole night long; and he in his lust for meat   660
makes straight for them, but achieves nothing; for showers of spears
fly against him from the men's strong hands
and burning torches, which he shrinks from, for all his urgent desire,
and at dawn he departs far away, his spirit aggrieved;
so from Patroclus Menelaos of the war cry
departed much against his will; for greatly did he fear lest the Achaeans
in the face of panic that cannot be endured should abandon the body of
     Patroclus as spoil for their enemies.
Much he enjoined on Meriones and the Aiantes:
"Aiantes, leaders of the Argives, and Meriones,
now let you each be mindful of gentle, unhappy Patroclus,   670
for to all men he knew to be kind
while he was alive; and now death and fate have swallowed him."
          So speaking fair Menelaos departed,
peering about in every direction, like an eagle, which they say
sees most keenly of all things on wing under heaven,
and which even on high does not fail to mark a swift-footed hare
lying low under a thick-leafed bush, but swoops for it,
and swiftly seizing it, snatches its life away;
so now, Menelaos cherished by Zeus, your shining eyes
wandered everywhere across the band of your many comrades,   680
with the hope of somewhere seeing the son of Nestor still alive.
And very soon he spotted him on the left wing of all the fighting,
encouraging his companions and stirring them on to battle.

And going to him fair Menelaos stood close and spoke to him:
"Antilochos, come over here, you whom Zeus cherishes, so you may learn
our disastrous news—would that it had never happened.
By now I think you know yourself by looking
that some god has rolled disaster against the Danaans
and victory is the Trojans'; the best of Achaeans has died,
Patroclus, and great is the loss befallen the Danaans.   690
Come, run at once to the ships of the Achaeans to tell Achilles,
that with all speed he might bring the body safe to his ship,
naked though it is; for Hector of the shimmering helm has his armour."

            So he spoke, and Antilochos was struck with horror hearing this
    word;
for a long while he was held speechless, his eyes
filled with tears, and his strong full voice was checked.
But even so he was not careless of Menelaos' behest,
and he left on the run; his armour he handed to his blameless companion
Laodokos, who was wheeling round his single-hoofed horses hard by.

            Antilochos' feet carried him, weeping, from the battle,   700
to bear his evil message to Achilles son of Peleus.
Then, Menelaos cherished by Zeus, your heart did not wish
to defend the exhausted comrades of Antilochos, those he had left—
for great was the yearning of the Pylians for him—
but instead he sent godlike Thrasymedes to them,
and himself went back to the warrior Patroclus,
running, and took his stand beside the two Aiantes, and straightway
    addressed them:
"I have sent that one to the swift ships,
to go to Achilles, the fleet of foot. But I do not think that he
is coming now, for all his great anger with shining Hector;   710
for in no way would he go unarmed to battle with the Trojans.
Let us ourselves consider the best plan,
and how we shall drag away this body, and also how we ourselves
shall escape death and fate out from under the shouting throng of Trojans

Then answered him great Telamonian Ajax:
"All these things you say properly, O glorious Menelaos.
Come, you and Meriones quickly get under
the body, and lifting it carry it from the field of battle; then behind
you two, we will fight shining Hector and the Trojans,
we two of like spirit, of the same name, who before this   720
have withstood the cut of war standing firm beside each other."

So he spoke; and they took the body in their arms
with a mighty effort, from the ground up on high. And thereon the
    Trojan host behind them
shouted out, as they saw the Achaeans lift the body;
and they charged for them like dogs that spring
at a wounded boar ahead of their young hunters;
and for a time they race along straining to rip it to pieces—
but when the boar at last turns on them, trusting in his courage,
they withdraw back and scuttle in fear hither and thither;
so for a while the Trojans followed keeping always in a group,   730
stabbing with their swords and double-edged spears,
but when at last the two Aiantes wheeled around and took their stand
against them, then their skin changed colour, nor did any dare
to wage a contest for the body by charging forward.

So with fierce resolve they bore the body from the fighting
towards the hollow ships; and the line of war was stretched tight upon
    them,
like a line of savage fire that, as it sweeps towards a city full of men,
rearing of a sudden, consumes it, and the houses are destroyed
in its great blazing, and the wind's force roars upon it;
so as they made their way, the incessant din of   740
horses and of spearmen was upon them.
And they like mules who throwing their steady strength around their work
drag from the mountain down a rocky path
a beam or a great timber for a ship, and their spirit within
is exhausted alike with toil and sweat as they press on,

so with fierce resolve they carried the dead man. And behind them
the two Aiantes held the Trojans off, as a wooded ridge holds off
water, a ridge that happens to jut across the plain,
and that holds off even the baneful coursings of mighty rivers,
swifly diverting the flow of each, and causes them to go across the plain, 750
nor do they shatter the ridge with their power as they gush forth;
so always the two Aiantes restrained the fighting of the Trojans
behind their comrades. But the Trojans followed close, and two among
     them more than most,
Anchises' son Aeneas and shining Hector;
and before them, as a cloud of daws or starlings goes
shrieking of their destruction, as they spy the coming of
a hawk that bears death to tiny birds,
so before Hector and Aeneas the young Achaeans
went shrieking of their destruction, and forgot their fire for battle.
And much fine armour fell around the ditch   760
from the Danaans as they fled; and there was no cessation in the battle.

So they fought like blazing fire;
but Antilochos went as swift-footed messenger to Achilles.
And he found him in front of his straight-horned ships,
foreboding in his heart those things that now had happened,
and troubled he addressed his own great-hearted spirit:
"Ah me, why now are the long-haired Achaeans again
driven to the ships in panicked confusion across the plain?
May the gods not have accomplished evil sufferings for my heart,
as once my mother plainly told me, and said to me
that while I yet lived, the best of Myrmidons,   10
at Trojan hands would leave the light of day.
Surely Menoetius' brave son has already died,
stubborn one; and yet I told him that when he had driven off the blazing fire
to come back to the ships, nor battle in his strength with Hector."
        While he churned these things through his mind and heart,
the son of noble Nestor drew close to him
shedding hot tears, and spoke his grievous message:
"Woe to me, son of brilliant Peleus, surely it is a baleful
message you will hear, would that it had never happened.
Patroclus lies dead, and they are fighting round his naked   20
body; for Hector of the shimmering helm has his armour."
        So he spoke; and a dark cloud of grief enveloped Achilles.
Taking with both hands the fire-blackened ashes,
he poured them down upon his head, and defiled his handsome face;

on his fragrant tunic the black ash settled;

and he lay outstretched in the dust,

a great man in his greatness, and with his own hands he defiled his hair,
    tearing at it.

And the female slaves, whom Achilles and Patroclus had seized as plunder,

stricken at heart cried loud, and ran outside

around brilliant Achilles, and all with their hands   30

beat their breasts, and the limbs of each went slack beneath them;

on his other side Antilochos wept, pouring tears,

holding the hands of Achilles as his noble heart groaned.

For he feared lest Achilles cut his own throat with iron.

      Dreadful were Achilles' cries of grief; his lady mother heard

as she sat in the depths of the sea beside her aged father.

Then she wailed in turn; and all the goddesses gathered round her,

who down in the depths of the sea were daughters of Nereus.

There was Glauke, Thaleia and Kymodoke,

Nesaie and Speio, Thoë and ox-eyed Halia,   40

Kymothoë and also Aktaia, and Limnoreia,

Melite, and Iaira, Amphithoë and Agauë,

Doto, Proto and Pherousa, Dynamene,

Dexamene, Amphinome and Kallianeira;

Doris and Panope and illustrious Galateia

and Nemertes and Apseudes and Kallianassa;

and Klymene was there and Ianeira and also Ianassa,

Maira and Oreithyia and Amatheia of the lovely hair,

and the others who in the depths of the sea were daughters of Nereus.

And the silvery cave was filled with them; and all together   50

beat their breasts. And Thetis led the lament:

"Hear me, sister Nereids, so that all of you

may know well as you listen, how many are the sorrows in my heart.

Ay me, wretched I am—ay me, unhappy bearer of the noblest son,

since I bore a son, blameless and strong,

outstanding among warriors, who shot up like a young shoot,

and having nurtured him like a growing tree on the high ground of an
    orchard
I sent him forth with the curved ships to Ilion,
to go to battle against the Trojans; him I shall not welcome again
returned home into the house of Peleus.   60
So long as he lives and sees the sun's light,
he has sorrow, nor can I help him at all by going to him.
But come, so that I may see my beloved child and hear of
what sorrow has come to him while he stayed away from the fighting."

      So speaking she left the cave; and her sisters went with her
in tears, and the swell of the sea broke around them.
And when they reached the rich soil of Troy,
up onto the shore of the sea they went, up one after the other, where the
    ships
of the Myrmidons had been drawn up, close-pressed round swift Achilles.
And his lady mother stood beside him as he groaned deeply,   70
and keenly wailing she held her son's head,
and in lament spoke winged words:
"Child, why do you cry? What sorrow has reached your heart?
Speak out, do not hide it. Those things have been accomplished for you
through Zeus, as at that time before you prayed with uplifted hands,
that all the sons of the Achaeans be pinned against the sterns of their ships
and for want of you suffer deeds that shamed them."

      Then groaning deeply swift-footed Achilles answered her:
"Mother mine, these things the Olympian indeed fulfilled for me;
but what pleasure do I have in them, since my beloved companion died,   80
Patroclus, whom I revered beyond all companions,
as equal to my own life? I have lost him, and after slaying him Hector
stripped the stupendous armour, a wonder to behold,
a thing of beauty; the armour the gods gave to Peleus as splendid gifts
on that day when they placed you in the bed of a mortal man.
Would that you had made your home with the immortal goddesses of the
    sea,

and Peleus had taken to himself a mortal wife.

But as it is, for you too there must be grief immeasurable in heart

for the death of your son, whom you will not receive again

returned to home, since my spirit does not bid me   90

to go on living nor take my part among men, unless, before all else,

Hector, beaten beneath my spear, lose his life,

and pay the penalty for making prey of Menoetius' son Patroclus."

          Then in turn Thetis spoke to him as she shed her tear:

"Then you will die soon, my child, from what you say;

for your fate is prepared straightway after Hector's."

Then greatly troubled swift-footed Achilles spoke to her:

"Straightway may I die, since I was not destined to help my companion

as he was killed; and a very long way from his fatherland

he perished, and lacked me to be his defender against harm.   100

Now since I am not returning to my beloved fatherland,

nor was I in any way salvation's light to Patroclus, nor to my other

companions, who have been broken in their number by shining Hector,

but sat beside the ships a useless burden on the earth,

I who am such as no other of the bronze-clad Achaeans

is in battle; though in the assembly there are others better—

would that strife perish from gods and men,

and anger, which incites even a man of sense to violence,

and which, far sweeter than dripping honey,

wells like smoke in the breast of men,   110

as Agamemnon lord of men then angered me.

But let us leave these things in the past for all our distress,

subduing the spirit in our own breasts by necessity;

for now I am setting out to find the destroyer of a dear life—

Hector. I will take death at that time when

Zeus and the other deathless gods wish to accomplish it.

For even the mighty Heracles did not escape from death,

for all that he was dearest to lord Zeus the son of Cronus,

but fate broke him and the hard anger of Hera;

so I too, if the same fate has been prepared for me,   120
shall lie when I have died. But now let me win outstanding glory,
and drive some woman of Troy, or deep-breasted Dardan woman,
wiping with both hands from her soft cheeks
the thick-falling tears, to moan aloud,
and may they know that I stayed too long from fighting.
Do not detain me from battle though you love me; you will not
    persuade me."

        Then answered him Thetis of the silver feet:
"Yes, all these things, my child, you have spoken truly; nor is it shameful
to ward off sheer destruction from your afflicted comrades.
Yet your beautiful armour is held among the Trojans,   130
the brazen, glittering armour. Hector of the shimmering helm
exults in this, wearing it on his own shoulders; but I do not think
he will exult in it for long, since his slaughter is near at hand.
But do not enter in the strife of battle
until you see me returned here with your own eyes;
for at dawn I shall come back with the rising of the sun
carrying splendid armour from lord Hephaestus."

        Then having so spoken she took herself away from her son,
and turned to speak to her sisters of the sea:
"All of you now make your way into the broad gulf of ocean,   140
to see the old man of the sea and the halls of our father,
and to tell him everything; and I am going to high Olympus,
to the side of Hephaestus, famed for his skill, to see if he might be willing
to give to my son glorious gleaming armour."
So she spoke; and they at once plunged beneath the ocean swell;
and she, the goddess Thetis of the silver feet, went again to Olympus,
so that she might carry splendid armour to her beloved son.

        Her feet brought her to Olympus; meanwhile the Achaeans
fleeing with inhuman shouts before man-slaughtering Hector
reached their ships and the Hellespont.   150
But Patroclus—the strong-greaved Achaeans could not drag

the body of Achilles' henchman out from under the flying spears and
    arrow shafts;
for again the Trojan host and horses came upon him,
as did Hector son of Priam, like fire in fighting spirit.
Three times shining Hector seized the body by the feet from behind,
determined to drag it off, and shouted loud to spur the Trojans.
And three times the two Aiantes, mantled in their fierce courage,
beat him from the corpse. But steadfastly trusting in his battle prowess
Hector would now spring forth through the press of battle, now again
take his stand and cry aloud, nor fell back at all;   160
but as from a carcass rustic herdsmen fail to drive away
a tawny lion in his great hunger,
so the two Aiantes, fully armed, were not able
to frighten Hector son of Priam from the corpse.
       And indeed he would have dragged it away and won for himself
    glory everlasting,
had not swift Iris with feet like the wind come to the son of Peleus
as messenger, racing from Olympus with word to prepare for battle,
in secret from Zeus and the other gods; for Hera it was who sent her;
and standing close to him she spoke her winged words:
"Rise up, son of Peleus, most terrifying of men;   170
protect Patroclus, for whose sake the dread fighting
is under way before the ships—they are killing one another,
both those who fight to defend the body of him who died,
and the Trojans who rush to haul it off to windy Troy.
Above all others shining Hector
is bent on dragging it away; and his heart is urgent to impale the head
upon spiked stakes, cut from its tender neck.
Come, rise up, don't lie still; shame be on your heart,
should Patroclus become a plaything for Trojan dogs.
Yours the dishonour, if he comes mutilated to the dead."   180
      Then answered her swift-footed godlike Achilles:
"Divine Iris, which of the gods sent you as messenger to me?"

Then in turn swift Iris with feet like the wind addressed him:
"Hera sent me, the glorious wife of Zeus;
nor does the high-throned son of Cronus know, nor any other
of the immortals, who dwell about snow-clad Olympus."
Then answering her spoke swift-footed Achilles:
"How then am I to go among the tumult? For those others have my
    armour.
And my beloved mother forbade me to arm for battle
before I see her coming with my own eyes;   190
for she pledged to bring splendid armour from Hephaestus.
And I do not know who else's illustrious arms I might put on,
unless it be the great shield of Telamonian Ajax.
But he too, I think, is engaged among the frontline fighters,
wreaking havoc with his spear around Patroclus who lies dead."
Then in turn swift Iris with feet like the wind addressed him:
"We too well know that they hold your glorious armour.
But go as you are to the ditch and show yourself to the Trojans—
perhaps in dread of you they might retreat from fighting,
the Trojans, and the warrior sons of the Achaeans draw breath   200
in their extremity; for respite in war is brief."
        So speaking swift-footed Iris departed;
and Achilles beloved of Zeus arose. And Athena
cast the tasselled aegis about his mighty shoulders;
the most divine of goddesses encircled round his head a cloud of
gold, and from it blazed bright-shining fire.
And as when smoke rising from a city reaches the clear high air
from a distant island, which enemy men fight round,
and they the whole day long are pitted in hateful warfare
around their city walls, but with the sun's setting   210
the beacon fires blaze, torch upon torch, and flaring upwards
the glare becomes visible to those who live around,
in the hope that they might come with ships as allies against destruction,
so from Achilles' head the radiance reached the clear high air.

And going away from the wall he stood at the ditch, nor did he mix with
the Achaeans; for he observed his mother's knowing command.
And standing there he shouted, and from the distance Pallas Athena
cried out too; unspeakable was the uproar he incited in the Trojans.
As when a clarion voice is heard, when cries the trumpet
of life-destroying enemies who surround a city,   220
such then was the clarion voice of Aeacides.

      And when they heard the brazen voice of Aeacides,
the spirit in each man was thrown in turmoil; the horses with their fine
   manes
wheeled their chariots back, for in their hearts they foreboded distress to
   come,
and the charioteers were struck from their senses, when they saw the
   weariless
terrible fire above the head of Peleus' great-hearted son
blazing; and this the gleaming-eyed goddess Athena caused to blaze.
Three times across the ditch godlike Achilles cried his great cry,
and three times the Trojans and their illustrious allies were thrown in
   panic.
Then and there perished twelve outstanding men   230
upon their own chariots and spears. And the Achaeans
with relief pulled Patroclus out from under the missiles
and laid him on a litter; and his beloved companions stood around it
weeping, and with them followed swift-footed Achilles
shedding hot tears, when he looked upon his trusted comrade
lying on the bier, torn with sharp bronze,
whom he had sent forth with horses and chariots
into war, but did not welcome him returned home again.

      And ox-eyed lady Hera caused the tireless sun
to return, unwilling, into the streams of Ocean;   240
the sun set, and the glorious Achaeans ceased
from the powerful din of battle and all-levelling war.
The Trojans in their turn on the other side, withdrawing from the

mighty combat, released their swift horses from under their chariots,
and gathered into assembly before taking thought for supper;
and the assembly took place with them standing upright, nor did any
    man dare
to take his seat; for trembling held them all, because Achilles
had appeared; he who for a long time had abandoned the painful battle.

      And to them Poulydamas, wise son of Panthoös,
was first to speak to the assembly; he alone looked both forward and
    behind him;   250
he was Hector's comrade, and born in the same night,
but the one greatly excelled in speech, and the other in the spear;
he with wise intent gave counsel to them and spoke:
"Consider well, my friends; I for my part urge
you now to go to the city, and not await the bright dawn
on the open plain beside the ships; we are far from our ramparts.
As long as that man harboured wrath at noble Agamemnon,
so long were the Achaeans easier to fight;
I myself used to welcome sleeping by the swift ships at night,
with the hope we would seize these double-ended ships.   260
But now terribly I dread the swift-footed son of Peleus;
such is the reckless might of that one's spirit, he will not wish
to remain upon the plain, in this middle ground where Achaeans and
    Trojans
both share between them battle's fury,
but he will fight for our city and our women.
Come, let us go to the city, be persuaded by me; for this is how it will be.
Now ambrosial night has curbed the swift-footed son of Peleus;
but if he finds us here
tomorrow when he rises under arms, well will a man come to know him;
and gladly will he make his way to sacred Ilion—   270
he who escapes; but the dogs and vultures will devour many
of the Trojans—but may this word never come to my hearing.
If you will be persuaded by my words, painful though they are,

this night we will harbour our strength in the place of assembly,
and our high walls and gates and the doors fitted to them—
the long, well-honed, barred doors—will guard our city;
and in early morning, having armed in our weapons with the dawn,
we will take up position along the ramparts. The worse for him, if he
    chooses
to come from his ships to do battle around our walls;
he will go back to the ships, when he has given his high-necked horses   280
their fill of running round about, as he roams beneath the city walls.
Even his courage will not permit him to storm inside,
nor will he ever sack our city. Before that the sleek dogs will devour him."

       Then looking at him from beneath his brows spoke Hector of the
    shimmering helm:
"Poulydamas, these things you declare are no longer pleasing to me,
you who bid us go back to cower down in the city.
Or have you all not had your fill of being penned inside the walls?
In days before, the city of Priam, as all men born of earth
were wont to say, was rich in gold, rich in bronze—
by now the splendid treasures have vanished from our houses,   290
and many possessions went for sale to Phrygia and lovely Maeonia,
since mighty Zeus conceived hatred for us.
And now, at this time when the son of devious Cronus grants me
to win glory by the ships and drive the Achaeans to the sea—
you fool, no longer disclose such thoughts among the people!
None of the Trojans will obey you, for I will not allow it.
But come, let us all be persuaded to do as I say.
Take your meal now at your posts throughout the army
and be mindful of your watches and each of you be alert;
and whoever of the Trojans is excessively distressed for his
    possessions,   300
let him gather them together and give them to the people to consume
    as common stock;
better that one of them have profit of them than the Achaeans;

and in early morning, having armed in our weapons with the dawn,
by the hollow ships we shall awaken cutting war.
And if in fact Achilles the godlike has stirred himself to action by his ships,
the worse it will be for him, if he so chooses, for I will not
flee from him out of this grievous war, but I will strongly
face him—we shall see whether he will win great glory, or I.
Enyalios the god of war is impartial; and often he kills the one who kills."

   Thus declared Hector, and the Trojans shouted their
  applause,   310
the fools, for Pallas Athena took their wits away;
all assented to Hector as he devised disaster,
but none to Poulydamas, who thought out excellent counsel.

   Then they took their meal throughout the army; but the Achaeans
through all the night groaned aloud as they mourned Patroclus.
And the son of Peleus led their impassioned lament,
placing his man-slaughtering hands on the breast of his companion,
groaning without ceasing, as a full-maned lion,
whose cubs a hunting man has stolen away
out from the dense forest, and who returning too late is stricken with
  grief,   320
and many is the valley he traverses, following after the footprints of the
  man,
in the hope he would find him in some quarter; for very bitter anger
  holds him;
so groaning deeply Achilles addressed the Myrmidons:
"Alas, alas, empty were the words I let fall that day
as I encouraged the warrior Menoetius within his walls;
I said to him that I would bring his son back to Opoeis surrounded in glory
after sacking Ilion and receiving a share of the spoils.
But Zeus does not fulfil men's every wish;
for it was fated that we both stain the same earth
here in Troy, since I will not be returning home   330
to be received by old Peleus, the horseman, in his halls,

nor by Thetis my mother, but the earth will cover me here.
But now, Patroclus, since I am following you beneath the earth,
I shall not honour you with funeral rites, until I lay here
the armaments and head of Hector, your slayer, great-hearted one;
and before your pyre I shall cut the throats of twelve
noble sons of Troy, in anger for your killing.
In the meanwhile you will lie as you are by my curved ships,
and around you women of Troy and deep-breasted Dardan women
shall wail for you night and day as they shed their tears,   340
those women whom we ourselves toiled to win by force and the long
    spear
when we two sacked the rich cities of earth-born men."
            So speaking godlike Achilles ordered his companions
to set a great cauldron on its three-legged stand astride the fire, so that
    with all speed
they could wash away the clotted blood from Patroclus;
and they set a cauldron for heating bathing water on the blazing fire,
then poured water in it, and took sticks of wood and kindled them
    beneath it.
And the fire caught the belly of the cauldron, and heated the water.
Then when the water had come to boil in the bright bronze,
they washed him and anointed him luxuriantly with oil,   350
and filled in his wounds with seasoned unguents;
and placing him on the bier, they covered him with soft linen
from his head to his feet, and over this with a shining mantle.
            Then nightlong the Myrmidons groaned aloud as around Achilles
of the swift feet they mourned Patroclus.
But Zeus addressed Hera, his sister and his wife:
"So once more, you have accomplished things your way, after all, my
    brown-eyed lady Hera,
having roused to action swift-footed Achilles. Surely the long-haired
    Achaeans
must be your own offspring!"

Then answered him ox-eyed lady Hera: 360
"Most dread son of Cronus, what sort of word have you spoken?
Surely, even a human tries to do what he can for another man,
one who is only mortal, and who does not know so many arts as we;
how then should not I—who claim to be the highest of the goddesses,
both by birth and because I am called your wife,
and you are lord of all the immortal gods—
how should I not contrive evil for the Trojans whom I hate?"

        Thus they were speaking such things to one another.
But silver-footed Thetis arrived at the home of Hephaestus,
imperishable, strewn with stars, conspicuous amongst the homes of the
        immortals,   370
made of bronze, which the crippled god had built himself.
And she found him dripping with sweat, twisting back and forth round
        about his bellows,
hard at work; for he was forging fully twenty tripods
to stand round the inside wall of his well-built palace.
He placed golden wheels beneath the legs of each,
so that of their own accord they might go into the divine assembly for him
and then return back to his house again, a wonder to behold.
And they were so far finished, but the elaborate handles were not
affixed; these he was fitting and striking the rivets.
And while he toiled at these things with his skilled understanding, 380
the goddess Thetis of the silver feet approached him;
and Charis of the shining headdress saw her as she was coming forward,
lovely Charis, whom the famed bent-legged god had wed,
and she clasped her hand, and spoke to her and said her name:
"Why, Thetis of the flowing robe, have you come to our house?
You are honoured and beloved, but you have not come frequently before.
But follow me in, so that I can set all hospitality before you."

        So speaking she, shining among goddesses, led Thetis forward.
Then she settled her on a beautiful elaborate silver chair,
and placed a stool beneath her feet;   390

and she called Hephaestus famed for his art and spoke a word to him:
"Hephaestus, come this way; Thetis has need of something from you."
Then the renowned god of the crooked legs answered her:
"Then surely in our house is a goddess whom I hold in awe and revere.
She saved me, that time I suffered bodily pain when I was made to fall a
   long way
by the efforts of my dog-faced mother, who wanted
to hide me away for being lame. At that time I would have suffered many
   cares at heart,
had not Thetis taken me to her bosom,
and Eurynome the daughter of Ocean of the shifting tide.
For nine years with them I forged many intricate objects,   400
brooches and curving spirals for the hair, buds of rosettes and necklaces
in their hollow cave; and all around the boundless currents of the Ocean
with its foam flowed murmuring; nor did any other being
know of this, neither of gods nor of mortal men,
but Thetis and Eurynome knew, they who saved me.
Now she has come to our house; therefore I must surely
repay to Thetis of the lovely hair all the value of my life.
But you now set before her fitting hospitality,
while I put away my bellows and all my tools."

      He spoke, and the huge craftsman rose from the anvil block   410
limping, but his shrunken legs moved nimbly beneath him.
He put the bellows aside from the fire, and all the tools
with which he worked he gathered into a silver box.
And with a sponge he wiped around his face and both his arms
and powerful neck and shaggy chest,
and he put on a tunic, took up his thick staff, and went out of the door,
limping; and supporting their master were attendants
made of gold, which seemed like living maidens.
In their hearts there is intelligence, and they have voice
and vigour, and from the immortal gods they have learned skills.   420
These bustled about supporting their master; and making his halting way

to where Thetis was, he took his seat upon a shining chair,
and clasped her hand, and spoke to her and said her name:
"Why, Thetis of the flowing robe, have you come to our house?
You are honoured and beloved, but you have not come frequently before.
Speak what you will; my heart compels me to accomplish it,
if I am able to accomplish it, and if it can be accomplished."

      Then Thetis answered him as she let her tears fall:
"Hephaestus—who of all the goddesses on Olympus
endures in her heart so many bitter cares   430
as the griefs Zeus the son of Cronus has given to me beyond all?
Out of all the other goddesses of the sea he made me subject to a mortal
    husband,
Peleus son of Aeacus, and I endured the bed of a mortal man
very much unwilling; he now worn out with bitter age
lies in his halls, but there are other troubles now for me;
for he gave me a son to bear and to raise
outstanding among warriors, who shot up like a young shoot,
and having nurtured him like a growing tree on the high ground of an
    orchard
I sent him forth with the curved ships to Ilion,
to go to battle against the Trojans; him I shall not welcome again   440
returned home into the house of Peleus.
So long as he lives and sees the sun's light
he has sorrow, nor can I help him at all by going to him.
The girl, whom the sons of the Achaeans picked out as prize for him,
she it was, from his hands, lord Agamemnon took back;
and he has been consuming his heart in grief for her, while the Trojans
pinned the Achaeans against the sterns of their ships, nor
let them go forth from that place; and the Argive elders
beseeched him, and promised many splendid gifts.
At this he refused to ward off their destruction,   450
but then put his own armour about Patroclus,
and sent him to the fighting, and gave a great host with him.

All the day they battled around the Scaean gates;
and surely that same day he would have sacked the city, had not Apollo
killed the brave son of Menoetius as he was wreaking much destruction
among the front fighters, and gave glory to Hector.
And it is for this reason I have now come to your knees, to see if you
        would be willing
to give to my short-lived son a shield and crested helmet
and fine greaves with silver fastenings
and a breastplate; for those that were his, his trusted comrade lost   460
when he was beaten down by the Trojans; and my son lies upon the
        ground grieving at heart."

            Then answered her the famous crook-legged god:
"Have courage; do not let these matters be a care to your heart.
Would that I were so surely able to hide him away from death and its
        hard sorrow,
when dread fate comes upon him,
as he will have his splendid armour, such as many a man
of the many men to come shall hold in wonder, whoever sees it."

            So speaking he left her there, and went to his bellows;
and he turned them to the fire and gave them their commands to get to
        work.
And all twenty bellows began to blow into the crucibles,   470
from every angle blasting up and forth their strong-blown gusts
for him as he hurried to be now in this place, now again in that,
in whatever manner Hephaestus wished, and accomplished the job.
And he cast on the fire weariless bronze, and tin
and treasured gold and silver; and then
he placed his great anvil on his anvil block, and with one hand grasped
his mighty hammer, and with the other grasped his tongs.

            And first of all he made a great and mighty shield,
working it intricately throughout, and cast around it a shining rim
of triple thickness, glittering, and from it a silver shield-strap.   480

Five were the layers of the shield itself; and on it
he wrought with knowing genius many intricate designs.

On it he formed the earth, and the heaven, and the sea
and the weariless sun and waxing moon,
and on it were all the wonders with which the heaven is ringed,
the Pleiades and Hyades and the might of Orion,
and Arctos the Bear, which men name the Wagon,
and which always revolves in the same place, watchful for Orion,
and alone has no part in the baths of Ocean.

And on it he made two cities of mortal men,   490
both beautiful; and in one there were weddings and wedding feasts,
and they were leading the brides from their chambers beneath the gleam
    of torches
through the city, and loud rose the bridal song;
and the young men whirled in dance and in their midst
the flutes and lyres raised their hubbub; and the women
standing in their doorways each watched in admiration.
And the people were thronged into the place of meeting; and there a
    dispute
had arisen, and two men were contending about the blood price
for a man who had been killed. The one was promising to pay all,
declaring so to the people, but the other refused to accept a thing;   500
and both desired the resolution be taken to a judge;
the people spoke out for both sides, favouring one or the other,
and heralds were holding the people in check. The elders
were sitting upon seats of polished stone in a sacred circle,
and holding in their hands the staves of the heralds with their ringing
    voices;
to these the two sides next rushed, and in turn the elders each gave
    judgement.
And there lay in their midst two talents of gold,
to give to him who might speak the straightest judgement among them.

But around the other city lay two armies of men,
shining in their armour. And they were torn between two plans,   510
either to sack the city, or to divide everything equally with its people,
as much wealth as the lovely town held within.
But the city was not yielding, and the men were secretly arming for
    ambush.
And their beloved wives and little children stood guard upon the
    ramparts
with those men whom old age held,
but the other men set forth; and Ares led them and Pallas Athena,
both made in gold, and the clothing on them was golden,
magnificent and mighty with their armour, like very gods,
standing out apart; and beneath them the people were smaller.
And when these arrived at the place where it seemed to them good for
    ambush,   520
on the river, at the watering place for all the grazing herds,
there they sat down, covered in their gleaming bronze.
And at a distance from them, their two lookouts were in position
waiting for when they might see sheep and twist-horned cattle;
and these soon came in sight, with two herdsmen following with them
taking pleasure in their flute, and did not at all foresee the plot.
And catching sight of them ahead, the men in ambush ran towards them,
and swiftly, on both sides, cut off the herds of cattle and splendid flocks
of white-woolled sheep, and killed the shepherds for good measure.
But the other men, when they heard the great uproar from the cattle   530
as they were sitting before the place of meeting, they at once mounted
    behind their high-stepping
horses and went after them in pursuit. They reached the place swiftly,
and having arrayed the battle, began fighting by the riverbanks,
smiting one another with their bronze-headed spears.
And Strife was joining the throng of battle, and Tumult, and painful
    Death,

holding now a living man new-wounded, now one unharmed,
now dragging a man who had died by his feet through the press of
    battle;
and Death wore around her shoulders a cape crimsoned with the blood
    of men.
And they clashed in battle and fought like living men,
dragging away the bodies of those slain by one another.   540
And on the shield he made a soft fallow field—fertile worked land
broad and thrice-ploughed; and on it many ploughmen
were driving their yoked teams of oxen turning up and down the field.
And when they came to the furrow end, after turning around,
then would a man come up to give into their hands a cup of
honey-sweet wine; and they would turn back along the row,
eager to reach the turning place of the deep fallow field.
And the earth darkened behind them, like land that has been ploughed,
made of gold though it was; a wonder indeed was that which was
    wrought.
      And on the shield he placed a royal estate; and there the
    labourers   550
were reaping, sharp sickles in their hands.
Some sheaths were thickly falling to the ground along the row,
others the sheaf binders bundled with bands.
Three binders stood by; but behind them
children were gathering handfuls, carrying them in their arms,
constantly nearby. And among them the king, in silence,
staff in hand, stood near the line rejoicing in his heart.
And to one side heralds were readying a feast beneath an oak,
dressing the great ox they had slaughtered. And the women
were scattering quantities of white barley for the workers as a meal.   560
      And on the shield he put a great vineyard heavy with clumps of
    grapes,
a thing of beauty, all in gold, and the dark clusters were along it.

And it was set up on vine poles of solid silver;
and on either side he drove a ditch of blue enamel, and around it a fence
of tin. One path alone was on it,
on which grape bearers made their way, when they gathered in the
     vineyard.
Maidens and young men with the giddy hearts of youth
carried the honey-sweet crop in woven baskets;
and in their midst a boy played his clear-sounding lyre
with enchantment, and beautifully sang to it the mournful harvest
     song   570
in his soft voice. And the others beating time all together
with song and cries followed, skipping with their feet.

               And on it he made a herd of straight-horned cattle,
and the cows were made of gold and tin,
and lowing they hastened from the farmyard to their pasture,
beside a rushing river, beside the waving reeds.
Golden herdsmen accompanied the cattle,
four in all, and nine sleek dogs followed at their feet;
but two dread lions held a bellowing bull
among the foremost cattle; and he lowing loudly   580
was being dragged away, and the dogs and sturdy youths followed
     after him.
And the two lions tearing open the great bull's hide
were gulping down the entrails and dark blood; at a loss,
the herdsmen set the swift dogs in pursuit, urging them on,
but they shrank from biting the lions,
and standing very close bayed and stayed away.

               And on the shield the famed crook-legged god made a meadow,
a great meadow for white-fleeced sheep lying in a lovely glen,
and farmsteads and huts for the shepherds and their folds.
And on it the famed crook-legged god made a patterned place for
     dancing,   590
like that which once in broad Knossos

Daedalus created for Ariadne of the lovely hair.

There the unwed youths and maidens worth many oxen as their bridal
    price

were dancing, holding each other's hands at the wrist;

and the girls were wearing finest linen, and the youths wore

fine-spun tunics, soft shining with oil.

And the girls wore lovely crowns of flowers, and the youths were
    carrying

golden daggers from their silver sword-belts.

And now the youths with practised feet would lightly run in rings,

as when a crouching potter makes trial of the potter's wheel   600

fitted to his hand, to see if it speeds round;

and then another time they would run across each other's lines.

And a great crowd stood around the stirring dance

filled with delight; and among them two acrobats,   604/5

leaders of the dance, went whirling through their midst.

       And Hephaestus set on it the great might of the river Ocean,

along the outmost edge of the thick-made shield.

       And when he had made the great and massive shield,

then he wrought a breastplate for Achilles more resplendent than the
    light of fire,   610

and he made a helmet for him, strong and fitted to his temples,

a thing of beauty, intricately wrought, and set a gold crest on it;

and then he made greaves for him of pliant tin.

       And when the famed crook-legged god had made all the armour
    with his toil,

lifting it up he set it before the mother of Achilles;

and she like a hawk leapt down from snowy summit of Olympus,

carrying the glittering armour from Hephaestus.

Dawn veiled in saffron rose from the streams of Ocean,
to carry light to the immortals and to mortal men,
and Thetis arrived at the ships carrying the gifts from Hephaestus.
She found her beloved son lying with his arms around Patroclus,
keening, and his many companions about him
dissolved in tears; and she stood among them, the shining among
    goddesses,
and clasped his hand, and spoke to him and said his name;
"My child, grieved though we be, we must leave this one
lie, since by the will of the gods he has been broken once for all;
you now take the splendid armour from Hephaestus,   10
exceeding in beauty, such as a mortal man has never worn upon his
    shoulders."

    Then so speaking the goddess laid the armour down
before Achilles; and it clashed loud, all that was elaborately wrought.
And trembling took all the Myrmidons, nor did any dare
to look upon it straight, and they shrank afraid; but Achilles
as he gazed upon it, so anger entered him all the more, and his eyes
terribly shone out beneath his lids like fire flare;
and he rejoiced as he held in his hands the glorious gifts of the god.

    And when he had satisfied his heart in looking at its elaborateness,
then he addressed his mother in winged words: 20
"My mother, the weapons the god has given me are fitting
handwork of the immortals, not such as mortal man can make.

Now I will arm myself; yet terribly do I fear
meanwhile for the brave son of Menoetius,
that flies burrowing down into his bronze-inflicted wounds
will breed worms, defile his body—
for the life is slain from him—and all the flesh be rotted."

      Then the goddess Thetis of the silver feet answered him:
"Child, do not let these things be a care to your heart.
I will set myself to ward off from him the savage throngs,   30
the flies, which consume men slain in battle.
Were he to lie for the turning of a year's completion,
his flesh would be firm always, or even firmer.
But summon into assembly the Achaean warriors,
renounce your wrath against Agamemnon the shepherd of the people,
arm for battle quickly, and put on your might."
So speaking she inspired a dauntless spirit in him;
and then into Patroclus she dripped ambrosia and red nectar
through his nostrils, in order that his flesh be firm.

      But he, godlike Achilles, went along the shore of the sea   40
crying his terrible cry, and roused the Achaean warriors.
And even those who before had remained in the gathering place of the
   ships,
those who were helmsmen and held the steering oars of the ships
and those who were stewards beside the ships, the distributors of food,
even they then came to assembly, because Achilles
had appeared; he who for a long time had abandoned the painful battle.
And the two companions of Ares came limping,
the son of Tydeus, steadfast in war, and brilliant Odysseus,
leaning on spears; for they still bore grievous wounds;
and coming they took their seats at the front of the assembly.   50
Then last to come was Agamemnon lord of men,
nursing a wound; since in the powerful combat
Koön son of Antenor had struck him too with his bronze-tipped spear.

      Then when all the Achaeans had come together,

rising up, Achilles of the swift feet addressed them:

"Son of Atreus, was this then the better way for us both,

for you and me, that we two, for all our grief at heart,

raged in life-devouring strife for the sake of a girl?

Artemis should have killed her with an arrow aboard the ships

on that day when I took her as a prize after destroying Lyrnessos;   60

then so many Achaeans would not have gripped the broad earth in their
     teeth

under the hands of enemy men, while I was deadly angered.

It was the better way for Hector and the Trojans; but I think that the
     Achaeans

will remember for a long time this strife of yours and mine.

But let us leave these things in the past for all our grief,

subduing the spirit in our own breasts by necessity.

Now I surely cease my anger; it is not fitting that I

be wrathful, unrelenting for ever. But come, the more quickly

rouse the long-haired Achaeans to war,

so that I can make trial of the Trojans as I go against them,   70

to see if they will indeed still want to keep watch beside our ships. But I
     think

that many a one will gladly bend his knee to rest, he who escapes

from under our spear, out of the deadly war."

     So he spoke; and the strong-greaved Achaeans exulted

at the great-hearted son of Peleus renouncing his wrath.

And the lord of men Agamemnon also addressed them,

from where he was, from his seat, not rising among them:

"O friends, Danaan warriors, henchmen of Ares,

it is good to listen to a man who stands to speak, nor is it seemly

to interrupt; for that is hard even for an experienced speaker.   80

Amid a great uproar of men how can one listen

or speak? Clear speaker though he be, he is made to stumble.

To the son of Peleus I shall declare myself; but you other

Argives pay heed, and each mark my word well.

Many times did the Achaeans speak this charge against me,
and kept faulting me; but it is not I who am to blame,
but Zeus and Fate and the Fury who walks in darkness,
they who in the assembly cast savage Delusion in my mind
on that day when, on my own authority, I took away Achilles' prize.
But what could I do? God accomplishes all things to fulfilment—   90
the elder daughter of Zeus is Delusion, who infatuates all men,
ruinous one. Her feet are soft; for they do not touch upon the earth,
but she walks over the heads of men
tripping up mankind; so she has trammelled other men before me.
For indeed even Zeus was once deluded, although they say he is the
     greatest
of gods and men; but even him
Hera, a mere female, deceived with her calculated guile
on that day when Alkmene was about to give birth to mighty Heracles
in Thebes, the city crowned with ramparts.
Bragging, Zeus kept telling all the gods: 100
'Hear me, all you gods, and all you goddesses too,
while I speak those things the spirit in my breast urges.
This day Eileithyia who brings on women's birth pain
will bring to light a man who is to rule all who dwell around him:
one of the race of those men, who are of my blood.'
Then with calculated guile the lady Hera addressed him;
'You are a liar, nor when the time comes will you fulfil your word.
Come on now, swear to me, Olympian, a mighty oath,
that indeed that man will rule all who dwell around him:
who shall drop between a woman's feet this day   110
a man of the race of men who are of your blood.'
So she spoke; and Zeus did not mark at all her calculated guile,
but swore a great oath, and therein he was greatly deluded.
In a flash Hera left the peak of Olympus,
and swiftly came to Achaean Argos, where she knew of
the stately wife of Sthenelos, son of Perseus;

she was pregnant with a dear son, a pregnancy of seven months' duration.

And Hera brought him forth early to the light of day though short of
    months,

but stopped the childbirth of Alkmene, holding back the birth pangs of
    Eileithyia.

Then she went to announce the news herself, and addressed Zeus the
    son of Cronus: 120

'Father Zeus of the bright thunderbolt, I am going to put some news in
    your mind.

Now has a noble man been born who will rule the Argives—

Eurystheus, the son of Sthenelos, son of Perseus—

your blood; it is not unfitting for him to rule the Argives.'

So she spoke; and piercing grief struck Zeus deep down through his heart,

and he at once seized Delusion by the lustrous tresses of her head,

raging in his heart, and swore a mighty oath

that not ever to Olympus and the star-strewn heaven

should she come again, she Delusion, who infatuates all men.

So speaking he whirled her with his hand and hurled her   130

from the star-strewn heaven; and she soon found herself in the world
    of men.

But Zeus would ever bemoan her, whenever he saw his beloved son

enduring shameful labour by reason of the trials set by Eurystheus.

So even I, in my turn, when great Hector of the shimmering helm

kept destroying Argives by the sterns of our ships,

could not forget Delusion, by whom I was first deluded.

But since I was deluded and Zeus took my wits from me,

I am willing to make amends and to offer untold recompense.

Come, rise up for war, and rouse the rest of the army.

And gifts—I am here to hand over everything, all that   140

brilliant Odysseus promised you yesterday in your shelter.

Or if you wish, wait a little, pressed though you be for war,

and retainers will take gifts from beside my ships

and bring them to you, so that you may see that I will give you abundant

     satisfaction."
              Then answering him spoke Achilles of the swift feet:
"Most glorious son of Atreus, lord of men Agamemnon,
hand over the gifts if you wish, as is fitting,
or keep them by you. But now let us recollect our fighting spirit
with all speed—there is no need to spin out time staying here,
nor to delay, for a great task still is unaccomplished—   150
so that each man may again behold Achilles among the frontline fighters
with his spear of bronze destroying the ranks of Trojans;
so let each of you be mindful to go to battle with your man."
              Then answering him, resourceful Odysseus spoke:
"Not in this way, skilled though you be, godlike Achilles,
urge the sons of the Achaeans toward Ilion to fight against the Trojans
without eating, since this battle din will last no little time,
when once the ranks of men have massed together,
and god has breathed fury in both sides.
Rather order the Achaeans to take food and wine   160
by their swift ships, for this is our strength and courage.
A man cannot battle the whole day long until the setting of the sun
in the face of the enemy without taking food;
for even if he burns in his heart to fight,
yet the heaviness of his limbs will catch him unawares, and
thirst and hunger will overtake him, and cause his knees to stumble as
     he goes.
But the man who has had his fill of wine and eating
will go to war with enemy men the whole day through,
and bold is the heart within him now, nor do his limbs
give way at all, until the last man has withdrawn from battle.   170
But come, disperse your men and order them to prepare their meal;
the gifts let Agamemnon lord of men
bring in the midst of the assembly, so that all Achaeans
can see with their eyes, and you gladden your heart.
And let him swear an oath to you, standing up among the Argives,

that he never mounted the girl's bed and lay with her;   176
and let the spirit in your own heart be gracious.
And then let him make atonement to you with a feast within his quarters,
a generous feast, so that you not in any way lack justice.   180
Son of Atreus, you also in future be more just to other men;
there is no blame for a king to make atonement
to a man, when the king was first to do the violence."

      Then in turn the lord of men Agamemnon addressed him:
"I rejoice, son of Laertes, hearing your word;
you went through and recounted everything in proper measure.
And I myself wish to swear to the same things, and my spirit urges me,
nor before the face of god will I swear false oath. Achilles—
let him wait here meanwhile, pressed though he be for war.
All you others wait gathered together, until the gifts   190
come from my shelter and we make solid oaths by sacrifice.
And on yourself, Odysseus, I lay this injunction and command;
choosing the most noble young men of all the Achaeans,
bring the gifts from beside my ships, all that to Achilles
we promised yesterday, and lead forth the women.
And let Talthybios at once make ready in the broad army of Achaeans
a boar for me to slay as sacrifice to Zeus and Helios."

      Then answering him spoke Achilles of the swift feet:
"Most glorious son of Atreus, lord of men Agamemnon,
far better you should busy yourself about these things another time,   200
when there is some interval in the fighting,
and the fury is not so great inside my heart.
For now they lie cut asunder, those whom
Hector son of Priam brought down, when Zeus gave glory to him—
and you two are urgent for eating! No, but I
would command the sons of the Achaeans to go to war now
without eating, without food, and at the setting of the sun
to prepare a great meal, after we have avenged the outrage.
Before this, nothing will go down my own throat,

neither drink nor food, with my companion dead,   210
who in my shelter, torn asunder by sharp bronze,
lies turned to face the door, his companions dissolved in tears
around him; food and drink—these things are of no concern at all within
    my heart,
but slaughter is, and blood, and the harsh groaning of men."
       Then answering him resourceful Odysseus spoke:
"O Achilles, son of Peleus, far greatest of Achaeans,
you are mightier than me and greater by no small degree
with the spear, but in reason I would surpass you
by much, since I was born first and know more;
therefore let your heart bear with my words.   220
Men soon have their fill of battle—
the bronze scythe strews cornstalks thickly on the ground,
but meagre is the harvest, when Zeus has tipped his scales,
Zeus who dispenses war for men.
It is not possible in any way for the Achaeans to mourn a dead man with
    their stomachs;
too many men fall, one after the other, day upon day.
When can a man pause for breath from this toil?
We must bury the one who has died
with pitiless hearts, weeping for the day alone,
and all who survive this hateful war   230
must remember their drink and food, so that all the more
we can do battle with enemy men, ceaselessly, forever,
our bodies clad in unyielding bronze. Let no man
of this army hang back waiting another summons,
for *this* is the summons—evil it will be for him who is left
by the Argive ships; rather attacking in a body
let us rouse bitter war against the Trojan horse-breakers."
       He spoke, and took as companions the sons of glorious Nestor,
and Meges son of Phyleus, and Thoas and Meriones and
Lykomedes son of Kreion, and Melanippos;   240

and they set out to go to the shelter of Agamemnon son of Atreus.
And as soon as the word was spoken, the deed was done;
seven tripods they carried from the shelter, which Agamemnon had
    pledged to Achilles,
and twenty gleaming cauldrons, and twelve horses;
then forthwith they led out seven women, skilled in flawless works of hand,
and the eighth was Briseïs of the lovely cheeks;
and Odysseus having weighed out fully ten talents of gold
led the way back, and the other young Achaean men carried other gifts
    along with him.
         And these things they set in the midst of the assembly, while
    Agamemnon
rose to his feet; then Talthybios like a god in voice,   250
restraining the boar with his hand, stood beside the shepherd of the
    people.
With his own hands the son of Atreus drew his knife,
which always hung beside the great scabbard of his sword,
and having cut the first bristles from the boar, raising his hands to Zeus,
he made his prayer; and all the Argives sat by themselves in silence
as was proper, listening to their king.
And in prayer, then, he spoke, looking to broad heaven:
"Let Zeus be witness first, the highest and greatest of the gods,
and the Earth and Sun and Furies, who from beneath the earth
bring low those men who swear false oath,   260
that I did not bring my hand to bear upon the girl Briseïs,
not desiring her for the purpose of my bed, nor for any other,
but she remained untouched in my shelters.
And if any word of this is falsely sworn, may the gods give me afflictions
in number, such as they bestow when a man who has sworn an oath
    transgresses them."
He spoke, and with pitiless bronze cut through the boar's throat.
Its body Talthybios, whirling round, then cast into the great gulf
of the grey salt sea, food for the fish; but Achilles

rising to his feet addressed the battle-loving Argives:

"Father Zeus, surely you afflict men with great delusions.   270
Otherwise the son of Atreus would never have made the heart within
my breast storm through and through, nor would he stubbornly
have led the girl away against my will. But Zeus it would seem
wished death to come to the Achaeans in great number.
Now go to your dinner, so that we may join the god of battle."
Then so speaking, he broke up the quickly-called assembly.

   The men dispersed each to his own ship,
and the great-hearted Myrmidons attended to the gifts,
and set out bearing them to the ships of swift Achilles.
And these they placed within his shelters, and bade the women sit,   280
and noble henchmen drove the horses to his herd.

   Then Briseïs, like to golden Aphrodite,
when she saw Patroclus cut asunder by sharp bronze,
wrapped herself about him and cried shrill, and with her hands tore at
her breasts and soft cheeks and lovely face.
Then weeping she spoke, a woman like the immortal goddesses:

"Patroclus, you who most rejoiced my wretched heart,
I left you alive when I went from the shelter,
but now, coming back, I find you dead,
O leader of men; how for me evil follows evil.   290
The man to whom my father and lady mother gave me in marriage
I saw cut asunder by sharp bronze before my city;
my three cherished brothers, whom my same mother bore,
all were driven to destruction in a day.
But never, when swift Achilles slew my husband,
and sacked the city of godlike Mynes,
never did you let me weep, but used to say
that you would make me godlike Achilles' wedded wife and take me on
 the ships
to Phthia, and give a marriage feast among the Myrmidons.
Therefore I have no fill of mourning your death, who were kind to me

always."   300

So she spoke, crying, and the women in response mourned
for the sake of Patroclus, but each mourned for her own cares.

And the Achaean elders gathered around Achilles,
begging him to take his meal; but he refused, groaning:
"I beg you, if any of my own companions will yield to my persuasion,
do not bid me sate my heart with food or drink,
when dire grief has come upon me—
for I will remain as I am until the setting of the sun and hold out all the same."
So speaking Achilles dismissed the other kings,
but the two sons of Atreus remained, and brilliant Odysseus,   310
and Nestor and Idomeneus and the old horseman Phoinix,
trying repeatedly to comfort him as he grieved; but in his heart
no comfort would he take at all, until he entered in the bloody maw of war.

And summoning his memories, Achilles deeply sighed and spoke:
"Once it was that you yourself, evil-fated always, dearest of companions,
set out a pleasing meal for me in my shelter
readily and deftly, when the Achaeans raced
to carry war and all its tears to the horse-breaking Trojans;
but now you lie cut asunder, and my heart
takes no part of food and drink, although this is in my shelter,   320
but yearns for you. For I could not suffer anything else more evil,
not if I should learn of the dying of my father,
who no doubt in Phthia now lets fall a soft tear
bereft of such a son; while I the son in a foreign land
am waging war with Trojans for the sake of Helen, at whom I shudder;
not if I should learn of the death of my beloved son, raised at my behest
    on Skyros—
if by chance he still lives—Neoptolemos the godlike in beauty.
Before this the heart within me had hoped
that I alone would die far from the horse-grazed pastures of Argos,
here at Troy, but that you would return to Phthia,   330
and that in your swift black ship you might fetch my son

away from Skyros and show him each and every thing I have,
my property, my slaves, and high-roofed great house.
I think Peleus is either already dead and altogether gone,
or perhaps still barely alive, he is worn down by grief
in hateful old age, dreading always
the baneful report of me, when he learns that I have died."
So he spoke weeping, and the old men in response mourned
as they remembered, each thinking of the things left in his own halls.

      And the son of Cronus as he saw them weeping pitied them,   340
and forthwith addressed Athena in winged words:
"My child, you have wholly forsaken your man.
Or is Achilles no longer any more your heart's concern?
For he sits before his straight-horned ships
mourning his beloved companion; the others
have departed for their dinner, but he is fasting, without food.
Come, go and drop nectar and delectable ambrosia
into his breast, so that hunger may not come upon him."

      So speaking he urged Athena, who had been eager even before;
she like some long-winged shrill-voiced bird of prey   350
leapt out and down from heaven through the high clear air. The Achaeans
were then swiftly getting under arms throughout the camp; and the
    goddess
dropped into Achilles' breast nectar and delectable ambrosia,
so that hunger's distress should not weaken his knees;
then she departed to the close-built house of her mighty father.
And from the swift ships the men poured forth;
as when thick-falling snow flies forth from Zeus above,
ice-cold beneath the blast of Boreas, the North Wind born of the high
    clear sky,
so then the close-pressed helmets gleaming bright
were borne forth from the ships, and the bossed shields,   360
strong-made breastplates and ash-wood spears.
And their gleam reached the heavens, and all the earth rang with

laughter round them

at the lightning flash of bronze; thunder rose beneath the feet

of men, and in their midst godlike Achilles began to arm.

With a gnashing of his teeth, his eyes

shining like fire flare, and sorrow beyond endurance

in his heart, raging at the Trojans,

he put on the gifts of the god, all that Hephaestus had toiled to make for
   him.

First he strapped the splendid greaves around his shins,

fitted with silver bindings around his ankles;   370

next he girt about his chest a breastplate,

and across his shoulders he slung his bronze sword

studded with silver; and then he took his great strong shield,

whose light shone afar, like the moon.

As when to sailors at sea there appears the light

of a watchfire burning, which blazes high on the mountains

in a lonely farmstead, as storm winds carry them unwilling

across the fish-filled sea far from their friends,

so the flare from Achilles' shield, beautiful and intricately wrought,

reached the high clear air. And lifting his heavy four-ridged helmet   380

he placed it about his head; and it shone far like a star,

the helmet crested with horsehair, the gold-maned plume flowing about it,

which Hephaestus had set thickly about its ridge.

And godlike Achilles made trial of himself in his armour,

to see if it fitted him and if his splendid limbs ran freely;

and for him it was as if they were wings that lifted the shepherd of the
   people.

Then from its stand he drew his father's spear,

heavy, massive, powerful; this no other of the Achaeans could

wield, but only Achilles knew how to wield it,

the spear of Pelian ash, which Chiron gave to his beloved father   390

from the heights of Mount Pelion to be death to warriors.

Then Automedon and Alkimos put the horses they were tending

into harness; and placed the fine breaststraps about them, and set the bits
in their mouths, and drew the reins back tight
toward the bolted chariot; and taking the shining whip
firmly in his hand, Automedon sprang up on to the chariot;
and behind him, under arms, mounted Achilles,
radiant in his armour like Hyperion the sun,
and in a voice of terror he commanded the horses of his father:
"Xanthos and Balios, far-famed foals of the mare Podarge,   400
consider some other way to bring your charioteer safely
back to the host of Danaans, when we have had enough of fighting,
nor leave him dead as you left Patroclus."
              Then from beneath the yoke answered him his horse of flashing
     feet,
Xanthos; abruptly he bowed his head, and all his mane,
streaming out from under the yoke-pad by the yoke, touched the ground;
for Hera the goddess of the white arms gave him voice:
"We shall surely save you for now, mighty Achilles;
but your day of destruction is near; it is not we who are to blame,
but a mighty god and powerful Fate.   410
For it was not by our slowness or slackness
that the Trojans took the armour from the shoulders of Patroclus,
but the best of gods, he whom lovely-haired Leto bore,
killed him among the front fighters and gave glory to Hector.
We two could run apace with even the West Wind's blowing,
which they say is swiftest; but for you Achilles
it is fated to be slain by the might of god and man."
              Then the Furies stopped his voice when he had so spoken.
And greatly troubled swift-footed Achilles answered him:
"Xanthos, why do you prophesy my death? You have no need.   420
I myself well know this, that it is my fate to die here,
far from my beloved father and my mother; but even so
I shall take no rest before I drive the Trojans to their fill of war."
He spoke, and giving shout held his single-hoofed horses into the
     frontlines.

So beside the curved ships the Achaeans,
insatiate of battle, armed around you, son of Peleus,
and the Trojans in turn armed on the other side, by the rising of the plain.
And Zeus from the peak of many-folded Olympus ordered Themis
to summon the gods to assembly; ranging everywhere she
ordered them to return to the house of Zeus.
None of the rivers were absent, except for Ocean,
nor any of the nymphs, who dwell in the lovely groves
and river springs and grassy water-meadows;
but coming to the house of Zeus who gathers the clouds   10
they took their seats in the polished colonnades that Hephaestus
had made with knowing craft for Zeus the father.
So they were gathered within the house of Zeus; nor was the Earth-Shaker
heedless of the goddess, but out of the salt sea he came with the others,
and took his seat in their midst, and asked of Zeus' plan:
"Why now, lord of the bright thunderbolt, have you summoned the gods
    to assembly?
Are you are concerned for the Trojans and Achaeans?
For now the war and fighting are set to blaze between them."
Then answering him spoke Zeus who gathers the clouds:
"Earth-Shaker, you know what is in my mind,   20
the reasons for which I have gathered you; I am concerned about them,
    dying as they are.
For my part, I will remain seated on a cleft of Olympus,

where I will pleasure my heart in watching; but the rest of you
go, until you come among the Trojans and Achaeans,
and give your aid to either side, whichever each of you desires.
For if Achilles goes to battle on his own against the Trojans,
not even for a little will they hold off Peleus' swift-footed son.
Even before—even seeing him—they used to tremble;
and now, when he rages in his heart for his comrade,
I fear even against fate he will storm their rampart."   30
So spoke the son of Cronus, and stirred up inescapable war.

      And the gods set out to go to war, their hearts divided;
to the assembled ships went Hera and Pallas Athena
and Poseidon who holds the earth, and the swift runner
Hermes, who excels in shrewd thought,
and Hephaestus went with them, exulting in his strength,
limping, yet his shrunken legs moved nimbly beneath him.
And to the Trojans went Ares of the shimmering helm, and with him
Phoebus with his unshorn hair and Artemis who showers arrows,
and Leto and the river Xanthos and laughter-loving Aphrodite.   40
And as long as the gods kept their distance from the mortal men,
so long did the Achaeans triumph, for Achilles
had appeared, he who for a long time had abandoned the painful battle,
and dreadful trembling seized the limbs of the Trojans, every man,
in terror, when they saw the swift-footed son of Peleus
shining in his armour, the equal of man-destroying Ares;
but when the Olympians came among the host of men,
then rose powerful Strife who drives the army into battle, and Athena
    shouted out,
coming up now to the trench dug outside the wall,
and now again giving her great cry by the far-thundering shore;   50
and from the other side shouted Ares, like a black storm-cloud,
calling aloud his sharp commands to the Trojans from their city heights,
then again running to Pleasant Hill beside the river Simoeis.

      So the blessed gods, goading both sides on,

clashed together, and let grave strife break loose among them.
The father of men and gods thundered terribly
from on high; and from below Poseidon shook
the boundless earth and sheer peaks of the mountains;
all the foothills of Ida and its many springs were shaken
and its peaks, as too the city of the Trojans and ships of the Achaeans;   60
Hades below, lord of the dead beneath the earth, in terror
leapt wailing from his throne in fear that
Poseidon, shaker of the earth, would split the earth above him,
and reveal his house to mortal men and the immortal gods
in all its mouldering horror, which even the gods abhor.

      Such was the thunderous crash arising as the gods converged in
   strife.
And against lord Poseidon
Phoebus Apollo took his stand, holding his feathered arrows,
and against the war god stood the gleaming-eyed goddess Athena;
and against Hera stood the goddess of the golden arrow and din of
   hunt,70
Artemis who showers arrows, sister of the Far-Shooter;
and against Leto stood strong Hermes the swift runner,
and against Hephaestus the mighty, deep-swirling river
that the gods call Xanthos, but men Scamander.

      So god was advancing against god; but Achilles
hungered above all else to enter the fray face to face with Hector
son of Priam; for beyond all others his heart drove him
to glut Ares, the shield-bearing warrior, with his blood.

      But Aeneas it was whom Apollo, driver of armies, sent straight
against the son of Peleus, and inspired mighty power in him,   80
and he likened his voice to that of Priam's son Lykaon;
and in this likeness, Apollo son of Zeus addressed him:
"Aeneas, adviser of Trojans, where are your boasts,
those threats you used to make as you drank wine with Trojan kings,
that you would go to battle, man to man, with Peleus' son Achilles?"

Then answering in turn Aeneas addressed him:
"Son of Priam, why do you urge me to do these things against my will,
to do battle against the high-hearted son of Peleus?
This is not the first time I will stand against Achilles the swift-footed,
but once before he put me to flight with his spear   90
from Mount Ida, when he came for our cattle,
and sacked Lyrnessos and Pedasos; but Zeus protected me,
and gave strength to me and swiftness to my knees.
Otherwise I would have been brought down beneath the hands of
    Achilles and Athena,
who going in advance bestowed the light of safety on him and bade him
kill with his spear the Leleges and the Trojans.
Therefore no man can do battle with Achilles;
always one of the gods stands by him, who wards off destruction.
And that apart, the spear he throws flies straight, nor stops
until it pierces human flesh. But if the gods   100
would stretch the rope of war equally, he would not so easily
be victorious, not though he boasts to be made of solid bronze."

Then in turn lord Apollo, son of Zeus, answered him:
"Come, warrior, and you too make prayer to the everlasting gods;
for it is said that you were born of Zeus' daughter Aphrodite;
that other is born of a lesser deity;
for Aphrodite is a daughter of Zeus, the other was born of the sea's old
    man.
Come, carry your unyielding bronze straight before you, do not let him
turn you aside with his contemptuous words and threatening."
So speaking he breathed great strength into the shepherd of the people,   110
and he set out through the frontline fighters armed in gleaming bronze.

Nor did the son of Anchises escape the notice of white-armed
    Hera
as he set out against the son of Peleus through the throng of men,
and she, summoning the gods together, made a speech:
"Consider you two, Poseidon and Athena,

in your minds, how this matter will be.
Here comes Aeneas armed in gleaming bronze
against the son of Peleus, and Phoebus Apollo sets him on;
come, let us turn him back
on the spot; or rather let one of us stand by Achilles,   120
and grant him great strength, so that he does not fail in spirit,
and so he may know that the best of immortals love him,
and the other gods are so much wind, they who before
warded off the battle host and fighting from the Trojans.
All of us have come down from Olympus to take our part
in this battle so that no harm befall Achilles at Trojan hands
today; though later he will suffer all that Fate
assigned to him with destiny's thread when he was born, when his
      mother bore him to life.
But if Achilles does not learn these things from the voice of gods,
then he will be afraid, should some other god come face to face against
      him   130
in the fighting; for gods are hard to bear when they appear in their own
      form."
            Then answered her Poseidon who shakes the earth:
"Hera, do not rage beyond reason; you should not.
I myself would not wish us to drive the other gods together in strife,
since we are much the stronger,
so let us go aside from the haunts of men
and seat ourselves upon a lookout point, and let the war be the concern of
      mortals.
But if Ares starts to fight, or Phoebus Apollo,
or if they should keep Achilles back and not let him fight,
there and then the strife of battle will arise   140
from our side too. And very swiftly, I think, they will break away,
and go back to Olympus among the company of other gods,
broken by force beneath our hands."
            So speaking the dark-haired god Poseidon led the way

to the wall of godlike Heracles, heaped up with earth,

a high place, which the Trojans and Pallas Athena

made, so that Heracles could escape the sea beast as he fled from its
     reach,

at the time when it chased him away from the shore toward the plain.

Here Poseidon took his seat as did the other gods,

and around their shoulders they wrapped impenetrable cloud;   150

and on the opposite side the gods of Troy settled down upon the brow of
     Pleasant Hill

around you, Phoebus to whom we cry aloud, and Ares, sacker of cities.

          And so they sat on either side taking counsel—

for to commence the painful warfare

was something both sides shrank to do, though it was Zeus who sits on
     high who urged them—

and all the plain was filled with men and shone with the bronze

of men and horses; and the earth quaked with the feet

of them on the move together. And two men, the best by far,

were advancing into the middle of both sides straining to do battle,

Aeneas son of Anchises and godlike Achilles.   160

And Aeneas, menacing, first strode forth,

gesturing with his heavy helmet; his charging shield

he held before his chest, and he shook his brazen spear.

And from the other side the son of Peleus rose up to face him like a

ravening lion, for whose sake men have assembled, which they strain to
     kill,

the whole village of them; and at first, paying them no heed,

the lion goes his way; but when some sturdy young man

strikes him with a spear-cast, then he crouches, jaws gaping, and foam
     forms

around his teeth, and in his heart his brave spirit groans,

and with his tail he lashes his ribs and flanks from side to side,   170

and goads himself for battle,

and, eyes gleaming, he is carried by his fury straight ahead, either to kill

one of the men, or himself to die at the forefront of the throng;
so the fury and heroic spirit of Achilles goaded him
to come face to face with great-hearted Aeneas.

    And when they had advanced almost upon each other,
swift-footed godlike Achilles addressed him first:
"Aeneas, why have you come to stand so far from your company?
Does your spirit urge you to fight with me
in the hope that you will rule the horse-breaking Trojans over Priam's
    domain?   180
But if you should kill me,
for all that, Priam will not drop any prize of honour in your hands;
for he has his sons, and his mind is steady and not witless.
Or have the Trojans cut out a plot of land for you surpassing all others,
a beautiful plot, with orchards and tilled fields, for you to enjoy,
if you should kill me? But I think you will do this with some difficulty.
For I believe another time before this you fled my spear.
Or do you not recall when I caught you alone and chased you smartly
    from your cattle
down from the Idaean hills in the swiftness of your feet?
And at that time you did not look behind you as you fled.   190
From there you escaped into Lyrnessos; but I sacked it
as I followed after in pursuit, with Athena's help and father Zeus,
and led the women away, captives, having stripped them of their day of
    freedom;
but Zeus protected you, Zeus and the other gods.
Yet I do not think they will protect you now, as you may believe
in your heart, and I urge you to retreat
back to your host, and not stand against me,
before you suffer some harm; even a fool learns after the event."

    Then in turn Aeneas spoke to him in answer:
"Son of Peleus, do not hope to frighten me with words   200
as if I were a child, since I too know well
how to speak both taunts and words of slander.

We know each other's birth, we know our parents,
having heard the words of old from mortal men;
yet with your own eyes you have never seen mine, nor I then yours.
They say you are born of blameless Peleus
from your mother, Thetis, lovely-haired daughter of the sea;
but I claim to be by birth the son of Anchises, the great of heart,
and my mother is Aphrodite.
And now one or the other of these will weep for their beloved son   210
this day; for I do not think it is thus, with foolish words,
we two will part and go home from battle.

        "But if indeed you wish to learn these things, so as to know well
my family's lineage, many men know of it.
Zeus who gathers the clouds first begat Dardanos;
and he founded the city Dardania, since sacred Ilion
was not yet established on the plain, the city of mortal men,
but at that time they dwelt in the foothills of Ida with its many springs.
And Dardanos in turn begat a son, Erichthonios the king,
who became the wealthiest of mortal men;   220
his three thousand horses grazed below the marshy meadow,
mares, delighting in their young fillies.
And the North Wind Boreas was enamoured of them as they grazed,
and likening himself to a dark-maned stallion, coupled with them;
and they conceived and bore twelve foals.
And when these gambolled over wheat-giving fields,
they ran upon the tip-top fruit of the tasselled grain, nor would they
    break it;
and when they gambolled over the broad back of the sea,
they would run upon the breaking foam of the grey salt water.
And Erichthonios begat Tros, who ruled the Trojans;   230
And three blameless sons were born in turn to Tros,
Ilos and Assarakos and godlike Ganymede,
who was born most beautiful of mortal men;
the gods plucked him up to be wine-pourer to Zeus

on account of his beauty, so that he would dwell among the deathless
    gods.
And Ilos in turn begat his blameless son Laomedon;
and Laomedon in turn begat Tithonos and Priam
and Lampos and Klytios and Hiketaon, companion of Ares.
And Assarakos begat Kapys, and he begat Anchises, his son;
and Anchises was father to me, as Priam was to shining Hector.   240
Of such descent and blood I claim to be.
Zeus gives men their valour and diminishes them too,
in whatever way he wishes, for he is mightiest of all.

        "But come, let us no longer debate these things like children
standing around in the middle of battle combat;
for both of us can speak many words
of insult, nor could a ship of a hundred benches bear their weight.
For the tongue of man is fickle, and there are many words
in everyone, and they cover, here and there, a wide field;
and whatever word you say, such you may also hear.   250
So why must we two hurl words of abuse and strife
in each other's faces, like women,
who enraged about some heart-devouring quarrel
go in the middle of the street and throw abusive words at each other,
many of them true, many not, which anger drives them to say?
You will not turn me, who am determined, from my prowess with your
    words
before we have fought man to man with bronze; but come,
with all speed let us taste each other's mettle with our bronze spears."

        He spoke, and into Achilles' dread and terrible shield Aeneas
    drove his
powerful spear; and the shield rang loud around the spear-point.   260
And the son of Peleus with his massive hand held his shield away from
    him,
alarmed; for he thought the long-shadowed spear
of great-hearted Aeneas would easily pierce it—

the fool; in mind and heart he did not understand
that the glorious gifts of gods are not so easily
broken by mortal men, nor do they give way.
So the powerful spear of brilliant Aeneas did not
shatter his shield; for the gold checked it, a gift of the god.
Two layers the spear did drive through, but three remained,
since the crippled god had hammered out five layers—   270
two that were bronze, two on the inside of tin,
and one of gold, in which was checked the ash-wood spear.

      But next Achilles let fly his long-shadowed spear,
and struck the perfect circle of Aeneas' shield,
at the extreme edge of the rim, where the bronze ran thinnest,
and the oxhide was fitted thinnest; right through
the Pelian ash-spear flew, and the shield crashed beneath it.
Aeneas crouched and held the shield from him,
terrified; and flying forward over his back the spear
stopped, standing in the ground, after breaking through two circled
    layers   280
of the man-surrounding shield. Escaping the great spear
Aeneas stood up, and great was the anguish that flooded his eyes
in his terror, because the weapon had fixed so close to him. And Achilles
in burning speed was rushing at him, sharp sword drawn,
shouting his terrifying cry; and Aeneas took in his hand
a boulder, a great feat, which two men could not lift,
such as mortal men are now; but he, even alone, brandished it with ease.

      Then Aeneas would have struck Achilles with the stone as he
    charged toward him
on his helmet or shield, which warded off fatal destruction from him,
and the son of Peleus, closing in, would have stripped Aeneas of his life
    with his sword,   290
had not Poseidon who shakes the earth paid sharp attention;
and at once he addressed the immortal gods:
"Alas, I grieve for great-hearted Aeneas,

who will soon go down to the house of Hades, broken by the son of
   Peleus,
having trusted in the words of Apollo who shoots from afar—
fool, for Apollo will be no use in warding off death's sorrow from him.
And why does this guiltless man suffer agonies now
to no end, for the troubles of others, and always
gives pleasing gifts to the gods who hold the broad heaven?
But come, let us take him away from the reach of death,   300
lest the son of Cronus too be provoked to anger if Achilles
kills this man; for it is fated for Aeneas to escape death,
so that the race of Dardanos not perish without seed, blotted out,
Dardanos whom the son of Cronus loved beyond all his sons
who were born to him from mortal women.
Yet the son of Cronus has come to hate the race of Priam;
and now it is strong Aeneas who will rule the Trojans,
and the sons of his sons, who will be born hereafter."

      Then answered him the ox-eyed lady Hera;
"Earth-Shaker, you decide in your own mind   310
about Aeneas, whether you will save him, or whether you will let
   him go;   311
but know this, that we two have sworn many oaths   313
before all the immortals, I and Pallas Athena,
never to fend off the day of evil from the Trojans,
not when all of Troy with raging fire is burning,
set ablaze, and the warrior sons of the Achaeans set it blazing."

      Then when Poseidon who shakes the earth had heard this,
he proceeded to go towards the battle and tumult of spears,
and came to where Aeneas was and glorious Achilles.   320
Swiftly he poured a cloud of mist down over his eyes,
over the eyes of Achilles son of Peleus, and pulled his ash-wood bronze-
   pointed
spear out of the shield of great-hearted Aeneas,
and laid it before Achilles' feet;

but Aeneas himself he hurled from the earth, lofting him on high;
over the many ranks of warriors, over the many ranks of horses
Aeneas vaulted, sped from the hand of the god,
and arrived at the farthest edge of the charging battle,
where the Kaukones were armed for war.
Then Poseidon who shakes the earth came up very close to him,   330
and addressed him with winged words:
"Aeneas, which of the gods bade you in this crazed manner
go to battle and fight against Achilles,
who is both stronger than you and very dear to the immortals?
Rather draw back, whenever you encounter him,
lest even beyond fate you arrive at the house of Hades.
But when Achilles meets his death and his fate,
at that time summon your courage to do battle with the frontline fighters;
for no other of the Achaeans will kill you."

         So speaking he left him there, since he had revealed all.   340
And forthwith from Achilles' eyes he scattered the divine
mist; and Achilles stared with all his might,
then troubled, spoke to his own great-hearted spirit:
"Oh shame! This is a great wonder I see with my eyes.
This spear lies upon the earth, and I do not see the man at all
at whom I let fly, as I raged to kill.
So, after all, Aeneas is beloved by the immortal gods;
and I thought he boasted idly of this.
Let him go. He will have no heart to make further trial of me,
as now, again, he was happy to flee death.   350
But come, I will command the warlike Danaans
and make trial of the other Trojans I come against."

         He spoke and sprang to the ranks, and began giving orders to
    every man:
"No longer, now, stand back from the Trojans, brave Achaeans,
but come, and let it be man against man, eager to do battle;
for it is hard for me, strong though I am,

to take in hand so many men and fight them all.
Nor could Ares, god immortal though he is, nor could Athena
for all their toil curb the jaws of so great a battle.
But as much as I am able—with hands and feet   360
and with my strength—I say, I will no more slacken, not a little,
but I am going right through their line; nor do I think that any Trojan man
will be happy, who should approach my spear."

          So he spoke urging them on; and to the Trojans shining Hector
shouted orders, for he was minded to go against Achilles:
"Trojans, high-hearted warriors, do not fear the son of Peleus.
With words I too might go to battle even with the gods;
but with a spear this is more difficult, since they are far stronger.
Nor does Achilles give fulfilment to all his words,
but one thing he accomplishes, another even he cuts short half done.   370
So I am going against him, though his hands are like fire—
though his hands are like fire and his strength like flashing iron!"

          So he spoke urging them on, and the Trojans, facing him, raised
their spears; and their fury massed together, and their cry of battle rose.
But just then Phoebus Apollo came up and spoke to Hector:
"Hector, do not think to battle with Achilles out in front of other men,
but wait among the crowd and away from the tumult of battle,
lest he strike you with a spear-cast, or stab you at close quarters with his
     sword."
So he spoke; and Hector at once plunged into the throng of men,
shaken, when he heard the voice of the god speaking.   380

          But Achilles, his heart clad in valour, sprang for the Trojans,
shouting his terrifying cry. And first he killed Iphition,
the brave son of Otrynteus, leader of many men,
whom a nymph of the river bore to Otrynteus, sacker of cities,
below snowy Mount Tmolos, in the rich land of Hyde;
this man godlike Achilles smote with his spear across the middle of the
     head
as he charged straight at him; and the whole of the head was split in two,

and he fell with a thud. And over him godlike Achilles vaunted:

"Lie dead, son of Otrynteus, most terrifying of all men.

Your death is here, but your people are by Lake   390

Gygaia, where the land of your fathers is,

by the fish-breeding river Hyllos and the eddies of Hermos."

So he spoke vaunting, and darkness closed the other's eyes.

   And the Achaean chariots cut him to pieces with their wheels

at the front of the fighting; and after him it was noble Demoleon,

who stems the tide of battle, a son of Antenor,

whom Achilles struck about the temple through the brazen cheek piece
 of his helmet;

nor did the bronze helmet withstand the blow, but right through it

the spear-point, straining forward, crushed bone, and the brains

were all spattered within it; so Achilles destroyed the man for all
 his fury.   400

   Then Hippodamas, as he leapt from his chariot,

fleeing before him, Achilles stabbed with his spear in the back;

the man gasped out his life bellowing, like a bull

bellows as it is dragged about lord Poseidon's shrine at Helike,

when the young men drag it, and the Earth-Shaker rejoices in them;

and so his brave spirit left his bones as he was bellowing.

   Then with his spear Achilles went after godlike Polydoros

son of Priam; always his father forbade him to go to battle,

because among his sons he was the youngest of his offspring

and was dearest to him; in speed of feet he excelled all men;   410

but this time, in his youthful folly, displaying his outstanding speed,

he raced on through the front ranks until he lost his life.

Swift-footed godlike Achilles struck him with his spear

midway in the back as he rushed past, there where the golden buckles

of his belt came together and the two halves of the breastplate met.

Straight on beside his navel the spear-point passed;

he dropped to his knees screaming, the dark mist embraced him,

and in his hands he held his bowels before him, as he sank.

BOOK 20

And Hector when he saw his brother Polydoros
holding his bowels in his own hands, sinking towards the earth,   420
then mist seeped down upon his eyes; he could no longer bear
to range about at a distance, but balancing his spear
he came at Achilles, like a flame of fire. And Achilles
sprang up when he saw him, and spoke a word in triumph:
"Here is the man, who above all others has touched my heart to the quick,
who slew my cherished companion; we will no longer
cower from each other between the lines of battle."
He spoke, and looking from beneath his brows addressed glorious Hector:
"Come nearer, so that you may come the quicker to death's border."
Then not at all afraid, Hector of the shimmering helm answered him: 430
"Son of Peleus, do not hope to frighten me with words
as if I were a child, since I myself well know too
how to speak both taunts and words of slander.
I know you are brave, and I am weaker than you.
But these things lie in the laps of the gods,
and it may be that weaker though I am, I shall take your life
as I cast with my spear, since even my spear has been sharp in time before."
        He spoke, and balancing his spear he hurled it forth; but Athena
with her breath turned it back from illustrious Achilles,
blowing very gently, and the spear came back again to glorious
    Hector,   440
and fell before his feet. Then Achilles
with blazing speed sprang forward, raging to kill,
shouting his terrifying cry; but Apollo snatched Hector away
lightly, god that he was, enfolded in dense mist.
Three times swift-footed godlike Achilles charged
with his bronze spear, and three times he struck at deep mist.   446
And with a terrible shout he flung at Hector winged words: 448
"You escaped death once again now, dog; yet very close it was the evil
came to you; now once more Phoebus Apollo saved you,   450
to whom no doubt you make prayer when you approach the thud of

spears.

Meeting again, I will surely finish you,

if one of the gods should be my ally too.

Now I will go after the other Trojans, whomever I catch."

So speaking he stabbed Dryops in the middle of the neck with his
   spear,

and he dropped before his feet. And Achilles left him,

and it was Demouchos son of Philetor, a good man and great,

he next checked with a spear strike to the knee. Then stabbing him

with his great sword he stripped his life away.

Next he charged at Laogonos and Dardanos, both sons of Bias,   460

thrusting both from their chariot to the ground,

striking one with his spear, and stabbing the other at close quarters with
   his sword.

But Tros the son of Alastor—he made straight for Achilles' knees,

in the hope that Achilles might somehow spare him, taking him alive to
   let him go,

and not kill him, pitying him as a youth of his own age—

fool, he did not see that Achilles had no mind to be persuaded;

for this was not some sweet-tempered or some gentle man,

but a man of urgent fury. Yet Tros grasped his knees with his hands

straining to make entreaty, and Achilles with his sword stabbed him
   beneath by the liver;

his liver slipped out from the wound, and its black blood   470

filled his lap; darkness covered him over his eyes,

his life gone. And Achilles coming up to Moulios stabbed

him with his spear beside his ear; right through the other ear drove

the bronze spear-point. And next he smote Echeklos the son of Agenor

in the middle of his head with his hilted sword,

and all the sword was made hot with blood; and over his eyes

crimson death and powerful fate took him.

Then Deukalion—there where the tendons of the elbow

join, there Achilles pierced him through his arm

with his bronze-pointed spear. And his arm hanging heavy, he awaited
    Achilles,   480
beholding death before his face; and Achilles striking his neck with his
    sword,
sent the head and helmet flying far away; the marrow
throbbed forth from his spine, and Deukalion lay stretched along the
    earth.
And Achilles set out after Peires' blameless son
Rhigmos, who had come from the rich soil of Thrace;
this man Achilles struck in the abdomen with his spear, and the bronze
    point fixed in his belly,
and he fell from his chariot. Then with his sharp spear he struck
    Areïthoös, his henchman,
in the back as he was turning the horses around,
and shoved him from the chariot; and the horses fled in panic.

       And as demonic fire rages through deep valleys   490
of a sun-parched mountain, and the dense forest is consumed,
and everywhere the careening wind rolls the flames along,
so Achilles swept everywhere with his spear like something more than
    human,
driving before him those whom he killed; and the earth ran black with
    blood.
As when a man puts a yoke to his broad-browed bull-oxen team
to crush white barley on a well-laid threshing-floor,
and it is quickly husked beneath the loud-bellowing oxen's feet,
so under the hands of great-hearted Achilles his single-hoofed horses
trampled alike the dead and their shields; and the axle beneath
was spattered all with blood, and the rails which ran around the
    chariot,   500
struck by droplets from the hooves of the horses
and rims of the wheels; and he strained to seize glory,
he the son of Peleus, his invincible hands spattered with gore.

And when they reached the crossing of the fair-flowing stream
of whirling Xanthos, born of immortal Zeus,
there Achilles split the Trojans, chasing half from the plain
towards their city, to where the Achaeans had fled bewildered with fear,
the day before, while shining Hector raged;
there the Trojans streamed in rout, but Hera
began to spread dense mist ahead to check them; and the other half
were crammed into the deep-flowing, silver-eddied river.
In they fell, with a great crashing splash, and the headlong flowing waters
   roared,
and the banks echoed loud all round; crying in distress, men   10
were trying to swim, spun here and there through the eddies.
As when from under rushing fire locusts take to the air,
fleeing towards a river, and the weariless fire blazes,
stirred of a sudden, and the locusts shrink into the water,
so before Achilles the flowing water of deep-eddying Xanthos
was filled with the mingled roar of men and horses.

      Then god-born Achilles left his spear there on the bank
propped against the tamarisks, and leapt in like something more than
   human,
gripping his sword, intent in his heart on dark deeds;
he struck, turning this side and that; abject groaning rose from those   20
stricken by his sword, and the water was made red with blood.
As before a great-mawed dolphin, other fish

seeking safety fill the inmost coves of a well-sheltered harbour
in their fear—for greedily it will devour whatever it catches—
so the Trojans all along the running waters of the terrible river
cowered under its steep banks; and Achilles, when he had wearied his
    hands with slaughtering,
picked out twelve youths alive from the river,
blood payment for the dying of Menoetius' son Patroclus;
these he led out of the river dazed with fear like fawns,
and bound their hands behind them with straps of well-cut leather,   30
which they wore around their own strong-woven tunics,
and gave them to his companions to lead away to the hollow ships;
then he charged back, raging still to cut more men to pieces.

           And there he encountered a son of Dardanian Priam
fleeing from the river, Lykaon, whom Achilles himself once
captured and took by force from his father's orchards
while on night excursion; the youth had been cutting with sharp bronze
    a wild fig tree
of its young branches, to be rails for his chariot;
then evil unforeseen had come to him in godlike Achilles;
at that time, Achilles sold him across the sea, leading him off   40
to strong-built Lemnos in his ships, and the son of Jason paid for him;
there a guest friend, Eëtion of Imbros, ransomed him,
paying a great price, and dispatched him to bright Arisbe.
From there, slipping away, he arrived at his father's house,
and for eleven days rejoiced his heart among his dear ones
after coming back from Lemnos; but on the twelfth day a god
cast him again into the hands of Achilles, who would
dispatch him, unwilling yet, on his way to the house of Hades.
When, then, swift-footed godlike Achilles saw Lykaon
naked, without helmet or shield, nor did he hold a spear—   50
but all these things he had flung away to the ground as, wringing with
    sweat,

he fled from the river, and exhaustion overwhelmed his limbs—
then Achilles, troubled, spoke to his own great-hearted spirit:
"What is this? A great wonder is this I see with my eyes.
Surely the great-hearted Trojans whom I killed
will rise again from under the misted realm of darkness,
seeing how this man appears, having escaped his pitiless day of death,
he who was sold into holy Lemnos, nor did the deep
of the grey salt sea keep hold of him, which detains so many against
    their will.
But come, and let him have a taste of my spear-point,   60
so that I may know in my mind and learn,
whether likewise he will return even from Hades, or
whether the life-giving earth will keep him, which detains even the
    mighty below."
        So his thoughts churned as he waited; but the other came close
    to him, dazed with fear,
seeking to lay hold of his knees; and beyond all measure he desired in
    his heart
to escape death and evil and dark fate.
He, godlike Achilles, lifted his great spear,
seeking to stab him; but Lykaon ran under it and seized his knees,
crouching, and the spear flying forward over his back
stuck in the ground, eager to sate itself on human flesh.   70
And with one hand holding Achilles' knees, he made supplication,
with the other he held the pointed spear, nor let it go;
and speaking winged words he addressed him:
"At your knees I implore you, Achilles; respect me and have mercy on me.
I am as your suppliant, god-cherished Achilles; respect my claim;
for it was in your presence first I tasted the bread of Demeter
on the day when you captured me in our well-laid orchard,
and sold me across the sea, taking me far from my father and friends
to holy Lemnos, and I earned you a hundred cattle.

Then paying three times as much I was freed for ransom; and this is the
    twelfth dawn   80
for me, since I came to Ilion,
after suffering much; now again deadly fate
has put me in your hands; I must surely be hated by father Zeus,
who handed me to you again; to a short life my mother
Laothoë bore me, the daughter of aged Altes,
Altes, who rules the battle-loving Leleges,
holding steep Pedasos by the river Satnioeis.
Priam took his daughter in marriage—among many other women—
and we two sons were born of her; and you will cut the throats of both.
One already you killed among the foremost warriors,   90
godlike Polydoros, when you struck him with your sharp spear;
and now you will be my death here; for I do not believe
I will escape your hands, since some divine force has brought me to this
    place.
Yet I will say one other thing to you, and put this within your heart;
do not kill me, since I am not born of the same womb as Hector,
who slew your strong and gentle comrade."

        So the glorious son of Priam addressed him,
entreating him with his words; but the voice he heard was implacable:
"Fool, do not with me propose ransom nor argue a case.
Before the day of fate reached Patroclus, it is true,   100
until then my heart chose to spare
the Trojans, and many I took alive and sold.
But now there is no one who will escape death, whom god
puts in my hands before the gates of Ilion,
of all the Trojans, but especially the sons of Priam.
Come friend, you die too; why bewail this so?
Even Patroclus died, who was far better than you.
Do you not see how magnificent and mighty I am?
I am born of a noble father, and a goddess the mother who bore me,
yet death and powerful fate is upon me too;   110

there will be a dawn or an afternoon or noon,
when someone will take the life from even me in battle,
striking with a spear or an arrow from a bowstring."
        So he spoke; and the knees and very heart of the other went
    slack.
He let go the spear, and sank to the ground spreading both arms wide;
and Achilles, drawing his sharp sword,
struck him on the neck by the collarbone, and the whole of his
double-edged sword plunged in; and Lykaon face down upon the earth
lay outstretched; and his dark blood flowed forth, and soaked the earth.
Seizing his foot, Achilles flung him to the river to be carried off,   120
and vaunting over him spoke winged words:
"Lie there now with the fish, who will lick you, your wounds,
your blood, with no care for you; nor will your mother
mourn you on a funeral bier, but Scamander
will carry you as he whirls towards the broad breast of the sea.
Many a fish leaping through the waves will dart up beneath the dark
    ruffling of the water,
to eat the white shining fat of Lykaon.
May you all die, until we fall upon the city of sacred Ilion,
you fleeing, and I ravaging from behind.
Nor will your river, for all its fair streams and silver eddies,   130
defend you, to which you have so long made sacrifice of many bulls,
and cast alive into its eddies single-hoofed horses;
but even so you will die, all, an evil death, until all
have atoned for the murder of Patroclus and the destruction of the
    Achaeans,
whom you slew by the swift ships while I was away."
        So he spoke; and the river was provoked to growing anger in his
    heart,
and turned over in his mind how he might stop godlike Achilles'
slaughter, and ward off destruction from the Trojans.
But holding his long-shadowed spear, the son of Peleus,

raging to kill, sprang for Asteropaios,   140
the son of Pelegon, born of the wide-flowing river Axios
and of Periboia, the eldest of the daughters of Akessamenos;
for the deep-eddying river lay in love with her.
At this man Achilles charged, and from the river Asteropaios
stood to face him, wielding two spears in his hands; and into his heart
Xanthos put strength, since he was angered for the young men slain in
    battle,
those whom Achilles tore apart along his waters, and had not pitied.
      And when they had advanced almost upon each other,
swift-footed godlike Achilles first addressed the other:
"What man are you, from where, who dares to come against me?   150
They are sons of brokenhearted men, who face my might."
Then in turn the glorious son of Pelegon addressed him:
"Great-hearted son of Peleus, why do you ask my lineage?
I come from the rich soil of Paeonia, far from here,
leading the Paeonian men with their long spears; and this is now
the eleventh dawn for me since I came to Ilion.
And my lineage is from the broad-running river Axios,
the Axios, who lets flow the loveliest water upon the earth,
who bore Pelegon famed for his spear; and men say that he begat me.
And now let us go to battle, illustrious Achilles."   160
      So he spoke, threatening; and godlike Achilles raised at the ready
his Pelian ash-spear, and the warrior Asteropaios at the same moment
with both hands cast with two spears, since he was ambidextrous.
And with one spear he struck the shield, but it did not
shatter through it; for the gold checked it, the gift of the god;
with the other he grazed Achilles on the elbow of his right arm,
and a dark cloud of blood gushed out; and passing over him
the spear fixed into the earth, longing to glut itself on flesh.
And then Achilles let fly his straight-flying ash-wood spear
at Asteropaios, raging to kill;   170

but missed him, and he struck the high bank of the river,
and the ash-spear was driven up to its middle in the bank.
Then the son of Peleus drawing his sharp sword beside his thigh,
sprang for the man, raging; and the other was not able to draw
Achilles' ash-spear from the steep bank with his strength of hand.
Three times he shook the spear, desperate to withdraw it,
and three times his strength failed; and on the fourth time, bending
the ash-spear of Aeacides toward him, he sought with all his heart to
    break it.
But before this Achilles stripped his life away at close quarters with his
    sword;
for he struck him in the stomach beside the navel, and all his bowels   180
poured out on the ground; then darkness covered his eyes
as he gasped for breath; and Achilles springing onto his chest
stripped his armour away and spoke vaunting:
"Lie there so; hard it is to compete with the sons
of the almighty son of Cronus, even for those born of a river.
You said you were born of a wide-flowing river,
but I claim the lineage of mighty Zeus.
The man who fathered me is lord over many Myrmidons,
Peleus the son of Aeacus; and Aeacus was born of Zeus.
So Zeus is greater than the rivers that flow to the sea,   190
and the descendant of Zeus in turn, is greater than a man born of
    a river.
And there is a great river here beside you, if he can somehow
help you; but it is not possible to do battle with Zeus the son of Cronus,
nor does the august river Achelous contend with him,
nor the mighty strength of deep-flowing Ocean,
from whom all rivers and all the sea
and all the fountains and deep wells flow;
but even he fears the lightning bolt of mighty Zeus
and his dread thunder, when it crashes from the heavens."

He spoke, and withdrew his bronze spear from the riverbank,   200
but left the man there, since he had stripped the dear life from him,
lying in the sands, the dark water soaking him.
Eels and fish attended to him,
feeding on his fat, nibbling at his kidneys;
then Achilles set out after the Paeonians, marshallers of the chariots,
who fled in terrified confusion still towards the swirling river,
when they saw their best man in the powerful combat
broken under the hands of the son of Peleus and by the strength of his
    sword.
There Achilles slew Thersilochos and Mydon and Astypylos and
Mnesos and Thrasios and Ainios and Ophelestes.   210

       And now swift Achilles would have killed yet more Paeonians,
had the deep-swirling river not addressed him in anger,
likening himself to a man, and shouted from the depths of his eddies:
"O Achilles, you are mighty beyond all men, and beyond all men you
perform outrageous deeds; for the gods themselves defend you always.
If the son of Cronus grants you to destroy every Trojan,
drive them away from me and commit your evil deeds upon the plain.
For my lovely flowing waters are full of corpses,
nor is there any place where I can pour forth my stream into the bright
    salt sea
crammed with corpses; your killing is annihilation.   220
Come and let me alone; I stand aghast, leader of the people."

       Then answering him Achilles of the swift feet spoke:
"As you will, god-cherished Scamander.
But I will not relax my killing of the high-handed Trojans
before driving them to their city and making trial of Hector
to his face, to see whether he will break me, or I him."
So speaking he charged at the Trojans like something more than human.

       And then the deep-eddying river called to Apollo:
"For shame! God of the Silver Bow, child of Zeus, you have not observed
the resolve of the son of Cronus, who many times enjoined you   230

to stand by the Trojans and defend them, until
the setting sun at last declines, and darkens the rich ploughland."

He spoke; and spear-famed Achilles leapt into midstream,
springing from the overhanging bank; and with a seething surge the
    river sped toward him,
and made turbulent all the streaming waters as he churned them and
    shoved aside the many
bodies that were clotted all along his stream, those whom Achilles
    killed;
these he hurled, roaring like a bull, from his banks
onto dry land; but the living he saved along his lovely flowing waters,
sheltering them in his great deep eddies.
And about Achilles rose a churning, dreadful wave;   240
its falling torrent drove against his shield; nor was he able to stand
with his feet, but with his hand he grabbed a mighty strong-grown
elm; and it, uprooted, falling,
tore the whole of the steep bank away, and checked the lovely flowing
    waters
with its close-set branches, and dammed the river itself
as it fell at full length. Springing out of the whirling water Achilles
made a dash to fly across the plain in the swiftness of his feet,
terrified; but the great god did not leave off, and reared against him
with a darkening crest, to stop Achilles the godlike
from his slaughter, and keep destruction from the Trojans.   250
The son of Peleus sprang as far as a spear is thrown,
with the rushing speed of a dark eagle, the hunter,
strongest and swiftest of all things on wings.
Like such he flashed, and on his chest the clash of bronze
was terrible to hear; and swerving out from under the water,
he fled, and behind him the river, racing, followed with a mighty roar.
As when a man who makes a ditch guides from a dark water spring
the water's flowing among his plants and gardens,
mattock in hand, striking the dams from the channel;

and all the small stones are dislodged beneath its flowing,   260
and falling on some sloping place it swiftly
comes gurgling forth, and then outstrips even him who guides it;
so the swell of water flowing always caught Achilles,
for all his swiftness; for gods are stronger than men.
And as many times as swift-footed godlike Achilles moved to
take a stand against it, and to determine if all the
immortal gods were driving him to flight, all who hold wide heaven,
as many times did the great wave of the rain-filled river
keep striking his shoulders down from above. He kept leaping, his feet
    high,
his heart harried with fatigue; but the torrential river overwhelmed his
    knees' strength   270
as it poured under, eating away the earth beneath his feet.

        And the son of Peleus wailed aloud, looking to broad heaven:
"Zeus, father, so not one of the gods undertook to save me, who am
    pitiable,
from the river—were I to be saved, I would suffer anything.
None of the heavenly gods is so to blame
as my own mother, who charmed me with false words;
for she told me that below the armoured Trojans' battlement
I would be destroyed by the swift arrows of Apollo.
Would that Hector had killed me, who is the best of warriors bred here;
then would a brave man have been the slayer, and brave the man he
    would have slain;   280
but now it is my fate to be taken by a mean death,
trapped in a big river, like a swineherd boy,
whom a gully sweeps away as he crosses in bad weather."

        So he spoke; and in a flash Poseidon and Athena went to him
and stood beside him, assuming the forms of men.
Taking his hand in their hands, they assured him with their words;
and Poseidon who shakes the earth was first of them to speak:
"Son of Peleus, do not shrink back, nor be alarmed;

such allies are we two gods who stand by you
with Zeus approving, I and Pallas Athena.   290
Since you are not destined to be killed by a river,
he will soon give way—you yourself will see this.
But we have close advice for you, if you will heed it;
do not rest your hands from war that levels all alike,
until you have penned within Ilion's famed walls the Trojan men,
those who should escape you. And after you have stripped the life from
    Hector,
return to your ships; we grant you to win glory."

        So speaking they both departed to the immortals;
then Achilles set out, for the injunction of the gods had stirred him
    greatly,
towards the plain. And the whole of it was filled with outpoured
    water,   300
and much splendid armour of sturdy young men killed in battle
was floating, and their corpses; and he sprang his knees high
as he rushed straight on against the current, nor did the broad-flowing
river check him; for Athena cast in him great strength.
But neither did Scamander restrain his fury, but all the more
raged against the son of Peleus, and rising high
he reared the crested wave of his flowing waters. And shouting he called
    to the Simoeis river:
"Dear brother, let us both together contain the strength of this man,
since he will soon sack the great city of lord Priam;
the Trojans will not stand firm throughout the press of battle.   310
Come, defend them with all speed, and fill the currents
of your water from the springs, and stir all the torrents in the gullies,
raise a great wave, stir a tumult
of timbers and stones, so that we stop this savage man,
who now is powerful and as determined as a god.
For I think his strength will not help him, nor at all his beauty,
nor that fine armour, which somewhere at the very bottom

of the flood will lie buried beneath the mud; and his own body
I will wrap around with sand, spreading more silted rubble than can be
    counted,
rubble in abundance, nor will the Achaeans know how to pick out   320
his bones; so much silt I will cover over him.
His grave-mound will have been built; he will have no need
of mound building, when the Achaeans perform his funeral rites."

        He spoke, and rushed upon Achilles, seething, racing to a height,
boiling with foam and blood and corpses,
and a surging wave of the rain-filled river
stood upraised; and began to overpower the son of Peleus.
But Hera shouted loud in great fear for Achilles,
lest the huge deep-swirling river sweep him away,
and called at once upon Hephaestus, her own son: 330
"Rise up, Crippled One, my child; against you,
we thought, swirling Xanthos was matched in battle.
Come, rescue Achilles quickly, conjure a great fire,
and I will press the West Wind Zephyr and Notos, wind of the south,
    who clears the bright sky of clouds,
to raise a violent whirlwind from the sea,
which will burn away the Trojan armaments and bodies,
as it spreads your deadly flame. Burn the trees along the banks of
Xanthos, set him on fire; do not let him by any means turn you back
with placating words or threats.
Do not stop your fury, until such time when   340
I shout out to you; then contain your weariless fire."

        So she spoke and Hephaestus made ready his divinely kindled fire.
First the fire blazed upon the plain, and consumed the dead
in their multitude, who lay in throngs all along it, those whom Achilles
    killed.
The whole plain dried out, and the bright water was contained;
as when a late summer wind from the north quickly dries
a new-flooded field, and delights him who must till it,

so the entire plain was made dry; and then Hephaestus
consumed the dead. Thence he turned his gleaming fire towards the river;
the elms were set alight and the willows and tamarisk trees,   350
the clover was burned and the rushes and the galingale,
which all around the lovely flowing waters of the river grew in
    abundance.
The eels and the fish below the whirling water were thrown into distress;
across the lovely flowing waters they tumbled here and there,
in their distress under the blasting breath of many-skilled Hephaestus.
The river's strength was burned away, and he spoke out and called the
    god by name:
"Hephaestus, none of the gods can set himself against you,
I cannot do battle with you, when you so blaze with fire.
Give over this strife, let godlike Achilles forthwith
drive the Trojans from their city; what have I to do with their war and
    helping them?"   360
        He spoke, burning with fire, seething all along his lovely waters.
As when a pot boils when set into a great fire,
melting down lard of a pig made plump with good feeding,
which bubbles up from every quarter when dry wood lies beneath it,
so the river's lovely streams were ablaze, and his water boiled,
nor had he will to flow on, but stopped his course; for the fiery breath
of skilled Hephaestus reduced him to extremity with its force. And
    imploring
urgently, he addressed Hera with winged words:
"Hera, why has your son attacked my streams to harry me
beyond all others? It is not I who am so much to blame   370
as all of them who are allies of the Trojans.
Come, surely I will make an end, if you bid me,
but let him stop too. And I will swear an oath to this—
never to fend off the day of evil from the Trojans,
not when all of Troy with raging fire is burning,
set ablaze, and the warrior sons of the Achaeans set it blazing."

And when the white-armed goddess Hera heard him,
she called at once to Hephaestus her dear son:
"Hephaestus, hold back, my splendid child, it is not seemly
to pummel an immortal god like this for the sake of mortals."　　　380
So she spoke; and Hephaestus quenched his divinely kindled fire,
and backwards flowed the wave down along its lovely running stream.

　　　　　And when the fury of Xanthos had been subdued, then the
two gods desisted; for Hera checked them, angry though she was;
but among the other gods hard and grievous conflict
fell, and the passions in their breasts blew in two directions.
They rushed together with a great crash and the wide earth rang,
and mighty heaven trumpeted around them; Zeus heard
as he sat upon Olympus, and his heart laughed
in sheer delight, as he saw the gods coming together in conflict.　　　390

　　　　　For no long time they stood apart; then shield-piercing Ares
led off, and first made for Athena,
bronze-pointed spear in hand, and spoke words of derision:
"Why again, you dog-fly, do you pit the gods together in strife
in your insatiate arrogance, your mighty passion setting you on?
Or do you not recollect, when you incited Diomedes son of Tydeus
to stab me, you yourself, in full view, snatching his spear
to charge straight for me, and tore through my splendid skin?
For this, I think, I will pay you back in turn, such things you have done
　　to me."

　　　　　So speaking he stabbed at her tasselled aegis,　　　400
a thing of dread, that not even Zeus' thunderbolt could rend;
murderous Ares stabbed her here with his long spear.
But drawing back, she seized a stone in her massive hand
that lay in the plain, dark and jagged and huge,
which men in time before placed to be a boundary marker of their field.
With this she struck furious Ares on his neck, and unstrung his knees.
Over seven acres he sprawled as he fell, his hair was fouled with dust,
and his armour clanged around him. Pallas Athena laughed,

and vaunting over him spoke winged words:

"Idiot, you did not take into your head, even now, how much greater   410
I claim to be, when you matched your strength with me.

So would you satisfy in full the curses of your mother

Hera, who in her rage plots evil things against you, because you
    abandoned

the Achaeans, and defend the reckless Trojans."

        So speaking she turned her shining eyes away.

And Aphrodite, daughter of Zeus, taking Ares' hand, led him off

as he groaned the while, trying to collect himself with difficulty.

And as the white-armed goddess Hera saw her,

she addressed at once winged words to Athena:

"Oh for shame, daughter of Zeus who wields the aegis, Atrytone,   420

there she is again, that dog-fly leads man-destroying Ares

from the deadly combat through the press of battle; up, go after her."

So she spoke; and Athena set off after her, glad at heart,

and speeding to her, struck Aphrodite on the breast with her powerful
    hand;

and on the spot unstrung her knees and very heart.

And vaunting over the two of them as they lay upon the nourishing earth,

Athena spoke winged words:

"May all be of such stuff as this who aid the Trojans,

when they go to battle with the armoured Argives—

as bold and daring as Aphrodite   430

came as helpmate to Ares, to encounter my might;

then would we long ago have done with war,

having sacked utterly the well-built city of Ilion."   433

        At that the lord Earth-Shaker addressed Apollo: 435

"Phoebus, why do we two stand apart? It is not right

when the others have begun; it would be shameful if without a fight

we should return to the bronze-floored house of Zeus upon Olympus.

Begin! For you are the younger in age; for me it would not do so well,

since I was born first and know more.   440

Young fool, how thoughtless your heart is; do you not recall at all   440
the ills we suffered in such number around Ilion,
we two alone of all the gods, when to bold Laomedon
we came from Zeus to serve as labourers for a year
for a stated wage, and overseeing our work he gave the orders?
And I built a wall around the city for the Trojans
a wide wall and of exceeding beauty, so that the city would be defended;
Phoebos, you were cowherd for their shambling, twist-horned cattle
in the foothills of many-folded, wooded Ida.
But when the gladdening seasons brought the due time of our payment,   450
then Laomedon in his violence robbed us both of all our wages,
and after threatening sent us on our way;
and he threatened that he would bind us hand and foot,
and sell us across the sea to far-off islands,
and he boasted that with his sword he would slice the ears off both of us;
and we two went back again with rancour in our hearts,
angered about our wages, which after promising he did not deliver.
And now you curry favour for the people of this man, nor try with us
to ensure the reckless Trojans be destroyed
utterly and shamefully, with their offspring and their honoured wives!"   460

          Then in turn lord Apollo who shoots from afar addressed him:
"Earth-Shaker, you would not say that I was sound in mind
if I were to go to war with you for the sake of pitiful
mortals, who now come into being like leaves
full of the flame of life, eating the fruit of their fields,
and then fade away without life. Come, with all speed
let us make an end of fighting, let them struggle on by themselves."
So speaking he turned back; for he forbore in shame
to fight hand to hand with the brother of his father.

          But his sister rebuked him greatly, the lady of wild creatures,   470
Artemis of the wild, and spoke words of revilement:
"So you flee, Far-Shooter? After yielding all victory to Poseidon,
making idle boast to him?

You fool, why do you vainly carry your useless bow?
Let me never now hear you in our father's halls
bragging, as you have done before in company of the immortal gods,
that you would go to war face to face against Poseidon."

So she spoke; Apollo who shoots from afar said nothing to her,
but the revered wife of Zeus spoke in anger: 479
"How now do you presume, shameless dog, to stand up against me?   481
I am dangerous to oppose, when it comes to might,
archer though you be, since Zeus made you a lion among only women,
and granted you to kill which of these you like.
But better that you kill wild beasts along the mountains,
and deer of the wild than contend in strength with those more powerful!
But if you wish to learn of warfare, so as to know well
how much greater I am, when you contend with me in strength—"
She spoke, and grabbed the other's hands at the wrist
with her left hand, and with her right she snatched the bow and quiver
    from her shoulders,   490
and, with a smile, struck Artemis on the ears with her own weapons
as she turned and twisted; and her swift arrows fell from her quiver.
Weeping, the goddess fled under and away like a wild dove,
which away from a hawk flies into the hollow cleft of a rocky cliff;
for it was not its fate to be seized;
so Artemis fled in tears, and there left her bow and archery.

Then Hermes the messenger, Slayer of Argos, addressed Leto:
"Leto, I will have no fight with you; for it is hard
to bandy blows with the wives of Zeus who gathers the clouds.
Rather boldly boast among the immortal gods   500
that you vanquished me with your powerful force."
So he spoke; and Leto gathered up Artemis' arrows and curved bow
scattered hither and there amid the whirling dust.
Taking the weapons she went back after her daughter,
who had arrived at the bronze-floored house of Zeus upon Olympus;
the girl was sitting in tears on her father's knees,

her ambrosial robes quivering around her. And her father, the son of
  Cronus,
took her to him, and lifted her, laughing softly:
"Now which of the heavenly gods did such a thing to you, dear child?"
Then in turn the fair-crowned lady of the hunting cry addressed him: 510
"Your wife beat me, father, white-armed Hera,
on whose account strife and fighting is the lot of the immortals."

      So they were speaking such things to one another;
but Phoebus Apollo made his way into holy Ilion,
troubled for the walls of the well-built city,
lest the Danaans sack it on that day, against fate.
The rest of the immortal gods went to Olympus,
some in anger, some in great triumph,
and took their seats beside the father of the dark clouds. But Achilles 520
kept on slaying alike the Trojans and their single-hoofed horses;
as when smoke reaches into the broad heaven arising
from a city that is in flames, and the wrath of the gods impels it,
and lays toil upon all, and sends suffering to many,
so Achilles laid toil and suffering upon the Trojans.

      And standing on the ramparts built by god was aged Priam;
and he looked out to huge Achilles, and the Trojans
roiled in panic-stricken flight before him, nor was there any fighting
  spirit
to be seen; and groaning he descended from the rampart to the ground,
urging the worthy keepers of the gates beside the wall: 530
"Hold the gates wide open in your hands, until my people
come to the city in their flight; for here is Achilles
very near, roiling them in fear; now I think there will be disaster.
But once they have thronged inside the walls to catch their breath,
immediately shut again the closely fitted gates;
for I fear lest this baneful man should leap into our battlements."
So he spoke; and they drove back the bolts and opened the gates,
which spread wide to be the light of safety. Apollo

sprang towards them, to ward off disaster from the Trojans.
And straight for the city and its high ramparts they fled,   540
their throats rough with thirst, covered with dust from the plain;
and Achilles, pressing hard, hung upon them with his spear, a great
    mad fury
ever gripping at his heart, as he raged to seize glory.
        Then the sons of the Achaeans would have taken high-gated
    Troy,
had Phoebus Apollo not stirred on godlike Agenor,
Antenor's son, a blameless and a powerful man.
Into his heart Apollo cast courage, and stood
near him to ward off the heavy hands of Death,
leaning against an oak tree, shrouded in dense mist.
And when Agenor saw Achilles, the sacker of cities,   550
he stood firm, but his heart pitched violently as he waited.
And troubled he spoke to his own great-hearted spirit:
"Ah me; if I should flee before powerful Achilles
to where the others in their fear have fled in panic,
he will take me all the same, and cut my coward's throat.
But suppose I let the others be driven in confusion before
Achilles, the son of Peleus, and with speed of my feet flee elsewhere,
    away from the wall
toward the plain of Ilion, until I reach
the foothills of Ida and make my way into the brush—
then at evening, having washed clean in the river,   560
having dried the sweat away, I could go home to Ilion.
But why does my heart debate these things?
He might mark me as I set off from the city to the plain,
and racing after catch me with the swiftness of his feet.
No longer then will it be possible to shun death and fate.
For he is strong beyond the measure of all men.
But what if, before the city, I came face to face against him—
for surely the flesh of even this man can be wounded by sharp bronze,

only one life is in him, and men say his is mortal!
It is Zeus the son of Cronus who hands him glory."   570

   So speaking, he collected himself to await Achilles, and the
 brave
heart in him was urgent to fight and go to battle.
As when a leopard steps into view out of her deep thicket
to face the man who hunts her, and in her heart
she feels neither dread nor fear, when she hears the howling of the dogs—
even if the hunter strikes or wounds her first,
even so, even pierced through by the spear, she does not relinquish
her fighting courage, until she either pits herself against him or is killed;
so the son of noble Antenor, godlike Agenor,
had no mind to flee, until he had made trial of Achilles.   580
But he held the circle of his shield before him,
and aimed at Achilles with his spear, and shouted loud:
"Surely you greatly hoped within your heart, illustrious Achilles,
on this day to sack the city of the noble Trojans—
fool; many hardships yet lie ahead on her account!
For inside we are many men and brave men,
and before our beloved parents, our wives and sons,
we will protect Ilion; you, in this place, will meet your fate,
terrible and daring warrior though you be."

   He spoke, and hurled the sharp spear from his mighty hand,   590
and it struck Achilles' leg below his knee, nor did he miss his aim;
But the greaves of new-wrought tin around it
rang with a dreadful sound; and back the bronze point sprang from
striking him, nor did it penetrate, but the gifts of the god protected him.
And the son of Peleus charged next at godlike Agenor;
but Apollo did not permit him to win glory,
and snatched Agenor away, and concealed him in dense mist,
and sent him forth from the war, to go home in peace.
Then with a trick he kept the son of Peleus from the Trojan people;

for likening himself in every way to Agenor, the Far-Shooting god   600
stood before Achilles' feet, and Achilles charged forth to pursue him in
   the swiftness of his feet.
And all the while Achilles chased him over the wheat-bearing plain,
turning beside the deep-eddying river Scamander,
Apollo always just a little out of reach—with trickery Apollo deceived him,
so that Achilles hoped always to overtake him with his speed of feet—
meanwhile the rest of the Trojans fleeing in a body came
gladly welcomed to their city; and the city was filled with their crowding,
nor did they dare any longer to await one another outside the city
and its walls to learn who might have escaped,
who died in the fighting, but in rushing haste they poured   610
into the city, every man whose feet and knees could save him.

So those who had fled terrorised like fawns into the city
dried off their sweat and drank and slaked their thirst,
slumped on the splendid ramparts. The Achaeans, however,
drew near the walls with shields inclined against their shoulders;
and there ruinous fate bound Hector to stand his ground,
before the Scaean gates of Ilion.
        Now Phoebus Apollo hailed Peleion:
"Why, son of Peleus, do you chase me, with those swift feet,
you a mortal, I an undying god? You must not yet know
that I am divine, you rage after me so furiously!   10
Is it of no concern, this business with the Trojans, whom you scattered in
    fear—
who are by now cowering in the city, while you slope off here?
You will never kill me; I am not marked by fate."
Then greatly stirred, swift-footed Achilles answered him:
"You have thwarted me, most malevolent of all the gods, you who strike
    from afar,
turning me here away from the city walls; otherwise many would
have bitten the dirt before they arrived at Ilion.
Saving them, you have robbed me of great glory,
lightly, without fear of retribution;
I would pay you back, if that power were in me."   20
So speaking, he made toward the city, intent on great things,
straining like a prizewinning horse who with his chariot

runs effortlessly, stretching over the plain—
so swiftly did Achilles move his feet and knees.

And old Priam first beheld him with his eyes
as, shining like a star, Achilles streaked across the plain,
the star that comes at summer's end, its clear gleaming
in the milky murk of night displayed among the multitude of stars—
the star they give the name Orion's Dog;
most radiant it is, but it makes an evil portent,   30
and brings great feverish heat on pitiful mortal men—
just so did his bronze breastplate shine about Achilles running.
The old man cried out and hammered his head with his hands,
lifting them on high; crying mightily he called,
imploring his beloved son; for before the gates Hector
continued to stand firm, intent on combat with Achilles.
To him the old man called piteously, reaching out his hands:
"Hector, for my sake, do not wait for this man
on your own, without allies, lest you straightway meet your fate,
broken by Peleion; since he is so much stronger,   40
he is pitiless; would that he were as dear to the gods
as he is to me—in short order would the dogs and vultures devour him
as he lay dead; and bitter pain would leave my heart.
This is the man who has bereaved me of many sons, brave sons,
killing them, or selling them to far-off islands.
Even now there are two, Lykaon and Polydoros,
whom I cannot see in the city of the cowering Trojans,
sons whom Altes' daughter Laothoë bore me, a queen among women.
If they are alive somewhere among the army, then
I will ransom them for bronze or gold; all this is inside—   50
old, illustrious Altes endowed his daughter richly.
But if they have already died and are in the house of Hades,
this is anguish to my heart and to their mother, we who bore them;
but to the rest of the people, it will be anguish shorter lived
than if you also should die, broken by Achilles.

Come inside the walls, my child, that you may save the
Trojan men and Trojan women, do not make a gift of glory to
the son of Peleus, who will rob you of your very life.
And on me—wretched, still feeling—have pity,
born to ill fate, whom on the threshold of old age father Zeus, son of
    Cronus,   60
will blight with my hard fate, when I have seen
the destruction of my sons, the abduction of my daughters,
my chambers ravaged, and innocent children
hurled to the ground in the terror of battle;
my daughters-in-law abducted by the wicked hands of Achaean men,
and me myself, last of all, at my very gates, my dogs
will rip raw, when some man with sharp bronze,
stabbing or casting, will strip the spirit from my limbs—
the dogs I raised in my halls and fed at my table as guardians of my gates,
these, maddened by the drinking of my blood,   70
will sprawl in my doorway. All is seemly for the young man
slain in war, torn by sharp bronze,
laid out dead; everything is honourable to him in death, whatever shows.
But when the dogs defile the white head and white beard
and the private parts of a dead old man—
this is most pitiable for wretched mortals."
So the old man spoke, and pulled his white hair with his hands,
tearing it from his head. But he did not persuade the heart of Hector.

      Now in turn his mother wailed, raining tears,
and loosening her robe, with a hand she exposed her breast   80
and raining tears addressed him with winged words:
"Hector, my child, be moved by this and have pity on me,
if ever I used to give you my breast to soothe you—
remember those times, dear child, defend yourself against this deadly man
from inside the walls; don't stand as champion against him,
my stubborn one. If he cuts you down, I will surely never
mourn you on your deathbed, dear budding branch, whom I bore,

nor will your worthy wife. But a long way from us
by the ships of the Achaeans the running dogs will eat you."

       Thus both of them weeping addressed their dear son,   90
repeatedly beseeching. But they did not persuade the heart of Hector,
and he awaited Achilles, who was looming huge as he drew near.
As a snake by its hole in the mountains waits for a man,
having eaten evil poisons, and a deadly anger comes upon it,
and it shoots a stinging glance, coiled by its hole,
so Hector keeping his spirit unquelled did not retreat,
but having leaned his shining shield against the jutting tower,
in agitation, he spoke to his great-hearted spirit:
"Oh me, if I enter the gates and walls
Poulydamas will be the first to reproach me,   100
who bade me lead the Trojans to the city
that baneful night when Achilles the godlike rose,
but I was not persuaded. It would have been far better if I had.
Now since I have destroyed my people by my recklessness,
I dread the Trojan men and the Trojan women with their trailing robes,
lest some other man more worthless than me say:
'Hector, trusting in his strength, destroyed his people'—
thus they will speak. It would be far better, then, for me
to confront Achilles, either to kill him and return home,
or to die with honour at his hands, before my city.   110
But what if I put aside my studded shield
and my strong helmet, leaned my spear against the walls,
and going out alone approached noble Achilles,
and pledged to him Helen and the possessions with her?
All those things—as much as Alexandros carried away to Troy
in his hollow ships, which was the beginning of our quarrel—
to give to the sons of Atreus to lead away; and in addition
to divide everything else with the Achaeans, whatever this city holds,
and after that to make a formal oath with the Trojan council
not to hide anything, but to divide it all, equally—   120

but why does my heart debate these things?   122
I could set forth to meet him and he not pity me,
nor even respect me, but kill me naked as I was,
as if I were a woman, since I would have put off my armour.
It is not now possible from rock or oak, in the country way,
to chatter to him those things that a girl and youth
chatter to each other, a girl and youth—
no, it is better to engage with him straightway;
we shall see to whom the Olympians give glory."   130

   Thus his thoughts churned as he waited, and Achilles drew near,
equal to the war god, the helmet-shaking warrior,
brandishing his Pelian ash-wood spear above his right shoulder,
terrifying. The bronze glinted around him like the flare
of blazing fire or the sun rising.
And as he watched him, trembling took hold of Hector; and he could no
 longer endure
there to stand his ground, but left the gates behind and, terrified, he ran.
The son of Peleus charged for him, trusting in the swiftness of his feet;
as a mountain hawk, lightest of all things on wings,
easily swoops after a terror-stricken dove,   140
which, away from under, flees, but crying sharply near
he swoops continuously and his spirit drives him to take her;
so Achilles flew straight for him, ravenous, and Hector fled
under the walls of Troy, working his swift knees.

   By the watch place and the wild fig tree twisted by wind,
always away from the walls, along the wagon path they ran
and reached the two fair-flowing streams, where the two springs
gush forth from the whirling waters of Scamander.
One flows with warm water, enveloping steam
rises from it as if from a burning fire.   150
The other even in summer runs as cold as hail,
or snow water, or ice that forms from water.
Near to these there are the broad washing hollows

of fine stone, where their lustrous clothes
the Trojan wives and their beautiful daughters washed,
in those days before, in peacetime, before there came the sons of the
      Achaeans.
By this place they ran, one fleeing, the other behind pursuing;
outstanding was he who fled ahead—but far better he who pursued him
swiftly; since it was not for a sacral animal, nor for an oxhide
they contended, prizes in the races of men—   160
but they ran for the life of Hector breaker of horses.

            As when prizewinning single-hoofed horses
tear around the turning post—a great prize awaits,
a tripod, or woman, in those games held when a man has died—
so three times around the city of Priam they whirled
in the swiftness of their feet, and all the gods looked on.
To them the father of men and gods spoke the first word:
"Alas; it is a dear man whom my eyes see
pursued around the wall; my heart grieves
for Hector, who has burned many thigh cuts of sacral oxen to me,   170
both on the summit of Ida of the many glens, and at other times
on the heights of his citadel. But now godlike Achilles
pursues him in the swiftness of his feet around the city of Priam.
But come, you gods, consider and take counsel
whether we shall save him from death, or
noble though he is, break him at the hands of Achilles son of Peleus."

            Then the gleaming-eyed goddess Athena answered him:
"O father of the bright thunderbolt and black clouds, what have you said?
This man who is mortal, consigned long ago to fate—
you want to take him back and free him from the harsh sorrow of
      death?   180
Do so; but not all the other gods will approve."
In answer, Zeus who gathers the clouds addressed her:
"Take heart, Tritogeneia, dear child. I did not now
speak in earnest, and I mean to be kind to you.

Act in whatever way your mind inclines, nor hold back any longer."
So speaking, he urged Athena, who had been eager even before;
and she went, slipping down from the peaks of Olympus.

      Relentlessly, swift Achilles kept driving Hector panicked before
    him,
as when a dog in the mountains pursues a deer's fawn
that he has started from its bed through glens and dells;   190
and though, cowering in fright, it eludes him beneath a thicket,
the dog runs on, tracking it steadily, until he finds it—
so Hector could not elude Achilles of the swift feet.
Each time he made to dash toward the Dardanian gates,
under the well-built tower,
in the hope that men from above might defend him with thrown missiles,
each time did Achilles, outstripping him, turn him back
toward the plain, and he himself sped ever by the city.
As in a dream a man is not able to pursue one who eludes him,
nor is the other able to escape, nor he to pursue,   200
so Achilles for all the swiftness of his feet was not able to lay hold of
    Hector, nor Hector to escape.
How then could Hector have eluded his fated death
had not Apollo for that last and final time joined closely with him
to rouse his spirit and make swift his knees?
And shining Achilles was shaking his head at his men,
nor allowed them to let their sharp spears fly at Hector,
lest whoever making the throw claim glory, and himself come second.

      But when for the fourth time they came to the springs,
then Zeus the father levelled his golden scales,
and placed in them two portions of death that brings enduring grief,   210
that of Achilles and that of Hector breaker of horses;
he lifted them, holding by the middle; and the measured day of Hector
    sank,
headed to Hades, and Phoebus Apollo abandoned him.

      Then the gleaming-eyed goddess Athena came up to the son of

Peleus
and standing near addressed him with winged words:
"Now I hope, illustrious Achilles, beloved of Zeus,
to carry honour for us two back to the Achaean ships,
after breaking Hector, insatiate though he may be for battle;
he can no longer get clear of us,
not if Apollo the Far-Shooter should suffer countless trials for
    his sake,   220
grovelling before Father Zeus who wields the aegis.
But you now stop and catch your breath, while I
make my way to Hector and convince him to fight man to man."
Thus spoke Athena, and Achilles obeyed and rejoiced in his heart,
and stood leaning on his bronze-flanged ash-spear.

        She left him and came up to shining Hector
in the likeness of Deïphobos, in form and steady voice.
Standing close, she spoke winged words:
"My brother, swift Achilles presses you hard,
pursuing you around the city of Priam in the swiftness of his feet.   230
Come; let us take our stand and standing firm defend ourselves."

        Then great Hector of the shimmering helm addressed her in
    turn:
"Deïphobos, even before you were far dearest to me
of my brothers, those sons whom Hecuba and Priam bore.
Now I am minded to honour you even more in my heart—
you who dared for my sake, when you saw me with your eyes,
to quit the walls where the others remain inside."

        Then the gleaming-eyed goddess Athena spoke to him:
"My brother, our father and lady mother implored me greatly,
entreating in turn, and the companions about them,   240
to remain there—for so great is the dread of all;
but my inner spirit was harrowed with impotent grief.
But now let us two press straight forwards and go to battle,
and let there be no restraint of our spears, so that we shall see if Achilles,

killing us both, will bear our bloodied arms
to his hollow ships, or if he will be broken by your spear."
Thus spoke Athena and with cunning led him on.

And when they had advanced almost upon each other,
great Hector of the shimmering helm spoke first:
"No longer, son of Peleus, shall I flee from you, as before   250
I fled three times around the great city of Priam, nor could then endure
to withstand your charge. But now my spirit stirs me
to hold firm before you. I will kill you, or be killed.
But come, let us take an oath upon our gods, for they
will be the best witnesses and protectors of agreements.
I will not, outrageous though you are, dishonour you if Zeus grants me
to endurance, and I take your life.
But when I have stripped you of your splendid armour, Achilles,
I will give your body back to the Achaeans; and do you the same."

Then looking at him from beneath his brows, Achilles of the
swift feet spoke: 260
"Hector, doer of unforgettable deeds—do not to me propose your
agreements.
As there are no pacts of faith between lions and men,
nor do wolves and lambs have spirit in kind,
but they plot evil unremittingly for one another,
so it is not possible that you and I be friends, nor for us two
will there be oaths; before that time one of us falling
will sate with his blood the shield-bearing warrior god.
Recollect your every skill. Now the need is very great
to be a spearman and brave warrior.
There will be no further escape for you, but soon Pallas Athena   270
will break you by my spear. Now you will pay in one sum
for all the sorrows of my companions, those whom you killed, raging
with your spear."

He spoke, and balancing his long-shadowed spear, he let it fly.
But, holding it in his sight as it came at him, shining Hector avoided it,

for as he watched, he crouched, and the bronze spear flew over
and stuck in the earth; but Pallas Athena snatched it up
and gave it back to Achilles, escaping the notice of Hector, shepherd of
   the people.
And Hector addressed the noble son of Peleus::
"You missed! It was not, then, godlike Achilles,
from Zeus you knew my fate—you only thought you did;   280
and you turn out to be a glib talker, cunning with words—
fearing you, you thought I would forget my strength and valour—
but you will not fix your spear in my back as I flee,
but drive it through my breast as I come at you,
if a god grants this. Now in your turn dodge my spear,
bronze-pointed; would that you carried the whole of it in your flesh.
Then would this war be the lighter to bear for the Trojans,
with you dead. For you are their greatest evil."

     He spoke, and balancing his long-shadowing spear, he let it fly
and hurled at the middle of the son of Peleus' shield, nor did he miss;   290
but the spear glanced off the shield, for a long way. And Hector was angry
that his swift cast flew from his hand in vain,
and he stood dejected, nor did he have any other ash-shafted spear.
Raising his great voice he called Deïphobos of the pale shield
and asked for his long spear—but Deïphobos was not near him.

     And Hector understood within his heart and spoke aloud:
"This is it. The gods summon me deathward.
I thought the warrior Deïphobos was by me,
but he is inside the walls and Athena has tricked me.
Hateful death is very near me; it is no longer far away,   300
nor is there escape. And for some long time this has been pleasing
to Zeus and to Zeus' son who shoots from afar, who before this
protected me willingly enough. Yet now destiny has caught me.
Let me not die without a struggle and ingloriously,
but while doing some great thing for even men to come to hear of."

     So speaking he drew his sharp sword

that hung down by his side, huge and strong-made,
and collecting himself he swooped like a high-flying eagle,
an eagle that plunges through lowering clouds toward the plain
to snatch a soft lamb or a cowering hare;   310
so Hector swooped brandishing his sharp sword.
But Achilles charged, his spirit filled with
savage passion. Before his breast he held his covering shield,
beautiful and intricately wrought, and nodded with his shining
four-ridged helmet; splendid horsehair flowed about it,
of gold, which Hephaestus had set thickly around the helmet crest.
As a star moves among other stars in the milky murk of night,
Hesperus the Evening Star, the most beautiful star to stand in heaven,
so the light shone from the well-pointed spearhead that Achilles
was shaking in his right hand, bent upon evil for Hector,   320
surveying his handsome flesh, where it might best give way.
The rest of his body was held by brazen armour,
the splendid armour he stripped after slaying strong Patroclus—
but at that point where the collarbone holds the neck from the shoulders
    there showed
his gullet, where death of the soul comes swiftest;
and at this point, shining Achilles drove with his spear as Hector strove
    against him,
and the spearhead went utterly through the soft neck.
Heavy with bronze though was, the ash-spear did not sever the windpipe
so that he could speak, making an exchange of words.
He fell in the dust. And shining Achilles vaunted: 330
"Hector, you surely thought when you stripped Patroclus
that you were safe, and you thought nothing of me as I was absent—
pitiable fool. For standing by, his far greater avenger,
I remained behind by the hollow ships—
I who have broken the strength of your knees. You the dogs and birds
will rip apart shamefully; Patroclus the Achaeans will honour with
    funeral rites."

Then with little strength Hector of the shimmering helm
    addressed him:
"By your soul, by your knees, by your parents,
do not let the dogs devour me by the ships of the Achaeans,
but take the bronze and abundance of gold,   340
the gifts my father and lady mother will give you;
give my body back to go home, so that
the Trojans and the Trojan wives will give my dead body its portion of
    the fire."
        Then looking at him from under his brows Achilles of the swift
    feet answered:
"Do not, you dog, supplicate me by knees or parents.
Would that my passion and spirit would drive me
to devour your hacked-off flesh raw, such things you have done;
so there is no one who can keep the dogs from your head,
not if they haul here and weigh out ten times and twenty times
the ransom, and promise more,   350
not if Dardanian Priam seeks to pay your weight in gold,
not in any way will your lady mother
mourn you laid out upon your bier, the child she bore;
but the dogs and the birds will devour you wholly."
        Then, dying, Hector of the shimmering helm addressed him:
"Knowing you well, I divine my fate; nor will I persuade you.
Surely, the soul in your breast is iron.
Yet now take care, lest I become the cause of the god's wrath against you,
on that day when Paris and Phoebus Apollo
destroy you, great warrior though you are, at the Scaean gates."   360
Then the closure of death enveloped him as he was speaking
and his soul flying from his limbs started for Hades,
lamenting her fate, abandoning manhood and all its young vigour.
        But shining Achilles addressed him, dead though he was:
"Lie dead. I will take death at that time when
Zeus and the other deathless gods wish to accomplish it."

He spoke and pulled his bronze spear from the dead body
and laying it aside he stripped the bloodied armour from Hector's shoulders.
But the other sons of the Achaeans ran up around him
and admired Hector's physique and beauty,   370
nor was there a man who stood by him without inflicting a wound.
And thus each would speak, looking at his neighbour:
"Well, well; he is softer to handle, to be sure,
this Hector, than when he torched our ships with blazing fire."
Thus they would speak, and stabbed him as they stood by.
      But when shining Achilles of the swift feet had stripped Hector
   of his armour,
he stood amid the Achaeans and pronounced winged words:
"O friends, leaders and counsellors of the Achaeans;
since the gods gave me this man to be broken,
who committed evil deeds, more than all the other Trojans together,   380
come, let us go under arms and scout around the city
so that we may learn the disposition of the Trojans, what they have in
   mind,
whether they will abandon their high city now this man is dead,
or desire to remain, although Hector is no longer with them—
but why does my spirit recite these things?
There lies by the ships a dead man, unmourned, unburied—
Patroclus. I shall not forget him as long as I am
among the living and my own knees have power in them.
And if other men forget the dead in Hades,
I will remember my beloved companion even there.   390
But come now, Achaean men, singing a victory song
let us return to our hollow ships, and bring him along.
We have achieved great glory; we have slain shining Hector,
whom the Trojans worshipped throughout their city as a god."
      He spoke, and conceived a shocking deed for shining Hector;
behind both feet he pierced the tendon
between the heel and ankle and fastened there oxhide straps,

and bound him to his chariot and let the head drag along.
Lifting his glorious armour, Achilles mounted his chariot,
and whipped the horses to begin, and they two, not unwilling,
      took off.   400
A cloud of dust rose as Hector was dragged, his blue-black hair
fanning around him, his head lolling wholly in the dust
that before was handsome; so Zeus gave him to his enemies
to be defiled in the land of his own fathers.

                  His head was wholly befouled by dust; and now his mother
ripped her hair and flung her shining veil
far away, shrieking her grief aloud as she looked on her child.
His beloved father cried out pitiably and around them the people
were gripped by wailing and crying throughout the city—
it was as if the whole of   410
lofty Ilion, from its topmost point, were consumed with fire.
With difficulty the people restrained old Priam in his grief
as he strove to go forth from the Dardanian gates.
Thrashing in the muck, he entreated all,
calling off each man by name:
"Hold off friend, for all your care for me, and let me
leave the city to go to the ships of the Achaeans.
I will entreat this reckless man of violent deeds,
if somehow he may respect my age and pity
my years. Even his father is of such years,   420
Peleus, who bore him and raised him to be the destruction
of the Trojans; and beyond all men he has inflicted hardship on me.
For so many of my flourishing sons he killed,
but for all my grief, I did not mourn as much for all of them
as for this one, bitter grief for whom will carry me down to the house of
      Hades—
Hector. Would that he died in my arms.
We would have glutted ourselves with crying and weeping,

his mother, she, ill-fated woman who bore him, and I."
Thus he spoke lamenting, and thereupon the people mourned.

       And Hecuba led the Trojan women in passionate lament: 430
"My child, I am nothing. Why should I live now, grievously suffering,
when you are dead? You who were night and day
my triumph through the city, a blessing to all,
to the Trojans and the Trojan women throughout the city, who received
    you,
like a god; for to them you were, indeed, their glory,
while you lived; and now death and fate have overtaken you."

       Thus she spoke, crying. But Hector's wife knew nothing.
For no trusty messenger had come to her
announcing that her husband remained outside the walls,
and she was weaving at her loom in the corner of her high-roofed house   440
a crimson cloak of double-thickness, and working intricate figures in it.
She called through the house to her attendants with the lovely hair
to set a great tripod over the fire, so that
there would be a warm bath for Hector, when he returned home from
    battle—
poor wretch, she did not know that far from all baths
gleaming-eyed Athena had broken him at the hands of Achilles.
Then she heard the keening and groaning from the tower
and her limbs shook, and the shuttle fell to the ground,
and she called back to her maids with the beautiful hair:
"Come, both of you follow me; I will see what trouble has happened.   450
I hear the voice of Hector's worthy mother,
the heart in my own breast leaps to my mouth, my limbs beneath me
are rigid; something evil is come near the sons of Priam.
May this word not come to my hearing; but terribly
I fear that shining Achilles has cut my bold Hector
from the city on his own, and driving him toward the plain
has stopped him of that fateful ardour

that possessed him, since he never remained in the ranks of men,
but rushed far to the front, yielding in his courage to no one."
So speaking she raced through the hall like a madwoman,   460
her heart shaking; and her two maids ran with her.
But when she reached the tower and the crowd of men,
she stood on the wall, staring around her; and saw him
dragged before the city. Swift horses
dragged him, unconcernedly, to the hollow ships of the Achaeans.
Dark night descended over her eyes,
she fell backwards and breathed out her soul;
far from her head she flung her shining headdress,
the diadem and cap and the braided binding,
and the veil, which golden Aphrodite gave her   470
on that day when Hector of the shimmering helm led her
out of the house of Eëtion, when he gave countless gifts for her dowry.
In a throng around her stood her husband's sisters and his brothers' wives,
who supported her among themselves, as she was stricken to the point of
    death.
        But when then she regained her breath and the strength in her
    breast was collected,
with gulping sobs she spoke with the Trojan women:
"Hector, I am unlucky. For we were both born to one fate,
you in Troy, in the house of Priam,
and I in Thebes, under forested Plakos,
in the house of Eëtion, who reared me when I was still young,   480
ill-fated he, I of bitter fate. I wish that he had not begotten me.
Now you go to the house of Hades in the depths of the earth,
leaving me in shuddering grief,
a widow in your house. The child is still only a baby,
whom we bore, you and I, both ill-fated. You will
be, Hector, no help to him, now you have died, nor he to you.
For even if he escapes this war of the Achaeans and all its tears,
there will always be for him pain and care hereafter.

Other men will rob him of his land;

the day of orphaning cuts a child off entirely from those his age;   490

he is bent low in all things, his cheeks are tear-stained.

In his neediness, the child approaches his father's companions,

he tugs one by the cloak, another by his tunic;

pitying him, one of them offers him a little cup

and he moistens his lips, but he does not moisten his palate.

But a child blessed with both parents will beat him away from the feast,

striking him with his hands, reviling him with abuse:

'Get away — your father does not dine with us'—

and crying the boy comes up to his widowed mother—

Astyanax; who before on his father's knees   500

used to eat only marrow and the rich fat of sheep,

then when sleep took him and he left off his childish play,

he would slumber in bed in his nurse's embrace,

in his soft bedding, his heart filled with cheery thoughts.

Now he will suffer many things, missing his dear father—

'Astyanax'—'little lord of the city'—whom the Trojans called by this name,

for you alone, Hector, defended their gates and long walls.

Now beside the curved ships, away from your parents,

the writhing worms devour you when the dogs have had enough

of your naked body; yet there are clothes laid aside in the house,   510

finely woven, beautiful, fashioned by the hands of women.

Now I will burn them all in a blazing fire,

for they are no use to you, you are not wrapped in them—

I will burn them to be an honour to you in the sight of the Trojan men

    and Trojan women."

So she spoke, crying, and the women in response mourned.

So they mourned throughout the city. And the Achaeans
when they reached their ships and the Hellespont,
scattered, each man to his own vessel;
yet Achilles did not let the Myrmidons disperse,
but spoke to his battle-loving companions:
"Myrmidons, you of the swift horses, my trusted comrades,
let us not yet unyoke our single-hoofed horses from their chariots,
but with our horses and their chariots let us draw close
and mourn Patroclus; for this is the honour of the dead.
And when we have taken solace in painful lamentation,   10
we will release the horses and all take our meal here."

      So he spoke; and together the men cried aloud, and Achilles led
  them.
Three times around the corpse they drove their fine-maned horses
weeping; and Thetis stirred among them desire for lamentation.
The sand of the shore, the arms of the men were soaked
with tears; for such was their grief for Patroclus, master of the rout.
And the son of Peleus led their passionate lament,
placing his man-slaughtering hands upon the breast of his companion:
"May it be well with thee, O Patroclus, even in the house of Hades;
I am fulfilling now all I pledged to you before,   20
dragging Hector here to give to the dogs to devour raw,
and before your funeral pyre I will cut the throats of twelve
of Troy's noble sons, in rage for your slaying."

He spoke, and conceived a shocking deed for shining Hector;
stretching him face down beside the bier of Menoetius' son Patroclus
in the dust. And his soldiers to a man took off their armour,
bronze and glittering, and loosed their high-necked horses.
And they sat themselves beside the ship of swift-footed Aeacides
in their great numbers; and to them he gave a funeral feast fit for their
　　desire.
Many sleek cattle stretched their necks across the iron blade,   30
their throats cut, many sheep and bleating goats;
many white-tusked pigs luxuriant with fat
were singed and spread across the fire of Hephaestus;
and everywhere around the corpse blood flowed in cups.

　　　　　And then the Achaean kings conducted him, their lord,
swift-footed Achilles, to the shelter of illustrious Agamemnon,
inducing him with difficulty, angered at heart as he still was for his
　　companion.
And when after setting out they came to Agamemnon's shelter,
they at once commanded the clear-voiced heralds
to set over the fire a great three-legged cauldron, in hope they could
　　persuade   40
the son of Peleus to wash away the bloody gore.
But adamantly he refused, and swore an oath:
"No by Zeus, who is the highest and most powerful god,
it is unseemly that cleansing water come near my head,
until I have placed Patroclus on his pyre and mounded up his grave
and cut my hair, since no second sorrow will come to my heart
like this, so long as I am among the living.
But now let us submit to this hateful feast,
and at dawn, Agamemnon, lord of men, dispatch your people
to bring in timber, and supply however much is fitting   50
that a dead man have when he journeys beneath the misty nether darkness,
so that weariless fire consumes him
all the swifter from our sight, and the men turn to their tasks."

So he spoke; and the men heard him well and obeyed.
With haste they each prepared their meal and
feasted, nor did any man's appetite lack his due portion.
And when they had put away desire for eating and drinking,
they departed to sleep, each to his shelter;
but the son of Peleus lay on the shore of the tumultuous sea,
groaning deeply, with his many Myrmidons,   60
in a clear place, where the waves washed upon the beach.

        And when sleep took hold of him, melting the cares of his heart,
sweet, enveloping sleep—for his shining limbs were exhausted
from hounding Hector to windswept Ilion—
there came to him the shade of poor Patroclus,
like to him in every way, his great stature, his fine eyes,
his voice, even the clothes such as his body wore.
And this stood above Achilles' head and spoke a word to him:
"You sleep, and have no thought of me, Achilles;
you were not careless of me when I lived, only when I died.   70
Bury me quickly, let me pass the gates of Hades;
the shades, the images of the worn-out dead, keep me a long way off,
nor let me mingle with them beyond the river,
and in vain I wander by the wide-gated house of Hades.
And give me too your hand, I beseech you; for never again
will I return from Hades, once you have given me my portion of the fire.
You and I will not in life sit apart from our beloved companions,
and make plans together, but hateful death
gapes round me, allotted to me at my very birth.
And your own fate, Achilles, you who are like the gods,   80
is to be slain beneath the wall of the prosperous Trojans.
And I will say and charge you with another thing, if you will be persuaded;
do not lay my bones apart from yours, Achilles,
but together, even as we were raised in your house,
when Menoetius brought me, when I was little, out of Opoeis
to your home, because of an evil murder,

on the day when I killed the son of Amphidamas—
I was a child, it was not intentional—in anger over a game of knuckle-
    bones.
Then the horseman Peleus received me in his house
and reared me with kindness and named me your companion;   90
so let the same urn enclose the bones of us both,
the golden amphora, which your lady mother gave you."
            And answering him swift-footed Achilles spoke:
"Dear friend, why have you come to me
and laid each of these injunctions on me? For you
I will surely accomplish everything and obey you, as you bid.
But stand near me, even for a little time let us embrace
each other and take solace in painful lamentation."
            So speaking he reached out with his arms,
but did not take hold of him; and the shade departed beneath the earth   100
like smoke, with a shrill cry. And Achilles started up in astonishment
and clapped his hands together, and spoke in lament:
"See now! There is after all even in the house of Hades
some kind of soul and image, though the power of life is not altogether
    there;
for night long the shade of poor Patroclus
stood by shedding tears and weeping,
and enjoined on me each thing to do; wonderful was the likeness to him."
So he spoke; and in the hearts of all he stirred desire for weeping.
            And Dawn appeared to them with fingers of rosy light
they wept around the pitiable corpse. And lord Agamemnon   110
dispatched mules and men from the shelters all around
to haul the timber; a good man oversaw them,
Meriones, companion of kind Idomeneus.
They set out, woodcutting axes and strong-spun ropes
in hand; and the mules went before them,
trudging many times up hill, down hill, around the hill, and crossways.
And when they drew near the spurs of Ida and its many springs,

they swiftly set to felling the high-crowned oaks with their honed blades
   of bronze,
leaning to the work; and the trees crashing mightily
dropped to the ground. Splitting them, the Achaeans   120
bound them on the mules; and these cut the earth to pieces with their feet
through the dense brush, in their eagerness to reach the plain.
All the woodcutters carried logs; for so ordered
Meriones, ready companion of generous Idomeneus;
then the men threw the logs down upon the shore in rows, there where
   Achilles
planned a great mound for Patroclus, and for himself.

      And when they had thrown down an immense pile of timber on
   all sides,
they sat there, waiting in a body. And Achilles
swiftly bade the battle-loving Myrmidons
to gird themselves in bronze and to yoke, each of them,   130
their horses. The men began to stir themselves and don their armour,
and the chariot fighters and charioteers mounted to their platforms,
the horsemen in front, and a cloud of foot soldiers followed with them,
by the thousand; and in their midst his companions bore Patroclus.
They covered his whole body with their locks of hair, which they cut
and cast upon him; and behind them godlike Achilles held his blameless
   companion's head
grieving, for he was sending him to the house of Hades.
And when they reached the place, there where Achilles showed them,
they set Patroclus down; and quickly piled abundant wood.

      Then swift-footed godlike Achilles thought of yet one more
   thing;   140
standing away from the pyre he cut his tawny hair,
which he was growing luxuriant and long for the river Spercheios,
and troubled, he then spoke, looking out to sea as dark as wine:
"Spercheios, in vain did my father Peleus vow to you
that returning there to my beloved fatherland I

would cut and dedicate my hair to you and perform a sacred hecatomb,
would sacrifice fifty rams, ungelded, right
in your springs, where your sanctuary is and your altar that smokes with
    sacrifice.
So the old man vowed, but you did not accomplish what he intended.
Now since I am not returning to my beloved fatherland,   150
I would give my hair to the warrior Patroclus to bear away."
So speaking he placed the hair in the hands of his beloved companion;
and in the hearts of all he stirred desire for weeping.

      And now the sun's light would have set upon their mourning,
had not Achilles swiftly come up to Agamemnon and spoken:
"Son of Atreus—for the men of Achaea
obey your words above all—there can be enough even of lamentation,
so now dismiss the men from the place where the pyre will be kindled
    and have them prepare
their dinner. Let us attend to these things, we to whom the dead is closest;
let those who are leaders remain beside us."   160
And when the lord of men Agamemnon heard this,
at once he dismissed the men to their well-balanced ships,
but the close mourners stayed by there, and piled up the wood,
and made a pyre a hundred feet long and wide;
and on the lofty pyre they laid the body, with grieving hearts.
Many fat sheep and shambling twist-horned cattle
they flayed and arranged before the pyre; then after taking the fat
from them all, great-hearted Achilles covered the corpse over
from foot to head, and piled the flayed bodies round.
And he placed upon this twin-handled jars of oil and honey,   170
resting against the bier; four high-necked horses
he fiercely flung upon the pyre, lamenting greatly,
and there were nine dogs fed at the table of their lord;
and cutting the throats of two of these he flung them on the pyre,
while slaying twelve noble sons of the great-hearted Trojans
with his bronze sword; and evil were the deeds his heart intended.

Then he unleashed the unyielding fury of the fire to feed upon them.
And Achilles wailed and called the name of his beloved companion:
"May it be well with thee, O Patroclus, even in the house of Hades;
for all things are now accomplished for you, as I promised.   180
The twelve noble sons of the great-hearted Trojans—
the fire will consume them all along with you; but I will never give Hector
son of Priam to the fire to devour, but to the dogs."

   So he spoke, threatening; but the dogs ignored Hector's body,
for Aphrodite, daughter of Zeus, warded them off
day and night, and anointed the body with rose-scented
ambrosial oil, so that Achilles would not tear it as he dragged it about.
And Phoebus Apollo caused a dark cloud to descend around it
from the heavens to the plain, and covered all the space
the body rested on, before the power of the sun   190
could wither all around the flesh on the limbs and sinews.

   But the pyre of dead Patroclus was not catching light.
Then swift-footed godlike Achilles thought of yet one more thing;
standing apart from the pyre he prayed to the two winds
Boreas of the north and Zephyr of the west, and promised splendid
 sacrifice;
and pouring out many libations from a cup of gold he entreated them
to come, so that with all speed the dead bodies should be set ablaze by fire
and the wood start to burn. And swift Iris
hearing his prayers went as messenger to the winds.
They were all together within the house of stormy Zephyr,   200
sharing a feast; and having run to them, Iris came and stood
upon the stone threshold. And when they saw her with their own eyes,
all sprang to their feet and each one called her to him.
But she in turn declined to be seated, and spoke her word:
"I cannot sit, for I am on my way back to the running streams of Ocean,
to the land of the Aethiopians, where they are sacrificing hecatombs
to the immortal gods, so that I too may share the sacred feasting.
But Achilles is praying for Boreas and boisterous Zephyr

to come, and promises splendid sacrifices,
so that you might set the pyre blazing, on which lies   210
Patroclus, for whom all the Achaeans raise lament."
Then so speaking she departed; and with noise sublime
the winds began to rise, driving a tumult of clouds ahead of them;
swiftly they arrived at the sea and blew upon it, and the waves rose
under the shrill blast of their breath. Then they came to Troy's fertile land,
and fell upon the pyre; and the divine blaze roared loud.

   All night long they beat upon the flames together,
blowing shrieking blasts; and all night long swift Achilles
from his golden mixing bowl, two-handled cup in hand,
drew out the wine and poured it to the ground and soaked the earth,   220
calling on the soul of poor Patroclus.
As a father weeps as he burns the bones of his newly married son,
whose dying brings grief to his wretched parents,
so Achilles wept as he burned the bones of his companion,
moving leadenly beside the burning pyre, mourning without cessation.

   And when the Morning Star came to herald light of day upon the
  earth,
and after him Dawn veiled in saffron spread herself across the seas,
then the burning pyre was quenched, and its flame extinguished;
and the winds set out again to return to their home
across the Thracian sea; and the sea moaned with raging swell.   230
And the son of Peleus, turning aside from the pyre,
lay down, exhausted, and sweet sleep swept upon him.

   But those who were with the son of Atreus gathered all together;
and the uproar and din of them approaching woke Achilles.
He sat upright and spoke his word to them:
"Son of Atreus and you others who are chiefs of all Achaeans,
first quench all the burning pyre with dark-gleaming wine
all that retains the fire's strength; and then
let us gather the bones of Menoetius' son Patroclus,

separating them carefully; they are easy to see;   240
for he lay in the middle of the pyre, and the others
were burned apart from him at the edge, horses and men in a mass
   together.
And let us place the bones in a golden urn, within a double fold of fat,
until the time when I myself journey to the realm of Hades;
and do not, I bid you, toil over a massive mound,
but as much as is fitting; hereafter, have the Achaeans make it
broad and high, those of you who are left after me
in your ships with their many benches."

        So he spoke, and the men obeyed the swift-footed son of Peleus.
And first they extinguished the pyre with dark-gleaming wine,   250
everywhere the flame reached and the ash had fallen deep;
and, weeping, they gathered up the white bones of their gentle comrade
into a golden urn, within a double fold of fat,
and after placing this within his shelter they covered it with fine linen;
and they marked a circle for the funeral mound, and threw foundation
   stones
around the pyre; then they piled heaped-up soil upon the ground,
and when they had piled the mound, they started back—but Achilles
held the people there and seated them in a wide assembly.
And from his ships he brought forth prizes—tripods and cauldrons,
horses and mules and the strong heads of cattle,   260
and fair-belted women and grey iron.

        First, he set forth glorious prizes for the drivers of swift-footed
   horses,
a woman skilled in flawless work of hand to lead away
and a handled tripod that held two-and-twenty measures
for first place; for second place he caused a horse to be led out,
untamed, pregnant with a mule foal;
then for third place he set aside a cauldron that had not yet been put upon
   the fire,

a splendid thing, holding four measures, still shining just as it was;
for fourth place he set out two talents' worth of gold;
and for fifth he set out a two-handled jar, untouched by fire.   270
Then he stood up and spoke his word among the Argives:
"Son of Atreus and you other strong-greaved Achaeans,
these prizes are set down in assembly and await the horsemen.
If we Achaeans were now contending in honour of any other man,
I myself would surely carry these to my shelter after coming first;
for you all know by how much my horses are superior in speed.
For they are immortal, and Poseidon gave them
to my father Peleus, and he in turn gave them into my hands.
But as it is I will stay here, as will my single-hoofed horses;
for such was the charioteer whose noble strength they lost,   280
so kind, who many a time poured limpid oil
upon their manes, after washing them with shining water.
They both stand grieving for him, and their manes
hang upon the ground, they both stand grieving in their hearts.
But the rest of you throughout the army, ready yourselves,
whoever of you trusts his horses and his bolted chariot."

            So spoke the son of Peleus, and the horsemen gathered swiftly.
First to rise by far was Eumelos, lord of men,
the beloved son of Admetos, who was pre-eminent in horsemanship;
and after him rose the son of Tydeus, powerful Diomedes,   290
and he led Trojan horses beneath his chariot yoke, horses that in
    time past
he took from Aeneas—but Aeneas himself Apollo had saved;
and after him rose the son of Atreus, fair-haired Menelaos
descended from Zeus, and swift were the horses he led beneath his
    chariot yoke,
Aithe, a mare of Agamemnon, and his own Podargos.
Echepolos, son of Anchises, gave the mare to Agamemnon
as a gift, so that he would not have to follow him beneath the walls of
    windswept Ilion,

but might enjoy himself remaining where he was; for great was the wealth
Zeus gave him; and he made his home in Sicyon's wide spaces.
This mare, then, Menelaos led beneath the yoke, as she strained mightily
    for the race.   300
Fourth to ready his fine-maned horses was Antilochos,
the glorious son of high-hearted lord Nestor,
Neleus' son, and swift-footed Pylos-bred horses
bore his chariot. Standing close to him his father
thoughtfully advised him, though his son himself was knowledgeable:
"Antilochos, young as you are
Zeus and Poseidon have loved you and taught you horsemanship
of every kind; therefore I surely have no need to instruct you;
you know well to round the turning post. But your horses
are the slowest running; therefore I think it will be difficult.   310
Yet while the horses of these men are swifter, they themselves do not
know more about strategy than you.
Come, dear boy, and summon in your heart every kind
of skill, so that the prizes do not slip from your grasp.
It is by skill the woodsman excels more than by strength;
by skill too the helmsman on a wine-dark sea
keeps his swift ship straight on course as it is torn by winds;
and by skill charioteer surpasses charioteer.
Another driver putting trust in his chariot and horses
recklessly wheels wide, this way and that,   320
and his horses veer along the course, nor does he control them;
but the man skilled in cunning, driving lesser horses,
turns close, looking always to the turning post, and knows well
from the start how to stretch his team with the oxhide reins,
and he holds them steadily and keeps his eyes on the man in front.
I will describe for you the conspicuous turning mark, it will not escape you;
a post of dried wood stands to the height of a man's outstretched arms
    above the earth,
of oak or pine; it has not been rotted by the rain;

two stones are propped on either side if it, two white stones
at the narrowing of the track, and the running for horses is smooth
   around it;   330
either it is the grave-mark of a man who died long ago,
or it was made as a turning point by men before us;
but now swift-footed godlike Achilles has made it the turning mark.
Drive your chariot and horses close enough to graze it,
and you yourself, in the strong-plaited straps of your chariot car,
lean slightly to their left; goad your right-hand horse,
shout him on and yield him the reins with your hands,
but bring your left-hand horse near to the turning post,
so the hub of your wrought wheel appears to come to
its very edge; but avoid touching the stone,   340
lest you harm the horses and shatter the chariot;
this would be joy to others, but disgrace to yourself.
Come, dear boy, use your wits and be on guard!
For if you overtake at the turning mark as you chase them,
there is not a man who could catch you, nor spring after and pass,
not even if the one behind were driving splendid Arion,
the swift horse of Adrastos, who is of the race of gods,
or the horses of Laomedon, who are the best bred in this place."
So speaking Nestor son of Neleus sat in his place again,
since he had told his son a strategy for each and every thing.   350
Then Meriones was the fifth man to make ready his fine-maned horses.

       The men mounted their chariots, and dropped their lots into a
   helmet;
Achilles shook them, and out leapt the lot of Nestor's son
Antilochos. After him lord Eumelos received his lot;
and after him Atreus' son spear-famed Menelaos;
after him Meriones drew his lot; and last in his turn
the son of Tydeus, far the best of them, drew to drive his horses.
All in a line they took position, and Achilles pointed out the turning
   place

in the distance on the level plain; he had set as lookout
godlike Phoinix, his father's attendant,   360
so that he might observe the running and make a true report.

       Together they all raised their whips above their horses,
and shook their reins and shouted with urgent words;
and straightway the horses set out across the plain,
far from the ships; beneath their chests the rising dust
hung like a cloud or whirling storm,
and their manes flowed along with the gusts of the wind.
And now the chariots skimmed close to the nourishing earth,
now again they would fly in mid-air; but their drivers
stood firm in their chariot cars, the heart of each beating hard   370
as he strained for victory. Each man called to his horses;
and they flew on raising dust across the plain.

       But when the swift horses were completing the last stretch of the
   course
back toward the grey salt sea, then was each man's prowess
displayed; now the horses ran full stretch; at once
the swift-footed mares of Eumelos, Pheres' grandson, shot ahead,
and after them raced Diomedes' stallions,
Trojan horses, nor were they far behind at all, but so close
they seemed ever on the point of mounting Eumelos' very chariot,
and the back and broad shoulders of Eumelos himself   380
were hot with their breath; so with their heads leaning over him, the
   horses flew on.
And now would Diomedes have driven past or made a dead heat,
had not Phoebus Apollo become angered with Tydeus' son,
and struck the shining whip from his hands.
The tears flowed from Diomedes' eyes in rage,
as he watched the mares of Eumelos advancing far ahead,
while his own horses were slowed, running without a whip.

       But Apollo's cheating of the son of Tydeus did not escape
Athena, and at once she rushed after the shepherd of the people,

and gave him his whip, and placed furious strength in his horses;   390
then in rage she made after the son of Admetos;
the goddess smashed the horses' yoke, his steeds
bolted the track to either side, and the yoke-pole was bent to the ground;
Eumelos himself was spun from his chariot beside the wheel.
All around his elbow he was torn, all around his mouth and nose,
his forehead smashed above the brows; his eyes
filled with tears, and his strong full voice was checked.
And the son of Tydeus, veering aside, drove on his single-hoofed horses,
bounding far ahead of the others; for Athena had cast
furious strength within his horses, and to him she gave glory.   400
        And after him came fair-haired Menelaos.
But Antilochos called to his father's horses:
"Get on, you two as well; stretch as fast as you can.
I am not ordering you to challenge them—
the horses of the brilliant son of Tydeus, to whom Athena
has now granted speed and given glory—
but catch the horses of the son of Atreus, quickly,
do not be left behind, lest Aithe, who is female,
pour disgrace upon you both. Why are you left behind, brave ones?
For I declare this, and it will surely be accomplished;   410
there will be no care for you two from Nestor shepherd of the people,
but he will straightway kill you both with his sharp bronze sword,
if for your slackness we carry the lesser prize.
Come, stick with them and make all speed you can;
I will think of a way and contrive things
to slip past where the track narrows—he will not escape me!"
        So he spoke; and in fear before their master's threats
they ran the harder in pursuit in a burst of speed. And soon
steadfast Antilochos spied the narrowing of the hollowed track;
there was a fissure in the ground, where gathered storm water   420
had broken off part of the track, and hollowed the land all round.
Here Menelaos drove, avoiding running the chariots together;

but Antilochos, veering, held his single-hoofed horses
off the track and, swerving a little, gave pursuit.
And Atreus' son became afraid and shouted out to Antilochos:
"Antilochos, you are driving recklessly; come, check your horses—
for the road looks narrow, it will soon be broader for you to pass—
check them, lest you harm us both as you hit me with your chariot!"
So he spoke; but Antilochos drove yet the harder
urging with his whip, as if he did not hear.   430
As far as the range of a discus that a young man
hurls from the shoulder, making trial of his youthful strength,
for so far did the two teams race neck and neck together; then the son of
    Atreus' mares
dropped behind; for by choice Menelaos slackened his driving,
lest the single-hoofed horses crash on the track
and upset the strong-bound chariots, and the men
fall in the dust as they pressed for victory.

          And rebuking him, fair-haired Menelaos cried:
"Antilochos, no other man is more dangerous than you!
Go to damnation—we Achaeans falsely said that you had sense!   440
But you will never bear off the prize like this without swearing to an oath."
So speaking, he urged and called to his horses:
"Do not hold back on me now, nor stand about for all your hearts are
    grieving;
their feet and knees will tire
before yours do; for they have been robbed of their youthful vigour."
So he spoke; and in fear before their master's rebuke
the horses ran the harder in pursuit, and soon closed on the others.

          And the Argives sitting in assembly were watching for
the horses, which were flying in a cloud of dust across the plain.
Idomeneus, commander of the Cretans, marked them first;   450
for he sat outside the assembly, higher up, on a place where he could see
    all round.
And hearing a driver in the distance urging his horses,

he recognised him, and made out the horse conspicuous in the lead,
who was almost completely chestnut, but on his forehead
was a white blaze, circular like the moon.
Then Idomeneus stood up and spoke his word among the Argives:
"O friends, leaders and counsellors of the Argives,
do I alone discern the horses, or do you too?
Other horses seem to me to be in front,
and some other charioteer appears; somewhere out there the mares   460
came to grief upon the plain, they who going out were strongest;
for those I saw racing first around the turn,
I can see nowhere now, though my eyes are looking everywhere
across the Trojan plain as I keep watching;
perhaps the reins escaped the charioteer, and he was not able
to hold them well around the post, and did not complete the turn.
I suspect he fell out there and smashed his chariot,
and the mares swerved off course, when frenzy seized them.
But stand and see for yourselves; for I do not
make them out well, but the man who leads seems to me to be   470
Aetolian by birth, and rules among the Argives—
the son of horse-breaking Tydeus, powerful Diomedes."

　　　　But Ajax, swift son of Oïleus, reviled him scornfully:
"Idomeneus, why do you always bluster? The high-stepping mares still
race far away over the vast plain.
You are not the youngest of the Argives,
nor do the eyes in your head see the sharpest.
Always you bluster with your words; there is no need for you
to be a windy speaker; other better men are here.
The same horses are at the front that were before,   480
the mares of Eumelos, and he it is who drives them."

　　　　Then in anger the Cretan commander spoke against him:
"Ajax, best in abuse, bad in counsel, and in all else
inferior to the Argives, because your mind is unyielding—
come now, let us wager a tripod, or a cauldron,

and let us both make Agamemnon son of Atreus the judge
as to which horses are first, so that you may learn when you pay the
   penalty."
So he spoke; and immediately swift Ajax son of Oïleus rose up
in anger to retort with hard words.
And now would the strife between them both have gone still further,   490
had not Achilles himself risen and spoken a word:
"No longer now exchange hard words,
Ajax and Idomeneus, evil words, since it is not becoming;
you would censure another man doing such things.
But take your seats in the assembly and watch for
the horses; soon they will arrive here
as they press for victory; then you will each know
which Argive horses are second, which are first."

      So he spoke; and the son of Tydeus soon came racing,
ever driving with a whip stroke from the shoulder, and his horses'   500
feet were lifted high as they sped along the course;
and always the gritty dust spattered the charioteer,
and the chariot plated with gold and tin
ran on the heels of the swift-footed horses; nor was there much
of a wheel track in the shallow dust
behind; and the horses, pressing hard, flew on.
Diomedes brought them to a stand in the middle of the assembly,
profuse sweat poured from the horses' necks and chests to the ground;
and he leapt down from his gleaming chariot,
and leaned his whip against the yoke. Strong Sthenelos   510
lost no time, and was quick to collect the prize,
and gave the woman to their high-hearted companions to lead away
and the handled tripod for them to carry; then he unyoked the horses.

      Antilochos, grandson of Neleus, drove his horses after him,
outstripping Menelaos by cunning, and not by speed;
even so Menelaos held his fast horses to follow close.
As far from the wheel as stands a horse who pulls his master

as he strains across the plain with his chariot—
and the tip of his tail just touches the wheel behind,
because he runs so close, nor is there much   520
space between, when he races over the great plain—
by so much was Menelaos left behind by blameless Antilochos;
although at first behind by as much as a discus throw,
he had swiftly gained on him, for the noble fighting spirit
of Agamemnon's mare, Aithe of the lovely mane, had surged.
And if the running had been yet farther for them both,
then would Menelaos have overtaken him, nor would there have been
     dispute.
Meriones, noble attendant of Idomeneus,
was left behind by glorious Menelaos by as much as a spear is thrown;
for his fair-maned horses were the slowest,   530
and he himself the weakest chariot driver in the race.
             And the son of Admetos came last of them all,
dragging his splendid chariot, driving his horses before him.
And seeing him, swift-footed godlike Achilles had pity,
and standing up he spoke winged words to the Argive assembly:
"The best man at driving single-hoofed horses came last.
Come, let us give him, as is fitting, a prize
for second place; and the first prizes let the son of Tydeus bear away."
So he spoke; and all the men expressed approval, as he urged.
And now he would have given Eumelos the mare, as the Achaeans
     approved,   540
had not Antilochos, son of great-hearted Nestor,
rising to speak, answered Peleus' son Achilles with a plea for justice:
"O Achilles, I will be greatly angered with you, if you fulfil
your word; for you intend to take away my prize,
thinking of this, that his chariot and fast horses came to harm,
as did he himself, for all his skill. Well, he should have prayed
to the immortal gods; then he would not have come last of all as he raced.
But if you pity him and he is dear to your heart,

you have much gold in your shelter, you have bronze
and cattle, and you have slave girls and single-hoofed horses;   550
take from them and give him a greater prize, later
or even right now, so the Achaeans will applaud you.
But the mare I will not give; and let the man who wants try his luck
for her and fight me with his hands."

　　　　So he spoke; and swift-footed godlike Achilles smiled,
delighting in Antilochos, since he was his dear companion,
and answering him he spoke winged words:
"Antilochos, if you now bid me add something else from my store
for Eumelos, so then I will accomplish this.
I will give him the breastplate that I took from Asteropaios,   560
of bronze, an overlay of shining tin set in a circle
about it; it will be worth much to him."
He spoke, and bade Automedon, his dear companion,
carry it from his shelter; and he left and brought it to him.   564

　　　　But Menelaos also rose among them aggrieved at heart,   566
filled with furious anger for Antilochos; and into his hands the herald
placed the speaker's staff, and ordered the Argives
to be silent. Then Menelaos, a man like a god, addressed them:
"Antilochos, you who had good sense before, what have you done?   570
You have discredited my valour, thwarting my horses,
hurling yours ahead, which were far inferior.
Now come, Argive leaders and counsellors,
judge between us impartially, without favour to either,
lest some one of the bronze-clad Argives ever say,
'Menelaos after besting Antilochos with his lies
went away leading the prize mare, because though his horses were far
inferior, he himself was greater in rank and power.'
Come now, I myself will propose judgement, and I think no other man
of the Danaans will fault me; for this is fair.   580
Antilochos, god-cherished, come on now over here, as is right and proper,
stand up before your horses and your chariot, take that supple whip

in hand, with which you drove before;

lay hold of your horses and swear by Poseidon, the earth-holding Shaker
    of the Earth,

that you did not intentionally impede my chariot with your cunning
    trick."

        Then in turn wise Antilochos gave him answer:

"Hold off now; for I am indeed much younger than you,

lord Menelaos, and you are older and more worthy.

You know what sort of transgressions arise from a man who is young;

his mind is more impetuous, and his judgement shallow.   590

So let your heart forbear; I will give the horse to you myself,

the mare I won. And if you should ask for something greater as well

from my store, then at once, without hesitation I would rather give it

to you, god-cherished one, than for all my days

fall from your heart's favour and be culpable before the gods."

He spoke, and leading the horse, the son of great-hearted Nestor

put her in Menelaos' hands. And the heart of Menelaos

melted, like dew about the grain

of a ripening stand of corn, when the ploughlands are bristling;

so, Menelaos, your heart melted within your breast.   600

And speaking winged words he addressed the other:

"Antilochos, although angered I will now

yield to you, since you were neither wild nor witless

before, and this time your youth won over your wits.

But stay clear of trying this trick on your betters again.

For any other of the Achaeans would not have prevailed on me so quickly;

but you have already suffered much and toiled much

because of me, you and your good father and brother, too.

Therefore I yield to your petition, and I shall even return the mare,

although she is mine, so that these men may know   610

that my heart was never arrogant or harsh."

        He spoke, and gave the mare to Noëmon, the companion of
    Antilochos,

to lead away; then he carried off the gleaming cauldron;
and Meriones took up the two talents of gold
in fourth place, as he had driven. And there remained the fifth prize,
the two-handled jar; this Achilles gave to Nestor,
carrying it through the Argive assembly, and coming up to him, he spoke:
"Here now, old sir, and let this be your treasure,
to be a remembrance of the funeral of Patroclus; for you will not again
see him among the Argives; I give this prize to you   620
without contest; for you will not fight with your fists, nor will you
     wrestle,
nor take part in the throwing of spears, nor race with your feet;
for already hard age bears upon you."

              So speaking he placed it in his hands; and Nestor received it
     rejoicing,
and speaking winged words, he addressed him:
"Truly, my son, you speak all these things properly:
for my limbs are no longer steady on my feet, dear boy, nor do my arms
nimbly shoot out from my shoulders, left and right!
Would that I were young and my strength were steadfast,
as that time when the Epeans buried lord Amarynkeus   630
at Bouprasion, and his sons laid on games for the king!
There no man was my equal, not among the Epeans,
not among the Pylians themselves, not among the great-hearted
     Aetolians.
With my fists I vanquished Klytomedes, the son of Enops,
and in wrestling Ankaios of Pleuron, who stood up to me,
and with speed of feet I outran Iphiklos, excellent though he was,
and with the spear I out-threw both Phyleus and Polydoros.
Only in chariot-racing did the two sons of Aktor outstrip me,
forging ahead by their superior numbers, grudging me victory,
because the greatest prizes were left for this contest.   640
And these men were twins; and one drove the horses steadily,
steadily, and the other urged them on with the whip.

Thus was I once; but now let younger men take part in
such games. I must yield to painful old age;
but at that time, in my turn, I was distinguished among warriors.
But come, honour your companion's funeral with contests.
And I receive this willingly, and my heart rejoices
that you remember always my kindness, and do not forget
the honour with which it is fitting I be esteemed among the Achaeans.
May the gods give you abundant favour for these things."   650

      So he spoke; and the son of Peleus departed through the great
throng of Achaeans, when he had listened to all of Nestor's story.
Then he set out prizes for a match of painful boxing;
leading out a hard-working mule, six years old and unbroken,
the hardest to break in, he tethered her in the assembly place;
and for the loser he placed a double-handled cup.
Then he stood up and spoke his word among the Argives:
"Son of Atreus and you other strong-greaved Achaeans,
for these prizes, we bid two men stand forth, the two who are best,
to square up and box. The one to whom Apollo   660
grants strength of endurance, and all Achaeans recognise as winner,
let him return to his shelter leading the hard-working mule.
And let the man who is beaten take away the two-handled cup."

      So he spoke; and there rose at once a good and mighty man
and one skilled in boxing, Epeios son of Panopeus,
and he laid a hand on the hard-working mule and spoke:
"Let the man approach who will win the double-handled cup;
for I say no other of the Achaeans will win at boxing
and lead off the mule, since I claim to be the greatest.
Is it not enough that I fall short in battle? For it is never possible   670
for a man to be skilled in everything he does.
This I declare, and it will be a thing accomplished;
I will tear his flesh outright and smash his bones together.
Let his kinsmen remain here in droves,
so they can carry him away when he has been broken under my hands."

So he spoke; and all the men were hushed in silence.
Euryalos alone stood up against him, a man like a god,
the son of lord Mekisteus, descended from Talaos,
who came to Thebes in time of old, to the burial of Oedipus
after he fell dead; and there he had defeated all Cadmeians.   680
Now the son of spear-famed Tydeus served as his second,
encouraging him with his words, and sought a great victory for him;
first he set out his loincloth, and then
gave him his knuckle-straps, well cut from field-ox hide.

And when the two contenders had girded themselves, they
    stepped into the middle of the assembly,
and squaring up against each other with their with massive arms, they both
at the same moment rushed together, and their heavy hands mingled in
    blows.
A dreadful grinding came from their jaws, and sweat poured
from every part of their bodies. Then godlike Epeios lunged,
and struck the other on the jaw just as he was looking for an opening;   690
he stood his ground no more and on the spot his shining limbs collapsed
    beneath him.
As when a fish leaps up from water roughened by the North Wind
in a seaweedy shoal, and the dark swell covers him over,
so Euryalos leapt as he was struck. But great-hearted Epeios,
taking him in his arms, set him upright; the other's close companions
    ringed
around him and led him, his feet dragging, through the assembly,
as he spat clotted blood, hanging his head to one side;
and having led him off, they set him down, still groggy, among them,
and they themselves went to see after the two-handled cup.

Then the son of Peleus straightway set out other prizes for the
    third contest,   700
the painful wrestling, after displaying them to the Danaans;
first, for the victor a great tripod to go upon the fire;
this the Achaeans valued among themselves as worth twelve oxen;

and for the vanquished man he put a woman in their midst,
one skilled in many works of hand, whom they valued at four oxen.
Then he stood up and spoke his word among the Argives:
"Rise up, you who would try for this prize."

      So he spoke; then arose great Telamonian Ajax,
and against him rose resourceful Odysseus, skilled in wiles.
Girding themselves, they both strode to the middle of the ring,   710
and grasped each other by the arms with their massive hands,
as when a gifted carpenter joins the gabled rafters
of a high-roofed house, to escape the force of the winds.
Their backs, pulled steadily, creaked under the force
of their bold hands; their running sweat poured down,
and thick welts along their sides and shoulders
broke out in red blood; but they ever
strained for victory, strained for the crafted tripod.
Nor could Odysseus trip Ajax and bring him to the ground,
nor could Ajax trip him, for Odysseus' great strength held out.   720

      But when then the strong-greaved Achaeans grew impatient,
then great Telamonian Ajax addressed the other:
"Zeus-descended son of Laertes, Odysseus of many stratagems,
either you lift me, or I you; all things lie in Zeus' hands."
So speaking, he hoisted the other; but Odysseus did not forget his
    cunning;
he caught and struck the hollow place behind the other's knee, and his
    limbs collapsed,
and Ajax fell down backward; and Odysseus fell on his chest.
And the crowd watched, astonished.
Next, in his turn, much enduring godlike Odysseus tried to lift;
he budged Ajax, a very little, from the ground, but lifted him no higher.   730
Then Odysseus hooked the other's knee, and both men fell upon the
    ground
close to each other, and were soiled in the dust.
And now they would have sprung up again and wrestled a third fall,

had not Achilles himself stood up and checked them:
"Struggle no longer, nor wear yourselves out with pain.
Victory goes to you both; and go your way with equal prizes,
so that the other Achaeans can compete in contests ."
So he spoke; and they heard him well and obeyed,
and wiping off the dust, they donned their tunics.

       Then the son of Peleus swiftly set out more prizes for racing,   740
a crafted silver bowl; six measures
it contained, and in beauty it surpassed anything on earth
by a long way, since skilled Sidonian men had beautifully formed it with
   their art.
Phoenician men had carried it across the misted sea,
and landed it in the harbour, and gave it as a gift to Thoas;
and as price of ransom for Priam's son Lykaon,
Euneos, son of Jason, gave it to the warrior Patroclus.
And this Achilles set as a prize in honour of his companion,
for that man who should run lightest in his speed of feet.
And for second place he then set out an ox, massive and heavy
   with fat;   750
and for last place he set out a half talent of gold.
Then he stood up and spoke his word among the Argives:
"Rise up, you who would try for this prize."
So he spoke; and at once there rose swift Ajax, son of Oïleus,
and resourceful Odysseus rose, then Nestor's son
Antilochos; for he surpassed all young men in his swiftness of feet.
All in a line they took position, and Achilles pointed out the turning place.

       And right from the start they ran at full stretch; swiftly
the son of Oïleus drew away. And godlike Odysseus pressed after him,
very close, as close as a weaving rod is pulled to the breast of   760
a fair-belted woman, the rod she skilfully draws with her hand
as she pulls the spool out past the warp, and holds it close
to her breast; as close as this did Odysseus run, and from behind
he pounded the tracks of Ajax with his feet before the dust had settled;

brilliant Odysseus poured his breath upon the other's head
running swiftly always. And all the Achaeans shouted
to him as he strove for victory, and were urging him as he sped on.

But when they were finishing the last of the course, now
   Odysseus
prayed within his heart to gleaming-eyed Athena:
"Hear me, goddess, come as ready ally to my feet!"   770
So he spoke in prayer; and Pallas Athena heard him,
and made his limbs light and his feet and his arms above.
And when they were just on the point of dashing for the prize,
then Ajax slipped as he ran, for Athena tripped him,
there where dung was scattered of the loud-bellowing oxen that had been
   slaughtered,
those that Achilles of the swift feet had slain in honour of Patroclus;
and Ajax's mouth and nostrils were filled with the ox dung;
then brilliant, much-enduring Odysseus took up the bowl,
as he got there first. And glorious Ajax took the ox;
he stood holding the horn of the field ox with his hands,   780
spitting out dung, and addressed the Argives:
"For shame, the goddess tripped up my feet, she who as before
stands by Odysseus like a mother and comes to his aid."
So he spoke; and the men all laughed heartily at him.

Then Antilochos bore off the prize for last place
with a smile, and spoke his word among the Argives:
"I say this to all of you who know, my friends, that still, even now,
the immortals honour men of the older generation.
For Ajax is older than me by a little,
but this other one, Odysseus, is of an earlier generation from the men
   of old;
his, men say, is unripe old age. And hard it is   790
for any Achaean to contend in speed of feet with him, except for
   Achilles."
So he spoke, giving glory to the swift-footed son of Peleus.

And answering his words, Achilles addressed him:
"Antilochos, your praise will not be said in vain.
Come, to you I will give an additional half talent of gold."
So speaking he placed this in his hands, and the other received it rejoicing.

    Then the son of Peleus brought into the arena and set down
a long-shadowed spear and a shield and crested helmet,
the weapons of Sarpedon, which Patroclus had stripped from him.   800
Then he stood up and spoke his word among the Argives:
"For these prizes, we bid two men stand forth, the two who are best;
let them don their armour, take up their flesh-rending bronze,
and before this assembled crowd, make trial of each other.
And whoever is first to reach and strike fair flesh,
who touches the inward parts through the armour and black blood,
to him I shall give this silver-studded sword,
a splendid Thracian piece; this I stripped from Asteropaios;
and let both men carry this armour off in common,
and let us set a noble feast before them in the shelters."   810

    So he spoke; then arose great Telamonian Ajax,
and after him rose the son of Tydeus, powerful Diomedes.
When then they had armed themselves on opposite sides of the throng,
they strode into the middle, burning to do battle,
looking terror at each other; and awe held all the Achaeans.
And when they had advanced almost upon each other,
three times they charged, and three times attacked at close quarters.
Then Ajax next struck the other's circled shield,
but did not reach his skin; for the breastplate beyond it guarded him.
But the son of Tydeus, with the point of his gleaming spear,   820
kept trying to touch the other's neck above his great shield.
And in fear for Ajax the Achaeans
urged the men to stop and take up the equal prizes.
And the warrior Achilles gave the great sword to the son of Tydeus,
bringing its scabbard with it, and a skilfully cut sword-belt.

    And then the son of Peleus placed a mass of unworked iron,

which in time before Eëtion used to hurl in his great strength;
but godlike swift-footed Achilles slew him,
and brought it onto his ships with his other possessions.
And he stood and spoke his word among the Argives: 830
"Rise up, you who would try for this prize.
Even if the winner's fields are very far away,
he will have use of this for the turning of five years;
and not for any lack of iron will his shepherd
or his ploughman have to venture to the city, for this will supply them."

    So he spoke; then there rose Polypoites, steadfast in battle,
and Leonteus godlike in his powerful strength,
and Ajax the son of Telamon rose up, and brilliant Epeios.
They stood in a row, and brilliant Epeios lifted the mass of iron,
and whirling it round, let it fly; and all the Achaeans burst out in
    laughter.   840
Next in his turn Leonteus, companion of Ares, made his throw;
and third in turn great Telamonian Ajax hurled it
from his mighty hand, and out-threw the marks of them all.
But when Polypoites the steadfast in battle took up the iron—
then as far as a herdsmen hurls his cattle staff,
which as it spins flies across his cattle herd,
thus far did he throw beyond the entire field; the men cried out,
and rising to their feet the companions of powerful Polypoites
carried the prize of their king to the hollow ships.

    Then Achilles set forth dark iron for the archers;   850
ten double-edged axes he set down, and ten of single-edge.
And he erected the mast of a dark-prowed ship
at a distance on the sand, and from it he bound a timorous wild dove
by her foot with a slender string, and bade them shoot at her
with the bow: "The man who should strike this timorous dove,
let him take up and bear to his home all the double-edged axes;
but the man who should strike the string, missing the bird,

since that man is loser, he will take away the axes with single edge."

      So he spoke; and lord Teucer rose in his strength,
and Meriones rose, noble henchman of Idomeneus.   860
They took their lots and shook them in a brazen helmet,
and by lot Teucer was first. Straightway, drawing powerfully,
he launched his arrow; but he did not make vow to lord Apollo.   863
He missed the bird; for Apollo grudged this to him;   865
he struck the string, with which the bird was bound by her foot,
and straight through the string the sharp arrow cut.
The dove shot toward the heavens, and the string went slack
toward the earth; and the Achaeans shouted in applause.
But Meriones hastily snatched the bow out of Teucer's hand—   870
the arrow he had been holding before, while Teucer shot—
and quickly vowed to Apollo who shoots from afar
to sacrifice a splendid hecatomb of firstborn sheep.
High up, below the clouds, he saw the timorous dove;
and there he struck her, as she wheeled, upon her breast beneath the
    wing.
Right through the arrow passed; then fixed back in the earth
before the feet of Meriones; and the bird
was brought to rest upon the mast of the dark-prowed ship
and hung her neck, and her beating wings went slack,
and the swift spirit flew from her body, and from the height of
    the mast   880
she dropped; and the men watched and marvelled again.
Then Meriones took up all ten of the axes,
and Teucer carried the single-edged axes to his hollow ships.

      Then the son of Peleus set out a long-shadowed spear,
and a cauldron unmarked by fire and patterned with flowers,
worth an ox, bearing them into the place of assembly; and the spearmen
    rose up;
the son of Atreus rose, wide-ruling Agamemnon,

and Meriones rose, the noble henchman of Idomeneus.
And these men swift-footed godlike Achilles addressed:
"Son of Atreus, we know by how much you are superior to all men   890
and by how much you excel in power and the throwing of spears;
come, you take this prize and go back to your hollow ships,
and let us give the spear to Meriones the warrior,
if you should in your heart so choose; for I, indeed, am urging this."
So he spoke and lord of men Agamemnon did not disobey;
and he gave the bronze spear to Meriones; and then the warrior
    Agamemnon
gave his splendid prize to his herald Talthybios.

The games were dispersed, and the men scattered to go
each to his own swift ship. And they began to think about their meal
and giving themselves over to the pleasure of sweet sleep; but Achilles
wept still, remembering his beloved companion, nor did sleep,
who masters all, take hold of him, but he turned himself this side and that
yearning for the manly strength and noble spirit of Patroclus,
and remembered with yearning all he had been through with him and all
  the woes he had suffered,
running through dangerous waves and the conflicts of men.
Recalling these things he let the warm tears fall,
as he lay now on his side, now again   10
on his back, and now face down; then starting up
he would wander in distraction along the salt-sea shore. He came to know
the dawn as she appeared over the sea and shore;
and when he had yoked his swift horses to his chariot,
he would tie Hector behind the chariot so as to drag him;
and after dragging him three times around the tomb of Menoetius' dead
  son
he would rest again in his shelter, and leave Hector
stretched in the dust upon his face. But Apollo warded off from Hector's flesh
all disfigurement, pitying the mortal man,
dead though he was, and covered him wholly round   20
with his golden aegis, so that Achilles would not tear the skin away as he
  dragged him.

        So in his rage Achilles kept outraging glorious Hector;
and as they watched, the blessed gods took pity on the son of Priam,
and kept urging sharp-sighted Hermes, Slayer of Argos, to steal him away.
And this found favour with all other gods, but not with Hera,
nor with Poseidon, nor with the gleaming-eyed maiden Athena,
for their hatred persisted, as at the start, for sacred Ilion,
and the people of Priam, because of the folly of Alexandros
who insulted the goddesses, when they came to his shepherd's steading,
and gave the nod to her, the goddess whose gift to him was ruinous
    lust.   30

            But when at length the twelfth dawn rose since Hector's death,
then it was that Phoebus Apollo addressed the immortals:
"You gods are relentless, destroyers of men! Did Hector never
burn as offerings to you the thighbones of oxen and of goats without
    blemish?
And now, dead though he is, you cannot bring yourselves to rescue him,
for his wife to look on, for his mother, for his child,
and for his father and his people, who would with all speed
burn him upon a pyre and honour him with funeral rites;
but you gods choose to abet murderous Achilles,
in whose breast the heart knows no justice,   40
nor does his purpose bend, but his skill is in savage things, like a lion,
who giving way to his great strength and bold heart
goes for the flocks of men, to snatch his feast.
So Achilles has destroyed pity, nor has he shame,
which does great harm to men but also profits them.
A man surely is likely to lose someone even dearer—
a brother born of the same womb, or his own son—
but having wept and mourned, he lets it go;
for the Fates placed an enduring heart within mankind;
but Achilles, after he has stripped brilliant Hector of his life,   50
fastens him to his chariot and drags him round the tomb of his
    companion.

This is neither good for Achilles, nor is it worthy;
let him beware lest, noble though he be, we gods be angered with him.
For in his rage he outrages the senseless earth."

　　　Then in anger white-armed Hera addressed him:
"This speech of yours, you of the silver bow, might be justified
if you gods hold Achilles and Hector in the same honour.
But Hector is mortal and sucked at the breast of a woman,
while Achilles is born of a goddess, one whom I myself
nurtured and reared and gave as wife to her husband,   60
to Peleus, who was exceedingly dear to the immortals' hearts;
and all you gods took part in the wedding. And you among them
partook of the feast, lyre in hand, you companion of evil, faithless forever."

　　　Then answering her spoke Zeus who gathers the clouds:
"Hera, do not be angered with the gods.
The men will not have the same honour; yet Hector too
was dearest to the gods of all mortal men in Ilion.
For so he was to me, since he never failed to offer pleasing gifts;
my altar was never lacking its fair share of sacrifice,
of libation and the savour of burnt offering; for this honour is our due.   70
But as for stealing bold Hector away, let that go, it is in no way possible
without Achilles' notice, for always
his mother is at his side night and day alike;
but perhaps one of the gods would summon Thetis to my presence,
so that I could speak a close word to her, so that Achilles would
accept gifts from Priam and release Hector for ransom."

　　　So he spoke; and storm-footed Iris sprang up to take his message.
Between Samothrace and rugged Imbros
she leapt into the dark sea; and the sea groaned about her;
she sped to the depths of the sea like a leaden weight,   80
which mounted upon a piece of field-ox horn
goes bearing death to the fish who eat its carrion bait.
She found Thetis in a hollow cave; and gathered round her were
the other goddesses of the sea, and she in the middle

was weeping for the fate of her blameless son, who was destined
to perish in the rich soil of Troy, far from his fatherland.
Standing close, swift-footed Iris addressed her:
"Rise up, Thetis; Zeus whose counsels are unfailing, summons you."
Then the goddess Thetis of the silver feet answered her:
"What does he, the great god, command of me? I dread   90
mingling with the immortals; for I have sorrows without end within my
   heart.
Yet I will go, his word will not be in vain, whatever he might say."

        So speaking the shining among goddesses took her blue-black
veil; and than this there is no darker garment;
and she set out, and swift Iris with feet like the wind led the way
before her; and on either side the waves of the sea parted for them.
Going up onto the shore, they darted to heaven;
and they found the far-thundering son of Cronus, and gathered round him
were sitting all the other blessed gods who live for ever.
Then beside Zeus the father Thetis took her seat, which Athena yielded
   to her.   100
Hera placed a beautiful cup of gold into her hands
and spoke kindly words; and Thetis gave it back after drinking.

        Then to them the father of gods and men began his speech:
"You have come to Olympus, divine Thetis, despite your cares,
bearing grief that cannot be forgotten in your heart; I know this.
But even so I will tell you the reason for which I have called you here.
For nine days a quarrel has arisen among the immortals
concerning Hector's body and Achilles, sacker of cities.
They urge sharp-sighted Hermes, Slayer of Argos, to steal the body away.
I however grant this honour to Achilles,   110
safeguarding your respect and loving friendship for time after:
go quickly to the army and lay a charge upon your son;
tell him the gods are angry, and that I beyond all
immortals am provoked to rage, because in his madman's heart
he holds Hector beside his curved ships, nor has surrendered him—

and that perhaps in fear of me he would give Hector back.
And I will dispatch Iris to great-hearted Priam, to tell him
to obtain the release of his dear son by going to the ships of the Achaeans,
and to bear gifts for Achilles, which would soften his heart."

      So he spoke; nor did the goddess Thetis of the silver feet
   disobey,   120
and she left, darting down from the heights of Olympus,
and made her way to her son's shelter; inside she found him
groaning without cessation; around him his close companions
busily attended to him and readied the morning meal;
a great fleecy sheep had been slain by them in the shelter.
His lady mother sat down close beside him,
and stroked his hand, and spoke to him and said his name:
"My child, how long will you devour your heart
in weeping and grieving, mindful neither of food
nor bed? Indeed, it is good to lie with a woman   130
in lovemaking; you will not be living long with me, but already
death stands close beside you and powerful destiny.
Now, mark me at once; I bring a message for you from Zeus;
he says the gods are angry with you, and that he beyond all
immortals is provoked to rage, because in your madman's heart
you hold Hector beside your curved ships nor have surrendered him.
But come, give him up, and accept ransom for his body."

      Then answering her spoke swift-footed Achilles:
"Let the man appear who would bring the ransom and bear the body,
if the Olympian himself in earnest bids."   140

      So they, amid the gathering of ships, mother and son,
were speaking many things, winged words, to one another;
and the son of Cronus dispatched Iris into holy Ilion:
"Come, swift Iris, leave this Olympian seat
and bear a message to great-hearted Priam inside Ilion,
that he ransom his beloved son, going to the ships of the Achaeans,
and that he bear gifts for Achilles, which would soften his heart,

he alone, and let no other man of Troy go with him.
A herald may accompany him, some older man, who can drive
the mules and the strong-wheeled wagon, to bring back   150
to the city the dead man, whom godlike Achilles killed.
And let no thought of death trouble his heart, nor any fear;
for we will have Hermes, Slayer of Argos, accompany him as escort,
who will lead him, conducting him until he comes to Achilles.
And when he has led him inside Achilles' shelter,
Achilles himself will not kill him and he will restrain all others;
for he is not witless, nor thoughtless, nor without morals,
but with great kindness he will have mercy on the suppliant."

           So he spoke; and storm-footed Iris sprang up to take his message.
And she came to the house of Priam, and there was met with crying and
     lamentation;   160
the sons sitting about their father inside the courtyard
stained their garments with their tears, and among them the old man
was wrapped in his mantle, moulded to it; much dung
was round about the neck and head of the old man,
which wallowing in he had scraped up with his own hands.
All through his house his daughters and the wives of his sons wailed in
     grief,
remembering those men who in such numbers and nobility
lay dead, having lost their lives at Argive hands.
And Iris, messenger of Zeus, stood by Priam and addressed him,
speaking softly; and trembling seized his limbs: 170
"Have courage in your heart, Priam son of Dardanos, nor fear at all.
For I do not come to you here bearing evil,
but with good intentions; for I am a messenger to you from Zeus,
who though far away takes great thought for and pities you.
The Olympian bids you redeem brilliant Hector by ransom,
and bring gifts to Achilles, which would soften his heart,
you alone, and let no other man of Troy go with you.
A herald may accompany you, some older man, who can drive

the mules and the strong-wheeled wagon, to bring back
to the city the dead man, whom godlike Achilles killed.   180
And do not let any thought of death trouble your heart, nor any fear;
for Hermes, Slayer of Argos, will follow with you as escort,
and will lead you, conducting you until he comes to Achilles.
But when he has led you inside Achilles' shelter,
Achilles himself will not kill you and will restrain all others;
for he is not witless, nor thoughtless, nor without morals,
but with great kindness he will have mercy on a suppliant."

  Then so speaking, Iris of the swift feet departed;
and Priam ordered his sons to prepare the strong-wheeled mule-drawn
  wagon
and to fasten upon it a wicker carrier.   190
And he went down into his storeroom, high-roofed
and fragrant with cedar, which held his many precious things.
And he called to his wife Hecuba and spoke to her:
"My poor wife, from Zeus an Olympian messenger came to me,
and bids me ransom our beloved son, going to the ships of the Achaeans,
to bring gifts to Achilles, which would soften his heart.
Come and tell me this—how to your mind does this seem to be?
For terribly does my spirit urge me, and my heart,
to go there to the ships, inside the broad army of the Achaeans."

  So he spoke; and his wife cried out and answered him in a
  word: 200
"Alas for me, where have your wits departed, for which you were
famed before, among even those from other lands, as well as those you
  ruled?
How can you wish to go to the Achaean ships alone,
into the sight of a man who killed your many and your noble
sons? Your heart is iron.
For if he sets eyes upon you, and seizes you,
ravening and faithless man as he is, he will not have pity on you,
nor will he in any way respect your standing. No, let us weep now

as we sit far from Hector in our halls; thus it seems powerful Destiny
spun her fated thread for him at his very birth, when I myself brought
   him to life,   210
to glut swift-footed dogs far from his parents
beside a violent man, whose liver I wish I could take hold of,
burying my teeth into its middle to eat; then would there be revenge
for my son, since he was not killed as he played the coward,
but as he took his stand in defence of the Trojans and the deep-breasted
Trojan women, taking thought of neither flight nor shelter."

     And old Priam, godlike, spoke to her again:
"Do not delay me in my wish to go, nor yourself,
in my own halls, be a bird of ill omen; you will not persuade me.
For if any other person on earth had commanded me,   220
the smoke-watching seers, or priests,
we would have said it was a lie and we would turn our backs on it;
but as it is, since I myself heard the god and looked her in the face,
I am going, and her word will not be in vain. And if it is my fate
to die beside the ships of the bronze-clad Achaeans,
then so I wish it; let Achilles slay me at once
after I have clasped in my arms my son, when I have put away all desire
   for weeping."

     He spoke, and opened up the fine covers of his chests.
There he drew out twelve splendid robes,
and twelve single-folded woollen cloaks, and as many blankets,   230
as many mantles of white linen, and as many tunics too,
and he weighed and brought out ten full talents of gold,
and brought out two gleaming tripods, and four cauldrons,
and he brought out a splendid cup, which Thracian men gave to him
when he went to them on a mission, a magnificent possession; not
even this did the old man withhold, as he desired with all his heart
to ransom back his beloved son. And the Trojans, all,
he kept away from his covered halls, reviling them with shaming words:
"Be gone, outrages, disgraces; is there no weeping

in your own homes, that you have come to trouble me?   240
Or do you think it too little, that Zeus the son of Cronus has given me
   suffering,
destroying my best of sons? But you will come to know what this means
   too;
for you will be all the easier for the Achaeans
to kill now my son has died. But
before I behold with my own eyes my city sacked and ravaged,
may I enter in the house of Hades."

        He spoke, and drove the men off with his staff; and they went out
before the old man's urgency. And to his own sons he shouted rebuke,
railing at Helenos and Paris and brilliant Agathon
and Pammon and Antiphonos and Polites of the war cry   250
and Deïphobos and Hippothoös, too, and noble Dios.
To these nine, the old man, shouting his threats, gave orders:
"Make haste, worthless children, my disgraces. I would the pack of you
together had been slain by the swift ship instead of Hector.
Woe is me, fated utterly, since I sired the best sons
in broad Troy, but I say not a one of them is left,
Mestor the godlike and Troilos the chariot fighter
and Hector, who was a god among men, nor did he seem to be
the son of mortal man, but of a god.
War destroyed these men, and all these things of shame are left,   260
the liars and dancers, and heroes of the dance floor,
snatchers of lambs and kids in their own land.
Will you all not prepare a wagon for me at once,
and place all these things in it, so that we can go upon our way?"

        So he spoke; and they trembling before the old man's threats
lifted out the strong-wheeled wagon for the mule,
a beautiful thing, newly made, and fastened the wicker carrier on it,
and took down from its peg the mule yoke
made of boxwood and with a knob upon it, well-fitted with rings to guide
   the reins;

and they brought out the yoke strap of nine cubits length together with
   the yoke.   270
Then they fitted the yoke skilfully onto the well-polished wagon pole,
at the front end, and cast the ring over its peg,
and they bound the thong three times on each side to the knob, and then
secured it with a series of turns, and tucked the end under.
And carrying it from the storeroom they piled onto the polished wagon
the vast ransom for the head of Hector.
They yoked the mules, strong-footed, working in harness,
which in time before the Mysians gave as glorious gifts to Priam.
And for Priam they led under the yoke the horses that the old man,
keeping them for himself, tended at their well-polished manger.   280

      So the herald and Priam were having the animals yoked in the
high-roofed house, a flurry of thoughts in their minds.
And Hecuba with stricken heart drew near them,
carrying in her right hand in a cup of gold
wine that is sweet to the mind, so that they might set out after making
   libation.
She stood before the horses, and spoke to Priam and said his name:
"Here, pour an offering to Zeus the father, and pray that you come home,
back from the enemy men, since your heart drives you
to the ships, although I do not wish it.
Come, pray then to the son of Cronus of the black cloud   290
on Ida, who looks down upon the whole of Troy,
and ask for a bird of omen, the swift messenger that for him
is most prized of birds and whose strength is greatest,
to fly to the right, so that you yourself, marking it with your eyes,
may go trusting in it to the ships of the Danaans of swift horses.
But if far-thundering Zeus does not send you his messenger,
I would surely not then urge or bid you
go to the Argive ships, for all you are determined."
      Then answering her spoke godlike Priam:
"O my woman, I will not disobey what you demand;   300

for it is good to raise one's hands to Zeus, that he might have mercy."
He spoke, and the old man called on the handmaid attendant
to pour clean water on their hands; and the maid came up beside him
holding in her hands both a water bowl and pouring jug.
And after washing his hands, Priam took the cup from his wife.
Then standing in the middle of his court he prayed, and poured a wine
    libation
as he looked toward the heavens, and lifting his voice he spoke:
"Father Zeus, ruling from Mount Ida, most glorious and greatest,
grant that I come as one welcomed to the shelter of Achilles and that he
    pity me.
And send a bird, your swift messenger, which for you yourself   310
is most prized of birds and whose strength is greatest,
to fly to the right, so that I myself, marking it with my eyes,
may go trusting in it to the ships of the Danaans of swift horses."

        So he spoke in prayer, and Zeus all-devising heard him,
and he sent at once an eagle, the surest omen of winged birds,
the dusky hunter men call the darkly-spangled one.
As wide as the door of a lofty room is made
in the house of a wealthy man, strong-fitted with bolts,
so wide were its wings on either side; and it appeared to them
on the right as it swept through the city. And seeing it they   320
rejoiced, and the spirit in the breasts of all was lifted.

        Then in haste the old man mounted his polished chariot,
and drove out of the gateway and echoing colonnade.
In front, drawing the four-wheeled wagon, went the mules,
which skilful Idaios the herald was driving; then the horses behind,
which the old man as he guided urged with his whip swiftly on
through the city. And all his dear ones followed with him
lamenting greatly, as if he were going to his death.

        Then when they descended from the city, and reached
    the plain,
the rest, turning back, returned to Ilion,   330

the sons and the husbands of his daughters; but the two men did not
   escape the notice
of far-thundering Zeus as they came into view upon the plain, and he
   pitied the old man as he saw him
and swiftly spoke to Hermes his dear son:
"Hermes, it pleases you beyond all other gods
to act as man's companion, and you listen to whomever you will;
go now, and lead Priam to the hollow ships of the Achaeans
in such a way that none of the other Danaans sees him,
no one notices, until he arrives at the shelter of the son of Peleus."

     So he spoke; nor did the messenger, the Slayer of Argos, disobey.
Straightway he bound beneath his feet his splendid sandals   340
immortal, golden, which carried him over the water
and over the boundless earth with the breath of the wind;
he took up his wand, with which he charms the eyes
of whichever men he wishes, and rouses them again when they have
   slumbered;
and taking this in his hands the mighty Slayer of Argos flew away.
Swiftly he arrived at Troy and at the Hellespont
then he set out in the likeness of a noble youth
with his first beard, which is when early manhood is most graceful.

     And when Priam and Idaios had driven beyond the great burial
   mound of Ilos,
then they brought the mules and horses to a stand at the river,   350
so they could drink; for dusk by now had come upon the earth.
And as he looked, the herald caught sight of Hermes
drawing close from nearby, and raising his voice he spoke to Priam:
"Take care, son of Dardanos; there is need for a cautious mind.
I see a man, and I think we two will soon be torn to pieces.
Come, let us flee with the horses, or if not
let us take hold of his knees and beg, in the hope that he have mercy."

     So he spoke; and the old man's mind was in turmoil, and he was
   dreadfully afraid,

and the hair stood up on his bent limbs,
and he stood stupefied. But the Runner himself drawing near   360
and taking the old man's hand, inquired of him and addressed him:
"Whither, father, do you guide your mules and horses so
through the ambrosial night, when other mortal men are sleeping?
Do you have no fear of the Achaeans, who breathe fury,
hostile men and your enemy, who are near?
If any one of them should see you leading so much treasure
through the black fast-moving night, what then would be your plan?
You yourself are not young, and this man who attends you is too old
for driving men away, who might step forth in violence.
But I will do nothing to harm you, and will keep any other man   370
from you who would; for I liken you to my own father."
          Then old Priam, like a god, answered him:
"These things are much as you say, dear child.
But still one of the gods has surely stretched his hands above me,
who sent such a lucky wayfarer as you to fall in with me,
for such is your build and wonderful beauty,
and you have good sense in your mind; yours are blessed parents."
          Then in turn the messenger and Slayer of Argos addressed him:
"Yes, all these things, old man, you rightly say.
But come and tell me this and relate it exactly;   380
either you are sending away somewhere your many fine possessions
to men in other lands, so that they stay there safe for you,
or you are all abandoning sacred Ilion
in fear; for such a man, the best, has fallen,
your son; for he held nothing back in fight with the Achaeans."
          Then old Priam, like a god, answered him:
"Who are you, my good friend, and who are your parents?
How well you tell the fate of my unhappy son."
Then in turn the messenger and Slayer of Argos addressed him:
"You test me, old man, when you ask of brilliant Hector.   390
The man whom many times I saw with my own eyes

in battle where men win glory, and when he drove the Argives
to the ships and kept killing them as he slashed with his sharp bronze
    sword.
We stood by looking on in wonder; for Achilles
did not permit us to join the fight, being angered with the son of Atreus.
For I am a companion in arms-of-Achilles, and the same well-made ship
    brought us both.
I come from the Myrmidons, and my father is Polyktor.
He is a wealthy man, but he is old now, just as you;
He has six sons, and I am his seventh;
having shaken lots among us, it fell to me to follow here.   400
And now I have come to the plain from the ships; for at dawn
the dark-eyed Achaeans will deploy for battle round the city.
For these men have grown impatient sitting around, nor can the
Achaean kings restrain them in their eagerness for war."

       Then old Priam, like a god, answered him:
"If you are a companion of Peleus' son Achilles,
come and tell me the whole truth,
whether my son is still by the ships, or whether Achilles
has cut him limb from limb and already thrown him to his dogs."

       Then in turn the messenger and Slayer of Argos addressed
    him: 410
"O old man, the dogs have not eaten him at all, nor the birds,
but he lies there still beside Achilles' ship
among the shelters, just as he was. It is now the twelfth day
he has been lying, and his body has not decayed at all, nor have the
    worms
gnawed at him, which consume men slain in battle.
It is true Achilles drags him heedlessly around the tomb
of his companion, when the bright dawn shows forth,
but does not disfigure him; you yourself would wonder at this, going there,
how he lies fresh like the dew, and he is wholly cleansed of blood,
there is no stain anywhere; all the wounds have closed together,   420

all the wounds that he was struck; for many men drove their bronze
    weapons into him.
So do the blessed gods care for your noble son
although he is dead, since he was very dear to their hearts."

        So he spoke; and the old man rejoiced, and answered with a word:
"O child, surely it is a good thing to give the immortals
their proper gifts, since never did my son—if ever he was—
forget in his halls the gods who hold Olympus;
they remembered in turn these offerings even in his fated death.
But come and accept this beautiful two-handled cup from me,
and give me your protection, and with the gods escort me,   430
until I come to the shelter of the son of Peleus."

        Then in turn the messenger and Slayer of Argos addressed him:
"You make trial of my youth, old man, but you will not persuade me,
who bid me accept your gifts behind Achilles' back.
I fear him and in my heart I shrink
to rob him, lest something evil befall me later.
But with all kindness I would be your escort even should we go all the way
to famous Argos, whether by swift ship, or accompanying you on foot;
and no man would fight with you, making light of your escort."

        He spoke, and springing onto the horse-drawn chariot the
    Runner   440
swiftly took the whip and reins into his hands,
and breathed a brave spirit into the mules and horses.
And when they reached the fortifications of the ships and the ditch—
the watch guards were just beginning to busy themselves with their
    meals—
then the messenger Argeïphontes poured sleep upon them
all, and straightway opened the gates and pushed back the bolts,
and led in Priam and the glorious gifts upon the wagon.

        And when they came before the towering quarters of the son of
    Peleus—
which the Myrmidons had built for their lord,

cutting logs of fir, and thatched it above   450
after gathering bristling reeds from the meadow;
and all around it they built for their lord a great courtyard
with close-set stakes; a single bolt made of fir secured its door,
a bolt that three Achaean men would drive shut,
and three men would draw the great bolt back from its door,
three other men, but Achilles would drive it shut even on his own—
there Hermes the Runner opened it for the old man,
and brought inside the illustrious gifts for the swift-footed son of Peleus.
He descended from behind the horses to the ground and spoke:
"Old sir, I, a divine god, came to your aid;   460
I am Hermes; for my father sent me to accompany you as escort.
Yet I shall be quick to go back, nor will I enter into Achilles' sight;
for it would be cause for anger
should a mortal man entertain a god in this way, face to face.
But you go in and take hold of the knees of the son of Peleus;
and make your prayer in the name of his father and his mother of the
    lovely hair and his son, so that you stir his heart."

          Thus speaking, Hermes departed for high Olympus.
And Priam leapt from behind his horses to the ground,
and left Idaios there; and he remained   470
guarding the mules and horses. The old man went straight toward the
    quarters,
where Achilles beloved of Zeus would always sit, and found him
inside; his companions were sitting apart; two alone,
the warrior Automedon and Alkimos, companion of Ares,
were busy by him. He had just finished his meal,
eating and drinking, and the table still lay beside him.
Unseen by these men great Priam entered, then standing close,
with his arms he clasped Achilles' knees and kissed the
terrible man-slaughtering hands, which had killed his many sons.
As when madness closes tight upon a man who, after killing
    someone   480

in his own land, arrives in the country of others,
at a rich man's house, and wonder grips those looking on,
so Achilles looked in wonder at godlike Priam,
and the others in wonder, too, looked each towards the other.

      And in supplication Priam addressed him:
"Remember your father, godlike Achilles,
The same age as I, on the ruinous threshold of old age.
And perhaps those who dwell round surround him and
bear hard upon him, nor is there anyone to ward off harm and destruction.
Yet surely when he hears you are living   490
he rejoices in his heart and hopes for all his days
to see his beloved son returning from Troy.
But I am fated utterly, since I sired the best sons
in broad Troy, but I say not a one of them is left.
Fifty were my sons, when the sons of the Achaeans came;
nineteen were born to me from the womb of the same mother,
and the rest the women in my palace bore to me.
Of these furious Ares has made slack the knees of many;
he who alone was left to me, he alone protected our city and those inside it,
him it was you lately killed as he fought to defend his country,   500
Hector. And for his sake I come now to the ships of the Achaeans
to win his release from you, and I bear an untold ransom.
Revere the gods, Achilles, and have pity upon me,
remembering your father; for I am yet more pitiful,
and have endured such things as no other mortal man upon the earth,
drawing to my lips the hands of the man who killed my son."

      So he spoke; and he stirred in the other a yearning to weep for
   his own father,
and taking hold of his hand he gently pushed the old man away.
And the two remembered, the one weeping without cessation for
man-slaughtering Hector as he lay curled before Achilles' feet,   510
and Achilles wept for his own father, and then again for
Patroclus; and the sound of their lament was raised throughout the hall.

But when godlike Achilles had taken his fill of lamentation
and the yearning had gone from his breast and very limbs,
he rose suddenly from his seat, and raised the old man by the hand,
pitying his grey head and grey beard,
and lifting his voice he addressed him with winged words:
"Poor soul, surely you have endured much evil in your heart.
How did you dare to go to the Achaean ships alone,
into the sight of a man, who killed your many and your noble   520
sons? Your heart is iron.
But come and seat yourself upon the chair, and let us leave these
    sorrows
lying undisturbed within our hearts, grieving though we are;
for there is no profit in grief that numbs the heart.
For thus have the gods spun the thread of destiny for wretched mortals,
that we live in sorrow; and they themselves are free from care.
For two urns lie stored on the floor of Zeus
full of such gifts as he gives, one of evil, the other of good.
Should Zeus who delights in thunder bestow mixed lots upon a man,
he will sometimes meet with evil, another time with good;   530
but should he give to a man only from the urn of woe, he renders him the
    object of abuse,
and grinding distress drives him across the shining earth,
and he roams, esteemed by neither gods nor mortals.
Thus to Peleus too the gods gave shining gifts
from his birth; for he surpassed all men
in happiness and wealth, and was lord of the Myrmidons,
and to him, mortal though he was, they gave a goddess as his wife;
but to even him god gave evil, since
in his halls was born no line of lordly sons,
but he begot a single all-untimely child; nor do I care for him   540
as he grows old, since very far from my fatherland
I sit at Troy, afflicting you and your children.
And you, old man, we have heard, were blessed in time before;

as much as Lesbos, seat of Makar, contains out there within its
   boundaries,
and Phrygia inland and the boundless Hellespont,
all these, they say, old man, you surpassed in sons and wealth.
But since the gods of heaven have brought this misery to you,
there is forever fighting and the killing of men about your city.
Bear up, nor mourn incessantly in your heart;
for you will accomplish nothing in grieving for your son,   550
nor will you raise him from the dead; before that happens you will suffer
   yet another evil."
      Then old Priam, like a god, answered him:
"Do not have me sit upon a chair, god-cherished one, while Hector
lies in your shelters unburied, but quick as you can
release him, so that I may see him with my eyes, and you accept the
   many gifts
of ransom, which we bring for you. And have enjoyment of them, and may
you return to your fatherland, since from the first you spared me."   557
      Then looking at him from under his brows swift-footed Achilles
   spoke: 559
"Provoke me no further, old man; for I myself am minded   560
to release Hector to you; from Zeus, my mother came to me as
   messenger,
she who bore me, daughter of the old man of the sea.
I recognise, Priam, in my mind, and it does not escape me,
that some one of the gods led you to the Achaeans' swift ships;
for no mortal man, not even a young man in his prime, would dare
to come to our camp; nor could he have slipped by the watch guards, nor
   could he
easily force back the bolts of our doors.
Therefore do not now stir my heart further in its sorrows,
lest, old man, I do not spare even yourself within my shelter,
suppliant though you be, but transgress the commands of Zeus."   570
      Thus he spoke; and the old man was afraid and obeyed his word.

And the son of Peleus like a lion sprang out of the door of his shelter,
and not alone; with him followed his two henchmen,
the warrior Automedon and Alkimos, whom beyond all other companions
Achilles honoured after Patroclus died.
They released the horses and mules from under their yokes,
and led in the herald, crier to the old man,
and they seated him upon a bench; and from the strong-wheeled wagon
they lifted the boundless ransom for the body of Hector.
But they left two fine-spun robes and a tunic,   580
so Achilles could wrap the body and give it to be carried home.
And summoning his maids, Achilles ordered them to wash the body and
    anoint it,
after taking it to a place apart, so that Priam should not see his son,
for fear the old man might not keep his anger hidden in his anguished heart
on seeing his son, and might stir Achilles' own heart to violence
and he kill Priam, and transgress the commands of Zeus.
And when then the maids had washed and anointed the body with oil,
they put around it the beautiful robe and tunic,
and Achilles himself lifted it and placed it upon a bier,
then his companions with him lifted this onto the polished wagon.   590
And Achilles groaned, and called his dear companion's name:
"Do not, Patroclus, be angered with me, if you should learn,
though you be in the house of Hades, that I released shining Hector
to his father, since the ransom he gave me was not unworthy.
And I in turn will give you a portion of it, as much as is fitting."

        He spoke, and godlike Achilles went back into his shelter,
and took his seat on the richly wrought chair, from which he had risen,
against the far wall, and spoke his word to Priam:
"Your son has been released to you, old man, as you bade,
and lies upon a bier; and with the dawn's appearance,   600
you will see yourself when you take him. But now let us not forget our
    supper.
For even Niobe of the lovely hair did not forget her food,

she whose twelve children were destroyed in her halls,
six daughters, and six sons in the prime of manhood.
The sons Apollo slew with his silver bow
in his anger with Niobe, and Artemis who showers arrows slew the
    daughters,
because Niobe equalled herself to Leto of the lovely cheeks—
for she would boast that Leto bore two children, while she herself had
    borne many.
So two only though they were, they destroyed the many.
And for nine days they lay in their own blood, nor was there anyone   610
to give them burial; for the son of Cronus had turned the people into stone.
Then on the tenth day the heavenly gods gave them burial,
and Niobe bethought herself of food, when she was worn out with
    weeping.
And now among the rocks somewhere, in the lonely mountains
of Sipylos, where they say are the sleeping places of the immortal
nymphs who race beside the river Achelous,
there, stone though she is, she broods upon the cares sent her from the
    gods.
But come, and let us two, illustrious old sir, take thought
of food. For you may weep for your dear son again
when you have brought him into Ilion; he will be the cause of many
    tears."   620
        He spoke, and springing to his feet swift Achilles, with a cut to
    the throat,
slaughtered a shining white sheep; his companions flayed it and with skill
    prepared it properly.
They sliced the flesh skilfully and pierced it on spits
and roasted it with care, and then drew off all the pieces.
Automedon took bread to distribute around the table
in fine baskets; but Achilles distributed the meat;
and they reached out their hands to the good things set ready before them.
And when they had put away desire for eating and drinking,

then did Priam son of Dardanos look in wonder at Achilles,
how massive he was, what kind of man; for he was like the gods to look
    upon;   630
and Achilles looked in wonder at Dardanian Priam,
gazing on his noble face and listening to his words.

        But when they had their fill of looking upon each other,
then old Priam the godlike addressed Achilles first:
"Let me go to bed now quickly, god-cherished one, so that
we may have solace when we lie down beneath sweet sleep.
For not yet have my eyes closed beneath my lids,
from the time my son lost his life at your hands,
but always I groaned in lament and brooded on my sorrows without
    measure,
wallowing in dung in the enclosure of my court.   640
But now I have tasted food and let gleaming wine
down my throat; before I had tasted nothing."

        He spoke; and Achilles ordered the companions and servant
    women
to set out a bed under cover of the porch and to throw upon it
splendid crimson blankets to lie upon, and to spread rugs over them,
and to place woollen cloaks on top of all to cover them.
And the maids went from the hall bearing torches in their hands,
and working in haste soon spread two beds.
Then bantering, Achilles of the swift feet addressed Priam:
"Sleep outside, old friend, for fear one of the Achaean   650
leaders come suddenly upon us here, who forever
devise their counsels beside me, as is right and proper.
If one of them were to see you through the swift black night,
he would at once make it known to Agamemnon, shepherd of the people,
and there would be delay in the surrender of the body.
But come and tell me this and relate it exactly;
how many days do you desire to give funeral rites to shining Hector—
for so long I will wait and hold back the army."

Then old Priam the godlike answered him:

"If then you are willing for me to accomplish Hector's funeral,   660

by doing as follows, Achilles, you would give me a kindness.

For you know how we are penned within the city, and it is a long way

to bring wood from the mountains; for the Trojans are greatly afraid;

nine days we would mourn him in our halls,

and on the tenth we would bury him and the people would feast,

and on the eleventh day we would make a tomb for him:

and on the twelfth we shall go to war, if indeed we must."

Then in turn swift-footed godlike Achilles addressed him:

"These things, old Priam, will be as you ask;

I will suspend the war for such time as you command."   670

And so speaking he took hold of the old man's right hand

by the wrist, lest he have any fear in his heart.

Then they lay down to sleep there in the forecourt of the shelter,

the herald and Priam, a flurry of thoughts in their minds.

But Achilles slept in the inner recess of his well-built shelter,

and Briseïs of the lovely cheeks lay at his side.

So the other gods as well as chariot-fighting men

slept through the night, overcome by soft slumber,

but sleep did not lay hold of Hermes the runner

as he turned over in his heart how he might send king Priam   680

from the ships unnoticed by the hallowed watchers of the gate.

And he stood above Priam's head and addressed him with his words:

"Old man, surely you have no thought of any evil, seeing how you sleep

in the midst of enemy men, since Achilles spared you.

And now you have won release of your beloved son, and gave many

things for him;

but your sons who were left behind would give yet three times

as much ransom for you alive, should Agamemnon

the son of Atreus recognise you, and all the Achaeans."

So he spoke; and the old man was afraid, and woke up his herald.

Then Hermes yoked the mules and horses for them,   690

and himself drove swiftly through the camp; nor did anyone see.

      But when they reached the crossing of the fair-flowing
   stream,   692
then Hermes departed for high Olympus;   694
and Dawn robed in saffron spread over all the earth;
the men with lamentation and groaning drove the horses on
to the city, and the mules carried the corpse. No man
saw them at first, nor any fair-belted woman,
but then Cassandra, like to golden Aphrodite,
having gone up to the height of Pergamos, saw her beloved father   700
standing in the chariot and the herald and city crier;
and then she saw Hector lying upon the bier drawn by the mules.
She wailed her grief aloud, then cried out to the whole city:
"Look upon Hector, men and women of Troy! Come,
if ever before you used to rejoice when he returned alive from battle,
since he was the great joy of the city and all its people."

      So she spoke; nor did any man remain there in the city
nor any woman; uncontrollable grief seized all;
close by the gates they met Priam as he brought Hector's body;
at the front his beloved wife and lady mother ripped their hair
   in grief   710
for him, lunging at the strong-wheeled wagon,
to touch his head; and the throng surrounded him weeping.
And for the whole day long until the sun's going down they would have
mourned Hector, pouring their tears before the gates,
had not the old man spoken among them from the chariot:
"Make way for me to pass with the mules; later
you can sate yourselves with weeping, when I have brought him home."
So he spoke; and they stood aside and made way for the wagon.

      And when they had brought him into the illustrious house, then
they laid him upon a fretted bed, and set beside it singers,   720
leaders of the dirges, who sang their mournful dirge song,
and the women keened in response.

And white-armed Andromache led the lament among them,
holding in her arms the head of horse-breaking Hector:
"My husband, you were lost from life while young, and are leaving me a
     widow
in your halls; and the child is still just a baby,
whom we bore, you and I, ill-fated both, nor do I think
he will reach young manhood; before that this city
will be wholly ravaged; for you its watchman have perished, who used to
     guard it,
who protected its devoted wives and tender children.   730
They soon will be carried away in the hollow ships,
and I with them; and you then, my child, either you will follow with me,
and there do work unworthy of you
toiling for a harsh master—or some Achaean man
seizing you by the arm will hurl you from the ramparts, unhappy death,
in his anger, one whose brother, perhaps, Hector slew,
or his father or even his son, since so many of the Achaeans
gripped the broad earth in their teeth at Hector's hands.
For your father was no gentle man in sad battle;
therefore the people mourn him through the city,   740
and cursed is the grief and lamentation you have laid upon your parents,
Hector. And to me beyond all others will be left painful sorrow;
for you did not reach out your hands to me from your bed as you were
     dying,
nor did you speak some close word to me, which I might always
remember through the nights and days as I shed my tears."
So she spoke, crying, and the women in response mourned.

     And Hecuba led them next in the passionate lament:
"Hector, far the dearest to my heart of all my sons,
while you were alive you were dear to the gods,
who now care for you even in your fated lot of death.   750
Other sons of mine Achilles of the swift feet would sell,
whomever he captured, beyond the murmuring salt sea,

into Samothrace, into Imbros and sea-spattered Lemnos;
but he plucked your soul from you with his tapered bronze spear,
and dragged you again and again around the tomb of his companion
Patroclus, whom you slew—nor did he raise him from the dead so
   doing—
yet now you lie as fresh as dew, unsullied in my halls,
like one whom Apollo of the silver bow
approaches and kills with his gentle arrows."
So she spoke weeping, and stirred unceasing wailing.   760

      Then third among the women, Helen led the lament:
"Hector, far dearest to my heart of all my husband's brothers;
too true, my husband is Alexandros of godlike beauty,
who led me to Troy; would that I had died before;
for this is now the twentieth year for me
since I set out from there and forsook my fatherland,
but never yet did I hear a harsh or abusive word from you,
but if someone else would revile me in these halls,
one of my husband's brothers, or his sisters, or one of my fine-robed
   sisters-in-law,
or my husband's mother—but my husband's father was like a kind father
   always—   770
you with soothing words would restrain them
with your gentle nature and kind speech.
Therefore I weep, grieving at heart, for you and for me, ill-fated, together;
for no longer is there anyone else in broad Troy
to be kind or friend to me, but all shudder at me."
So she spoke crying, and in response all the great multitude moaned.

      Then old Priam spoke his word among the people:
"Men of Troy, now fetch timber to the city. Have no fear in your heart
of cunning ambush by the Argives; for Achilles,
as he sent me from the black ships, gave orders thus,   780
that he would do no harm before the twelfth dawn comes."
So he spoke; and the men yoked the oxen and mules to the wagons,

and soon they were gathered before the city.

      For nine days they brought an immense pile of timber;
and when at length the tenth dawn showed, bringing light to mortals,
then, shedding tears, they carried forth bold Hector.
On the very top of the pyre they placed his body, and on it flung the fire.

      And when Dawn born of the morning showed forth her fingers
  of rosy light,
then around the pyre of illustrious Hector the people gathered;   789
first they extinguished the burning pyre with dark-gleaming wine   791
entirely, all that retained the fire's strength; and then
his brothers and his comrades picked out his white bones
as they wept, and the swelling tears fell from their cheeks.
And taking the bones they placed them in a golden box,
after covering them round with soft purple cloth;
swiftly they placed these in a hollowed grave, and covered it
from above with great stones set close together.
Lightly they heaped up the burial mound—lookouts were set all round,
lest the strong-greaved Achaeans should attack before—   800
and when they had piled up the mound they started back. Then
having come together they duly gave a glorious feast
in the house of Priam, king nurtured by Zeus.
Thus they tended the funeral of Hector, breaker of horses.

NOTES

1.39 *God of Plague*: In the Greek, Chryses invokes Apollo as *Smintheus*. According to ancient commentary, *sminthos* was the word for "mouse" in Mysian, a language of the region east of the Troad. Modern scholars have suggested that Apollo Smintheus may have origins in an east-central European mouse-god of the second millennium B.C. There is much evidence that the Greeks of antiquity associated mice with pestilence.

1.263–68 *Peirithoös and Dryas . . . slaughtered them*: Peirithoös, Dryas, Kaineus, Exadios, and Polyphemos are all of the Lapith tribe in Thessaly. Their battle with the Centaurs, wild creatures that were half-man and half-horse living in the mountains of Thessaly, was a favourite subject in later Greek art. The Greek word used of the Centaurs here, *phêr*, literally "wild animals", is Aeolic, reflecting a native Thessalian tradition.

1.402–4 *the Hundred-Handed One . . . Briareos . . . Aigaion*: The poet Hesiod (*Theogony*, vv. 148–53) tells of three hundred-handed brothers—Briareos (meaning "strong"), Cottus, and Gyes—who are sons of Uranus and Gaia (or Heaven and Earth). In the *Iliad*'s mythology, however, the father in question is perhaps Poseidon. There are a number of examples in Homeric epic of a person or thing having both a divine and human name. The incident Achilles references was a revolt against Zeus by the Olympians (in Hesiod's poem the revolt was by the Titans, the generation of gods older than Zeus). As the commentator G. S. Kirk observes, "much remains obscure".

1.423 *the river of Ocean*: Like a mighty river, Ocean encircles the Earth, and is the source of all other rivers.

1.538 *the old man of the sea*: Nereus, the father of Thetis and her sister Nereids.

1.594 *the Sintian men*: Inhabitants of the island of Lemnos who were said to be originally from Thrace.

2.103 *Hermes, the messenger and slayer of Argos*: The first appearance of a common epithet for Hermes, a messenger of the gods also known as "the runner".

The Greek word *Argeïphontes* is generally taken to mean "slayer of Argos", a monstrous giant with one hundred eyes. Among other interpretations, some take the word to mean "swift to appear".

2.157 *who wields the aegis*: This fearsome if obscure talisman of divine power is wielded by Zeus, Athena and Apollo. Literally it means "goatskin", but it has been suggested that the aegis was originally a thunderbolt, and goats are linked with some northern thunder-gods. In the *Iliad* the aegis is uncertainly described as a kind of shield with shaggy tassels.

2.157 *Unwearied One*: Athena is called by the ancient title *Atrytone* five times in the epic; different texts differ as to whether this should be capitalised as a formal epithet, or left as a simple adjective. The term is thought to mean "unwearied", "weariless".

2.336 *Gerenian*: Apparently Gerenia was a place associated with Nestor.

2.651 *equal to Enyalios*: Another name for Ares.

2.718 *Philoctetes*: Abandoned on Lemnos on account of his noxious wound, Philoctetes was later sought out by the Achaeans, who had learned of a prophecy that Troy could not be taken without his bow and arrow, which he had inherited from Heracles.

2.782 *Typhoeus*: The monster offspring of Tartaros and Gaia who attempted to overthrow Zeus, but Zeus defeated him and cast him beneath the earth.

3.6 *Pygmy men*: Literally "fistlike men". A popular subject in Greek art, the battle of Pygmies with cranes may have been the subject of a lost Egyptian folk tale.

4.2 *Lady Hebe*: Daughter of Zeus and Hera whose name means "youth", Hebe is an attendant to the gods.

4.8 *Athena who stands guardian in Boeotia*: In the Greek she is Athena *Alalkomeneïs;* the latter word refers to a cult site in Boeotia, dedicated to a local hero, Alalkomenees.

4.101 *Lycian Apollo*: In the Greek Apollo's epithet, *Lukïgenes*, could be derived from *lukos* ("wolf"), or Lycia, a region in Southwest Anatolia, with which Pandaros is associated.

4.219 *Chiron*: The most civilised of the wild centaurs who dwelt in the wooded mountains of Thessaly, Chiron was the mentor of many heroes, including Achilles, to whom he taught his healing arts.

4.365 *Tydeus*: The father of Diomedes, Tydeus was one of the Seven Against Thebes, the band of heroes who marched against the tyrant of Thebes, one of the sons of Oedipus (who is referred to later at 23.679), when he refused to relinquish power to his brother. All Seven were killed, and it was left to

their sons, the Epigoni ("Descendants") to capture the city. Tydeus, a hero
of old, was associated with many feats.

4.385 *Thebans from the city of Cadmus*: Literally Cadmeians, men of Cadmeia, or
Thebes (not to be confused with Egyptian Thebes), a Greek city in Boeotia
named after its founder, Cadmus.

4.515 *Tritogeneia*: an obscure epithet of Athena, variously explained by associa-
tions with Lake Tritonis in Libya; by the several rivers Triton in Greece; by
the sea deity Triton; or by *tritos*, Greek for 'third'.

5.236 *single-hoofed*: A common attribute of horses, referring to their uncloven
hoofs, which form a "single" unit.

5.266 *Ganymede*: The most handsome man on earth and one of the sons of Tros,
one of the founding kings of Troy, Ganymede was snatched away by Zeus to
be cup bearer to the gods.

5.333 *city-sacking Enyo*: Enyo is a goddess of war, associated with Ares.

5.392 *powerful son of Amphitryon*: This is Heracles, son of Zeus by Alkmene, whose
mortal husband was Amphitryon. Zeus' fathering of Heracles by a mortal
woman incited Hera's undying fury. This is the first of many references to
Heracles in the *Iliad*.

5.401 *Paiëon*: A god of healing whose name appears as far back as the Linear B
tablets. In later tradition he is merged with Apollo, who takes the title Apollo
Paiëon. A paiëon, or paean, becomes a song of praise to Apollo.

5.638ff. *Heracles they say . .* : A reference to one of the many feats of Heracles
(Hercules in Latin). The story is embedded in a longer mythological narrative
that begins with Zeus' punishment of Apollo and Poseidon for rebellion
against him. Dispatched by Zeus to work as servants for Laomedon, the
grandson of Tros and the father of king Priam, the two gods were set to
build the walls of Troy. When they sought due payment, Laomedon refused,
and in retribution Poseidon sent a monster to terrorise the land. Laomedon
then offered the semi-divine horses descended from those given to his
forebear Tros (in recompense for the abduction of Ganymede to Olympus) to
whomever could kill the monster. Heracles did this, but Laomedon reneged
again, attempting to pass off mortal horses for the divine. Heracles then
attacked and sacked Troy, killing Laomedon and all his sons, save Priam.

5.741 *Gorgon*: A snake-haired monster whose dread gaze, even dead, turned men
to stone.

5.845 *cap of Hades*: A cap of invisibility belonging to Hades, god of the under-
world, the "unseen one".

5.898 *the fallen Titans*: In the Greek these are the *Ouraniones*, or children of Ouranos (Heaven), also known as the Titans, whom Zeus overpowered and consigned to the depths of Tartaros.

6.132 *nurses of raving Dionysus*: Here the god of wine is a mere baby, whom, according to tradition, his father Zeus handed to nymphs to raise in the glens of Mount Nysa.

6.168 *gave him baneful signs*: The only reference to writing in the Homeric poems. See the introduction, where these lines are discussed (XXIX).

6.216 *Oineus*: King of Calydon and the father of Tydeus, hence grandfather of Diomedes.

6.319 *eleven cubits length*: A cubit is the approximate length of a forearm (*pêku*), or about seventeen to twenty inches.

7.452–53 *that wall, which I and Phoebus Apollo built for the warrior Laomedon*: A reference to the legend referred to above (5.638ff), that Apollo and Poseidon built the walls of Troy while in servitude to King Laomedon.

7.468 *Euneos son of Jason*: One of three references in the *Iliad* (the others being at 21.41 and 23.747) to Jason, the hero of the saga of the Argonauts.

8.363 *I kept on saving his son Heracles who was worn down by the trials set by Eurystheus*: Another extended reference to Heracles (see note for 5.638ff above). Heracles, despised by Zeus' wife Hera, was compelled to serve his brutal cousin King Eurystheus, performing a series of "trials" (the Greek word, *athloi*, literally means "contests"), including descending into Hades to bring back Cerberus, "the hound of hateful Hades" (v. 368), who guards the entrance to Erebus, or the Underworld. The twelve labours of Heracles are not yet standardised in the *Iliad*.

8.479 *Iapetos and Cronus*: Titan sons of Ouranus and the fathers of, respectively, Prometheus and Zeus, Zeus; overthrew them and confined them in the depths of Tartaros.

8.480 *Helios Hyperion*: The sun.

9.142–45 *Orestes . . . Chrysothemis and Laodike and Iphianassa*: The son and three daughters of Agamemnon and his wife Clytemnestra. The names of the daughters do not accord with well-known classical tradition, which knows of Iphigenia and Electra.

9.188 *Eëtion*: Here, king of Thebes and father of Andromache; there are several men by this name mentioned in the *Iliad*.

9.405 *Pytho*: Another name for Delphi, the oracular site sacred to Apollo, who is sometimes referred to as Pythian Apollo for his slaying of a great python. Pytho is also mentioned in the Catalogue of Ships, at 2.519.

9.571 *Erinys*: The Fury; one of the Furies (in Greek *Erinyes*), vengeful spirits beneath the earth, agents of the gods of the underworld.

Book 10, the Doloneia: Even in antiquity there was a question as to whether this very Odyssean interlude represented by the entirety of Book 10 originally belonged to the Iliad. Modern opinion runs the whole gamut, from those who believe it is Iliadic, to those who believe it is the work of Homer but not original to the Iliad, to those who believe it to be the work of an unrelated hand. See Bryan Hainsworth, The Iliad: A Commentary, vol. 3, Books 9–12 (Cambridge, 2000), 151–55. To the ear of this translator, the book sounds Homeric, but not native to the Iliad. That said, it is not badly integrated into the Iliad's action, and it gives audiences a chance to see Odysseus, that favourite hero of the Trojan War, in action.

11.1 Tithonos: Priam's half-brother, whom Dawn took to be her lover.

11.270 the spirits attending birth-pain: In Greek, these are the Eileithyiai, possibly meaning "the goddesses who come", either because their coming signifies the onset of birth-pain or because they come in time of need; but there is much evidence that they are pre-Greek. Compere with 16.187.

11.682 Neleian Pylos: Pylos the city of Neleus, Nestor's father.

11.690 Heracles had committed outrages: According to legend Heracles fought Neleus, Nestor's father, who was the son of Poseidon, at Pylos; Poseidon came to his son's rescue.

11.709 two Moliones: This means "the two sons of Molos", Molos being their mother (or possibly referring to their mother's father). In the Iliad the brothers Kteatos and Eurytos are simply twins, but later tradition has them as Siamese twins. They are named in the Catalogue of Ships at 2.621.

11.750–51 Molione boys, from the line of Aktor, had not their father, the wide-ruling Earth-Shaker Poseidon: Poseidon was the real father of the twins, Aktor being their human father-in-name.

13.4–6 Thracians . . . Mysians . . . Hippemolgoi . . . the Abioi: All four are pastoralist tribes of the northern steppes. Hippemolgoi literally means "Mare-milkers".

13.669 Achaeans' harsh fine for deserters: A reminder that not every man at Troy was there for glory.

14.201–4. Ocean, the source of the gods, and mother Tethys: Elsewhere in mythology, Ocean and Tethys are children of Ouranos and Gaia (Heaven and Earth), the ultimate "source" of gods. Here, the implication is that Ocean and Tethys are the primordial source. Rhea, the wife of Cronus and the mother of Zeus and his sister Hera, gave Hera to Ocean and Tethys for safekeeping, while Zeus battled with their father and the other Titans.

14.250ff. Heracles, that overbearing son of Zeus: Following Heracles' sack of Ilion

(5.638ff., above), Hera induced Sleep to visit Zeus, so that she could torment his hated son with yet another trial, this time by driving him off course at sea, to the island of Kos.

14.279 *Tartaros*: The lowest part of the underworld—no place on earth is lower.

14.290–91 *a clear-voiced bird, which in the mountains the gods call* chalkis, *but men* kymindis: This is a kind of large owl, possibly the eagle-owl, and another example of the dual terminology used by gods and men (see note for 1.402–4).

14.296 *in secret from their beloved parents*: Zeus and Hera are brother and sister as well as husband and wife. Evidently, their sexual relationship began while in their parents' home.

14.434 *Xanthos, which is born of immortal Zeus*: The river Xanthos, also called Scamander, is born of Zeus in that Zeus, the god of weather, fills the river with rain.

15.87 *Themis of the lovely cheeks*: The Greek word *themis* means "accepted practice", "custom", "that which is permitted or decent". Significantly, the goddess Themis presides over orderly feasting. She is asked by Zeus to call a key assembly at 20.4

15.204 *the Furies*: The Erinyes (see note to 9.571), here in the plural, punish various transgressions, especially violations of family bonds and order, such as disrespect for an older brother.

16.175 *whom the daughter of Peleus bore, beautiful Polydora*: Polydora, the half-sister of Achilles, lay with the river god Spercheios; Spercheios was the principal river in Achilles' homeland, Phthia.

16.184 *Hermes the healer*: Hermes' epithet *akákēta* is usually taken to derive from a verb meaning "to heal"; other interpretations have it meaning something along the lines of "without guile", or an association with a cult located on Mount Akakesion in Arcadia.

16.187 *Eileithyia, the goddess who causes pain in birth*: At 11.270 the "spirits attending birth pain" are called Eileithyiai in the plural form; here a single goddess is named, a daughter of Zeus and Hera.

16.233–35 *Lord Zeus of Pelasgian Dodona . . . with unwashed feet*: This most solemn prayer evokes Zeus of Dodona, a sanctuary sacred to Zeus in northwest Greece, known for its oracle, which spoke through the leaves of a sacred oak; in its antiquity it rivalled the oracle at Delphi. The Pelasgians were a prehistoric tribe whom ancient writers regarded as indigenous to Greece. The Selloi (there is good support for reading "Helloi" here), the priests interpreting the oracular pronouncements may have gone barefoot so as to draw strength from the earth. Long without a temple or other major structure, Dodona evokes the open-air, direct worship of the great god of the sky and storms. Its substantial ruins can be seen today some twelve miles south-west of modern Ioannina.

16.543 *at the hands of Patroclus*; Glaukos' words indicate that the Trojans and their allies now realise that Achilles has not returned to battle after all, but recognise that the warrior in Achilles' armour is Patroclus.

18.39–49 *There was Glauke . . . daughters of Nereus*: The names of these thirty-three Nereids are "speaking names", which—like the names of many of the minor warriors—evoke their attributes. Roughly, they translate as Glauke/Gleaming, Thaleia/Blooming, Kymodoke/She Who Calms the Sea, Nesaie/Girl of the Island, Speio/Cave, Thoë/Swift, Halia/Of the Salt Sea, Kymothoë/Swift-Wave, Aktaia/She of the Shore, Limnoreia/Guardian of the Harbour, Melite/Honey Sweet, Iaira/Fleet, Amphithoë/Very Swift, Agauë/Wondrous, Doto/Giver, Proto/First Lady, Pherousa/She Who Bears the Ships, Dynamene/Enabler, Dexamene/Protector, Amphinome/Rich in Pasture, Kallianeira/Beautiful, Doris/Gift of the Sea, Panope/All-Seeing, Galateia/Milk White, Nemertes/Unfailing, Apseudes/Truthful, Kallianassa/Beautiful Lady, Klymene/Famous, Ianeira/Strong, Ianassa/Strong One, Maira/Sparkler, Oreithyia/Mountain Rushing, and Amatheia/Sandy.

For further discussion of these names, see Mark W. Edwards, *The Iliad: A Commentary*, vol. 5, *Books 17–20* (Cambridge, 1991), 147ff.

18.489 *alone has no part in the baths of Ocean*: The constellation Arctos, the Bear, also known as the Wagon, the Plough or the Big Dipper, never dips below the horizon into the Ocean.

18.570 *the mournful harvest song*: Or "the *Linos*-song". Linos was the son of Apollo and one of the Muses. According to one account, he was killed by his father, who was jealous of his singing. The *Linos*-song seems to have been a mournful lament. Linos may also have been a vegetation god of eastern origin, who dies in the autumn; here his song seems to be associated with harvest time.

19.119ff *but stopped the childbirth of Alkmene*: Alkmene was seduced by Zeus, who deceitfully took the form of her husband; as a consequence, she became pregnant with Heracles. Hera's first act of vengeful wrath was to ensure that Eurystheus, also of the line of Zeus, would be firstborn on this day, and therefore the more powerful of the two men. See also note on 5.392.

19.327 *Neoptolemos the godlike in beauty*: This is the only mention in the *Iliad* of Achilles' son, Neoptolemos, whose name is Greek for "new war". His mother was the daughter of a king of Scyros, where according to tradition Thetis had hidden her son, so as to escape his fated death at Troy.

20.145ff. *to the wall of godlike Heracles*: Yet another reference to the story of the sea monster sent by Poseidon when Laomedon reneged on his payment to the gods, and Heracles' slaying of the monster and subsequent sack of Troy (see also 5.638ff. and 7.452–3.).

20.297ff *And why does this guiltless man suffer agonies now*: Although of the royal house of Troy, descended from Zeus' son Dardanos, Aeneas was not a son of Laomedon, and therefore not tainted by Laomedon's guilt in cheating Poseidon and Apollo of their wages. A later tradition held that descendants of Aeneas still ruled in the Troad. The survival of Aeneas after the fall of Troy was the basis for the Roman legend celebrated by Vergil in the *Aeneid*.

21.42 *Eëtion of Imbrios*: Not the Eëtion who is Andromache's father (in the Greek text, this is line 21.43).

21.194 *the august river Achelous*: The Achelous in northwest central Greece is the longest river in Greece (another Anatolian Achelous is referred to at 24.616).

21.443–44 *when to bold Laomedon we came from Zeus to serve as labourers for a year*: This differs from the earlier reference to the year of servitude (7.452–3), which has both gods toiling on the walls.

21.483–84 *a lion among only women, and granted you to kill which of these you like*: The sudden death of a woman was attributed to the arrows of Artemis; so Andromache recalls the death of her mother at 6.428.

23.441 *without swearing to an oath*: That he did not intentionally foul Menelaos. He is indeed required to take the oath (at 23.581ff.).

24.29–30 *who insulted the goddesses, when they came to his shepherd's steading, and gave the nod to her, the goddess whose gift to him was ruinous lust*: This is the only reference in the *Iliad* to the Judgement of Paris, a story told in many ancient sources. At the wedding feast of Peleus and Thetis, the goddess Eris (whose name means "strife") tossed a golden apple among the assembled guests, saying it should go to the most beautiful goddess. Reluctant to be judge, the gods gave the task to Paris, Priam's son, who was tending sheep on the slopes of Mount Ida. Each of the contending goddesses offered a bribe: Hera offered power, Athena wisdom and battle-victory, and Aphrodite the love of Helen, the most beautiful woman in the world. Awarding the apple to Aphrodite, Paris incurred the unflagging hatred of Hera and Athena for Troy and all Trojans. The passage in which the Iliadic reference occurs, and especially lines 24.29–30, have a vexed history, leading some scholars to believe they are later interpolation (Nicholas Richardson, *The Iliad: A Commentary*, vol. 6, *Books 21–24* [Cambridge, 1996], 276ff.).

24.544 Makar is a legendary ruler of Lesbos. This passage delineates the range of Priam's power, from Lesbos to the south, Phrygia to the east, and north to the Hellespont.

24.617 *stone though she is*: In other traditions, only Niobe was turned to stone. The origin of the story is thought to lie in a natural rock formation on Mount Sipylos, roughly suggesting a woman's head, down which water coursed like tears.

24.700 *the height of Pergamos*: The citadel of Troy, above the lower city.

24.735 *will hurl you from the ramparts*: According to later tradition, this was indeed to be Astyanax's fate.

24.765 *the twentieth year for me*: The number of years perhaps should be taken as a poetic figure, with twenty representing "a long time". The war has been of ten years' duration, and there is a tradition that it took Paris and Helen some time to make their way from Sparta to Troy.

SELECTED FURTHER READING

COMMENTARIES AND REFERENCES

The most comprehensive commentary is the six-volume series published by Cambridge University Press. While the line-by-line remarks are often technical, the series' many essays on general themes ("The gods in Homer"; "Typical motifs and themes") are generally clear and readable.

G. S. Kirk, *The Iliad: A Commentary; Volume I: books 1-4* (Cambridge, 2000).

G. S. Kirk, *The Iliad: A Commentary; Volume II: books 5-8* (Cambridge, 2000).

Bryan Hainsworth, *The Iliad: A Commentary; Volume III: books 9-12* (Cambridge, 2000)

Richard Janko, *The Iliad: A Commentary; Volume IV: books 13-16* (Cambridge, 2000).

Mark W. Edwards, *The Iliad: A Commentary; Volume V: books 17-20* (Cambridge, 2000)

Nicholas Richardson, *The Iliad: A Commentary; Volume VI: books 21-24* (Cambridge, 2000).

Other general reference works

Margalit Finkelberg (ed.). *The Homer Encyclopedia.* 3 vols. (Oxford, 2011).

Timothy Gantz. *Early Greek Myth: A Guide to Literary and Artistic Sources.* (Baltimore, 1993).

Ian Morris and Barry Powell (eds.). *A New Companion to Homer.* (Leiden, 1997).

OTHER EARLY GREEK POETRY

J.S. Burgess. *The Tradition of the Trojan War in Homer and the Epic Cycle.* (Baltimore, 2001).

Homer, *The Odyssey;* Translations by Richmond Lattimore (New York, 1967), and Robert Fagles, (New York, 1996) are recommended.

Glenn W. Most (ed. and trans.). *Hesiod: Volume I: Theogony; Works and Days; Testimonia; Volume II: The Shield; Catalogue of Women; Other Fragments* (Cambridge, Mass., 2007).

M.L. West. *The Epic Cycle: A Commentary on the Lost Troy Epics* (Oxford, 2013).

M.L. West (ed. and trans.) *Homeric Hymns. Homeric Apocrypha. Lives of Homer,* (Cambridge, MA., 2003).

M. L. West (ed. and trans.) *Greek Epic Fragments from the Seventh to the Fifth Centuries BC* (Cambridge, MA., 2003).

THE BRONZE AGE AND THE TROJAN WAR

Greece and Mycenae

John Chadwick. *The Decipherment of Linear B* (Cambridge, 1958)

John Chadwick. *The Mycenaean World* (Cambridge, 1976).

Oliver Dickinson, *The Aegean Bronze Age* (Cambridge, 1994).

Nic Fields. *Mycenaean Citadels c. 1350-1200 BC* (Botley, Oxford, 2004).

Elizabeth French. *Mycenae: Agamemnon's Capital* (Oxford, 2002)

K. A. Wardle and Diana Wardle. *Cities of Legend: The Mycenaean World* (London, 1997).

Anatolia and Troy

Trevor Bryce. *Life and Society in the Hittite World* (Oxford, 2004).

Trevor Bryce. *The Trojans and Their Neighbours* (Abingdon, Oxon, 2006).

Nic Fields. *Troy c. 1700-1250 BC* (Botley, Oxford, 2004).

John Victor Luce. *Celebrating Homer's Landscapes: Troy and Ithaca Revisited* (New Haven, 1998).

Craig H. Melchert. (ed.) *The Luwians* (Leiden, 2003).

Studia Troica: Interdisciplinary periodical dedicated to Troy and the Troad through all the many historical phases; includes the annual report of excavations at Troy between 1991 and 2011. Topics can be browsed and copies of the reports purchased through the University of Tübingen's website: http://www.ufg.uni-tuebingen.de/ju engere-urgeschichte/forschungsprojekte/aktuelle-forschungsprojekte/troia/ publikationen.html

Trojan War

Eric H. Cline. *The Trojan War: A Very Short Introduction* (Oxford, 2013).

G.S. Kirk. "History and fiction in the *Iliad*", in Kirk, *The Iliad: a commentary; Volume II: books 5-8* (Cambridge, 1990), reprinted 2000; 36-50.

Joaquim Latacz. *Troy and Homer: Towards a Solution of an Old Mystery.* Translated from the German by Kevin Windle and Rosh Ireland (Oxford, 2004).

Carol G. Thomas and Craig Conant. *The Trojan War* (Westport, Conn., 2005).

Michael Wood. In Search of the Trojan War, rev. ed. (London, 2005).

AGE OF HOMER

Jane B. Carter and Sarah P. Morris, (eds.). *The Ages of Homer: A Tribute to Emily Townsend Vermeule* (Austin, 1998).

J. N. Coldstream, *Geometric Greece: 900-700 BC*, 2nd ed. rev. (New York, 2003).

Robin Osborne. "Homer's society", in Robert Fowler (ed.), *The Cambridge Companion to Homer* (Cambridge, 2007), 206-219.

Carol G. Thomas and Craig Conant. *Citadel to City-State: The Transformation of Greece, 1200-700 B.C.E.* (Bloomington, Ind., 1999).

ORAL POETRY AND TRANSMISSION OF THE HOMERIC POEMS

Robert Fowler. "The Homeric question", in Robert Fowler (ed.), *The Cambridge Companion to Homer* (Cambridge, 2007), 220-232.

M. Haslam. "Homeric Papyri and the Transmission of the Text", in Ian Morris and Barry Powell, eds, *A New Companion To Homer* (Leiden, 1997) 55-100.

Richard Janko. "The origins and evolution of the epic diction" and "The text and transmission of the *Iliad*", both in *The Iliad: A Commentary; Volume IV: books 13-16* (Cambridge, 1992), 8-19 and 20-38 respectively.

Minna Skafte Jensen. *The Homeric Question and the Oral-Formulaic Theory* (Copenhagen, 1980).

G.S. Kirk. *The Songs of Homer* (Cambridge, 1962).

Albert B. Lord. *The Singer of Tales* (Cambridge, Mass., 1981).

Gregory Nagy. *Homeric Questions* (Austin, Tex., 1996).

Barry Powell. "Homer and Writing", Ian Morris and Barry Powell (eds.), *A New Companion to Homer* (Leiden, 1997) 3-32.

Benjamin A. Stoltz and Richard S. Shannon. (eds.), *Oral Literature and the Formula* (Ann Arbor, Mich., 1976); see especially Ruth Finnegan, "What is oral literature anyway? Comments in the light of some African and other comparative material", 127-66.

CRITICAL STUDIES

The works below represent useful treatments of the epic's different themes and features.

Caroline Alexander. *The War That Killed Achilles* (New York, 2009).

Jasper Griffin. *Homer on Life and Death* (Oxford, 1983).

Katherine Callen King. *Achilles: Paradigms of the War Hero from Homer to the Middle Ages* (Berkeley, 1987).

Sarah Morris. "Homer and the Near East", in Ian Morris and Barry Powell (eds.). *A New Companion to Homer* (Leiden, 1997), 599-623.

Gregory Nagy. *The Best of the Achaeans* (Baltimore, 1981).

Adam Nicolson. *The Mighty Dead: Why Homer Matters* (London, 2014)

J. M. Redfield. *Nature and Culture in the Iliad: The Tragedy of Hector.* rev. ed. (Durham, N.C., 1994).

Ruth Scodel. *Listening to Homer* (Ann Arbor, Mich, 2009)

Jonathan Shay. *Achilles in Vietnam: Combat Trauma and the Undoing of Character* (New York, 1995).

Laura M. Slatkin. *The Power of Thetis: Allusion and Interpretation in the Iliad* (Berkeley, 1991).

Simone Weil. "The Iliad, or the Poem of Force", translated by M. McCarthy, in Christopher Benfey (ed.) *War and the Iliad* (New York, 2005) 1-37.

ACKNOWLEDGEMENTS

The first debt of any translator is to the original author; and so my immeasurable gratitude is to the master poet Homer, whose work has informed and directed so much of my life.

My second debt is to Martin L. West, whose Greek text was the basis of my translation. As this book was going into production, I learned with great and unexpected sadness of his death. A towering figure in the world of early Greek poetry and epic, his many works of scholarship have defined this difficult and exciting field. His kind words of support to me meant and mean a great deal, and it is hard to accept that I will now never meet him. Nonetheless, I give my great thanks to him for his personal interest, and for his peerless work.

My great gratitude goes to Laura Hassan and to Vintage Classics for the leap of faith that made this work possible. I am further indebted to Frances Macmillan for her close work on all stages of this work's production. I would like to thank Suzanne Dean and Lily Richards for going an extra mile or two on behalf of the book design. I also thank illustrator David Cain for another beautiful map.

This translation had its roots in a previous book, *The War That Killed Achilles* (Viking Penguin, 2009), which featured my translation of *Iliad* Book 22, as well as some historical material that I have used in the introduction to this work. My thanks, therefore, to Wendy Wolf and Viking Penguin for being there at the beginning.

I would also like to thank for supportive words along the way Richard

Janko and Jean Strouse; and Glen Bowersock, who inadvertently prodded me to this undertaking.

I owe thanks to friends and family for encouragement over the years; to George Butler and Belinda and John Knight who were there at the origin of this effort; to Hugh Van Dusen and to Annette Worsley-Taylor; to Jenny Lawrence, Simon Prebble and the New York Society Library; to my departed friend Marjorie Shuer; to Bruce and Gabriele Dempsey for both moral and practical support over many years; and to my mother who matter-of-factly indicated that whatever else I might do, she expected the *Iliad*.

My thanks to Anthony Sheil, my dear friend and agent, who, I suspect, always had this project lurking in the back of his heart and mind; and whose close reading of the Greek was an immeasurable asset.

And my greatest thanks to Frank Blair, whose unflagging faith, enthusiasm, warm support and sharp reading eye—especially for words relating to "wine" and "the sea"—greatly enabled this work; and to Mac and Tybalt.

penguin.co.uk/vintage-classics